THE PURITANS IN AMERICA

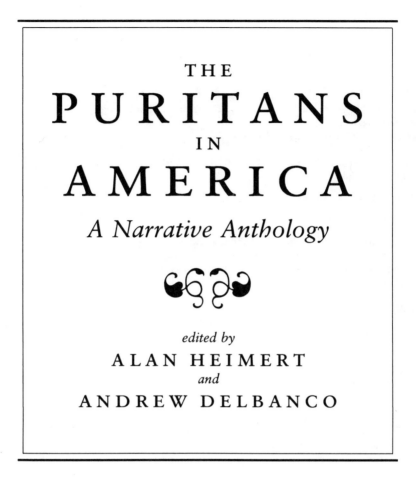

THE PURITANS IN AMERICA

A Narrative Anthology

edited by

ALAN HEIMERT
and
ANDREW DELBANCO

HARVARD UNIVERSITY PRESS
Cambridge, Massachusetts
and London, England

Printed in the United States of America
10 9 8 7 6 5 4 3
LIBRARY OF CONGRESS CATALOGING IN PUBLICATION DATA
Main entry under title:

The Puritans in America.

Bibliography: p.
Includes index.
1. Puritans—United States—Doctrines—Addresses, essays, lectures.
2. Puritans—United States—Addresses, essays, lectures.
I. Heimert, Alan. II. Delbanco, Andrew, 1952–
BX9318.P87 1985 285'.9'0974 84-10926
ISBN 0-674-74065-3 (alk. paper)
ISBN 0-674-74066-1 (pbk.)

Designed by Gwen Frankfeldt

To our students and colleagues in English 70 who showed us that the Puritans can still find the readers they deserve

CONTENTS

PREFACE

THIS BOOK is an outgrowth and expansion of a selection of seventeenth-century writings that we began to compile some years ago for our courses in American literature. In teaching those courses, we discovered that for us the most effective way of presenting the major works of colonial New England differed somewhat from that of the ground-breaking anthology, *The Puritans*, edited by Perry Miller and Thomas H. Johnson, which has been the standard text since it was first published in 1938. *The Puritans* is organized generically around what the editors deemed to be the ideas and concepts that controlled a century or more of American Puritan thought and expression. As one of those rare "textbooks" that can be accurately described with that overused word "seminal," it inspired several generations of scholars (including the present editors) and should still be consulted by all serious students of American culture. If, as we believe, a need has been felt in recent years for a book that could make the Puritans accessible to a new and differently trained generation of students, this has been so in large part because Miller and Johnson succeeded so brilliantly at opening a once-closed field to inquiry, and, inevitably, to revision. It is in a spirit of gratitude that we say, even as Jefferson said on his arrival in Paris in 1784, "No one can *replace* Dr. Franklin; I am only his successor."

We nevertheless found ourselves disposed, pedagogically as well as intellectually, to a treatment of Puritanism that grew increasingly chronological, until, we discovered, we were offering our students a *narrative*, as well as analytic and critical, exposition of Puritan utterance. While not ignoring the place of the sermon, of history, biography, or poetry, in and for the Puritan literary imagination, we each year moved further away from purely generic distinctions, and introduced our students to varieties of utterance, as they emerged concurrently in time, or as grouped around a single event or issue. Such an approach, we came to believe, better allowed our students to witness the Puritans responding to historical change, or participating in a succession of intellectual crises, thus providing them a fuller and richer sense of how different was, say, the intellectual world of Cotton Mather from that of his grandfathers (and by what steps it evolved as so different)—as well as the degree to which the New England mind was, at any moment, divided within itself.

Several of the texts included in this volume are not "Puritan" at all; they bespeak criticisms of the reigning Puritan orthodoxy of New England or even, at last, reversions from it. Moreover, we have provided, we believe, evidence that the New England mind was seldom, if ever—despite many protestations to the contrary—a single or simple one. The well-known "debate" between John Cotton and Roger Williams is given its hearing; so too are some of the central issues behind the trial and banishment of Anne Hutchinson, as well as the largely generational dispute over the Half-Way Covenant, and the ecclesiastical contentions of the early eighteenth century that disclosed how fragmented New England had become. Through a necessarily small sampling of pre-migration sermons by the towering figures of the first generation, we have sought to demonstrate that there were subtle differences (and some not so subtle) even among those who first banded together to build a nation, as we have so often been told, where none before had stood.

Indeed, one of the longer and more complex sections of the anthology represents our attempt to show just how tortuous and complicated was the process by which a variety of English nonconformists came to see themselves as not only different from those of the brethren they had left behind, but, in the final analysis, profoundly separate from them. This early chapter of New England's intellectual history seems to us central to any understanding of how (and for that matter why) some Puritans chose to become (or were forced to become) *American* Puritans.

At the other end of the volume, we had once thought to carry our textual narrative through the Great Awakening and thereby introduce students to the culmination of the first century of New England literature: the sermons and dissertations of Jonathan Edwards. To carry out this plan adequately, however, would have required virtually a second volume, and so instead we offer only a glimpse of the glories of his mind and prose. It is our hope that another of those "textbooks" that have been indispensable to our field, Clarence Faust and Thomas H. Johnson's *Jonathan Edwards: Representative Selections,* already once risen from the publishing world's dead, will in time rejoice in yet another resurrection.

We assume that neither the teacher not the student will feel confined to our anthology for an understanding of the period which we treat. We have provided bibliographical suggestions for further reading, not only of primary materials but of secondary works—works, for that matter, that are as likely to challenge as to confirm our narrative interpretation of seventeenth-century New England. Both our choice of texts and the manner in which we unfold and interpret the first century of New England literature may well be—indeed we hope will be—disputed by the teachers and students who use this anthology. Like Emerson, we would greatly regret it if we have written anything that is capable of "proof." We have not been sparing in our commentary, however, both because we believe that the material in this book can only be approached with a sense of its intellectual and historical context, and also because we believe that learning generally involves resistance (or possibly considered assent) to a point of view. For a decade or more we have admonished our own students to hear us much as John Cotton asked his parishioners to hear him—to accept nothing on mere authority, but to expend their time and energies, through their own reading and thinking, in deciding whether what we have said has validity. We will have succeeded in our goal, therefore, if—and only if—this anthology provokes individual and independent thinking about the first century of New England literature, and thus about the complex and endlessly fascinating beginnings of the American nation.

ACKNOWLEDGMENTS

MANY PEOPLE gave us aid and comfort over the years in which this book took shape. Arline Heimert and Dawn Delbanco exemplified the un-Puritan virtue of tolerance. For various kinds of advocacy we owe thanks to William B. Goodman, Maynard Mack, and Daniel Aaron, who believed early and steadfastly in the project. To Herschel Baker, chairman of the Committee on Administration of the Hyder Edward Rollins Fund, and to his colleagues W. J. Bate, Larry Benson, and Jerome Buckley, we are indebted for material support that has helped make publication possible. Aida Donald was a champion of our idea from the start and patient with our ways. Without her, this book would not have reached print in anything like its present form. Elizabeth Suttell supported the project all along with good humor and understanding. Camille Smith's firmness, tact, and editorial skill made the book vastly better than it was, and we are very grateful. At different stages in preparing the manuscript, the following persons assisted with xeroxing, book-hunting, proofreading, and the like: Walter Hughes, Phoebe Koehler, Veronica Lee, M. David Samson, and David Watt. Andrew Delbanco owes special thanks to John Klause, who gave his introduction a searching critique and whose knowledge of the classics, the church fathers, and the renaissance generally was of consistent help. Professor Klause, whose erudition is matched by his modesty and generosity, also supplied many of the translations of Latin and checked the rest. David Sacks offered guidance on some questions in Stuart history. Patricia Caldwell and Albert J. von Frank were willing and thoughtful consultants. All along, Mary Johnson and Edie Holway were splendid typists and boosters of morale. Members of the staffs of Widener, Houghton, and Andover libraries were unfailingly cooperative.

Several individuals and publishers kindly granted us their permission to use some of the texts in this volume; we acknowledge them on the first page of each text.

Our largest debts are to Judith Baumel and Frederick Wertheim. Ms.

Baumel waited patiently during our long silences, and then, when suddenly assaulted by hundreds of pages of crammed seventeenth-century type, she transformed them into a readable text from which this book could be printed. She also read and improved the introduction and several headnotes. Her combination of literary sensitivity and command of computer technology has saved us from many pitfalls. Mr. Wertheim tracked down much elusive information and helped enormously during the final stages of manuscript preparation. His skill and stamina have been a great boon to us. His commitment to the project went far beyond the call of duty—for which he has our warm thanks.

A Note on Editorial Method

WITH CERTAIN exceptions, we have changed the spelling and punctuation of the texts in this volume to conform to modern usage. The exceptions are the poetry and those works (such as Sewall's *Diary*) that are reprinted from widely used scholarly editions. We have not changed archaic forms of words where the change would affect sound: for example, *divers* has not become *diverse; salvages* has not become *savages.* We have edited the texts in this way because one important aim of this book is to recover inaccessible works for the modern reader. Many seventeenth-century sermons were transcribed by unknown hands from oral delivery, and such aspects of the original texts as italicization, capitalization, irregular spelling, sometimes even marginal scriptural citations, were not necessarily stipulated by the author. Moreover, we believe that faithfully preserving such features from the early editions would, in some cases, lend the texts an air of eccentricity that they did not have for contemporary readers. The editions upon which our texts are based are identified in each case. (The date given for each selection is the year of composition, not necessarily that of first publication.)

We have supplied annotation in the same spirit. Foreign phrases have been translated; some (by no means all) biblical paraphrases and citations have been identified; archaic words and references that are not immediately clear have been explained. We have kept the annotation at a minimum, however. Our aim is to remove stumbling blocks without burdening the reader with exhaustive commentary.

We indicate with ellipses those places where writing has been omitted. To avoid a text cluttered with endless dots, we do not always indicate small deletions (such as biblical references or Greek phrases that are translated by the author). In choosing what to include in the volume, we concentrated on works that are hard to come by outside the rare-book libraries; we do not supply long excerpts from those which are more readily available, such as Bradford's *History.*

This book is best used in the company of the Oxford English Dictionary and the Authorized or the Geneva Bible. (Puritans used both biblical texts; citations have been given from the more familiar King James version.) Often, a minister quotes a fragment of scripture to illustrate or introduce a point, safely assuming that his auditors will instantly recall the rest of the passage. In such instances we usually give the remainder of the quotation in a note.

Our work has been cooperative from the start, much of it taking shape as we talked over how best to teach the literature of colonial New England and what kind of book would be most useful in the classroom. In the realization of our plans, there has been a division of labor: Andrew Delbanco is responsible for the Introduction and the selections and introductory materials in Parts I, III, and V; Alan Heimert for Parts II, IV, and VI and the Afterword.

INTRODUCTION

"WE CALL YOU PURITANS," wrote an English clergyman named Oliver Ormerod at the beginning of the seventeenth century, "not because you are purer than other men . . . but because you think yourselves to be purer." That sentence, contemptuous as it is, contains a fundamental insight into the phenomenon called Puritanism: Ormerod understood that the Puritans had received their name, and even their sense of who they were, from those who reviled them. Theirs was a movement invented, in some respects, by its enemies.

This was not the first time a name had been given to English dissenters in a spirit of mockery. A group of monastics in the fourteenth century, for instance, who objected to what they called a "flour god" (a reference to the Catholic claim that the bread and wine of the communion service were miraculously "transubstantiated" into the body and blood of Christ), became known as Lollards. "Lollard" was a derisive term taken from a Middle English word meaning to mumble—one among many examples of religious dissidents who were defined by the language of English culture as deviants. Any reader of the *Canterbury Tales*—a poem populated by scheming pardoners and flatulent friars—knows that the minor English clergy had been targets of abuse and ridicule long before Puritan satirists took on the bishops in the sixteenth century.

Not just the functionaries, of course, but the whole structure of the English national church was permanently changed when Henry VIII declared its independence from Rome in the 1530s, and much of the religious turmoil of Tudor and Stuart England can be understood as a struggle to complete the severance that Henry had begun. He had transferred authority over English Christians from pope to king, but to reform-minded Englishmen this was only a beginning. Roger Williams, roughly a century later, put it this way: "He despoiled the Pope . . . upon a grudge about his wife . . . and left the church half-Popish, half-Protestant."

The basic program of the Catholic church, which Martin Luther had repudiated early in the century, remained in force. It has often seemed (both to contemporaries and to historians) a system of propitiation based on the idea that one could purchase exoneration for sin. It is true that a man could—in individual confession to a priest, or through recitation of the *confiteor* at Mass—beseech and expect God's mercy for his sins. Yet Catholic doctrine always maintained that such forgiveness was granted not for any merit in the supplicant but because of Christ's sacrifice on behalf of man. Even confessed sins, moreover, still carried a sentence of temporal punishment. It was here that the traditional procedures of the church might seem a crude system of barter, a *quid pro quo* between God and man: the penitent, by saying a prescribed number of Hail Marys, or in more serious cases by making a pilgrimage to Canterbury, could hope to reduce his time in purgatory. In such established practices of confession and penitence, the niceties of theological distinctions between God's freely dispensed forgiveness and man's capacity to earn it tended to be lost. That loss encouraged an image—often a caricature—of the church as an enterprise in the business of selling God's forgiveness.

Even after Henry broke the papal grip, more than the vestiges of such a propitiatory religion remained: the English countryside was filled with chantry priests—clergymen settled on privately owned land, the income of which paid their livings, who were devoted entirely to the daily performance of Mass for the soul of the deceased landlord. It was not unusual for such a parish priest to say his Mass and perform the ritual of the Eucharist without a single person in attendance. By the middle of the sixteenth century, many parsons had still never read the Bible, and many, according to Bishop Hooper's survey of Gloucester, could not recite the Ten Commandments. Plural livings (in which a clergyman drew income from several parishes), clerical immunity to civil punishment, and a general association of the clergy with corruption, ignorance, and foreign allegiances—to Rome and Spain in particular—created an atmosphere of hostility between ordinary Englishmen and their spiritual advisers.

When lay people did come to church, they were likely to find a place lit through stained glass and by candles, perfumed with incense, its quiet broken by the priest's Latin chant and the sound of the communion bell. Attending church was above all a visual experience, and heavy with mystery—what the Puritans would later call a "dumb show"—and the Mass had an imperial and sensual aloofness. It should be noted, however, especially in view of later Puritan claims to a populist legitimacy, that there was also a great deal of affection among common people for the old style of worship. In the summer of 1549, for example, Devon and Cornwall filled with rioting that was at least partly triggered by discontent over the imposition of a Protestant prayer book.

Through this first Book of Common Prayer, issued under Edward VI in 1549, the English language invaded the English church. The new text, which prescribed vernacular substitutes for the old Latin incantations, spoke carefully of the communion bread and wine as a "memorial" of Christ, rather than of his body made present through a miracle. Auricular confession was forbidden; clerical education started to improve, especially at the University of Cambridge; but as is often the case, the beginnings of reform stimulated the appetite for more. As the century progressed, Parliament was besieged by petitions—against papist vestments, episcopal greed, rule by absentee clergy—and one monarch after another faced endless agitation for change.

Succeeding her deeply Protestant brother Edward and her Catholic sister Mary, Queen Elizabeth I displayed an extraordinary delicacy in brokering her subjects' competing demands. Depending especially on two archbishops, Richard Hooker and John Whitgift, she managed to maintain ecclesiastical discipline, and with it an uneasy peace—known as the Elizabethan settlement—for nearly forty years. This required silencing the Catholics who pined for Queen Mary or even for the days before Henry's break with Rome, as well as those who by the 1560s were being called Puritans. These dissatisfied Protestants, with their insatiable appetite for "prophesyings"—gatherings of clergy who met to discuss their religious vocation—drove the queen to fury. In 1577 she commanded her bishops to see to it that no "manner of person be suffered within your diocese to preach, teach, read, or any wise exercise any function in the Church but such as shall be lawfully approved and licensed as persons . . . conformable to the ministry in the rites and ceremonies of the Church of England." Edmund Grindal, Archbishop of Canterbury, was less outraged by the Puritans and said so—and got a brisk upbraiding from his queen. Sensing that a potent grass-roots movement was being born, he had the gall to stand his ground and admonish her: "Remember, Madam, that you are a mortal creature."

Such open chastisement of established authority was rare, and by the end of the century Puritanism had been forced underground. With the accession of James VI of Scotland to the English throne in 1603, however, fresh hope was stirred that the hold of the bishops might be broken, that this Scotsman might lead his new kingdom toward Presbyterian reform—the elimination of bishops and the delegation of authority to councils (presbyteries) of ministers who would be ultimately answerable to their individual congregations. In this changed climate, one outspoken minister, William Bradshaw, offered to a curious nation an openly sympathetic analysis of Puritanism (which had become a catch-word for radical religion): "They hold," he explained, "that the pastors, teachers, and ruling elders of particular congregations, are, or ought to be the highest spiritual officers in the church, over whom (by any divine ordinance) there is no superior Pastor but only Jesus Christ; and that they are led by the spirit of Antichrist, that arrogate or take upon themselves to be pastors of pastors." These were harsh words in a society whose church still operated through an elaborately hierarchical structure; indeed it was a direct affront to the authority of bishops and king. The king himself had at first seemed sympathetic to those who now renewed complaint about the sorry state of England's clergy. He even seemed willing to implement some of the requests incorporated in the moderate Millenary Petition of 1603, a document designed to foster a "learned and godly" ministry and to curb such abuses as excommunication "for trifles"—in short, a manifesto for gradualism in returning the church to conformity with what the Puritans deemed its apostolic origin. (The petition was signed by more than eight hundred members of the clergy.) But James rightly sensed that the Puritans' logic, no matter how deferentially posed, would eventually challenge his own authority: "No Bishop, No King," he declared with unconscious prophecy at the Hampton Court Conference, and added his famous threat: "I will harry them out of the land." It is at this point that we can intelligibly speak of a Puritan movement heading toward rebellion, or at least of a Puritan element in what would become the English revolution.

For his campaign to suppress the Puritans, James enlisted new ideologies and new allies. A distinctive brand of thought had begun to emerge in the religious establishment, associated with such polished preachers as Lancelot Andrewes—a devotional style that inherited and refashioned the rationalism upon which Richard Hooker had built his magnificent defense of the Church of England in the 1590s. To this school—characterized by oratorical elegance, a taste for ritual and splendor, a tendency to elevate human reason to autonomy, and a frank Erastianism (the idea that the church was an arm of the state)—James turned for support. English Calvinists thus began to feel a slippage from orthodoxy in the highest quarters of their church, and soon another convicting epithet entered the language: "Arminian," a reference to Jacobus Arminius, a Dutch theologian who had questioned the doctrines of predestination and irresistible grace. These doctrines held that at the beginning of time God had decided, with a permanence beyond appeal, who would be saved and who damned; and that God's grace could be neither earned nor resisted. Arminius implied that man, like a beggar, could at least stretch out his hand to accept or ward off God's proffered grace. The will of God, in short, was not entirely immune to the will of man.

Along with what seemed his tolerance of such dilutions, James shocked the Puritans by issuing a *Declaration of Sports* (1618) that encouraged revels when planting and harvest were done instead of honoring the weekly Sabbath by enforcing church attendance and introspection. James was not being obtuse to the currents of his time. On the contrary, he knew exactly what he was opposing, for since before the death of Elizabeth the Puritan movement had quietly strengthened its own structures for what it considered devotion and what James considered subversion. Tudor Cambridge, for instance, had become a breeding ground for "precise" preachers, whose sermons were likely to stray from traditional biblical subjects and linger on such topics as the proper response to enclosure (the use of hedges and fences to turn a village common into pasture for sheep or cattle), or obedience to the poor laws, or the obligations of debtors. Many Puritan sermons were lopsidedly focused on the "applications" (or "uses") of the biblical text under discussion; they seemed as much political speeches with highly specific policy recommendations as pious homilies. Many parish churches, too, had adopted Puritan practices during Elizabeth's waning years. Some put an end to kneeling at communion, to the ceremonial ring in marriage rites, to crossing the child in baptism. A pastor with a Puritan tinge might prefer administering communion to his entire congregation rather than calling up the worshippers one by one; such a procedure accorded with the developing Puritan concept of the church as an organic whole, rather than as a haphazard meeting of individual worshippers at which virtually anyone might drop in. A few churches—some of which followed precedents established in Holland and eventually declared themselves separate from the Church of England—began to require an indication of worthiness from those who wished to take communion. Such attempts to distinguish between the sheep and the goats would be carried much further in New England, where a public profession of faith began to be required for church admission, and where the power to accept a new member was vested in the congregation alone.

By the late 1620s such encroachments were coming under blistering attack from William Laud, who became Charles I's Bishop of London three years after James's death and Archbishop of Canterbury in 1633. To the Puritans, Laud quickly rivaled the pope himself as a human embodiment of Antichrist. He epitomized the pomp and bluster that had made previous bishops so unpopular, and he outdid them all in what one of his predecessors, Bishop Jewel, had called "scenic apparatus." "Room, room for my Lord's Grace," Laud's ushers cried when he rode past with fifty mounted attendants, "Gentlemen be uncovered; my Lord's Grace is coming." Laud had, in fact, a powerfully incisive mind, and he assumed his imperial posture by design rather than as a vain indulgence. He was openly Arminian and determined to restore the centrality of the sacraments to the English church—literally to bring the altar out of the dark corner to which Puritan congregations had banished it, and to dignify it with ceremonial rails. But perhaps most important, it was Laud who seemed capable of carrying out James's threat to "harry them out of the land." As Thomas Shepard, who emigrated to New England as a result of Laud's harrying, recalled:

> As soon as I came in the morning about eight of the clock, falling into a fit of rage, [Laud] asked me what degree I had taken in the University. I answered him, I was a Master of Arts. He asked me, Of what College? I answered, Of Emmanuel. He asked how long I had lived in his diocese. I answered, Three years and upwards. He asked who maintained me all this while, charging me to deal plainly with him, adding withal that he had been more cheated and equivocated with by some of my malignant faction than ever was man by Jesuit, at the speaking of which words he looked as though blood would have gushed out of his face and did shake as if he had been haunted with an ague fit, to my apprehension by reason of his extreme malice and secret venom. I desired him to excuse me. He fell then to threaten me and withal to bitter railing, calling me all to naught, saying, You prating coxcomb! Do you think all the learning is in your brain? He pronounced his sentence thus: I charge you that you neither preach, read, marry, bury, or exercise any ministerial function in any part of my diocese, for if you do, and I hear of it, I will be upon your back and follow you wherever you go, in any part of the kingdom, and so everlastingly disenable you. I besought him not to deal so, in regard of a poor town. Here he stopped me in what I was going to say. A poor town! You have made me a company of seditious, factious Bedlams, and what do you prate to me of a poor town? I prayed him to suffer me to catechise in the Sabbath days in the afternoon. He replied, Spare your breath; I will have no such fellows prate in my diocese. Get you gone, and now make your complaints to whom you will!

It is important, if less than exhilarating for Americans, to acknowledge that the American faction of the Puritan movement—however brutally exiled—was a minor offshoot of English events. For most Englishmen, whether they looked on in approval or horror, the climax of the English Reformation was now at hand—first in the open defiance of Episcopacy in the 1630s, then in the struggle against Charles and Laud in the 1640s. Both men were eventually beheaded. Compared to this holy war at home, the settlement of the New World seemed an instance of diverted energy, even a mistake. "A poor, cold, and useless" place was Cromwell's assessment of Massachusetts Bay—an opinion not without adherents among New Englanders themselves. After the New Model Army took to the battlefield in the mid-1640s, about half of New England's university-educated men returned home, some quite literally to join the fight. It is necessary, therefore, to understand that the founders of Puritan New England had to contend almost immediately with an articulated sense, both from abroad and from within their own ranks, that they were missing the main event. This helps to explain the many Puritan pages of self-justification. Defensiveness was a part of New England's initiation.

There were also, however, powerful elements in the American Puritans' inheritance that countered their fear of being what Thomas Brattle called, in a somewhat different context, "the last of all the Lags." That inheritance included the long-standing Christian fascination with the Bible's many clues to the nature and timing of the world's end. By the middle of the seventeenth century, many Puritans believed that the end was imminent, and that they would take part in the coming triumph of the saints.

During the twelve centuries between Augustine and the Puritan moment, such biblical interpretations underwent a development much too complex to treat adequately here. But it may be said that Augustine's relatively cautious reading of the prophetic books, especially Revelation, became the basis for official church doctrine until the Reformation. The devil's desperation, for example, as narrated in Revelation 20—"Satan shall be loosed out of his prison, And shall go out to deceive the nations which are in the four quarters of the earth"—signaled to Augustine a last Satanic gasp, permitted by God for the edification of his earthly servants: "in the end," he argued, Satan "shall be loosed; that the city of God may see what a potent adversary she has conquered." With similar interpretive calm, Augustine read the crucial opening verses—"And I saw an angel come down from heaven, having the key of the bottomless pit and a great chain in his hand. And he laid hold on the dragon, that old serpent, which is the Devil, and Satan, and bound him a thousand years"—as a prediction that Christ's church will endure for a millennium, after which humankind's fleshly bodies (as prophesied in verse 12) will be resurrected, and the saved sorted out from the damned. Placing this cataclysmic event far away, Augustine thus held the ecstatic dream-visions of Revelation more or less outside the imaginable limits of human history;

his sense of the apocalypse was not so much a divine intervention, a disruption of temporal history, as a distant conclusion, a wrapping up.

Throughout the Middle Ages, especially at the approach of ominous round-numbered years such as the year 1000 and during devastations like the Black Death, there had been times of intensified expectation of a sudden second coming. But with the beginning of modern science and the rise of Renaissance humanism, such anticipations grew more abstract. (All such generalizations must, of course, be extended only with due caution from those Europeans who left a written record of their opinions to the vast majority who did not.) It is in this context that we may understand Thomas Shepard's paradoxical remark, made shortly after his emigration to New England: "It may be the last and great coming of the Lord is not very nigh (although we are doubtless in the last times)." Shepard's parenthesis encloses an idea that has become a convention; he acknowledges the march toward judgment, but he does not tremble at it.

Shepard's sobriety was a deliberate dissent from the prophetic fervor of many English Puritans in the early seventeenth century. His conviction that the world had a long way to go before redemption ran counter to the recent facts of church history. For one thing, the Augustinian interpretation that Shepard echoed was more than a millennium old itself, and its fulfillment, even if the thousand years of Revelation were construed as an approximation, seemed imminent or overdue. Furthermore, the pace of events since Martin Luther had nailed his theses to the Wittenberg church door made many Puritans feel that history was not merely advancing but hurtling toward its final act. Victories over the papacy had seemed for a while to prepare the way for the realization of verse 10: "the devil that deceived them was cast into the lake of fire and brimstone, where the beast and the false prophet are, and shall be tormented day and night for ever and ever." John Cotton, in his *Pouring Out of the Seven Vials* (1641), extracted this meaning from Revelation 16:8, "And the fourth angel poured out his vial upon the sun": "If you look through all the antichristian world," he wrote, "what should be the most eminent, and most glorious, and most illustrious light that shines in the greatest glory amongst them all? What doth more readily offer itself then the House of Austria, the chief governor in the antichristian state, of eminent luster, and hath been so for two hundred years, as they call it, the *Lumen* and *Columen* of that state, the light and pillar of that state?" With Turkish armies barely one hundred miles from Vienna, there seemed reason to credit Cotton's theory. But more generally the pace of events had seemed to slow since the 1620s, with the intransigency of James and Charles, the spreading hegemony of the Hapsburgs throughout the Continent, the plight of the Huguenots in France the loss of the Palatinate. "It is God's work," explained Cotton in his later sermons on Ecclesiastes, "to set good and evil times in a vicissitude or enterchange." The darker the night, the brighter would be the day.

In part, therefore, to meet potential discouragements, an ecstatic eschatology began to take hold in the Puritan imagination. Such figures as Joseph Mede, the aptly named Thomas Brightman, and among those who emigrated to America, John Cotton, applied the prophecies to temporal history as it was unfolding before their eyes. The resurrection of Revelation 20, for example—"And I saw the dead, small and great, stand before God"—formerly interpreted as a literal ascent of bodies at the end of time, now was frequently taken to predict the imminent triumph of the true church on earth. Among anticipated events was the conversion of the Jews, often identified with the pouring of the sixth vial (Revelation 16), just before "a great voice [came] out of . . . heaven . . . saying it is done." Since God's redemptive plan was to proceed in orderly sequence, each stage depended on completion of the one before, and those who dared to place obstacles in its path would pay dearly. One byproduct, therefore, of Puritan ascendancy in England was a novel hospitality toward the Jews. In 1656 Cromwell struck down restrictions on Jewish immigration and extended toleration to them—a solicitousness applauded by many who believed the Jews would soon no longer be Jews.

Puritan millenarianism, then, was filled with a remarkable hopefulness in the face of local and international defeats—an optimism that promised a thousand-year reign of God's elect as the blissful prelude to Christ's return. Prognostication of just when the final stage of history would arrive became widespread, and the talent of foretelling had many sophisticated claimants. Cotton, for instance, calculated that the Roman Church would collapse in 1655. John Milton, after his own hopes for a durable Puritan government had been dashed, composed the final books of *Paradise Lost* (1667) around the figure of a prophetic angel who unfolded for Adam and Eve the prospect of the human future as it stretched forward all the way to the second coming. Milton's England was filled with such seers, of whom many were sure that they spoke with angelic authority: Joseph Mede, for instance, proclaimed that the world would be purged by fire of all its "wicked statesmen, high and low ones, princes and peasants." It was a compelling dream, and it crossed the Atlantic with the founders of New England.

The rediscovery by contemporary historians of this millenarian mood has significantly affected our view of the Puritans in America. Several scholars have argued that what Englishmen regarded, in Sacvan Bercovitch's phrase, as a "temporary, probational concurrence"—namely, that the true church was expanding within the same political entity (England) that was carrying on the worldly battle against Catholic power—became in New England an unprecedented fusion. In England, writes Bercovitch, "no soldier in Cromwell's army . . . could *ipso facto* claim regeneration, no English patriot could confuse his country *per se* with the Heavenly City," but in New England, "as nowhere else, the saint prepared for salvation within a corporate historic undertaking destined to usher in the millennium." This expectancy, regarded by onlooking Europeans (and by some New Englanders, such as Roger Williams) as outlandish pride, played an important part in the development of a distinctively New England mind. Samuel Sewall, for instance, writing in 1696, interpreted the pouring out of the sixth vial on the River Euphrates as God's assault upon the Spanish empire in the New World. Nearly twenty years later, Sewall found the same geographic promise in the Gospels: "I have for several years supposed that something of a local consideration is couched in the parable of the Sower . . . Why may we not, without being envied, or derided, hope that the *Americans* shall be made the good ground that shall once at last prove especially and wonderfully fruitful?"

Sewall's excitement at New England's scripturally inscribed destiny was not uncritically shared by his peers: he made his assertion of equivalence between the Euphrates and Spanish America in a letter to his old friend Edward Taylor, who flatly disagreed. In 1713 he reported in his diary the following response from the Mathers, to whom he had written asking how best to distribute *Proposals Touching the Accomplishment of the Prophecies,* the book in which his patriotic reading of the parable of the sower appears: "Dr. Cotton Mather not having answer'd my Letter nor look'd upon me on his Lecture day last Thorsday; I was in a strait to know what to do, as to the disposal of my Proposals; and let none go. Now Dr. Incr. Mather spake pleasantly to me; of his own accord thank'd me for my book, said his Son had shew'd it him; I was fond of America." Sewall, in short, found himself humored for his eschatological opinions. Such domestic debate (of which examples abound) should be borne in mind when assessing the Puritans' sense of their American errand. The New England Puritans were unanimous about precious few issues—and the question of their own centrality in God's redemptive plan was not among that number.

In close company with their millenarian expectancy, the founders brought with them a technique for reading scripture and for understanding history, a technique called typology. This typological method was nearly as ancient as the prophetic tradition. Paul, for example, speaks in his letters to the Corinthians and the Romans of *typoi,* explaining that certain Old Testament figures such as Adam and Moses were foreshadowings or embodied prophecies of Christ. In the view of the Church Fathers, who made typology into a tool for linking the two Testaments, the types were not restricted to individuals (Moses at Sinai foreshadowing Christ on the Mount, or Jonah in the belly of the whale foreshadowing Christ in the tomb); types could also be national: the Jews enslaved in Egypt, for example, might typify Christ's agony in Gethsemane. One of the attractions of the typological approach was that it solved the persistent problem of reconciling a Jewish with a Christian book—it unified the Bible into one truth, a holy narrative whose end is contained in its beginning, a story that collapses time into one divine instant. Bearing this in mind, it becomes clear how Increase Mather, for example, could speak of a Babylonian king (Daniel 2) dreaming of "the kingdom of Jesus Christ."

Especially as the types were put to use by the Reformers, Christ did not represent the end-point of all scriptural prophecies, since he stood not at the conclusion of history, but in its midst. Bercovitch, who has led the resurgence of scholarly interest in the impact of typology on American culture, puts it this way: "Sacred history did not end, after all, with the Bible; it became the task of typology to define the course of the church ('spiritual Israel') and of the exemplary Christian life. In this view Christ, the 'antitype,' stood at the center of history, casting His shadow forward to the end of time as well as backward across the Old Testament." Thus the Eden and Canaan of the Old Testament not only bear a typological relation to one another but also look forward to the greater paradise promised in Revelation. Some New Englanders went so far as to construe their own crossing of the sea as an antitype of the exile of the Jews; like Sewall, some concluded that their American refuge might actually be the New Jerusalem promised in Revelation 22.

In the context of such intoxicating hopes—not quite assumptions, not quite willed fantasies—it is possible to understand the insistence with which New Englanders spoke of themselves as a covenanted people, a people living in unique reciprocal relation to God. Indeed, the typological frame of mind turned sacred history, as Bercovitch says, into "a sort of relay race toward eternity, whose participants were essentially identical (all one in Christ), while temporally they represented ascending steps in the work of redemption." It is also possible, in this context, to understand why the Puritan "plain style" was often not plain at all: the typological strategy, in combination with the Puritans' first literary principle—reverence for the language of scripture—allowed the faintly heathenish imagery of certain Old Testament books to enter their permissible lexicon. The apparently carnal images of the Song of Solomon, for example, could be interpreted allegorically, so that the breasts and belly and lips of Solomon's bride became symbols of the spiritual beauties of the true church. As types, these symbols carried the promise that the union they stood for would be realized not only in the believer's mind but in history as well. What might, to an uninitiated reader, seem merely the bridegroom's lust becomes the holy devotion of Christ to his betrothed, the elect.

Since every type was an interpretable symbol, and every biblical figure potentially a type, their meanings could be hotly contested. Some of the fiercest colonial disputes—between John Cotton and Roger Williams, for example, over the disciplinary authority of the civil magistrate—were at bottom literary disagreements. Not until American politics split between "strict" and "loose" constructions of the Constitution did the reading of a prescriptive text again matter so much in American public life. And the disagreements lingered: more than a century after the Great Migration, Jonathan Edwards could claim that "this new world is probably now discovered, that the new and most glorious state of God's church on earth might commence there." Reading the same text and watching the same events, Edwards' contemporary Charles Chauncy asked whether "any good end [may] be answered in endeavoring, upon evidence absolutely precarious, to instill into the minds of the people a notion of the millennium state, as what is now going to be introduced; yea, and of America, as that part of the world which is pointed out in the Revelations of God." In 1743 this was already an old dispute, and it remains, perhaps, unresolved by Edwards' and Chauncy's posterity.

It is, in some respects, easier to see conflict within Puritanism and among the heirs of Puritanism than to grasp the original antagonism that separated Puritan from "Anglican"—a word invented in the later seventeenth century to denote those committed to the Elizabethan settlement. There were, as Perry Miller stressed, much larger areas of agreement than of contention between these groups who seem so distinct in retrospect. Both regarded the Church of England as a true church; both believed that God had predestined some human beings for damnation and others for salvation; both believed that those favored were saved not by works but by faith. Many historians have tried to single out the Puritans as somehow more deeply committed to the "harsh" doctrines of Calvinism, such as human impotence and divine wrath. They were, according to this view, a grimmer, more pessimistic lot than their moderate Anglican counterparts. But what we know now about Puritan eschatology, with its liberating effects on language and sensibility, calls this into question. And long before the recovery of the Puritans by modern scholarship, their great Anglican enemy, Richard Hooker, had hinted that they did not finally accept the doctrine of depravity they so loudly proclaimed: "[they] impute all faults and corruptions, wherewith the world aboundeth, unto the kind of ecclesiastical government established." Hooker understood that the Puritan appetite was first of all for an unmediated relation to God; he grasped, as Larzer Ziff has put it in our own time, that the "antinomian belief [was] at the core of Puritanism," that the Puritan longed for a sense of communion with the Holy Spirit, for a closeness to God unattainable through religious duties and prescriptions, through sacraments, priests, saints—the whole panoply of religious apparatus as it still existed in England.

Understanding the Puritans as well as he did, Hooker was most exasperated by their inexhaustible taste for talk: they disliked the regularity of the Anglican service, with its prayer-book readings and formal homilies, and preferred a lengthy sermon from a preacher who used words fit, as William Perkins put it, "for the people's understanding." "They tell us," Hooker reported with studied amazement at their presumption, that "the profit of reading [scripture] is singular, in that it serveth for a preparative unto sermons." To Hooker this relation between reading and preaching seemed exactly the reverse of the truth:

> Unless, therefore, clean contrary to our own experience, we shall think it a miracle if any man acknowledge the divine authority of the scripture, till some sermon have persuaded him thereunto, and that otherwise neither conversation in the bosom of the church, nor religious education, nor the reading of learned men's books, nor information received by conference, nor whatsoever pain and diligence in hearing, studying, meditating day and night on the law, is so far blest of God as to work this effect in any man; how would they have us to grant that faith doth not come but only by *hearing sermons*?

Hooker did not stumble, as modern readers might, over an apparent contradiction between the Puritans' determinism and their stress on the converting efficacy of sermons. They avoided this discrepancy by what they called the doctrine of means—the conviction that God was likeliest to dispense his predetermined grace through a gospel preacher. This was God's preferred way of awakening sinners to their condition, and, should he choose to release them from their bondage to sin, to their obligations as his regenerate children. Meditating on the Puritans' passion for preaching, Hooker saw—and few later commentators have been as sensitive—that the essence of their movement lay not in any body of peculiar doctrine nor in specific prophecies or exegetical technique nor even in a program for ecclesiastical reform—but in their relentless need to feel God's will.

In a remarkable outpouring of commentary on seventeenth-century Anglo-American culture, contemporary scholars have confirmed that the Puritan temperament is an elusive thing—often they have resorted to figurative language in order to describe it. One authority on Elizabethan Puritans, Patrick Collinson, has called them "the hotter sort of Protestants." Historians who deal with more measurable material than attitude have done a great deal of fruitful work in correlating the Puritan temper with the economic and social standing of those who displayed it. Since the enormously influential books of Max Weber and R. H. Tawney, a consensus has emerged that Puritanism found especially congenial conscripts among those who were beginning to live within the structures and rhythms of early capitalism—as merchants, entrepreneurs, craftsmen in other men's employ. Such people, whom Christopher Hill (borrowing a seventeenth-century phrase) calls "the industrious sort," had economic grievances against a crown still committed to mercantile patterns of authority, and they led a disciplined way of life that fit well with a religion of self-scrutiny. Identifying such social alignments has been a substantial achievement of modern historiography, but it is also important to bear in mind that among the leading emigrants to America were ministers (such as Davenport and Cotton) from cosmopolitan ports like London where trade was the lifeblood of the town, and others (such as Hooker and Shepard) from Essex villages that lived on subsistence farming and modest country markets. Puritanism remains resistant to categories.

Of the many efforts to sum up what may be called the Puritan difference, one by John S. Coolidge is exceptionally valuable: "It cannot be explained in logical or epistemological terms; it is a difference, rather, in the way in which the mind is conscious of being affected in its operations by the Bible . . . For the Puritan, obedience to God's word must be something more than a rational adjustment of man's behaviour to God's truth, although undoubtedly it is that. He insists on trying to hear God's voice of command in all his thoughts and cannot feel that he is obeying God if it is 'shut out.' " As Coolidge implies, the Puritan difference is beyond paraphrase; it was an experience, not a position. It can be evoked, perhaps even recreated (as it almost is in the great opening chapter of Perry Miller's *The New England Mind*), but it cannot be stated in summary.

The same caution is in order if we wish to understand the motives and experiences of those Puritans who came to the New World. To economic historians the depression in the wool trade looms large. To some intellectual historians, the promise of a New Canaan furnished by scriptural types and prophecies seems at the root of the migration. To a recent writer, Charles Hambrick-Stowe, who is interested in the forms of Puritan piety, the journey to America was a "devotional act," a self-removal from a land of buzzing distraction to a place better suited for concentrated worship. But despite the lively interest the Puritans continue to inspire, one sensible way of approaching them has not been sufficiently pursued. That way is to think of them as a minority that came suddenly into the possession of power. James Truslow Adams put the matter succinctly more than fifty years ago in a chapter heading of *The Founding of New England:* "an English opposition becomes a New England oligarchy." As much as an ideology, as much as a coherent critique of the standing church, Puritanism was an emotion of dissent. And one of the fascinating aspects of its transplantation to America, where enemies seemed weak and far away, was its complex adjustment to being unopposed. The American Puritans turned inward with merciless demands on the self that can make their English brethren seem lenient; it was not long before they were rooting out their own deviants from their midst. The irony of this transformation from dissenters to lawgivers is manifold and deep; with it comes a certain queasiness in the Puritan voice as it tries to find its proper American pitch.

One must take care that the search for a functional generalization about Puritanism does not obscure the human uncertainty, the confusion of many purposes, in the American adventure. "I thought I should find feelings," was the exquisitely simple explanation offered by one of Thomas Shepard's Newtowne flock. This was perhaps the vaguest and most personal promise of America—that it might deliver or revive the *feeling* of belonging to God as a cherished child. As Patricia Caldwell puts it in her eloquent study of New England conversion relations (statements of religious experience that candidates were required to make upon application for church membership)—America was "irradiating [the relations] with the speaker's hope to be pure and new and whole in a new and holy place."

Much of the beauty and power of Puritan literature comes out of its struggle toward self-knowledge. If the Catholic question had been "what shall I do to be saved?" and the question of the Reformers became "how shall I know if I am saved?" perhaps the American Puritans asked, more elementally, "What am I in the eyes of God?" This was a question that would lead to relentless introspection, even to a tortured solipsism. Especially in the writings of the first generation, a palpable urgency arises out of a terrible conjunction: between the Puritans' insistence that no matter is of indifference to God and their uncertainty over whether, in coming to America, they had rightly read God's will. The burden of such doubt has never quite lifted from what we once would have called the American soul.

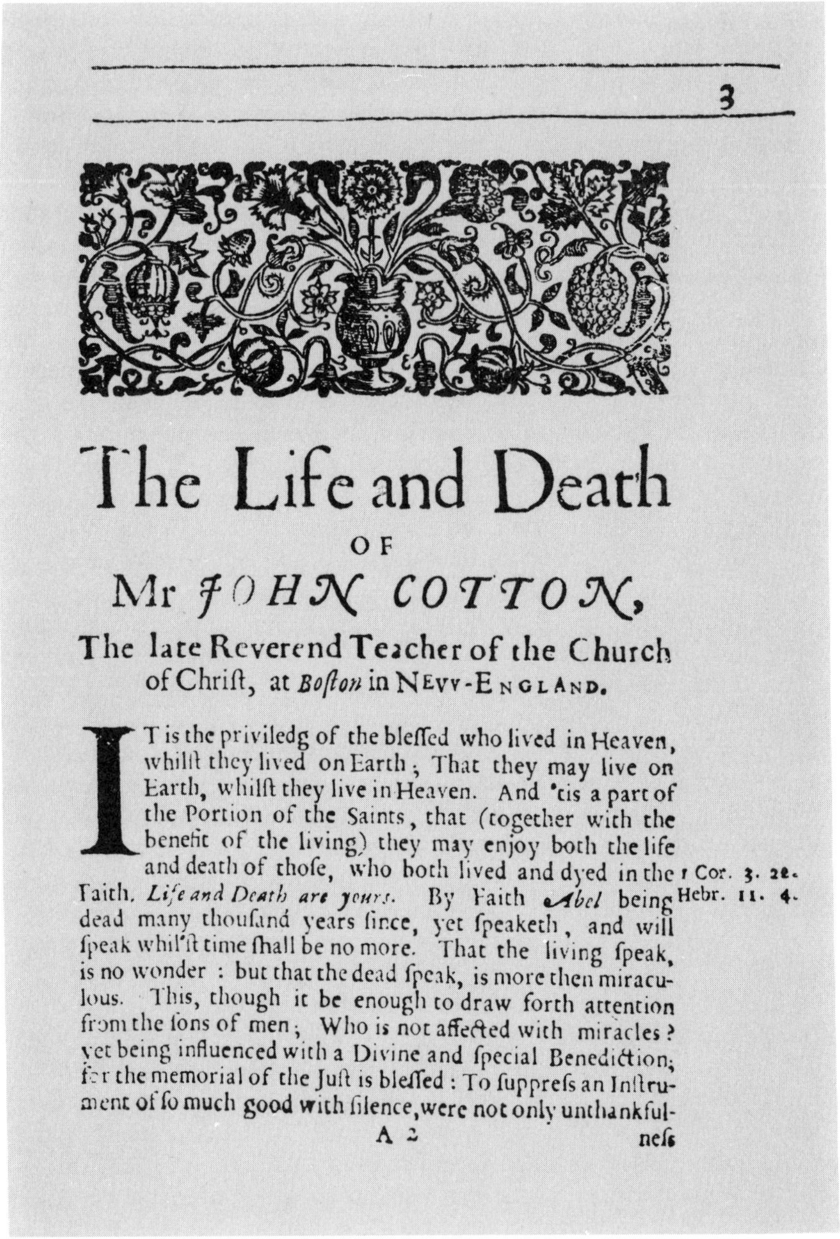

3

The Life and Death
OF
Mr JOHN COTTON,
The late Reverend Teacher of the Church of Chriſt, at *Boſton* in NEVV-ENGLAND.

IT is the priviledg of the bleſſed who lived in Heaven, whilſt they lived on Earth; That they may live on Earth, whilſt they live in Heaven. And 'tis a part of the Portion of the Saints, that (together with the benefit of the living) they may enjoy both the life and death of thoſe, who both lived and dyed in the Faith. *Life and Death are yours.* By Faith *Abel* being dead many thouſand years ſince, yet ſpeaketh, and will ſpeak whil'ſt time ſhall be no more. That the living ſpeak, is no wonder: but that the dead ſpeak, is more then miraculous. This, though it be enough to draw forth attention from the ſons of men; Who is not affected with miracles? yet being influenced with a Divine and ſpecial Benediction; for the memorial of the Juſt is bleſſed: To ſuppreſs an Inſtrument of ſo much good with ſilence, were not only unthankful-

1 Cor. 3. 22.
Hebr. 11. 4.

A 2 neſs

The opening page of John Norton's biography of John Cotton, *Abel Being Dead Yet Speaketh,* published in 1658. (By permission of the Houghton Library, Harvard University.)

ONE

LOOMINGS

FOR PURITAN clergy and laymen in the 1620s the lure of America grew in proportion to the pressure to conform. Especially in such Puritan strongholds as Essex County, where entrepreneurs had to cope with uncontrollable fluctuations in the wool market, landholding gentry with fixed rents and rising prices, and everyone with the vagabond poor, it became dangerous to express open discontent with royal policies such as ship money, poor laws, and monopolies, that many thought were making things worse. Among the Puritan "brethren,"—a term that was becoming the seventeenth-century equivalent of "comrade," as far as their enemies were concerned—a debate began to take shape over the question of emigration. The sermons of the great Puritan preachers of the twenties tell us that the prospect of departure was very much in the air: "Shall we leave [God's] subjects and children," asked Richard Sibbes, "for this or that fear? Let our condition be never so uncomfortable, he can make it comfortable." Sibbes, revered as a man whose generosity of spirit transcended the usual religious divisions, preached with a serene eloquence that remains undiminished by time. His teachings were consolatory, filled with a hope that England could somehow be restored to harmony. For example, he expressed what is perhaps the central paradox of Puritan piety, an idea that explains why so many troubled people could find solace in predestinarian doctrine: "None are fitter for comfort than those that think themselves furthest off."

In this language of reassurance, Sibbes continued until his death in 1630 to describe God's ministers as "ambassadors . . . of a gentle savior." But there was also gathering anger in the Puritan brotherhood—an increasingly articulated impatience which Laud, for one, construed as incitement to treason: "to suffer imprisonment and disgraces for good causes, this is a good work," said John Preston in his stirring sermons on *The Breast-Plate of Faith and Love,* but he also made clear that Puritans would not be satisfied much longer with passive martyrdom:

"Let us not say we must be moderate . . . [We] must be men of contention." And such they ultimately became.

As Puritanism developed an increasingly organized opposition to church and crown—eventually creating a potent fighting machine called the New Model Army—it helped to bring into English life what William Hunt has called the "culture of discipline." Its success with social, parliamentary, and finally military organization had a common starting point: the discipline of the self. The Puritan project sometimes seemed nothing less than a wholesale revision of the values by which English men and women lived. At the heart of its program was a prescription for rigorous introspection—readying the soul for the reception of grace. Puritans called this process "preparation." "Beginnings of preparation," explained William Perkins (who died in 1603, but not before he had nurtured a legion of Cambridge disciples), "are such as bring under, tame and subdue the stubbornness of man's nature, without making any change at all." In other words, preparation was a preliminary step toward salvation, one that man could take on his own initiative. Perkins and other English preparationists were careful to point out—as in the phrase, "without making any change at all"—that this was not the transforming work that only God's freely dispensed grace could perform: "Beginnings of composition I term all those inward motions and inclinations of God's spirit, that follow after the works of the law and rise upon the meditation of the gospel."

This was a distinction that proved harder to keep clear in America, where such critics from within as Anne Hutchinson would accuse the heirs of Perkins and Sibbes of reverting to a covenant of works—of arrogating to man the capacity to earn grace as a reward for his disciplined behavior. In fact the nature of grace itself had already been subject to varying accounts in England. Where Perkins described it as a new capacity for self-control, Preston (who also died before the Great Migration, in 1628) put more stress on its renovation of the senses—for him, the saint was "able to discern things" which once had been hidden, able to "relish" tastes and sounds to which he had once been numb. These differences were to take on dramatic importance in New England when the colonists struggled to find their bearings and purpose. John Cotton, who first felt the stirrings of grace at a sermon by Sibbes and who, in turn, converted Preston, was to find himself more and more isolated in America as he resisted the growing prestige of preparation as the favored technique for entering sainthood.

But whatever their differences, and however serious these became once the Episcopal enemy had been left an ocean behind, the Puritans in

England agreed on one central fact: that ministers must not "preach for fear of the law . . . [nor] for fashion sake . . . [nor] for ostentation sake," but always and only to "deliver a man from hell." The brief selections that follow represent the thought and feeling of three English ministers who later made the journey to America.

THOMAS HOOKER (1586–1647)

The Soul's Preparation for Christ (c. 1626)

THOMAS HOOKER, according to one contemporary, could "put a king in his pocket." It is still possible, through his many surviving sermons, letters, and ecclesiastical tracts, to see why he struck those who knew him as larger than life, as a man beyond intimidation: "When Christ hath given us weapons," he wrote while still in England, "and taught us to fight, and made us conquerors, then he will crown us." Despite the militancy of his English career (Moses Coit Tyler compared the movement of his sermons to the "tramp of an advancing army") Hooker was able as late as 1626 to please a wary Bishop Montaigne, who conceded that he spoke "learnedly and well." Montaigne showed no displeasure at the young man's sermon except to warn him against meddling with questions of church governance. The bishop had a good instinct for trouble. Already restless within the episcopal organization, Hooker had instigated regular "conferences" among Essex ministers and was gaining a reputation as a spellbinding preacher. In 1628 he received the inevitable summons to appear before Laud, Montaigne's less tolerant successor as Archbishop of London. Under real suspicion now, Hooker sensed a crisis coming that would separate Englishmen into the loyal and the faithless: "If the Lord should try us, all those that are fearful to suffer will fly to the low countries."

Within three years of making that remark, Hooker left for Holland. Except by his actions, he never recanted his imperative to stay. One suspects, to put it mildly, that he had a painfully divided mind on the question of withdrawing his own destiny from England's, and the low countries proved no more sustaining for him than they had been for earlier expatriates. Another leading refugee from conformity, William Ames, had put it this way during his own Dutch exile: "We have the good orders here; you have the good Christians in England." In a letter written in 1633 to John Cotton, who had remained in England, Hooker echoed Ames's discontent: "For the better part [with respect to] heart religion they [the Dutch] content themselves with mere forms though much blemished; but the power of godliness, for aught I can see or hear, they know not." In July he returned home for the last time. After settling family affairs he joined Cotton and Samuel Stone—all three disguised to avoid Laud's police—and boarded a ship bound for Massachusetts Bay.

By 1636, Hooker was on the move again. From Newtowne, where he was pastor, he journeyed west with most of his congregation (many of whom had followed him across the sea) to the virtually uncharted Connecticut River Valley. His wife, the legends say, was carried all the way on a horse litter. Many reasons for the secession of the Newtowne church, including a personal rivalry between Hooker and Cotton, have been proposed by historians, but no real consensus has been reached; we do know that Cotton had fought hard against the departure, and there is some evidence that Hooker was unhappy with admissions procedures in the churches of the Bay. The explanation the migrants themselves offered was that they wanted more land.

At Hartford, Hooker produced a major defense of the New England polity, *A Survey of the Sum of Church Discipline,* and preached for at least the third time in his career a systematic series of sermons tracing the soul's journey toward salvation. The excerpt below is from *The Soul's Preparation for Christ,* a sermon sequence delivered in England as part of what Perry Miller called "the most coherent and sustained expression of the essential religious experience ever achieved by the New England divines." Hooker did not finish his American revision of the whole work until *A Comment on Christ's Last Prayer,* completed just before his death in 1647.

The length and complexity of these writings reflect Hooker's refining of the preparatory process outlined by William Perkins. Hooker identified six essential stages: contrition, humiliation, vocation, implantation, exaltation, possession. These are subdivided still further until Hooker's version of the journey toward grace becomes a sequence of enormously subtle gradations.

The sample of Hooker in England given below represents a preacher still defining his relation to his audience. It is in some ways preliminary to the corrosive soul-search they will be expected to undertake. Perhaps the clearest and briefest gloss was long ago provided by Herman Melville in a dictum from Father Mapple (*Moby Dick*, ch. 9): "Woe to him who seeks to please rather than to appall."

The text of *The Soul's Preparation* is from the edition of 1632, pp. 52–55, 228–230.

The Soul's Preparation for Christ

. . . we poor ministers find too often by woeful experience, that when we have taken away all cavils from wicked men, and then if we could weep over them, and mourn for them, and beseech them to consider of it aright, mark what they say: "Good sir, spare your pains, we are sinners, and if we be damned, then every tub must stand upon his own bottom. We will bear it as well as we can." What, is the wind in that door? Is that all you can say? O woe to thee that ever thou wert born! O poor creature! If I should cease speaking, and all of us join together in weeping, and lamenting thy condition, it were the best course; it is impossible thou shouldest ever bear God's wrath with any comfort. And let these three considerations be remembered and retained, which will make any man come to a stand; even the vilest wretches who will blaspheme and swear, and if they be damned (they say) they have borne something, and they will also bear this as well as they can.

First, judge the lion by the paw. Judge the torments of hell by some little beginnings of it; and the dregs of God's vengeance by some little sips of it; and judge how unable thou art to bear the whole by thy inability to bear a little of it in this life. In the terror of conscience (as the wise man saith), a wounded spirit who can bear? When God lays the flashes of hellfire upon thy soul, thou canst not endure it. Whatsoever a man can inflict upon a poor wretch may be borne; but when the Almighty comes in battle array against a poor soul, how can he undergo it? Witness the saints that have felt it, as also witness the wicked themselves that have had some beginnings of hell in their consciences. When the Lord hath let in a little horror of heart into the soul of a poor sinful creature, how is he transported with an insupportable burthen? When it is day, he wisheth it were night, and when it is night, he wisheth it were day. All the friends in the world cannot comfort him; nay, many have sought to hang themselves, to do anything rather than to suffer a little vengeance of the Almighty. And one man is roaring and yelling as if he were now in hell already and admits of no comfort: if the drops be so heavy, what will the whole sea of God's vengeance be? If he cannot bear the one, how can he bear the other?

Secondly, consider thine own strength, and compare it with all the strength of the creatures, and so if all the creatures be not able to bear the wrath of the Almighty (as Job saith), *is my strength the strength of stones, or is my flesh as brass that must bear thy wrath?* As if he had said, it must be a stone, or brass, that must bear thy wrath. Though thou wert as strong as brass or stones, thou couldst not bear it; when the mountains tremble at the wrath of the Lord, shall a poor worm or bubble and a shadow endure it?

Conceive thus much; if all the diseases in the world did seize on one man, and if all the torments that all the tyrants in the world could devise were cast upon him, and if all the creatures in heaven and earth did conspire the destruction of this man, and if all the devils in hell did labor to inflict punishments upon him, you would think this man to be in a miserable condition. And yet all this is but a beam of God's indignation. If the beams of God's wrath be so hot, what is the full sun of his wrath, when it shall seize upon the soul of a sinful creature in full measure?

Nay, if yet thou thinkest to lift up thyself above all creatures, and to bear more than they all, then set before thine eyes the sufferings of the Lord Jesus Christ, he that creates the heavens, and upholds the whole frame thereof. When the wrath of God came upon him, only as a surety, he cries out with his eyes full of tears and his heart full of sorrow, and the heavens full of lamentation, *My God, my God, why has thou forsaken me*? Oh thou poor creature, if thou hast the heart of a man, gird up the loins of thy mind, and see what thou canst do! Dost thou think to bear that which the Lord Jesus Chrst could not bear without so much sorrow? Yet he did endure it without any sin or weakness; he had three sips of the cup[1], and every one of them did sink his soul; and art thou a poor sinful wretch, able to bear the wrath of God forever? . . .

When you do nakedly open your sins to a faithful minister, you go out in battle against sin, and you have a second in the field to stand by you. But especially there is comfort in this particular, for the minister will discover the lusts, and deceits, and corruptions, that you could not find out, and he will lay open all those holds of Satan, and that means of comfort that you never knew. I am able to speak it by experience; this hath broke the neck of many a soul, even because he would go out in single combat against Satan, and (do what he could) not revealing himself to others for help, was overthrown forever.

As it is with the impostumed[2] part of a man's body, when a man lets out some of the corrupt matter, and so skins it, never healing it to the bottom, at last it cankers inwardly, and comes to a gangrene, and the part must be cut off, or else a man is in danger of his life. So when you let out some corruptions by an overly[3] confession, but suffer some bosom

1. Matthew 26:42: "O my Father, if this cup may not pass away from me except I drink it, thy will be done."

2. Abscessed.

3. Cursory.

lust to remain still, as malice, or uncleanness, &c. Then the soul cankers, and Satan takes possession of it, and the soul is carried into fearful abominations . . .

I say, the only way for secrecy is to reveal our sins to some faithful minister. For if we confess our sins, God will cover them. If you take shame to yourselves, God will honor you: but if you will not confess your sins, God will break open the door of your hearts, and let in the light of his truth and the convicting power of his spirit, and make it known to men and angels, to the shame of your persons for ever . . .

So you that keep your sins as sugar under your tongues, and will be loose, and malicious, and covetous still, well, you will have your thirty pence still, and they are laid up safe, as Achan's wedge of gold was.[4] Remember this, God will one day open the closets of your hearts, and lay you upon your deathbeds, and then haply ye will prove mad, and vomit up all: were it not better to confess your sins to some faithful minister now? . . .

4. Judas' price for his betrayal of Christ was thirty pieces of silver (Matthew 26:15); Achan defied God's injunction to reject the spoils of conquered Jericho, and was stoned to death by his fellow Israelites when his booty was discovered (Joshua 7:19–26).

JOHN COTTON (1584–1652)

Christ the Fountain of Life (c. 1628)

IN SEPTEMBER 1633, shortly after John Cotton arrived in Massachusetts Bay aboard the *Griffin,* Governor John Winthrop committed a piece of understatement to his journal: "He was desired to divers places." If there was a generally recognized spiritual leader of the Puritan colony, it was Cotton, whose stature in England among the preaching brethren was commensurate with the size of his church in the busy Lincolnshire seaport of Boston. One of Cotton's English counterparts, Samuel Ward, was frank about his preeminence: "Of all men in the world, I envy Mr. Cotton, of Boston, most; for he doth nothing in way of conformity, and yet hath his liberty, and I do everything that way, and cannot enjoy mine." With the fall from influence of the Bishop of Lincoln—who looked the other way when Cotton declined to wear the surplice and officiate at ceremonies—pressure from the Episcopal authorities increased. Cotton was well known to be a magnet for the young men fresh out of Cambridge who were beginning to seem a disciplined phalanx in training for war against the church. By 1632 (two years after he had preached the farewell sermon to Winthrop's fleet) he was under warrant from the High Commission and had decided for America.

Unlike Shepard, Cotton left no explicit record of the process by which he reached this decision, but it had a long foreground. His many volumes of sermons delivered in England are an extraordinary record of development from a rather brittle-minded ideologue—demanding that "a man [should] find his sin as bitter as death"—to a tender comfort-preacher who seemed to know the generosity of Christ from within, who offered hope to those living in perplexity and foreboding. "Ministers," he declared in his first great series of sermons on *Canticles,* "should be as doors to open a wide entrance for the people to come to Christ; not as those scribes and Pharisees, which Christ complains of which neither enter in themselves, nor would suffer others: such are rather portcullises, yea, gates of hell." Here lies the secret of the Puritan appeal; this is not the exclusionary righteousness we still tend to associate with the Calvinist idea of predestination; it is an invitation, offered through the preached word, to those who feel bereft, a promise of community at a time when people felt more and more alone. Yet Cotton did not speak his promises lightly; the essential paradox of his thought is that although he believed anybody might qualify for membership in the community of true believers he nevertheless maintained the highest standards of admission. He spoke, it often seemed, in riddles: "Christ cannot be had for money, yet sometimes without expense of money he cannot be had." This kind of intellectual tease was his characteristic rhetorical strategy, especially in England, where he demanded ceaseless mental effort from his listeners, requiring that they think through the subtle distinctions dividing, for example, public generosity (a mark of the saint) from pecuniary display (a mark of those headed for hell).

Cotton's language of holy paradox reaches its height in two series of sermons preached in the 1620s, *The Way of Life* and *Christ the Fountain of Life*. In these works he described the spirit by which men and women might live in, but not of, the world; how a man can give his best to his vocation and yet withhold his desire from worldly reward. These were, and are, hard distinctions to grasp—and the delicate intellectual balance with which Cotton expressed them was soon to be threatened, as he sailed away from England, still proclaiming his loyalty to her church.

The text of *Christ the Fountain of Life* is from the edition of 1651, pp. 109–112, 114–115, 118–121.

Christ The Fountain of Life
Sermon VIII

I John 5:12. He that hath the Son, hath life, and he that hath not the Son, hath not life.

. . . the sum of what I shall now say is thus much: there are certain variety of the graces of God in themselves so different and opposite as that in nature they are seldom compatible to one person at one and the same time, or least of all to be found in one and the same business, and yet are found wherever the heart of a man is sanctified by the spirit of grace. Where you have the life of sanctification in a Christian you shall find variety of graces in them, some of them of such diversity and opposition one to another that in nature the like temper is not to be found in one person at the same time, and in the same business. There are certain kind of conjugations, or companions of grace so fitted and joined together in the heart of a man, as that nature is not able to compact such sanctified affections unto such uses upon any occasion, much less able to bring them forth upon any occasion—they are so different in themselves. To name some of them in particular:

First, if you look at the grace of God as it works in the heart and exercises itself in the conversion of a sinner, you shall find that when the soul discerns any life of grace in its heart, that sin is now pardoned, and God is pleased to frame it anew and to give it a new life. At that time the heart is taken up with these two contrary effects: it is both enlarged with no small measure of joy, that ever God should redeem him from such a desperate condition as his soul lay in, and yet withal full of grief of heart, that ever he should have so much displeased that God that hath done so much for him; and so plain, as that you shall evidently discern the voice of your own joy from the voice of your own grief . . .

Secondly, in the worshiping of God in those duties of the life of sanctification, you shall find another combination of mixed affections, the like of which are not and cannot be found in nature; and that is joy and fear. According to Psalms 2:11, *Serve the Lord with fear, and rejoice with trembling.* A Christian man, when he is in a good frame, and the life of grace most stirs in his spirit, he never comes to an holy duty but with some holy fear and trembling before God, before whom he then stands, and yet there is no duties he goes about with more comfort and joy then those, when his heart is not dead . . .

You shall have gentleness and meekness sometimes mixed in a man with much austerity and strictness, which is very much [strange] they should meet in one man at one and the same time.

It was said of Moses, *He was the meekest man upon earth* (Numbers 12:3). Take Moses in his own case, and his carriage towards men, as they had respect to himself, and then he was a meek man, soon persuaded. Yet the same Moses, when he saw the matter concerned the cause of God, he is so stiff and unmoveable as that he will not yield one jot, he will not *leave an hoof behind, of all that appertained to the children of Israel* (Exodus 10:26).[1] He would not only have men and women and children go forth to serve the Lord, but their cattle and their stuff; he will not yield a little here, no not for the king's pleasure's sake. A man would much wonder that such a man, so meek and gentle, and so easy to be persuaded in his own cause, that yet when it comes to a matter of importance and concerns God, he will not there yield. He is now inflex-

1. "Our cattle also shall go with us; there shall not an hoof be left behind; for thereof must we take to serve the Lord our God; and we know not with what we must serve the Lord, until we come thither."

ible; nothing can persuade him to give way to it. This is a combination of graces that are not wont to be found in men thus mixed together, but it is found in the people of God that live a sanctified and holy life. I know not better what to instance it, than in the liquid air, of all other things the most easiest to be pierced through. Of itself it gives way to every creature, nor the least fly, or least stone cast into it, but it gives way to it of itself, yet if God say it shall be as a firmament between the waters above and the waters below, it then stands like a wall of brass and yields not. It will not suffer the water in the clouds to fall down, but if it do fall to water the earth, it shall strain through the air as through a sieve. The clouds sometimes are so full that one would think they would burst through the air and fall upon the earth, but God having set the air to be a firmament or expulsion between the waters above and waters below, though of itself a very liquid thing, yet it stands like to a wall of brass. And truly so is it with a Christian spirit, though of himself he is as liquid as the air, you may easily pass through him and go an end with him easily; he is easy to be entreated, very gently, but take him now in anything wherein God hath bid him keep his stand in his course, and there he stands like a wall of brass, that were never such high and great matters put upon him, ready to bear him down, he will not shrink nor give any way at all . . . A strange kind of combination in the spirit of grace [is] wrought in such hearts: they can call upon their hearts to be lifted up to the high things of God, nothing then too great for them to exercise themselves in; no mercies nor judgments too great, no not the unsearchable counsel of God, the depths of the mysteries of God, nothing is too high for them. It will be prying and looking into the secret counsels of God, and yet both together with most modesty, when the soul is most lifted up in the ways of God. Yet at the same time he looks at himself as nothing, and yet notwithstanding so far forth as God will be pleased to reveal it to him, he will be searching into the deep things of God, and yet all this will he do with a very modest spirit.

Thus you have seen [the] combinations severally of the gracious affections that are not to be found in nature, no not set upon civil objects, much less upon spiritual, but upon civil objects they cannot be so combined together . . .

There is another combination of virtues strangely mixed in every lively holy Christian, and that is diligence in worldly business and yet deadness to the world; such a mystery as none can read but they that know it. For a man to *rise early, and go to bed late, and eat the bread of carefulness,* not a sinful but a provident care, and to avoid idleness, cannot endure to spend any idle time, takes all opportunities to be doing something, early and late, and loseth no opportunity [to] go any way and bestir himself for profit—this will he do most diligently in his calling. And yet be a man dead-hearted to the world, *the diligent hand maketh rich* (Proverbs 10:4). Now if this be a thing which is so common in the mouth of the Holy Ghost, and you see was the practice of the greatest women then upon the earth, [of] the greatest princes in those times, the more gracious, the more diligent and laborious in their callings: you see it will well stand with the life of grace, very diligent in worldly business. And yet notwithstanding, the very same souls that are most full of the world's business, the more diligent they be in their callings, yet the same persons are directed to be *dead with Christ* (Colossians 3:1–3). *Set not your affections upon things below, but on things that are above, for we are dead with Christ.* Meaning dead to all these earthly things and all the comforts here below; they are not our life, but our *life is hid with Christ in God* and therefore to this world are we dead . . . Be busy like ants, morning and evening, early and late, and labor diligently with their hands and with their wits, and which way soever as may be the best improvement of a man's talent, it must be employed to the best advantage, and yet when a man hath labored thus busily, yet his heart and mind and affections are above . . . Say not therefore when you see two men laboring very diligently and busily in the world, say not, here is a couple of worldlings, for two men may do the same business, and have the same success, and yet a marvelous difference between them: the heart of the one may be dead to these things, he looks at them as they be; indeed, *but crumbs that fall from the children's table.* He looks not at them as his chiefest good; but *the bread of life,* the spiritual food of his soul, that is the thing which he chiefly labors after. And another man places his happiness and felicity in them and makes them his chiefest good, and so there is a manifest difference between them . . .

The last virtue is a single one, and that is love of enemies. *I say unto you, love your enemies* (Matthew 5:44), *that you may be the children of your heavenly Father.* Love your enemies. This very grace whereby we do love our enemies, it hath a contrary work to nature, for naturally, this we shall find to be the frame of our hearts towards our enemies: we are cold and undisposed to do any good office unto them, very hard and cold, and frozen towards them. Those who are our enemies, we take no pleasure in them, but now in such a case as this, the love of a Christian will come and warm the heart and thaw this cold frostiness that is in our souls; whereas before a man was cold toward his enemies, his heart now begins to reflect upon him in pity and compassion . . .

This is the nature of love, as it is the nature of water to cool hot distempers, and as it is the nature of fire to thaw and soften hard frozen spirits, and so though it be but as one entire grace. Yet in the act it puts forth a kind of variety of work, whereby one would think it did cross itself, but it doth not, but doth all by the life of Christ. Thus you see what the effects of the life of sanctification is in the heart of a man, after that God hath begun to root the life of justification in us, and he discerns that God hath wrought a change in him, and then these several graces, though in themselves, and work, one opposite to another—yet in a Christian heart they can meet and join together . . .

THOMAS SHEPARD (1605–1649)
The Sound Believer (c. 1633)

BARELY THIRTY, Thomas Shepard was the youngest of the leading ministers who emigrated to New England during the Puritan flight from Laud. He was, like virtually all his colleagues except Davenport, a product of Cambridge, where he had been awakened by John Preston from "gaming, bowling, and drinking" into a life of piety. As lecturer in the small Essex village of Earle's Colne, he built a reputation for what Edward Johnson called "soul-ravishing" preaching, and thereby earned the archbishop's rage.

In his memoir, Shepard left an unusually candid record of his personal struggle to decide between exile and resistance. When he finally did arrive in the New World, it is not surprising that he took a leading role in the colonists' effort to explain their decision to their brethren who stayed behind. The *Defense of the Answer,* which Shepard wrote together with John Allin, minister of Dedham, was composed as part of the transatlantic dialogue over New England's legitimacy; it made its essential appeal to the primacy of preaching: "when some freely in zeal of the truth preached against . . . the corruptions of the times . . . we might easily have found the way to have filled the prisons." It was not cowardice, Shepard implied, that sent them out of England; it was commitment to the Word, which would have been shut up with them if they had allowed themselves to be apprehended. What he did not address in the *Defense,* and only hinted at in his memoir, was his personal craving for a sense of renewal, for liberation from the confusions of daily life in oppressive England, where, as he put it in a series of sermons later published as *The Sincere Convert,* many are "taken up with suits in law, and almost eaten up with suretyship, and carking cares how to pay debts." What Shepard fled was not so much the difficulty of making ends meet—though this may have been a real concern for him as well as for his parishioners—as it was the moral vertigo that life in England seemed more and more to entail. Although his English sermons show Shepard to have been a preparationist in the lineage of Perkins and Hooker, his emphasis on working toward a "true sight of sin," and on the ceaseless struggle with sin that God demanded, could sometimes give way to an ecstatic language of expectation—of anticipatory delight in the fleshless serenity that would be the saints' reward. The urgency of Shepard's need for such a release had, it would seem, something to do with his hopes for the future in America.

The text of *The Sound Believer* is from volume 1 of John Albro's edition of Shepard's *Works* (1853), pp. 267–271.

The Sound Believer

Glorification

This is the sixth and last privilege and benefit, and you all know is the last thing in the execution of God's eternal purpose toward all his beloved and chosen ones . . . Hereby we are made perfect in holiness; no more sin shall stir in us; perfect also in happiness; no more tears, nor sorrows, nor temptations, nor fears, shall ever molest us, and all this shall be in our immediate communion with God in Christ. *We shall be then,* saith Paul, *forever with the Lord.* If the Lord would but open our eyes and give us one glimpse of this, what manner of persons should we be! How should we then live! How willingly then should we embrace fagots and flames, prisons and penury! The light afflictions here, would not they work for us glory? Nay, the Apostle useth such a phrase which I believe may pose the most curious orator in the world to express to the life of it—*an exceeding weight of glory* (2 Corinthians 4:17). What is our life now but a continual dying, carrying daily about us that which is more bitter than a thousand deaths? . . . O that I were able therefore to give you a blush and a dark view of this glory, that might raise up our hearts to this work!

Consider the glory of the place: the Jews did and do dream still of an earthly kingdom, at the coming of their Messiah; the Lord dasheth those dreams, and tells them *his kingdom is not of this world,* and that he *went away to prepare a place for them, that where he is they might be* (John 14:2–3), and *be with him to see his glory* (John 17:23–24). The place shall be the third heaven, called our father's house, built by his own hand with most exquisite wisdom, fit for so great a God to appear in his glory to all his dear children; called also a *kingdom. Come, ye blessed, inherit the kingdom* . . . This inheritance, he tells us, is (1) *incorruptible,* whereas, *all this world waxeth old as a garment.* (2) It is undefiled, never yet polluted with any sin, no, not by the angels that fell, for they fell in paradise, when guardians to man; whereas *this whole creation groaneth under burden and bondage of corruption* (Romans 8:21–22). (3) This never fadeth away; it is not like flowers, whose glory and beauty soon wither, but this shall be most pleasant, sweet, and ever delightsome after we have been ten thousand years in it, as it was the first day we entered into it . . . whereas in this world (suppose a man should ever enjoy it, yet) there grows a secret satiety and fullness upon our hearts, and it grows common, and blessings of greatest price are not so sweet as the first time we enjoy them; they clog the stomach and glut the soul. But here our eyes, ears, minds, hearts, shall be ever ravished with that admirable glory which shines brighter than ten thousand suns, the very fabric of it being God's needlework (if I may so say), quilted with variety of all flowers, in divers colors, by the exactest art of God himself, as the Apostle intimates.

Secondly: Consider of the glory of the bodies of the saints in this place: the Lord shall change our vile bodies, which are but as dirt upon our wings and clogs at our feet, as the Apostle expresseth it. Paul was in the third heaven and saw the glory, doubtless, of some there: see what he saith of them (I Corinthians 15:42–44):

It shall be an incorruptible body: it shall never die, nor rot again; no, not in the least degree tending that way; it shall never grow weary (as now it is by hard labor, and sometimes by holy duties), nor faint, nor grow wrinkled and withered. Adam's body in innocency *potuit non mori,* we say truly; but this *non potest mori,* it cannot die: and hence it is, that there shall be no more sickness, pains, griefs, faintings, fits, etc., when it comes there.

It shall be a glorious body: it shall *rise in honor,* saith Paul; and what glory shall it have! Verily, it shall be like *unto Christ's glorious body* (Philippians 3:21), which, when Paul saw, did *shine brighter than the sun;* and therefore here shall be no imperfection of limbs, scars, or maims, natural or accidental deformities; but as the third heaven itself is most lightsome, so their bodies that inhabit that shall exceed the light and glory thereof, these being more compacted, and thence shining out in greater luster, that the eyes of all beholders shall be infinitely ravished to see such clods of earth as now we are advanced to such incomparable beauty and amiableness of heavenly glory . . .

It shall be a spiritual body: our body now is acted by animal spirits, and being earthly and natural, grows, feeds, eats, drinks, sleeps, and hath natural affections and desires after these things, and is troubled if it wants them. But then these same bodies shall live by the indwelling of the spirit of God poured out abundantly in us and upon us, and so acting our bodies, and swallowing up all such natural affections and motions as those be here; as Moses, being with God in the mount forty days and nights, did not need any meat or drink, the Lord and his glory being all unto him: how much more shall it be thus then! I do not say we shall be spirits like the angels, but our bodies shall be spiritual, having no natural desires after any earthly blessing, food, raiment, etc., nor troubled with the want of them. And hence also the body shall be able as well to ascend up as now it is to descend down; as Austin[1] shows by a similitude of lead, which some artists can beat so small as to make it swim: we are now earthly, and made to live on this earth, and hence fall down to the center; but we are made then to be above forever with the Lord . . .

It shall not be with us there as it was with the wicked Israelites, who when they came into the good land of rest, they then forgot the Lord and all his works past: no, no, all that which God hath done for you in this world, you shall then look back and see, and wonder, and love, and bless, and suck the sweet of forevermore. It is a fond, weak question, to think whether we shall know one another in heaven. Verily, you shall remember the good the Lord did you here; by what means the Lord humbled you; by what ministry the Lord called you; by what friends the Lord comforted and refreshed you: and there you shall see them with you . . .

You shall sit down with Abraham, Isaac, and Jacob in the kingdom of God; be taken into the bosom of Abraham, and there we shall speak with them of the Lord's wonders, of his Christ and kingdom (Psalms 145:11), and every sentence and word shall be milk and honey, sweeter than thy life now can be unto thee. We shall know, and love, and honor one another exceedingly . . .

1. Augustine, *City of God*, XIII, 18; XXIII, 11.

TWO

THE MIGRATION

WELL BEFORE there was a Puritan literature in New England—in fact before any of those who became the intellectual architects and spokesmen of Massachusetts Bay even hinted of a migration from England—another settlement was founded in southeastern Massachusetts. Those who sailed aboard the *Mayflower* in 1620 and founded Plymouth Plantation were representative of a distinctive brand of English nonconformity: Separatists. Separatism had emerged in England in the 1580s, inspired by one Robert Browne (hence the epithet "Brownists"), who formed what was called a conventicle and published *Reformation without Tarrying for Any* (1582), in which he proclaimed it unavailing to look to the English state to reform the church. He and his followers sought a return to Pauline purity: churches formed not out of whole parishes but only by "the worthiest," each of them forswearing membership in the "false church" established in England and communion with the faithless and corrupt. They feared and fled contamination by a world filled with sins (chiefly, as they defined sin, those of the flesh). Early in the seventeenth century large numbers of Separatists exiled themselves from English society by moving to Holland, where they practiced and began to perfect their comparatively simple Reformed faith.

Late in the second decade of the century, many of these Leyden Separatists concluded that yet another "removal" was needed if their purity was to be preserved. Their reasons were not widely different from those which inspired the subsequent and larger migration of "non-Separating" Puritans to Massachusetts Bay. Both treated the question of removal as a "case of conscience"; both were overcome with a sense of impending spiritual desolation in Christian Europe—even of divine judgments about to befall the Old World. Yet it took nearly the whole decade of the 1620s for some English Puritans to despair ultimately of their native country. The literature of both plantations, moreover, places emphasis on the difficulties of settling a new land, in part to discourage wrongly motivated migration, in larger part, it would seem, in order to assure their remaining brethren they had not chosen the morally easy path of simply fleeing from the sins and plague of the Old World. In the literature of both groups, moreover, one discerns a slow but inexorable reordering of their visions of the past, as events, in Old England and in New, demanded reinterpretation of God's "general providence" in bringing his saints across the Atlantic. The long process of reconceiving the reasons and the motives of the first settlers of New England—a process that eventually was to see John Adams ascribing to them a desire for political as well as religious liberty, and Daniel Webster, a seeking after economic opportunity—began in the memories and imaginations of the first New England generation.

ROBERT CUSHMAN (1579–1625)

Reasons and Considerations Touching the Lawfulness of Removing out of England into the Parts of America (1622)

THE EARLIEST expression of Plymouth Plantation was the work of Robert Cushman, deacon of the Leyden congregation and business agent of the proposed colony. Although Cushman intended to sail with the first migrants, events held him behind for nearly a year, during which he secured from British officialdom a broad patent for settling the land and devised a rather demanding contract with English merchant-investors: a bonded indebtedness that for more than a decade controlled the economic destiny of the colony. He was in Plymouth in November and December 1621, during which time he won the colonists' acceptance of the contract and delivered an eloquent lay sermon on "The Sin and Dangers of Self-Love," in which he admonished the brethren against an individualism that threatened the colony's economic survival and, more important, its Christian social cohesiveness.

On his return to England, Cushman helped to compile and wrote the dedication to a collection of narrative and description concerning the Atlantic voyage and the colony's first tentative months. This tract concluded with a lengthy sermon-like utterance entitled *Reasons and Considerations Touching the Lawfulness of Removing out of England into the Parts of America.* Clearly Cushman's own work, it has often and quite erroneously been labeled "promotional" literature. This it was only in the sense that it was addressed to Separatists still living in England, who might be considering joining their brethren in the New World. The genre to which it can most appropriately be assigned is that of "cases of conscience," for the title, as well as the text itself, shows Cushman addressing those Englishmen who were uncertain as to the morality—not the expediency, and surely not the economic advantage—of permanently departing their native land. It bears comparison with John Winthrop's *Reasons to Be Considered,* composed at the end of the decade; both manifest the degree to which by the onset of the 1620s some separatists had come to despair of Old England—perhaps of all Europe—as a "moral wilderness" filled with temptations and ethical dilemmas from which escape seemed an almost unquestionable imperative. Cushman's certitude in refuting objections to removal is among the first of the many ironies in our literature. For it was composed, and promulgated, after Cushman's visit to Plymouth and his discovery, disclosed in the sermon on self-love, that a simple change of location did not, in fact, redeem human nature or cleanse or preserve it from all impurities.

The text of *Reasons and Considerations* is from Dwight B. Heath, ed., *A Journal of the Pilgrims at Plymouth* (New York: Corinth Books, 1963), pp. 88–95.

Reasons and Considerations Touching the Lawfulness of Removing out of England into the Parts of America

Forasmuch as many exceptions are daily made against the going into and inhabiting of foreign desert places, to the hindrances of plantations abroad, and the increase of distractions at home, it is not amiss that some which have been ear-witnesses of the exceptions made, and are either agents or abettors of such removals and plantations, do seek to give content to the world, in all things that possibly they can . . .

Being studious for brevity, we must first consider that whereas God of old did call and summon our fathers by predictions, dreams, visions, and certain illuminations to go from their countries, places, and habitations, to reside and dwell here or there, and to wander up and down from city to city, and land to land, according to his will and pleasure, now there is no such calling to be expected for any matter whatsoever, neither must any so much as imagine that there will now be any such thing . . .

Neither is there any land or possession now, like unto the possession which the Jews had in Canaan, being legally holy and appropriated unto a holy people, the seed of Abraham, in which they dwelt securely and had their days prolonged, it being by an immediate voice said, that he (the Lord) gave it them as a land of rest after their weary travels and a type of eternal rest in heaven but now there is no land of that sanctimony, no land so appropriated, none typical, much less any that can be said to be given of God to any nation as was Canaan, which they and their seed must dwell in, till God sendeth upon them sword or captivity. But now we are all in all places strangers and pilgrims, travellers and sojourners, most properly, having no dwelling but in this earthen tabernacle; our dwelling is but a wandering, and our abiding but as a fleeting, and in a word our home is nowhere, but in the heavens, in that house not made with hands, whose maker and builder is God, and to which all ascend that love the coming of our Lord Jesus.

Though then there may be reasons to persuade a man to live in this or that land, yet there cannot be the same reasons which the Jews had, but now as natural, civil and religious bands tie men, so they must be bound, and as good reasons for things terrene and heavenly appear, so they must be led. And so here falleth in our question, how a man that is born and bred, and hath lived some years, may remove himself into another country.

I answer, a man must not respect only to live, and do good to himself, but he should see where he can live to do most good to others; for, as one saith, "He whose living is but for himself, it is time he were dead." Some men there are who of necessity must here live, as being tied to duties, either to church, commonwealth, household, kindred, etc. But others, and that many, who do no good in none of those, nor can do none, as being not able, or not in favor, or as wanting opportunity, and live as outcasts, nobodies, eye-sores, eating but for themselves, teaching but themselves, and doing good to none, either in soul or body, and so pass over days, years, and months, yea, so live and so die. Now such should lift up their eyes and see whether there be not some other place and country to which they may go to do good . . .

But some will say, what right have I to go live in the heathens' country?

Letting pass the ancient discoveries, contracts and agreements which our Englishmen have long since made in those parts, together with the acknowledgment of the histories and chronicles of other nations, who profess the land of America from the Cape de Florida unto the Bay of Canada (which is south and north three hundred leagues and upwards, and east and west further than yet hath been discovered) is proper to the King of England—yet letting that pass, lest I be thought to meddle further than it concerns me, or further than I have discerning, I will mention such things as are within my reach, knowledge, sight and practice, since I have travailed in these affairs.

And first, seeing we daily pray for the conversion of the heathens, we must consider whether there be not some ordinary means and course for us to take to convert them, or whether prayer for them be only referred to God's extraordinary work from heaven. Now it seemeth unto me that we ought also to endeavor and use the means to convert them, and the means cannot be used unless we go to them or they come to us; to us they cannot come, our land is full; to them we may go, their land is empty.

This then is a sufficient reason to prove our going thither to live lawful: their land is spacious and void, and there are few and do but run over the grass, as do also the foxes and wild beasts. They are not industrious, neither have art, science, skill or faculty to use either the land or the commodities of it, but all spoils, rots, and is marred for want of manuring, gathering, ordering, etc. As the ancient patriarchs therefore removed from straiter places into more roomy, where the land lay idle and waste, and none used it, though there dwelt inhabitants by them (as Genesis 13:6,11,12, and 34:21, and 41:20), so it is lawful now to take a land which none useth, and make use of it . . .

It being then, first, a vast and empty chaos; secondly, acknowledged the right of our sovereign king; thirdly, by a peaceable composition in part possessed of divers of his loving subjects, I see not who can doubt or call in question the lawfulness of inhabiting or dwelling there . . .

As for such as object the tediousness of the voyage thither, the danger of pirates' robbery, of the savages' treachery, etc., these are but lions in the way, and it were well for such men if they were in heaven, for who can show them a place in this world where iniquity shall not compass them at the heels, and where they shall have a day without grief, or a lease of life for a moment; and who can tell, but God, what dangers may lie at our doors, even in our native country, or what plots may be abroad, or when God will cause our sun to go down at noon-days, and in the midst of our peace and security, lay upon us some lasting scourge for our so long neglect and contempt of his most glorious Gospel?

But we have here great peace, plenty of the Gospel, and many sweet delights, and variety of comforts.

True indeed, and far be it from us to deny and diminish the least of these mercies, but have we rendered unto God thankful obedience for this long peace, whilst other peoples have been at wars? Have we not rather murmured, repined, and fallen at jars amongst ourselves, whilst our peace hath lasted with foreign power? Was there ever more suits in law, more envy, contempt and reproach than nowadays? Abraham and Lot departed asunder when there fell a breach betwixt them, which was occasioned by the straitness of the land; and surely, I am persuaded that howsoever the frailties of men are principal in all contentions, yet the straitness of the place is such as each man is fain to pluck his means, as it were, out of his neighbor's throat . . .

Let us not thus oppress, straiten, and afflict one another, but seeing there is a spacious land, the way to which is through the sea, we will end this difference in a day . . .

"G. MOURT"

Mourt's Relation (1622)

THE TRACT to which Cushman appended his *Reasons and Considerations* was a compilation of several reports describing (according to the lengthy original title) the "safe arrival" of the planters, and "their joyful building of, and comfortable planting themselves in the now well-defended town of New Plymouth." Although it was probably Cushman who saw it through the press, the introduction was signed by one "G. Mourt"—which signature has been variously identified as a misprint for George Morton (another of the Leyden group's negotiators) and as an outright pseudonym, designed to suggest that the tract was sponsored by someone other than a "subversive" Separatist. Since 1736, when Thomas Prince so referred to it in his *Chronological History of New England*, the tract has been known simply as *Mourt's Relation*, but the actual identity of "G. Mourt" remains a mystery.

Mourt's Relation is commonly characterized as a promotional tract, which, as the original title along with Cushman's *Reasons* suggests, it in some sense was. But it differs markedly from the counterpart literature of Virginia, with its initially extravagant description of the New World's commodities. The advocates of Plymouth settlement were not addressing those who might lust after a fecund, even tropical, new Eden, and, more precisely, they viewed their colony as a haven solely for "spiritual" refugees, whatever the social and economic conditions that disturbed them in the Old World. The prevailing tenor of *Mourt's Relation* is matter-of-fact, even utilitarian, almost photographic in its descriptions, and devoid of any high drama in its narrative—notably in its recounting of the first landfall.

The text is from Dwight B. Heath, ed., *A Journal of the Pilgrims at Plymouth*, pp. 39–41.

A Relation or Journal of the beginning and proceedings of the English Plantation settled at Plymouth *in New England, by certain English adventurers both merchants and others*
With their difficult passage, their safe arrival, their joyful building of, and comfortable planting themselves in the now well defended town of New Plymouth

... Monday the 18th day, we went a-land, manned with the master of the ship and three or four of the sailors. We marched along the coast in the woods some seven or eight miles, but saw not an Indian nor an Indian house; only we found where formerly had been some inhabitants, and where they had planted their corn. We found not any navigable river, but four or five small running brooks of very sweet fresh water, that all run into the sea. The land for the crust of the earth is, a spit's[1] depth, excellent black mould, and fat[2] in some places, two or three great oaks but not very thick, pines, walnuts, beech, ash, birch, hazel, holly, asp, sassafras in abundance, and vines everywhere, cherry trees, plum trees, and many others which we know not. Many kinds of herbs we found here in winter, as strawberry leaves innumerable, sorrel, yarrow, carvel, brooklime, liverwort, watercresses, great store of leeks and onions, and an excellent strong kind of flax and hemp. Here is sand, gravel, and excellent clay, no better in the world, excellent for pots, and will wash like soap, and great store of stone, though somewhat soft, and the best water that ever we drank, and the brooks now begin to be full of fish. That night, many being weary with marching, we went aboard again.

The next morning, being Tuesday the 19th of December, we went again to discover further; some went on land, and some in the shallop. The land we found as the former day we did, and we found a creek, and went up three English miles. A very pleasant river, at full sea a bark of thirty tons may go up, but at low water scarce our shallop could pass. This place we had a great liking to plant in, but that it was so far from our fishing, our principal profit, and so encompassed with woods that we should be in much danger of the savages, and our number being so little, and so much ground to clear, so as we thought good to quit and clear that place till we were of more strength. Some of us having a good

1. Spade's.
2. Fertile.

mind for safety to plant in the greater isle, we crossed the bay which is there five or six miles over, and found the isle about a mile and a half or two miles about, all wooded, and no fresh water but two or three pits, that we doubted of fresh water in summer, and so full of wood as we could hardly clear so much as to serve us for corn. Besides, we judged it cold for our corn, and some part very rocky, yet divers thought of it as a place defensible, and of great security.

That night we returned again a-shipboard, with resolution the next morning to settle on some of those places; so in the morning, after we had called on God for direction, we came to this resolution: to go presently ashore again, and to take a better view of two places, which we thought most fitting for us, for we could not now take time for further search or consideration, our victuals being much spent, especially our beer, and it being now the 19th of December. After our landing and viewing of the places, so well as we could we came to a conclusion, by most voices, to set on the mainland, on the first place, on a high ground, where there is a great deal of land cleared, and hath been planted with corn three or four years ago, and there is a very sweet brook runs under the hill side, and many delicate springs of as good water as can be drunk, and where we may harbor our shallops and boats exceeding well, and in this brook much good fish in their seasons; on the further side of the river also much corn-ground cleared. In one field is a great hill on which we point to make a platform and plant our ordnance, which will command all round about. From thence we may see into the bay, and far into the sea, and we may see thence Cape Cod. Our greatest labor will be fetching of our wood, which is half a quarter of an English mile, but there is enough so far off. What people inhabit here we yet know not, for as yet we have seen none. So there we made our rendezvous, and a place for some of our people, about twenty, resolving in the morning to come all ashore and to build houses . . .

THOMAS MORTON (1575–1646)

New English Canaan (1634–35)

THOMAS MORTON first visited New England in 1622 or 1624 and returned in 1625 to lead a settlement (on the site of what is now Quincy, Massachusetts) that came to be known as Merrymount. Morton was an Anglican who employed the Book of Common Prayer and engaged in what the Plymouth settlers considered licentious activities—among them dancing around a Maypole. Morton's colony became—in nineteenth-century fictional treatments by Hawthorne and John Lothrop Motley and even in an opera composed in the 1930s—an emblem of the Elizabethan jollity threshed out of the American grain by a stern-visaged and iron-willed Puritanism. But Myles Standish's military assault on Merrymount in 1628 was chiefly provoked not by Morton's antics but by his selling firewater and firearms to the Indians and thereby interfering with Plymouth's fur trade.

In 1630 Morton was arrested, his property confiscated, and his house burned; he returned to England, where within a few years he was conspiring with Sir Ferdinando Gorges for the revocation of the Massachusetts Bay Colony charter and the transfer of all New England, including Plymouth Colony, to a company loyal to both church and crown. His *New English Canaan* was clearly intended as propaganda in this campaign, focused on the schismatic intentions of the nonconformist settlers of New England and on the beauties and commodities they had "hidden" from general view. Yet Morton's celebratory prose, illuminated by a bright ray of humor, reveals, for all its formulaic qualities, a genuine delight in the New England setting. In 1643, after Laud's downfall, Morton returned to New England, was ordered to leave Massachusetts, wandered to Rhode Island and Maine, returned to Massachusetts, was imprisoned for a year in 1645, and spent the final two years of his life in the District of Maine.

The text of *New English Canaan* is from the edition by Charles Francis Adams (Boston, 1883), pp. 110, 179–181.

New English Canaan or New Canaan

The Epistle to the Reader

Gentle Reader,

I present to the public view an abstract of New England, which I have undertaken to compose by the encouragement of such genious spirits as have been studious of the enlargement of his majesty's territories, being not formerly satisfied by the relations of such as, through haste, have taken but a superficial survey thereof, which thing time hath enabled me to perform more punctually to the life, and to give a more exact accompt of what hath been required. I have therefore been willing to do my endeavor to communicate the knowledge which I have gained and collected together by mine own observation in the time of my many years' residence in those parts to my loving countrymen, for the better information of all such as are desirous to be made partakers of the blessings of God in that fertile soil, as well as those that, out of curiosity only, have been inquisitive after novelties. And the rather for that I have observed how divers persons (not so well affected to the weal public in mine opinion), out of respect to their own private ends, have labored to keep both the practice of the people there, and the real worth of that eminent country concealed from public knowledge; both which I have abundantly in this discourse laid open. Yet if it be well accepted, I shall esteem myself sufficiently rewarded for my undertaking, and rest,

Your wellwisher.
Thomas Morton.

. . . . .

The Second Book. Containing a description of the beauty of the country with her natural endowments, both in the land and sea with the great Lake of Erocoise[1]

CHAPTER I
THE GENERAL SURVEY OF THE COUNTRY

In the month of June, anno salutis 1622, it was my chance to arrive in the parts of New England with 30 servants and provision of all sorts

1. Associating Lake Champlain with the Iroquois Indians, Morton conceived of it as a vast inland sea that fed the rivers of the Northeast—probably confusing it with the Great Lakes.

fit for a plantation. And whiles our houses were building, I did endeavor to take a survey of the country. The more I looked, the more I liked it. And when I had more seriously considered of the beauty of the place, with all her fair endowments, I did not think that in all the known world it could be paralleled, for so many goodly groves of trees, dainty fine round rising hillocks, delicate fair large plains, sweet crystal fountains, and clear running streams that twine in fine meanders through the meads, making so sweet a murmuring noise to hear as would even lull the senses with delight asleep—so pleasantly do they glide upon the pebble stones, jetting most jocundly where they do meet, and hand in hand run down to Neptune's court, to pay the yearly tribute which they owe to him as sovereign lord of all the springs. Contained within the volume of the land [are] fowls in abundance, fish in multitude; and [I] discovered, besides, millions of turtledoves on the green boughs, which sat pecking of the full ripe pleasant grapes that were supported by the lusty trees, whose fruitful load did cause the arms to bend; [among] which here and there dispersed, you might see lilies and of the daphnean tree, which made the land to me seem paradise; for in mine eye 'twas nature's masterpiece; her chiefest magazine of all where lives her store. If this land be not rich, then is the whole world poor . . .

I will now discover[2] . . . a country whose endowments are by learned men allowed to stand in a parallel with the Israelites' Canaan, which none will deny to be a land far more excellent than Old England, in her proper nature . . .

I must applaud the judgment of those that have made choice of this part (whereof I now treat), being of all other most absolute . . . Among those that have settled themselves in New England, some have gone for their conscience sake (as they profess), and I wish that they may plant the gospel of Jesus Christ, as becometh them, sincerely and without schism[3] or faction, whatsoever their former or present practices are, which I intend not to justify. Howsoever, they have deserved (in mine opinion) some commendations, in that they have furnished the country so commodiously in so short a time. Although it hath been but for their own profit, yet posterity will taste the sweetness of it, and that very suddenly . . .

2. Reveal.
3. The 1637 edition has "satism," presumably a misprint for "schism."

WILLIAM BRADFORD (1590–1657)
Of Plymouth Plantation (1630–1650)

William Bradford, governor of Plymouth Colony almost continuously from 1620 until his death in 1657, began to write his history of Plymouth Plantation in 1630, the year in which the first waves of migrants reached the shores of Massachusetts Bay. Bradford, who as a youth had joined William Brewster's Separatist conventicle in England and in 1609 had migrated with them to Holland, seems to have sensed almost immediately that the larger and far wealthier plantation to the north threatened the communal integrity of Plymouth. He appears to have sought, through his history, to preserve both the record and the fact of Plymouth's separate identity. But the history reflected other developments as well: the outbreak of civil war in England and the overthrow of Episcopacy, and the internal disintegration (as he saw it) of the Plymouth community, particularly as his contemporaries began to pass from the stage. The work is a highly artful document, not merely in its finely balanced sentences or in its rolling cadences, drawn from and built upon the language of the Geneva Bible. It is in its larger structure—an effort to understand and relate God's purpose in the founding of Plymouth—that Bradford's creative artistry and its implications are most conspicuously revealed. The history is organized around two themes: the failure of Plymouth to fulfill its original purpose as a selfless community and the concurrent completion of the Reformation through Cromwell's victories in Old England. The themes, which emerge almost contrapuntally, both contradict and reinforce one another. For even as Bradford hints (or wants to believe) that Plymouth's congregational polity informed Massachusetts Bay and that the example of the larger colony in turn inspired the ecclesiastical revolution in England, he acknowledges that the golden day of Plymouth lay in its distant past—perhaps in Leyden, which he recalls both as the great good place and (in his recollections of how the migrants' "case of conscience" was formulated there) as demanding the departure of at least some of the Separatist brethren.

If one reads *Of Plymouth Plantation* in its entirety—as any serious student of American literature should, not only because the manuscript served as a source for generations of historians but also because it is the first fulfilled literary achievement of New England—one senses that Bradford is uncertain of his audience. At times he seems to be addressing the saints still in Europe, seeking to justify those who had fled to America and who remained there even after the triumphs of the New Model Army. At other moments, his mind's eye is on Massachusetts Bay and its apologists, whom he reminds that they were preceded into the New World by a more pitiable and more resolute handful of reformers. In the 1650s Bradford several times argued that his people, unlike those of Boston, were the victims of persecution. But as the work progresses, it becomes clear that his chief concern is with the rising generation—a concern disclosed as well in a long poem written in 1654, and in his *Dialogue between Some Young Men Born in New England and Sundry Ancient Men that Came out of Holland* (1648).

In the context of these late-life concerns, Bradford's famous "description" of New England as it was first espied emerges neither as a factual record nor as meant to be one. (It bears comparison with the much earlier account of the landfall in *Mourt's Relation,* which Bradford himself may have had a hand in composing.) This later reconstruction was a reminder, perhaps an inspiration, to the forgetful and backsliding children of the first settlers of what God had accomplished for and through their fathers. In stating what the younger generation "ought to say," Bradford piles one Old Testament phrase upon another and thus nearly completes in a single sustained passage the process that, among the interpreters of Massachusetts Bay, took almost a full generation. Bradford and his fellow-Separates had gone first to Leyden and then to Plymouth in the hope and expectation of recapturing the Pauline purity of the primitive churches of the New Testament. Yet here, if only in his language, Bradford derives both comfort and judgment from parallels between his people's history and that of the children of Israel.

The manuscript of Bradford's history, probably looted during the British occupation of Boston in 1775–76, was rediscovered in London in 1855. The text here is from the edition by Samuel Eliot Morison (New York: Knopf, 1953), copyright © by Samuel Eliot Morison, pp. 23–27, 58–63. Reprinted by permission of Alfred A. Knopf, Inc.

Of Plymouth Plantation

Chapter IV. Showing the Reasons and Causes of Their Removal

After they had lived in this city [Leyden] about some eleven or twelve years (which is the more observable being the whole time of that famous truce between that state and the Spaniards) and sundry of them were taken away by death and many others began to be well stricken in years (the grave mistress of Experience having taught them many things), those prudent governors with sundry of the sagest members began both deeply to apprehend their present dangers and wisely to foresee the future and think of timely remedy. In the agitation of their thoughts, and much discourse of things hereabout, at length they began to incline to this conclusion: of removal to some other place. Not out of any newfangledness or other such like giddy humor by which men are oftentimes transported to their great hurt and danger, but for sundry weighty and solid reasons, some of the chief of which I will here briefly touch.

And first, they saw and found by experience the hardness of the place and country to be such as few in comparison would come to them, and fewer that would bide it out and continue with them . . .

Secondly. They saw that though the people generally bore all these difficulties very cheerfully and with a resolute courage, being in the best and strength of their years; yet old age began to steal on many of them; and their great and continual labours, with other crosses and sorrows, hastened it before the time. So as it was not only probably thought, but apparently seen, that within a few years more they would be in danger to scatter, by necessities pressing them, or sink under their burdens, or both. And therefore according to the divine proverb, that a wise man seeth the plague when it cometh, and hideth himself, Proverbs 22:3, so they like skillful and beaten soldiers were fearful either to be entrapped or surrounded by their enemies so as they should neither be able to fight nor fly. And therefore thought it better to dislodge betimes to some place of better advantage and less danger, if any such could be found.

Thirdly. As necessity was a taskmaster over them so they were forced to be such, not only to their servants but in a sort to their dearest children, the which as it did not a little wound the tender hearts of many a loving father and mother, so it produced likewise sundry sad and sorrowful effects . . .

Lastly (and which was not least), a great hope and inward zeal they had of laying some good foundation, or at least to make some way thereunto, for the propagating and advancing the gospel of the kingdom of Christ in those remote parts of the world; yea, though they should be but even as stepping-stones unto others for the performing of so great a work.

These and some other like reasons moved them to undertake this resolution of their removal; the which they afterward prosecuted with so great difficulties, as by the sequel will appear.

The place they had thoughts on was some of those vast and unpeopled countries of America, which are fruitful and fit for habitation, being devoid of all civil inhabitants, where there are only savage and brutish men which range up and down, little otherwise than the wild beasts of the same. This proposition being made public and coming to the scanning of all, it raised many variable opinions amongst men and caused many fears and doubts amongst themselves. Some, from their reasons and hopes conceived, laboured to stir up and encourage the rest to undertake and prosecute the same; others again, out of their fears, objected against it and sought to divert from it; alleging many things, and those neither unreasonable nor unprobable; as that it was a great design and subject to many unconceivable perils and dangers; as, besides the casualties of the sea (which none can be freed from), the length of the voyage was such as the weak bodies of women and other persons worn out with age and travail (as many of them were) could never be able to endure. And yet if they should, the miseries of the land which they should be exposed unto, would be too hard to be borne and likely, some or all of them together, to consume and utterly to ruinate them. For there they should be liable to famine and nakedness and the want, in a manner, of all things. The change of air, diet and drinking of water would infect their bodies with sore sicknesses and grievous diseases. And also those which should escape or overcome these difficulties should yet be in continual danger of the savage people, who are cruel, barbarous and most treacherous, being most furious in their rage and merciless where they overcome, not being content only to kill and take away life, but delight to torment men in the most bloody manner that may be; flaying some alive with the shells of fishes, cutting off the members and joints of others by piecemeal and broiling on the coals, eat the collops of their flesh in their sight whilst they live, with other cruelties horrible to be related . . .

It was answered, that all great and honourable actions are accompanied with great difficulties and must be both enterprised and overcome with answerable courages. It was granted the dangers were great, but not desperate. The difficulties were many, but not invincible . . .They lived here but as men in exile and in a poor condition, and as great miseries might possibly befall them in this place, for the twelve years of truce were now out and there was nothing but beating of drums and preparing for war, the events whereof are always uncertain. The Spaniard might prove as cruel as the savages of America, and the famine and pestilence as sore here as there, and their liberty less to look out for remedy.

After many other particular things answered and alleged on both sides, it was fully concluded by the major parts to put this design in execution and to prosecute it by the best means they could . . .

Chapter IX. Of Their Voyage, and How They Passed the Sea; and of Their Safe Arrival at Cape Cod

September 6 [1620]. . . . now all being compact together in one ship, they put to sea . . . with a prosperous wind, which continued divers days together, which was some encouragement unto them; yet, according to the usual manner, many were afflicted with seasickness. And I may not omit here a special work of God's providence. There was a proud and very profane young man, one of the seamen, of a lusty, able body, which made him the more haughty; he would alway be contemning the poor people in their sickness and cursing them daily with grievous execrations; and did not let to tell them that he hoped to help to cast half of them overboard before they came to their journey's end, and to make merry with what they had; and if he were by any gently reproved, he would curse and swear most bitterly. But it pleased God before they came half seas over, to smite this young man with a grievous disease, of which he died in a desperate manner, and so was himself the first that was thrown overboard. Thus his curses light on his own head, and it was an astonishment to all his fellows for they noted it to be the just hand of God upon him.

After they had enjoyed fair winds and weather for a season, they were encountered many times with cross winds and met with many fierce storms with which the ship was shroudly[1] shaken, and her upper works made very leaky; and one of the main beams in the midships was bowed and cracked, which put them in some fear that the ship could not be able to perform the voyage. So some of the chief of the company, perceiving the mariners to fear the sufficiency of the ship as appeared by their mutterings, they entered into serious consultation with the master and other officers of the ship, to consider in time of the danger, and rather to return than to cast themselves into a desperate and inevitable peril. And truly there was great distraction and difference of opinion amongst the mariners themselves; fain would they do what could be done for their wages' sake (being now near half the seas over) and on the other hand they were loath to hazard their lives too desperately. But in examining of all opinions, the master and others affirmed they knew the ship to be strong and firm under water; and for the buckling of the main beam, there was a great iron screw the passengers brought out of Holland, which would raise the beam into his place; the which being done, the carpenter and master affirmed that with a post put under it, set firm in the lower deck and otherways bound, he would make it sufficient. And

1. Harshly.

as for the decks and upper works, they would caulk them as well as they could, and though with the working of the ship they would not long keep staunch, yet there would otherwise be no great danger, if they did not overpress her with sails. So they committed themselves to the will of God and resolved to proceed.

In sundry of these storms the winds were so fierce and the seas so high, as they could not bear a knot of sail, but were forced to hull[2] for divers days together. And in one of them, as they thus lay at hull in a mighty storm, a lusty young man called John Howland, coming upon some occasion above the gratings was, with a seele[3] of the ship, thrown into sea; but it pleased God that he caught hold of the topsail halyards which hung overboard and ran out at length. Yet he held his hold (though he was sundry fathoms under water) till he was hauled up by the same rope to the brim of the water, and then with a boat hook and other means got into the ship again and his life saved. And though he was something ill with it, yet he lived many years after and became a profitable member both in church and commonwealth. In all this voyage there died but one of the passengers, which was William Butten, a youth, servant to Samuel Fuller, when they drew near the coast.

But to omit other things (that I may be brief) after long beating at sea they fell with that land which is called Cape Cod; the which being made and certainly known to be it, they were not a little joyful. After some deliberation had amongst themselves and with the master of the ship, they tacked about and resolved to stand for the southward (the wind and weather being fair) to find some place about Hudson's River for their habitation. But after they had sailed that course about half the day, they fell amongst dangerous shoals and roaring breakers, and they were so far entangled therewith as they conceived themselves in great danger; and the wind shrinking upon them withal, they resolved to bear up again for the Cape and thought themselves happy to get out of those dangers before night overtook them, as by God's good providence they did. And the next day they got into the Cape Harbor where they rid in safety . . .

Being thus arrived in a good harbor, and brought safe to land, they fell upon their knees and blessed the God of Heaven[4] who had brought them over the vast and furious ocean, and delivered them from all the perils and miseries thereof, again to set their feet on the firm and stable earth, their proper element. And no marvel if they were thus joyful, seeing wise Seneca was so affected with sailing a few miles on the coast of his

2. Drift.
3. Roll.
4. Daniel 2:19.

own Italy, as he affirmed, that he had rather remain twenty years on his way by land than pass by sea to any place in a short time, so tedious and dreadful was the same unto him.

But here I cannot but stay and make a pause, and stand half amazed at this poor people's present condition; and so I think will the reader, too, when he well considers the same. Being thus passed the vast ocean, and a sea of troubles before in their preparation (as may be remembered by that which went before), they had now no friends to welcome them nor inns to entertain or refresh their weatherbeaten bodies; no houses or much less towns to repair to, to seek for succour. It is recorded in Scripture as a mercy to the Apostle and his shipwrecked company, that the barbarians showed them no small kindness in refreshing them,[5] but these savage barbarians, when they met with them (as after will appear) were readier to fill their sides full of arrows than otherwise. And for the season it was winter, and they that know the winters of that country know them to be sharp and violent, and subject to cruel and fierce storms, dangerous to travel to known places, much more to search an unknown coast. Besides, what could they see but a hideous and desolate wilderness, full of wild beasts and wild men—and what multitudes there might be of them they knew not. Neither could they, as it were, go up to the top of Pisgah[6] to view from this wilderness a more goodly country to feed their hopes; for which way soever they turned their eyes (save upward to the heavens) they could have little solace or content in respect of any outward objects. For summer being done, all things stand upon them with a weather-beaten face, and the whole country, full of woods and thickets, represented a wild and savage hue. If they looked behind them, there was the mighty ocean which they had passed and was now as a main bar and gulf to separate them from all the civil parts of the world. If it be said they had a ship to succour them, it is true; but what heard they daily from the master and company? But that with speed they should look out a place (with their shallop) where they would be, at some near distance; for the season was such as he would not stir from thence till a safe harbor was discovered by them, where they would be, and he might go without danger; and that victuals consumed apace but he must and would keep sufficient for themselves and their return. Yea, it was muttered by some that if they got not a place in time, they would turn them and their goods ashore and leave them. Let it also be considered what weak hopes of supply and succour they left behind them, that might bear

5. Acts 28:2 (Bradford's note).
6. Deuteronomy 34:1; the summit from which Moses saw Canaan.

up their minds in this sad condition and trials they were under; and they could not but be very small. It is true, indeed, the affections and love of their brethren at Leyden was cordial and entire towards them, but they had little power to help them or themselves; and how the case stood between them and the merchants at their coming away hath already been declared.

What could now sustain them but the Spirit of God and His grace? May not and ought not the children of these fathers rightly say: "Our fathers were Englishmen which came over this great ocean, and were ready to perish in this wilderness; but they cried unto the Lord, and He heard their voice and looked on their adversity,"[7] etc. "Let them therefore praise the Lord, because He is good: and His mercies endure forever." "Yea, let them which have been redeemed of the Lord, shew how He hath delivered them from the hand of the oppressor. When they wandered in the desert wilderness out of the way, and found no city to dwell in, both hungry and thirsty, their soul was overwhelmed in them. Let them confess before the Lord His loving kindness and His wonderful works before the sons of men."[8]

7. Deuteronomy 26:5, 7 (Bradford's note).
8. Psalm 107: 1–5, 8 (Bradford's note).

WILLIAM AMES (1576–1633)

Conscience with the Power and Cases Thereof (c. 1630)

BRADFORD'S DESIRE to assert a role for Plymouth in the unfolding of history, together with an incidental reference to a meeting between an elder of his church and one of the founders of the first Massachusetts Bay congregation, helped to inspire a long-held view that the Bay Colony first learned of the "Congregational Way" through tutorial in the New World. However, as Williston Walker's *Creeds and Platforms of Congregationalism* (1893) made manifest, and as Perry Miller convincingly argued in *Orthodoxy in Massachusetts* (1933), the idea of nonseparating congregationalism emerged independently within English Puritanism in the decade prior to the Great Migration of 1630. The idea was tested, modified (quite possibly in light of the Plymouth experience), and eventually codified in response to New World conditions. But neither the founding of Massachusetts nor the development of its orthodoxy can be understood without a realization that many of those who built the Bay Colony were inspired and driven by some of the same concerns and aspirations that lay behind the Plymouth settlement.

Among the recognized leaders of English Puritan thought in the first third of the century was William Ames, perhaps the chief intellectual architect of both the theology of the covenant and the morphology of preparation. His influence on those Puritans who came to America, particularly on Thomas Hooker, was profound and enduring. Unlike such Puritan leaders as Richard Sibbes and John Preston, who persisted in contending for the faith in England, Ames removed to Holland, where he composed many of his major utterances, including the *Marrow of Sacred Divinity*. A gifted "casuist," Ames in 1630 published a collection of "cases of conscience" in which he, like many another English Puritan of the 1620s, addressed the variety of moral dilemmas confronting the faithful in a time of change. One of the more significant of his cases touched on the issue of schism—on what circumstances justified renunciation of membership in an established parish church and even, implicitly, the sort of exile Ames had chosen for himself.

The text of *Conscience with the Power and Cases Thereof* is from the edition of 1639, pp. 62–63, 140–141.

Conscience with the Power and Cases Thereof

Of the Church

Question 2. *To what a kind of church ought we to join ourselves?*

Answer 1. To none but a true one, that is, professing the true faith.

2. Of true ones, we ought to choose the purest as far as we are able.

3. Although we may join ourselves to one in which many defects are necessarily to be tolerated, yet not to one in which we must of necessity partake in any sin (Ephesians 5:11). Neither is it lawful to adjoin ourselves to any church with a mind, by our silence, to cherish any of its defects, but that (as far as we may with edification) we may do our endeavor to take them away.

Question 3. *Whether we may communicate with such a church as doth tolerate the wicked and oppose the good?* . . .

From such a church, in which some wicked men are tolerated, we must not presently separate (III John 9–11). First, because it may be the error or infirmity of the church. Secondly, because patience and long-suffering is to be exercised toward a private brother offending (Galatians 6:1), much more towards a whole society of brethren, or a church. Thirdly, because by the rash departure of the godly the correction of the evil ones is not promoted, but hindered. Fourthly, because ofttimes there cannot be a departure made from such a church to one more pure, without grievous discommodities, which must be avoided as much as we can, without sin. Yea sometime they make an affirmative precept to cease to bind, which otherwise could not be left undone without sin.

If any one either wearied out with unjust vexation, or providing for his own edification, or for a testimony against wickedness, shall depart from such a society to one more pure, without a condemnation of that church which he leaves, he is not therefore to be accused of schism or of any sin . . .

Of Schism

Question 3. *Whether or not all schism be a sin?*

Answer: Schism, properly so called, is a most grievous sin.

First, because it is against charity toward our neighbor, and robs him of a spiritual good.

Secondly, it is against the edification of him which maketh the separation, in regard it deprives him of all communion in that spiritual good.

Thirdly, it is against the honor of Christ, in regard that after its manner, it destroyeth the unity of Christ's mystical body.

Fourthly, it maketh way for heresy, and a separation from Christ.

Nevertheless, a withdrawing from the true church is in some cases both lawful and necessary. As first, if a man cannot continue his communion without a communication of their sins. Secondly, if there be any eminent danger of being seduced. Thirdly, if by oppression or persecution, a man be compelled to withdraw himself.

Howsoever a total secession or withdrawing, with all absolute renunciation and rejection of all communion with that which is the true church, can by no means lawfully be undertaken; but a partial secession only is allowed of, as far as there can be no communion had without a participation of the sin.

Question 4. *Whether or no, schismatics are members of the church?*

Answer. Schism doth in so much separate from the church, as it doth renounce the communion with the church. If therefore, first, a separation be made from some certain actions or persons only, although that separation be schismatical, yet doth it not presently separate from the church.

If the separation be made from one or more particular churches, yet the party separated may nevertheless remain a member of some other churches, in which he findeth not that cause of separation which he did in the other . . .

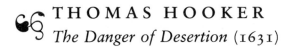

THOMAS HOOKER
The Danger of Desertion (1631)

AMES'S *CASES*, with its strict and limited definition of how and when willful abandonment of one's parish could be justified, evinces the dread of "schism" among even those nonconformists most disaffected from aspects of the Church of England. But ecclesiastical concerns were hardly the primary driving force, much less the exclusive one, behind the Great Migration of the 1630s. The literature of the 1620s discloses an increasing preoccupation among the Puritan clergy with the accelerating social and economic "sins" of English culture. Even while such leaders as John Preston were exhorting the faithful to contend earnestly for the faith, others were slowly drawing quite different conclusions—and imperatives.

On November 5, 1626 (Gunpowder Day), Thomas Hooker delivered a sermon of Thanksgiving, in which he proclaimed that only God's sovereign love and mercy had spared England the plagues and devastations that had been visited on continental Protestantism during the Thirty Years' War:

> . . . for whence comes it, whence is it, that the Lord hath had an eye unto me above all the rest, when the fire of God's fury hath flamed and consumed all the country round about us; Bohemia, and the Palatinate, and Denmark; when the fire hath thus burnt up all; yet this little cottage, this little England, this span of ground, that this should not be searched? Nay, when the sword hath ruinated and overcome all the other parts of Christendom where the name of the Lord Jesus is professed, we sit under our vines and fig trees, there is no complaining in our streets, our wives are not husbandless, our children are not fatherless. Mark the reason and ground of all is nothing else but God's mercy toward us. And above all, here is seen the abundant goodness of the Lord: not-

> withstanding our thankfulness and carelessness, we yet continue to be a nation.
>
> There is no other reason to be given of this but God's love will have it so . . .

Hooker's eloquent echo of Shakespeare reminds us that the Puritans were far more familiar with the poetic letters of their culture than we have sometimes supposed. Elsewhere Hooker invokes Chaucer as writing a pure and plain English, undefiled by French and Italian importations—an emblem, for Hooker, of an earlier national innocence. Hooker's nationalism—in tension for him as for other Puritans with the commitment to a Calvinism that knew no nation—was a two-edged sword: even as he stressed God's special mercies toward his English people, Hooker sketched the special "ruin and desolation" likely to be visited on a people that failed to return God's favor. In a later sermon of 1626 he invoked the precedent of Sodom and Gomorrah, even as he bewailed the "hypocrisy" prevailing among the professed children of God in England. ("Look as it is among stage-players.") Sometime in the next two years he preached his celebrated lecture "The Faithful Covenanter"—its controlling metaphors those of contract, bargain, and money—in which he reminded his audience that most were "behind hand" in their rents: "Good words pay no debts, brethren."

The sermon Hooker preached on Maundy Thursday, 1631, even though it was probably first delivered after the fleet sailed for Boston, establishes *the* context for the Great Migration. It is often wrongly called Hooker's "Farewell Sermon" and assumed to have accompanied his own sailing for New England. In fact, one printed version of the sermon makes no reference to New England whatsoever, and another, which speaks of New England as a refuge, contains no hint that Hooker himself anticipated migrating. It is not Hooker but Hooker's God who, in the sermon, is saying "Farewell England." Nor surely is the desertion of which he speaks that of the departing Puritans, but that of a God about to abandon his almost-chosen people because they have not upheld their part of the contract. The version published in 1657 carries the title "The signs of God forsaking a people."

It bears noting that Hooker's text for the sermon is Jeremiah 14:9, the prophet's plea that God not abandon his children. *The Danger of Desertion,* together with Hooker's earlier sermons, contains nearly all the intellectual premises and rhetorical techniques that were to be identified with the "jeremiad" so characteristic of second-generation New England. But it was as an Englishman that Hooker spoke in 1631, and to an audience that was English as well. Twenty years were to elapse before Englishmen, transplanted to New England, could again believe, with anything approaching Hooker's premigration certainty, that God had selected them as a specially covenanted people.

The Danger of Desertion was transcribed and published in two somewhat different versions in 1641 and 1657. The text reproduced here is from the later edition as established by George H. Williams in his *Thomas Hooker: Writings in England and Holland* (Cambridge, Mass.: Harvard University Press, 1975), pp. 228–236, 238–239, 241–242, 244–246.

The Danger of Desertion

Jeremiah 14:9. And we are called by thy name; leave us not.

Two things, brethren and beloved in Christ Jesus, are intended and expressed by the holy prophet, from the first verse to the thirteenth verse.

There is first a denomination[1] of a judgment, and that is: dearth or famine, from the first verse to the seventh.

Secondly, the sword is threatened, to the thirteenth verse; he will send the famine, then the sword, and he will not be entreated.

Then in the eighth and ninth verses, we have the importunate prayer of the church to turn away these judgments. And the prayer is marvelous sweet, in confession, where they confess their sins, and seek to God for succor . . .

First, they desire God that he would not take his providence from them: *Why stayest thou but for a night?*, verse the eighth, as if they should have said: "It is marvelous strange that thou behavest thyself so like a stranger; thou seest our sorrows and dost not help us. Thou perceivest our troubles and thou regardest us not. It is strange that the God of Israel stands as a man astonished; that thou that hast heretofore received us should now stand as a man amazed and astonished, as if thou shouldst say, 'Jerusalem cannot be saved, and Judah cannot be succored.' "

Secondly, they desire that God would not take away his presence from them: "Leave us not to ourselves," say they. "Let us see thy face. Though we die, yet let it be in thy presence . . .

"To whom should wives go, but to their husbands? To whom should children go, but to their fathers, to whom should servants go, but to their masters, to whom then should we go, but to thee, our God and Savior. Leave us not therefore, and we will meddle with none but thee" . . .

1. Definition.

And this is the greatest request of the saints: they desire not to be left of God, although God might leave them, whence learn that God might cast off a people, and unchurch a nation.

Israel did fear it and it is that which they prayed against, God might leave them. I do not say that God will cast off his elect eternally, but those that are only in outward covenant with him he may . . . See Isaiah 1:7: "your cities are burned with fire, strangers devour your land in your presence, and it is desolate like the overthrow of strangers."

[For] there is an outward calling, as well as an effectual calling. God may reject, "for many are called, but few are chosen," says our Savior. My brethren, cast your thoughts afar off, and see what is become of those famous churches of Pergamum and Thyatira and the rest mentioned, Revelation 1:11. And who would have thought that Jerusalem should have been made an heap of stones, and a vagabond people, and yet we see God hath forsaken them, showing us thereby that, although God will never forsake his own elect ones, yet he may forsake such as are in outward covenant with him.

The Lord is said to dischurch or discharge a people, Hosea 1:9 . . . and, as I may so say, he sues out a bill of divorcement, as it was in the old law. They that had anything against their wives, they sued out a bill of divorcement against them, and so doth God . . . as if God should now say to England, "Plead, plead with England, all ye that are my ministers in the way of my truth, and say unto her, let her cast away her rebellions, lest I leave her as I found her in the day of captivity and bondage under the blindness of popery and superstition!"

Objection: But how doth God cast off a people?

Solution: I answer, first, when he takes away his love and respect from a people; and as his love, so the token of his love, which is his word and sacraments, the means of salvation.

Secondly, when he takes away his providence, I mean when he takes down his walls, that is, his magistracy and ministry.

Thirdly, when instead of counseling, there comes in bribing; and instead of true teaching, there comes in daubing with untempered mortar when God takes away the hedge thereof [of the vineyard], Isaiah 5:5, or the stakes grow rotten, and are not renewed, then is God going away . . .

Use: May God unchurch or discharge a people, and cast a nation off? Oh, then let this teach us to cast off all security; for miseries are nigh at hand in all probability! When we observe what God hath done for us, all things are ripe to destruction, and yet we fear it not, but we promise to ourselves safety, and consider not that England is ready to be harrowed, and yet we cannot entertain a thought of England's desolation. When there are so many prophecies in it of its destruction, yet we cannot be persuaded of it. According to the conviction of our judgments, either it must not be, or not yet, as if it were unpossible that God should leave England, as if God were a cockering[2] father over lewd (and stubborn) children. God may leave a nation, and his elect may suffer, and why may not England (that is but in an outward covenant with him)? England's sins are very great, and our warnings are and have been great; but yet our mercies are far greater. England hath been a mirror of mercies. Yet now God may leave it, and make it the mirror of his justice . . .

Even so England: "Thou hast the temple and the priests, and yet may not God that destroyed Shiloh, destroy thee?" Go to Bohemia, and from thence to the Palatinate (and so to Denmark)[3] and from thence to other parts of Germany. Do but imagine that you were there, or do but mark what travelers say. God's churches are made heaps of stones, and those Bethels[4] wherein God's name was called upon, are now defiled temples for Satan and superstition to reign in. You cannot go three steps but you shall see the head of a dead man. And go a little further, and you shall see the heart picked out by the fowls of the air, or some other sad spectacle. And then surely you will say, "[Count von] Tilly hath been here or there."[5] Now are these churches become desolate, and may not England? Do but go into their cities and towns, and there you may see many compassed about with chains of captivity, and every man bemoaning himself. Do but look under a tree, and there you may see a poor fatherless child sending out his breath and crying unto his helpless mother. Step but a little further, and you shall see the helpless wife, the sad wife, bemoaning her husband, and this is her misery, she cannot die [soon] enough.

But she shall see greater misery; for either she shall, as she thinks, see her little ones dashed against the stones, or tossed upon the pikes, or if they live, that then they shall be brought up in popery . . . and then she weeps again, and thinks that if her husband be dead it is well, but it may be he is upon the rack, or put to some other torment, and then she dies an hundred times before she can die . . . May not this be the condition of England? . . .

Oh, my beloved, be not high-minded, but fear; for as we have God's bounty on the one side, so, for ought I know, we may have his severity on the other side! Prank not then yourselves with foolish imaginations, saying: "Who dare come to hurt England? The Spaniard hath his hands

2. Doting.
3. Sites of recent Protestant defeats.
4. From the Hebrew, meaning house of God.
5. A military leader of anti-Protestant forces during the Thirty Years' War.

full, and the French are too weak." But beloved, be not deluded. Who would have thought that Jerusalem, the lady city of all nations, whither the tribes went up to worship, should become a heap of stones and a vagabond people? But yet you see it was, and is to this day. And I pray, why may it not be England's case? Learn therefore, hear, and fear God; for assuredly God can be God without England's prosperity . . .

It is the importunate desire of the saints of God still to keep God present with them. They cared not so much for sword or famine, as they did for the loss of God's presence. "O Lord, leave us not," say they. This was their prayer. And blame them not, for consider what a grief it is that God should stand by and not help them. "Good Lord," say they, "leave us not; we cannot abide to think that God should leave us, much less can we endure to feel it or taste it" . . .

Thus they did, and thus the saints of God should do . . .

[*Objection:*] But what is the presence of God?

[*Answer:*] In a word, it is the particular favor of God which he expresseth in his ordinances; it is all the good and sweetness that flows from the purity of God's worship, whereby God reveals himself unto us. It is not gold, wealth, nor prosperity, that makes God to be our God; for there is more gold in the West Indies than in all Christendom. But it is God's ordinances purely administered that brings God's presence to a people.

God forsook Shiloh because his ordinances were not purely kept there. When the people left the ark, viz., his pure worship, then God left the people . . . Hence it was that Cain is said (Genesis 4:14) to be cast out of God's presence, because he was cast out from the church; he was cast out from God's ordinances. If a people do outwardly reform, and sincerely worship God, they may remain . . . If Sodom and Gomorrah had but legally repented, they had remained, they had not been destroyed.

All the helps in the world cannot help the heart of man, if God and Christ be wanting. You were as good offer a journey to refresh a weary man, or the air to feed a hungry man, as to offer riches, honors, and ease to help a distressed soul . . .

Woe be unto that heart, county, or kingdom, that God is departed from . . .

God will be God over thee in destruction, yea, when he hath spurned thousands and ten thousands into hell, such as thou art, then shalt thou be the everlasting object of his never-dying wrath. Then (though thou couldst scale the heavens with thy tears) notwithstanding all thy shrill cries, though thou couldst be heard out of that dungeon, yet were thy help never the near[er]; for God is God still. I advise thee therefore what to do, whilst thou art here in this life: make thy peace with God in Christ, and lay thyself low before him, and bear patiently his hand in his wrath which thou hast deserved. And mark what I say. Thou hast deserved to be in hell a hundred times, that is the least; and therefore be contented with thy condition. For thou hast chosen death rather than life (Jeremiah 31:8), and God should wrong himself and thee also, if he should not let thee have thy choosing.

Will not these things move you, my brethren? Methinks I see your colors rise. I am glad of it. I hope it is to a good end. You may be wise, and happily so wise as to choose life rather than death. Now the Lord grant it, for he delights not in your destruction . . .

I will deal plainly with you. As sure as God is God, God is going from England. Shall I tell you what God told me? Nay, I must tell you on pain of my life. Will you give ear and believe me? I am a poor ambassador sent from God to do his message unto you; and, although I be low, yet my message is from above, and he that sent me is great, and from above; and O that he would grant that this my message might be believed (for his sake)!

What if I should tell you what God told me yesternight that he would destroy England and lay it waste? What say you to this, my beloved? It is my message, by meditation in God's word, that he bid me do to you, and he expects an answer from you. I do my message as God commanded me. What sayest thou unto it, England? I must return an answer to my master that sent me, yea, this present night I must return an answer; for the Lord hath appointed a set time, saying, Exodus 9:5, *Tomorrow the Lord will do this thing*[6] *in the land.* Why speak you not? An answer you must give. Do you think well of it? Will you have England destroyed? Will you put the aged to trouble, and your young men to the sword? Will you have your young women widows, and your virgins defiled? Will you have your dear and tender little ones tossed upon the pikes and dashed against the stones? Or will you have them brought up in Popery, in idolatry, under a necessity of perishing their souls forever, which is worst of all? Will you have these temples wherein we seem to worship God, will you have them and your houses burnt with fire? And will you see England laid waste without inhabitants? Are you well-contented it shall be so? (God bade me ask. Why do you not answer me? I must not stir without it, I must have it.) I am an importunate suitor for Christ. Oh send me not sad away, but speak comfortably and cheerfully! What are you resolved of? Are you willing to enjoy God still, and to have him dwell with you? (You are, are you not?) It is well, I am glad of it if it be so.

6. The plague on the cattle of the Egyptians.

But you must not only say so, but you must use the means, and you must plead importunately with your God; for, although his sword be drawn and in his hand, lifted up and ready to strike, yet suffer him not to destroy, but rather to sheath his sword in the blood of his enemies. (God grant it.) I would be glad to have England flourish still. (And so are you, are you not? You are.) But if desolation do come, thank yourselves for it, it is your own fault if you be destroyed, and not God's; for he delights not in the death of any . . .

Look to it, for God is going, and if he do go, then our glory goes also. And then we may say with Phineha's wife, I Samuel 4:22, *The glory is departed from Israel.* So glory is departed from England; for England hath seen her best days, and the reward of sin is coming on apace; for God is packing up of his gospel, because none will buy his wares (not come to his price). God begins to ship away his Noahs, which prophesied and foretold that destruction was near; and God makes account that New England shall be a refuge for his Noahs and his Lots, a rock and a shelter for his righteous ones to run unto; and those that were vexed to see the ungodly lives of the people in this wicked land, shall there be safe. Oh, therefore my brethren, lay hold on God, and let him not go out of your coasts. (He is going!) Look about you, I say, and stop him at the town's end, and let not thy God depart! Oh, England, lay siege about him by humble and hearty closing with him, and although he be going, he is not yet gone! Suffer him not to go far, suffer him not to say farewell, or rather fare-ill, England! . . .

JOHN WINTHROP (1588–1649)
Reasons to Be Considered for . . . the Intended Plantation in New England (1629)

THE FIRST SETTLEMENT of Massachusetts Bay was undertaken in 1623, on Cape Ann, by fishermen sponsored by a group of English merchants chartered by the Council of New England as the Dorchester Adventurers, to whom James I had granted all New England. The fishing proved unprofitable, and the grant was transferred to the New England Company, which in turn obtained a new charter from the Council in 1628, and in 1629 yet another from the king himself. Now known as the Massachusetts Bay Company, the new group clearly had something other than fishing in mind: they envisioned, and began to organize, an expansive enterprise to provide refuge and opportunity for disaffected English nonconformists.

The central figure in this venture was John Winthrop, the first and frequent governor of the Bay Colony. Educated at Cambridge, trained as a lawyer, Winthrop was a member of the still prosperous landed gentry of England. But he was also a Puritan, vexed by economic changes, the revolution in status attending them, and, above all, the seemingly irresolvable ethical challenges posed by the changing order. To Winthrop, and to many others, it became increasingly evident that the faithful could not preserve the "ancient" faith in England, that all portents (among them the death of John Preston) called for something other than earnest contention against the evils overcoming England.

Only portions of Winthrop's correspondence from the years 1628–1630 survive, but several letters suggest that relatives, as well as friends, responded to his tentative proposals for a New England settlement with what came down to a single question and challenge: If England's moral deterioration is as grave as you say, how can you excuse a desertion by the handful of Puritan saints? Winthrop offered partial answers to his correspondents, and in the winter of 1628–1629 he drew up a systematic response to all the "objections" raised against the Massachusetts Bay enterprise by his Puritan brethren. His *Reasons to Be Considered* can be read, therefore, as a record of the dialogue between those who promoted and those who resisted the idea of Puritan migration. But it must also be read as testimony to debate within Winthrop's mind, as evidence not only of the reservations (even the guilt) carried as part of his psychological baggage to the New World, but of the extraordinary lengths—including the repudiation of the notion that God identifies his church with place or nation—to which he went in clearing his conscience for the impending voyage.

The text of *Reasons to Be Considered* is from the Massachusetts Historical Society, *Proceedings*, 8 (1864–65), 420–425.

Reasons to Be Considered for Justifying the Undertakers of the Intended Plantation in New England and for Encouraging Such Whose Hearts God Shall Move to Join with Them in It

First, it will be a service to the church of great consequence to carry the gospel into those parts of the world, to help on the coming in of fullness of the Gentiles and to raise a bulwark against the kingdom of Antichrist, which the Jesuits labor to rear up in those parts.[1]

2. All other churches of Europe are brought to desolation, and our sins, for which the Lord begins already to frown upon us, do threaten us fearfully, and who knows but that God hath provided this place to be a refuge for many whom he means to save out of the general calamity; and seeing the church hath no place left to fly into but the wilderness, what better work can there be than to go before and provide tabernacles, and food for her, against she cometh thither?

3. This land grows weary of her inhabitants, so as man who is the most precious of all creatures is here more vile and base than the earth we tread upon, and of less price among us than a horse or a sheep; masters are forced by authority to entertain servants, parents to maintain their own children, all towns complain of the burthen of their poor . . . And we use the authority of the law to hinder the increase of people, as urging the execution of the state against cottages and inmates; and thus it is come to pass that children, servants and neighbors (especially if the[y] be poor) are counted the greatest burthen, which, if things were right, it would be the chiefest earthly blessing.[2]

1. Since 1604 there had been a strong French presence in North America, and missionaries from the Society of Jesus led the French effort to convert the Indians.

2. A statute of 1589 prohibited the erection of any cottage on fewer than four acres of land, which was judged the minimum necessary for supporting a family. The harboring of "inmates" became an increasing problem in the seventeenth century as casual, untaxed inhabitants threatened to become a burden on the poor rates.

4. The whole earth is the Lord's garden and he hath given it to the sons of men, with a general condition, Genesis 1:28, *Increase and multiply, replenish the earth and subdue it,* which was again renewed to Noah. The end is double moral and natural, that man might injoy the fruits of the earth and God might have his due glory from the creature—why then should we stand here striving for places of habitation (many men spending as much labor and cost to recover or keep sometimes a[n] acre or two of land as would procure them many hundred as good or better in another country), and in the mean time suffer a whole continent, as fruitful and convenient for the use of man, to lie waste without any improvement?

5. We are grown to that height of intemperance in all excess of riot, as no man's estate almost will suffice to keep sail with his equals, and he who fails herein must live in scorn and contempt; hence it comes that all arts and trades are carried in that deceitful and unrighteous course, as it is almost impossible for a good and upright man to maintain his charge and live comfortably in any of them.

6. The fountains of learning and religion are so corrupted (as beside the unsupportable charge of the education) most children (even the best wits and fairest hopes) are perverted, corrupted, and utterly overthrown by the multitude of evil examples of the licentious government of those seminaries . . .

7. What can be a better work and more honorable and worthy a Christian than to help raise and support a particular church while it is in the infancy? . . .

8. If any such who are known to be godly and live in wealth and prosperity here shall forsake all this to join themselves to this church and to run a hazard with them of a hard and mean condition, it will be an example of great use both for removing the scandal of worldly and sinister respects which is cast upon the adventurers to give more life to the faith of God's people in their prayers for the plantation, and to encourage other[s] to join the more willingly in it.

9. It appears to be a work of God for the good of his church in that he hath disposed the hearts of so many of his wise and faithful servants (both ministers and others) not only to approve of the enterprise but to interest themselves in it, some in their prisons and estates, others by their serious advice and help otherwise: and all by their prayers for the welfare of it . . .

Divers objections which have been made against this plantation, with their answers and resolutions

Objection 1: We have no warrant to enter upon that land which hath been so long possessed by others.
Answer 1: That which lies common and hath never been replenished or subdued is free to any that will possess and improve it, for God hath given to the sons of men a double right to the earth: there is a natural right and a civil right; the first right was natural when men held the earth in common, every man sowing and feeding where he pleased, and then as men and the cattle increased, they appropriated certain parcels of ground by enclosing and peculiar manurance, and this in time gave them a civil right. Such was the right which Ephron the Hittite had in the field of Machpelah, wherein Abraham could not bury a dead corpse without leave, though for the out parts of the country which lay common, he dwelt upon them and took the fruit of them at his pleasure . . . The natives in New England, they inclose no land neither have any settled habitation nor any tame cattle to improve the land by, and so have no other but a natural right to those countries. So as if we leave them sufficient for their use we may lawfully take the rest, there being more than enough for them and us.

Secondly, we shall come in with the good leave of the natives, who find benefit already by our neighborhood and learn of us to improve part to more use than before they could do the whole, and by this means we come in by valuable purchase: for they have of us that which will yield them more benefit than all the land which we have from them.

Thirdly, God hath consumed the natives with a great plague in those parts so as there be few inhabitants left.[3]

Objection 2: It will be a great wrong to our church to take away the good people and we shall lay it the more open to the judgment feared.

Answer 1: The departing of good people from a country doth not cause a judgment but foreshow it, which may occasion such as remain to turn from their evil ways that they may prevent it, or to take some other course that they may escape it.

Secondly, such as go away are of no observation in respects of those who remain and they are likely to do more good there than here, and since Christ's time the church is to be considered as universal, without

3. Even before the establishment of Plymouth in 1620, the New England Indians had been ravaged by a series of epidemics brought on by contact with Europeans. Some historians estimate that the native population of New England was ultimately reduced by as much as 90 percent.

distinction of countries, so as he who doeth good in any one place, serves the church in all places in regard of the unity . . .

Objection 3: We have feared a judgment a great while, but yet we are safe: it were better therefore to stay till it come, and either we may fly then or, if we be overtaken in it, we may well content ourselves to suffer with such a church as ours is.

Answer: It is likely this consideration made the churches beyond the seas, as, the Palatinate, Rochelle,[4] &c., to sit still at home and not to look out for shelter while they might have found it, but the woeful spectacle of their ruin may teach us more wisdom, to avoid the plague when it is foreseen, and not to tarry as they did till it overtake us . . .

4. Sites of Protestant defeats by Catholic armies.

JOHN COTTON
God's Promise to His Plantations (1630)

WHILE PREPARING for their voyage, Winthrop and his company composed *The Humble Request of . . . the Company Late Gone for New England,* in which they denied any intention of separating from the Church of England. Their protestations, often plausibly interpreted by later readers as an attempt to keep Laud off the scent, can also be read as a rejoinder to those English Puritans who were dubious about what seemed desertion from the ranks of the faithful. Also in 1630 there appeared *The Planter's Plea,* written by John White, one of the founders of the Dorchester Company and later of the Massachusetts Bay Company, who rehearsed many of Winthrop's arguments in defense of migration. White too insists that the planters are no Separatists, but in his extended analysis of English social, economic, and political conditions, as in his answers to "objections," White's presumed audience and intentions are ambiguous: is he seeking to soothe the bishop, or is he, like Winthrop, attempting to dispel the aspersions of other Puritans? In some respects, his plea can be read as addressed to those who have removed to New England, seeking once more to salve their consciences.

The most effective balm for those aboard the Winthrop fleet was, however, John Cotton's appearance at Southampton to preach a sermon blessing the venture. In 1630 Cotton was recognizably the pre-eminent English Puritan clergyman and intellectual, and his *nihil obstat* served as the ultimate in reassurance to both those who sailed and those who remained behind. But Cotton's blessing was far from unqualified. Although he notes a variety of social and economic circumstance that might lead some to choose exile, his depiction of England's condition and destiny falls far short of Hooker's nearly apocalyptic sense of impending national doom. Moreover, Cotton views migration neither as flight to avoid contamination nor as refuge from an irredeemably corrupt England. He carefully limits his characterization of the proper frame of mind in which to undertake removal, and he sketches, however briefly, the more positive opportunities open to those about to settle in New England.

Most pointedly, Cotton reminds Winthrop's company of what lay in store should its members forswear, or forget, their brethren still in England, and the church of which all, he insists, are fellow members. Clearly at this point Cotton had no intention of joining in the migration himself. Though he spoke in other sermons of the possibility that God might "transplant us," he also consoled his people in Old Boston with the reminder that those who kept the faith amid the briars and thorns of Old England also had a promise from God: "fear not; there are more with us than against us." Indeed, not too long after the settlement of Massachusetts Bay, Cotton was writing to its clergy as a spokesman of English Puritanism, angrily asking an explanation for what he had heard of the practice, in some of the Bay churches, of refusing to accept English credentials of communion. His fears that those whom he had blessed were forming into Separate conventicles underlay many of the challenges he mounted after his own arrival in New England: his definition of the proper test of church membership (which divided him almost immediately from Thomas Hooker), his long debate with Roger Williams, and his sometimes rancorous disdain for the history and polity of Plymouth. But in 1630 his Southampton sermon was less a harbinger of his own later career than a vigorous reminder to the Winthrop company of just how sharp was the razor's edge on which their consciences were balanced.

The text of *God's Promise to His Plantations* is from *Old South Leaflets,* no. 53. Reprinted by permission.

God's Promise to His Plantations

II Samuel 7:10. Moreover I will appoint a place for my people Israel, and I will plant them, that they may dwell in a place of their own, and move no more.

. . . In this tenth verse is a double blessing promised:

First, the designment of a place for his people.

Secondly, a plantation of them in that place, from whence is promised a threefold blessing.

First, they shall dwell there like freeholders[1] in a place of their own.

Secondly, he promiseth them firm and durable possession; they shall move no more.

1. Freeholders owned their land outright—as opposed to copyholders, who held their land by a contract that subjected their heirs to "entry" fees and could be terminated by the landlord at virtually any time.

Thirdly, they shall have peaceable and quiet resting there. The sons of wickedness shall afflict them no more . . .

Now God makes room for a people three ways:

First, when he casts out the enemies of a people before them by lawful war with the inhabitants, which God calls them unto, as in Psalms 44:2, *Thou didst drive out the heathen before them* . . .

Secondly, when he gives a foreign people favor in the eyes of any native people to come and sit down with them either by way of purchase, as Abraham did obtain the field of Machpelah; or else when they give it in courtesy, as Pharaoh did the land of Goshen unto the sons of Jacob.

Thirdly, when he makes a country though not altogether void of inhabitants, yet void in that place where they reside. Where there is a vacant place, there is liberty for the sons of Adam or Noah to come and inhabit, though they neither buy it, nor ask their leaves . . .

It is a principle in nature, that in a vacant soil he that taketh possession of it, and bestoweth culture and husbandry upon it, his right it is . . .

This placing of people in this or that country is from God's sovereignty over all the earth, and the inhabitants thereof, as in Psalms 24:1, *The earth is the Lord's, and the fullness thereof* . . . Therefore it is meet he should provide a place for all nations to inhabit, and have all the earth replenished. Only in the text here is meant some more special appointment, because God tells them it by his own mouth; he doth not so with other people, he doth not tell the children of Seir[2] that he hath appointed a place for them: that is, he gives them the land by promise; others take the land by his providence, but God's people take the land by promise: and therefore the land of Canaan is called a land of promise. Which they discern, first, by discerning themselves to be in Christ, in whom all the promises are yea, and amen.

Secondly, by finding his holy presence with them, to wit, when he plants them in the holy mountain of his inheritance, Exodus 15:17. And that is when he giveth them the liberty and purity of his ordinances. It is a land of promise, where they have provision for soul as well as for body. Ruth dwelt well for outward respects while she dwelt in Moab, but when she cometh to dwell in Israel, she is said to come under the wings of God, Ruth 2:12. When God wraps us in with his ordinances, and warms us with the life and power of them as with wings, there is a land of promise.

2. The land given by God to Esau and his descendants: "I gave unto Esau Mount Seir to possess it, but Jacob and his children went down into Egypt" (Joshua 24:4). Cotton here distinguishes between the people in covenant and "the children of Seir," who have been separated from God's ancient promise to Abraham: "I will give unto thee, and to thy seed after thee . . . all the land of Canaan; for an everlasting possession" (Genesis 17:8; restated to Moses in Exodus 3).

This may teach us all where we do now dwell, or where after we may dwell. Be sure you look at every place appointed to you, from the hand of God: we may not rush into any place, and never say to God, "By your leave"; but we must discern how God appoints us this place. There is poor comfort in sitting down in any place, that you cannot say, "This place is appointed me of God." Canst thou say that God spied out this place for thee, and there hath settled thee above all hindrances? Didst thou find that God made room for thee either by lawful descent, or purchase, or gift, or other warrantable right? . . . If a man do remove, he must see that God hath espied out such a country for him . . .

Question: But how shall I know whether God hath appointed me such a place; if I be well where I am, what may warrant my removal?

Answer: . . . First, we may remove for the gaining of knowledge. Our Savior commends it in the queen of the south, that she came from the utmost parts of the earth to hear the wisdom of Solomon, Matthew 12:42. And surely with him she might have continued for the same end, if her personal calling had not recalled her home.

Secondly, some remove and travail for merchandise and gain-sake: *Daily bread may be sought from far,* Proverbs 31:14. Yea our Savior approveth travail for merchants, Matthew 13:45–46, when he compareth a Christian to a merchantman seeking pearls: for he never fetcheth a comparison from any unlawful thing to illustrate a thing lawful. The comparison from the unjust steward, and from the thief in the night, is not taken from the injustice of the one, or the theft of the other; but from the wisdom of the one, and the suddenness of the other; which in themselves are not unlawful.

Thirdly, to plant a colony, that is, a company that agree together to remove out of their own country, and settle a city or commonwealth elsewhere. Of such a colony we read in Acts 16:12, which God blessed and prospered exceedingly, and made it a glorious church. Nature teacheth bees to do so when as the hive is too full, they seek abroad for new dwellings: so when the hive of the commonwealth is so full that tradesmen cannot live one by another, but eat up one another, in this case it is lawful to remove.

Fourthly, God alloweth a man to remove, when he may employ his talents and gifts better elsewhere, especially when where he is, he is not bound by any special engagement. Thus God sent Joseph before to preserve the church: Joseph's wisdom and spirit was not fit for a shepherd, but for a counsellor of state, and therefore God sent him into Egypt . . .

Fifthly, for the liberty of the ordinances . . . This case was of seasonable use to our fathers in the days of Queen Mary, who removed to France and Germany in the beginning of her reign, upon proclamation of alteration of religion, before any persecution began.

There be evils to be avoided that may warrant removal. First, when some grievous sins overspread a country that threaten desolation . . . as in a threatening a wise man foreseeth the plague, so in the threatening he seeth a commandment, to hide himself from it. This case might have been of seasonable use unto them of the Palatinate, when they saw their orthodox ministers banished, although themselves might for a while enjoy liberty of conscience.[3]

Secondly, if men be overburdened with debts and miseries, as David's followers were: they may then retire out of the way (as they retired to David for safety) not to defraud their creditors (for *God is an avenger of such things,* I Thessalonians 4:6) but to gain further opportunity to discharge their debts, and to satisfy their creditors, I Samuel 22:1–2 . . .

Use: . . . when you have found God making way and room for you, and carrying you by his providence into any place, learn to walk thankfully before him, defraud him not of his rent, but offer yourselves unto his service: serve that God, and teach your children to serve him, that hath appointed you and them the place of your habitation . . .

Question: What is it for God to plant a people?

Answer: It is a metaphor taken from young imps;[4] I will plant them, that is, I will make them to take root there; and that is, where they and their soil agree well together, when they are well and sufficiently provided for, as a plant sucks nourishment from the soil that fitteth it . . .

He would give his people a *nail,* and *a place in his tabernacle,* Isaiah 56:5. And that is to give us part in Christ; for so the temple typified.[5] So then he plants us when he gives us root in Christ . . .

Question: What course would you have us take?

Answer: Have special care that you ever have the ordinances planted amongst you, or else never look for security. As soon as God's ordinances cease, your security ceaseth likewise; but if God plant his ordinances among you, fear not, he will maintain them . . .

Secondly, have a care to be implanted into the ordinances, that the word may be ingrafted into you, and you into it: if you take rooting in the ordinances, grow up thereby, bring forth much fruit, continue and abide therein, then you are vineyard of red wine, and the Lord will keep you . . .

Thirdly, be not unmindful of our Jerusalem at home, whether you leave us, or stay at home with us. *Oh pray for the peace of Jerusalem, they shall prosper that love her,* Psalms 122:6. *They shall all be con-*

3. The Protestant clergy was expelled from the Palatinate by Duke Maximilian in 1623.

4. Saplings.

5. "Even unto them will I give in mine house and within my walls a place and a name better than of sons and of daughters: I will give them an everlasting name, that shall not be cut off" (Isaiah 56:5).

founded and turned back that hate Sion, Psalms 129:5. As God continueth his presence with us (blessed be his name), so be ye present in spirit with us, though absent in body: forget not the womb that bare you and the breast that gave you suck. Even ducklings hatched under an hen, though they take the water, yet will still have recourse to the wing that hatched them: how much more should chickens of the same feather, and yolk? In the amity and unity of brethren, the Lord hath not only promised, but commanded, a blessing, even life forevermore, Psalms 133:1–2.

Fourthly, go forth, every man that goeth, with a public spirit, looking not on your own things only, but also on the things of others, Philippians 2:4. This care of universal helpfulness was the prosperity of the first plantation of the primitive church, Acts 4:32.

Fifthly, have a tender care that you look well to the plants that spring from you, that is, to your children, that they do not degenerate as the Israelites did; after which they were vexed with afflictions on every hand. How came this to pass? Jeremiah 2:21, *I planted them a noble vine, holy, a right seed, how then art thou degenerate into a strange vine before me?* Your ancestors were of a noble divine spirit, but if they suffer their children to degenerate, to take loose courses, then God will surely pluck you up . . .

Sixthly, and lastly, offend not the poor natives, but as you partake in their land, so make them partakers of your precious faith: as you reap their temporals, so feed them with your spirituals: win them to the love of Christ, for whom Christ died. They never yet refused the gospel, and therefore more hope they will now receive it. Who knoweth whether God have reared this whole plantation for such an end.

Use: . . . for consolation to them that are planted by God in any place, that find rooting and establishing from God, this is a cause of much encouragement unto you, that what he hath planted he will maintain. Every plantation his right hand hath not planted shall be rooted up, but his own plantation shall prosper, and flourish. When he promiseth peace and safety, what enemies shall be able to make the promise of God of none effect? Neglect not walls, and bulwarks, and fortifications for your own defense, but

ever let the name of the Lord be your strong
tower; and the word of his promise the
rock of your refuge. His word
that made heaven and earth
will not fail, till hea-
ven and earth be
no more.
Amen.

JOHN WINTHROP
A Model of Christian Charity (1630)

BOTH AMONG the Separates of Plymouth (where Cushman delivered his sermon on self-love) and within Winthrop's group, it was not unusual for members of the laity to deliver sermons. Since these lay sermons were not constrained by the customary fourfold divisions (text, doctrine, reasons, uses), they were often more flowing and less staccato than the utterances of the clergy. Winthrop's *A Model of Christian Charity,* delivered aboard the *Arbella* prior to its landfall in Massachusetts Bay, is without question the most famous and most eloquent of American lay sermons. (The practice was forbidden once Anne Hutchinson had revealed how threatening to social order it could be.)

Winthrop's *Arbella* sermon was never published in his lifetime, so his contemporaries had no fixed test from which to measure how rapidly and in what ways his earlier, happier vision of New England dimmed and even darkened as he accommodated himself to the realities of the New World. *A Model of Christian Charity* seems a shining moment of light between the dark judgment of England of his *Reasons* and the harsh practicalities of *Defense of an Order* (which appears later in this volume). Its argument and its language betray little of Winthrop's training as an advocate, much less the adversarial relationship to ideas that might be expected of a lawyer. It can be read, as can so many Puritan utterances, as "restorationist," that is, as envisioning a social order in New England that would recapture the serenity of a recollected (or imagined) English past of well-defined place for all, and of clearly understood and easily fulfilled obligations within the social hierarchy. But it is not feudal nostalgia that inspires Winthrop's sermon. Rather, Winthrop envisions an American future in which a Pauline growth in grace might be possible, as it was not, to his mind, amid the economic and ethical tangles of Old England. He speaks of "a due form of government, both civil and ecclesiastical," but he defines neither (although he safely could have, since his sermon was not intended as a public document), for his emphasis is on the spiritual opportunities available under such forms. The opportunity, and the imperative, is that of the spiritually thriving community, in which private good gives way almost inexorably to the general welfare. Having preserved themselves from the "common corruptions" of the Old World, the New World saints were now free to work out their salvation and, in Winthrop's telling, were in fact under solemn obligation to do so: to return God's favor by committing their hearts and wills to the community.

The most famous and frequently quoted of Winthrop's many eloquent passages is that in which he speaks of New England as being like "a city upon a hill." Many readers have taken this as evidence that Winthrop and his fellow voyagers undertook the New England venture in the hope of serving as an example, especially by way of forms of church government, to the saints and churches of Old England. Eventually, New Englanders did so conceive their "errand into the wilderness," especially after the question arose (both in England and in their own minds) as to why they were *here,* rather than marching with the New Model Army. But Winthrop suggests only that New England might, if a spiritual success, be emulated by "succeeding plantations." As for the other "eyes" looking toward New England, Winthrop depicts them not as hoping for a new revelation but as, it would seem, ready and even eager to see those who had deserted England as participants in a spiritual failure. In this larger sense, then, it was hardly necessary for Cotton to abjure Winthrop's people from "being unmindful" of their English brethren, since the settlers were acutely aware of those who, having questioned the entire enterprise, would continue to serve as a challenging and often oppressive superego.

The text of *A Model of Christian Charity* is from *Old South Leaflets,* no. 207. Reprinted by permission.

A Model of Christian Charity
Written on Board the Arbella *on the Atlantic Ocean*

I

A Model Hereof

God Almighty in his most holy and wise providence hath so disposed of the condition of mankind, as in all times some must be rich, some poor, some high and eminent in power and dignity, others mean and in subjection.

The Reason Hereof

First, to hold conformity with the rest of his works, being delighted to show forth the glory of his wisdom in the variety and difference of the creatures; and the glory of his power, in ordering all these differences for the preservation and good of the whole; and the glory of his greatness, that as it is the glory of princes to have many officers, so this great king will have many stewards, counting himself more honored in dispensing his gifts to man by man, than if he did it by his own immediate hands.

Secondly, that he might have the more occasion to manifest the work of his spirit: first upon the wicked in moderating and restraining them, so that the rich and mighty should not eat up the poor, nor the poor and despised rise up against their superiors and shake off their yoke; secondly in the regenerate, in exercising his graces in them, as in the great ones, their love, mercy, gentleness, temperance, etc.; in the poor and inferior sort, their faith, patience, obedience, etc.

Thirdly, that every man might have need of other, and from hence they might be all knit more nearly together in the bonds of brotherly affection. From hence it appears plainly that no man is made more honorable than another or more wealthy, etc., out of any particular and singular respect to himself, but for the glory of his creator and the common good of the creature, man. Therefore God still reserves the property of these gifts to himself as [in] Ezekiel 16:17. He there calls wealth his gold and his silver. [In] Proverbs 3:9 he claims their service as his due, *honor the Lord with thy riches,* etc. All men being thus (by divine providence) ranked into two sorts, rich and poor, under the first are comprehended all such as are able to live comfortably by their own means duly improved; and all others are poor according to the former distribution.

There are two rules whereby we are to walk one towards another: justice and mercy. These are always distinguished in their act and in their object, yet may they both concur in the same subject in each respect; as sometimes there may be an occasion of showing mercy to a rich man in some sudden danger of distress, and also doing of mere justice to a poor man in regard of some particular contract, etc.

There is likewise a double law by which we are regulated in our conversation one towards another in both the former respects: the law of nature and the law of grace, or the moral law or the law of the gospel, to omit the rule of justice as not properly belonging to this purpose otherwise than it may fall into consideration in some particular cases. By the first of these laws man as he was enabled so withal [is] commanded to love his neighbor as himself.[1] Upon this ground stands all the precepts of the moral law, which concerns our dealings with men. To apply this to the works of mercy, this law requires two things. First, that every man afford his help to another in every want or distress. Secondly, that he performed this out of the same affection which makes him careful of his own goods, according to that of our Savior. Matthew: "Whatsoever ye would that men should do to you." This was practiced by Abraham and Lot in entertaining the angels and the old man of Gibeah.[2]

The law of grace or the gospel hath some difference from the former, as in these respects. First, the law of nature was given to man in the estate of innocency; this of the gospel in the estate of regeneracy. Secondly, the former propounds one man to another, as the same flesh and image of God; this as a brother in Christ also, and in the communion of the same spirit, and so teacheth us to put a difference between Christians and others. *Do good to all, especially to the household of faith;* upon this ground the Israelites were to put a difference between the brethren of such as were strangers though not of Canaanites. Thirdly, the law of nature could give no rules for dealing with enemies, for all are to be considered as friends in the state of innocency, but the Gospel commands love to an enemy. Proof: If thine enemy hunger, feed him; *love your enemies, do good to them that hate you,* Matthew 5:44.

This law of the gospel propounds likewise a difference of seasons and occasions. There is a time when a Christian must sell all and give to the poor, as they did in the Apostles' times. There is a time also when a Christian (though they give not all yet) must give beyond their ability, as they of Macedonia (II Corinthians 11:9). Likewise community of perils calls for extraordinary liberality, and so doth community in some special service for the church. Lastly, when there is no other means whereby our Christian brother may be relieved in his distress, we must help him beyond our ability, rather than tempt God in putting him upon help by miraculous or extraordinary means.

This duty of mercy is exercised in the kinds, *giving, lending,* and *forgiving*—

Question: What rule shall a man observe in giving in respect of the measure?[3]

Answer: If the time and occasion be ordinary he is to give out of his abundance. Let him lay aside as God hath blessed him. If the time and

1. In Matthew 5:43.

2. The story of Abraham's hospitality to the angels is in Genesis 18; the old man of Gibeah gives aid to a needy stranger in Judges 19.

3. What rule shall govern the size of a man's charity?

occasion be extraordinary, he must be ruled by them; taking this withal, that then a man cannot likely do too much, especially if he may leave himself and his family under probable means of comfortable subsistence . . .

Question: What rule must we observe in lending?

Answer: Thou must observe whether thy brother hath present, or probable, or possible means of repaying thee. If there be none of these, thou must give him according to his necessity, rather than lend him as he requires. If he hath present means of repaying thee, thou art to look at him not as an act of mercy, but by way of commerce, wherein thou art to walk by the rule of justice; but if his means of repaying thee be only probable or possible, then is he an object of thy mercy, thou must lend him, though there be danger of losing it, Deuteronomy 15:7, *If any of thy brethren be poor, etc., thou shalt lend him sufficient* . . .

Question: What rule must we observe in forgiving?

Answer: Whether thou didst lend by way of commerce or in mercy, if he have nothing to pay thee, [thou] must forgive (except in cause where thou hast a surety or a lawful pledge), Deuteronomy 15:2. Every seventh year the creditor was to quit that which he lent to his brother if he were poor, as appears [in] verse 8, *Save when there shall be no poor with thee.* In all these and like cases, Christ was a general rule, Matthew 7:22, *Whatsoever ye would that men should do to you, do ye the same to them also.*

Question: What rule must we observe and walk by in cause of community of peril?

Answer: The same as before, but with more enlargement towards others and less respect towards ourselves and our own right. Hence it was that in the primitive church they sold all, had things in common, neither did any man say that which he possessed was his own. Likewise in their return out of the captivity, because the work was great for the restoring of the church and the danger of enemies was common to all, Nehemiah exhorts the Jews to liberality and readiness in remitting their debts to their brethren, and disposing liberally of his own to such as wanted, and stand not upon his own due, which he might have demanded of them.[4] Thus did some of our forefathers in times of persecution in England, and so did many of the faithful of other churches, whereof we keep an honorable remembrance of them . . .

Having already set forth the practice of mercy according to the rule of God's law, it will be useful to lay open the grounds of it also, being

4. Nehemiah rebuilt the walls of Jerusalem, in part by persuading the moneylenders to place the common welfare above their own profit (Nehemiah 3).

the other part of the commandment, and that is the affection from which this exercise of mercy must arise. The Apostle tells us that this love is the fulfilling of the law,[5] not that it is enough to love our brother and so no further; but in regard of the excellency of his parts giving any motion to the other as the soul to the body and the power it hath to set all the faculties on work in the outward exercise of this duty. As when we bid one make the clock strike, he doth not lay hand on the hammer, which is the immediate instrument of the sound, but sets on work the first mover or main wheel, knowing that will certainly produce the sound which he intends. So the way to draw men to works of mercy is not by force of argument from the goodness or necessity of the work; for though this course may enforce a rational mind to some present act of mercy, as is frequent in experience, yet it cannot work such a habit in a soul, as shall make it prompt upon all occasions to produce the same effect, but by framing these affections of love in the heart which will as natively bring forth the other, as any cause doth produce effect.

The definition which the scripture gives us of love is this: "Love is the bond of perfection." First, it is a bond or ligament. Secondly, it makes the work perfect. There is no body but consists of parts and that which knits these parts together gives the body its perfection, because it makes each part so contiguous to others as thereby they do mutually participate with each other, both in strength and infirmity, in pleasure and pain. To instance in the most perfect of all bodies: Christ and his church make one body. The several parts of this body, considered apart before they were united, were as disproportionate and as much disordering as so many contrary qualities or elements, but when Christ comes and by his spirit and love knits all these parts to himself and each to other, it is become the most perfect and best proportioned body in the world. Ephesians 4:16, *Christ, by whom all the body being knit together by every joint for the furniture thereof, according to the effectual power which is in the measure of every perfection of parts, a glorious body without spot or wrinkle,* the ligaments hereof being Christ, or his love, for *Christ is love,* I John 4:8. So this definition is right: *Love is the bond of perfection.*

From hence we may frame these conclusions. First of all, true Christians are of one body in Christ. I Corinthians 12:22, 27, *Ye are the body of Christ and members of their part.* Secondly, the ligaments of this body which knit together are love. Thirdly, no body can be perfect which wants its proper ligament. Fourthly, all the parts of this body being thus united are made so contiguous in a special relation as they must needs

5. Paul, in Romans 9:31.

partake of each other's strength and infirmity; joy and sorrow, weal and woe. I Corinthians 12:26, *If one member suffers, all suffer with it; if one be in honor, all rejoice with it.* Fifthly, this sensibleness and sympathy of each other's conditions will necessarily infuse into each part a native desire and endeavor to strengthen, defend, preserve and comfort the other . . .

The like we shall find in the histories of the church in all ages, the sweet sympathy of affections which was in the members of this body one towards another, their cheerfulness in serving and suffering together, how liberal they were without repining, harborers without grudging and helpful without reproaching; and all from hence: because they had fervent love amongst them, which only make the practice of mercy constant and easy.

The next consideration is how this love comes to be wrought. Adam in his first estate[6] was a perfect model of mankind in all their generations, and in him this love was perfected in regard of habit. But Adam rent himself from his creator, rent all his posterity also one from another; whence it comes that every man is born with this principle in him, to love and seek himself only, and thus a man continueth till Christ comes and takes possession of the soul and infuseth another principle, love to God and our brother. And this latter having continual supply from Christ, as the head and root by which he is united, gets the predomining in the soul, so by little and little expels the former. I John 4:7, *Love cometh of God and everyone that loveth is born of God,* so that this love is the fruit of the new birth, and none can have it but the new creature. Now when this quality is thus formed in the souls of men, it works like the spirit upon the dry bones. Ezekiel 37, *Bone came to bone.* It gathers together the scattered bones, or perfect old man Adam, and knits them into one body again in Christ, whereby a man is become again a living soul.

The third consideration is concerning the exercise of this love which is twofold, inward or outward. The outward hath been handled in the former preface of this discourse. For unfolding the other we must take in our way that maxim of philosophy *Simile simili gaudet,* or like will to like; for as it is things which are turned with disaffection to each other, the ground of it is from a dissimilitude arising from the contrary or different nature of the things themselves; for the ground of love is an apprehension of some resemblance in things loved to that which affects it. This is the cause why the Lord loves the creature, so far as it hath

6. Before the fall.

any of his image in it; he loves his elect because they are like himself, he beholds them in his beloved son. So a mother loves her child, because she thoroughly conceives a resemblance of herself in it. Thus it is between the members of Christ. Each discerns, by the work of the spirit, his own image and resemblance in another, and therefore cannot but love him as he loves himself . . .

If any shall object that it is not possible that love should be bred or upheld without hope of requital, it is graunted; but that is not our cause; for this love is always under reward. It never gives, but it always receives with advantage; first, in regard that among the members of the same body, love and affection are reciprocal in a most equal and sweet kind of commerce. Secondly, in regard of the pleasure and content that the exercise of love carries with it, as we may see in the natural body. The mouth is at all the pains to receive and mince the food which served for the nourishment of all the other parts of the body, yet it hath no cause to complain; for first the other parts send back by several passages a due proportion of the same nourishment, in a better form for the strengthening and comforting the mouth. Secondly the labor of the mouth is accompanied with such pleasure and content as far exceeds the pains it takes. So is it in all the labor of love among Christians. The party loving, reaps love again, as was showed before, which the soul covets more than all the wealth in the world. Thirdly, nothing yields more pleasure and content to the soul than when it finds that which it may love fervently, for to love and live beloved is the soul's paradise, both here and in heaven. In the state of wedlock there be many comforts to bear out the troubles of that condition; but let such as have tried the most, say if there be any sweetness in that condition comparable to the exercise of mutual love.

From former considerations arise these conclusions:

First, this love among Christians is a real thing, not imaginary.

Secondly, this love is as absolutely necessary to the being of the body of Christ, as the sinews and other ligaments of a natural body are to the being of that body.

Thirdly, this love is a divine, spiritual nature: free, active, strong, courageous, permanent; undervaluing all things beneath its proper object; and of all the graces, this makes us nearer to resemble the virtues of our heavenly father.

Fourthly, it rests in the love and welfare of its beloved. For the full and certain knowledge of these truths concerning the nature, use, and excellency of this grace, that which the Holy Ghost hath left recorded, I Corinthians 13, may give full satisfaction, which is needful for every true member of this lovely body of the Lord Jesus, to work upon their hearts by prayer, meditation, continual exercise at least of the special [influence] of this grace, till Christ be formed in them and they in him, all in each other knit together by this bond of love.

II

It rests now to make some application of this discourse by the present design, which gave the occasion of writing of it. Herein are four things to be propounded: first, the persons; secondly, the work; thirdly, the end; fourthly, the means.

First for the persons. We are a company professing ourselves fellow members of Christ, in which respect only though we were absent from each other many miles, and had our imployments as far distant, yet we ought to account ourselves knit together by this bond of love, and live in the exercise of it, if we would have comfort of our being in Christ. This was notorious in the practice of the Christians in former times; as is testified of the Waldenses,[7] from the mouth of one of the adversaries *Æneas Sylvius,*[8] "mutuo [ament] pene antequam norunt," they use to love any of their own religion even before they were acquainted with them.

Secondly for the work we have in hand. It is by a mutual consent, through a special overvaluing[9] providence and a more than an ordinary approbation of the churches of Christ, to seek out a place of cohabitation and consortship under a due form of government both civil and ecclesiastical. In such cases as this, the care of the public must oversway all private respects, by which not only conscience but mere civil policy doth bind us. For it is a true rule that particular estates cannot subsist in the ruin of the public.

Thirdly, the end is to improve our lives to do more service to the Lord; the comfort and encrease of the body of Christ whereof we are members; that ourselves and posterity may be the better preserved from the common corruptions of this evil world, to serve the Lord and work out our salvation under the power and purity of his holy ordinances.

Fourthly, for the means whereby this must be effected. They are twofold, a conformity with the work and end we aim at. These we see are extraordinary, therefore we must not content ourselves with usual ordinary means. Whatsoever we did or ought to have done when we lived

7. A French Protestant sect founded in the twelfth century.
8. Pope Pius II.
9. Supremely valuable.

in England, the same must we do, and more also, where we go. That which the most in their churches maintain as a truth in profession only, we must bring into familiar and constant practice, as in this duty of love. We must love brotherly without dissimulation; we must love one another with a pure heart fervently. We must bear one another's burthens. We must not look only on our own things, but also on the things of our brethren, neither must we think that the Lord will bear with such failings at our hands as he doth from those among whom we have lived; and that for three reasons:

First, in regard of the more near bond of marriage between him and us, wherein he hath taken us to be his after a most strict and peculiar manner, which will make him the more jealous of our love and obedience. So he tells the people of Israel, "You only have I known of all the families of the earth, therefore will I punish you for your transgressions." Secondly, because the Lord will be sanctified in them that come near him. We know that there were many that corrupted the service of the Lord, some setting up altars before his own, others offering both strange fire and strange sacrifices also; yet there came no fire from heaven or other sudden judgment upon them, as did upon Nadab and Abihu,[10] who yet we may think did not sin presumptuously. Thirdly, when God gives a special commission he looks to have it strictly observed in every article. When he gave Saul a commission to destroy Amalek, he indented[11] with him upon certain articles, and because he failed in one of the least, and that upon a fair pretense, it lost him the kingdom which should have been his reward if he had observed his commission.[12]

Thus stands the cause between God and us. We are entered into covenant with him for this work. We have taken out a commission, the Lord hath given us leave to draw our own articles. We have professed to enterprise these actions, upon these and those ends, we have hereupon besought him of favor and blessing. Now if the Lord shall please to hear us, and bring us in peace to the place we desire, then hath he ratified this covenant and sealed our commission, [and] will expect a strict performance of the articles contained in it. But if we shall neglect the observation of these articles which are the ends we have propounded and, dissembling with our God, shall fall to embrace this present world and prosecute our carnal intentions, seeking great things for ourselves and

10. Aaron's sons, whom God destroys by fire in anger at their disobeying his injunction against burnt offerings.

11. Made a formal agreement.

12. Saul spared the livestock of the Amalekites, thereby incurring the wrath of God, who had ordered their total destruction (I Samuel 15).

our posterity, the Lord will surely break out in wrath against us, be revenged of such a perjured people, and make us know the price of the breach of such a covenant.

Now the only way to avoid this shipwrack, and to provide for our posterity, is to follow the counsel of Micah, to do justly, to love mercy, to walk humbly with our God. For this end, we must be knit together in this work as one man. We must entertain each other in brotherly affection, we must be willing to abridge ourselves of our superfluities, for the supply of others' necessities. We must uphold a familiar commerce together in all meekness, gentleness, patience, and liberality. We must delight in each other, make others' conditions our own, rejoice together, mourn together, labor and suffer together, always having before our eyes our commission and community in the work, our community as members of the same body. So shall we keep the unity of the spirit in the bond of peace. The Lord will be our God, and delight to dwell among us as his own people, and will command a blessing upon us in all our ways, so that we shall see much more of his wisdom, power, goodness, and truth, than formerly we have been acquainted with. We shall find that the God of Israel is among us, when ten of us shall be able to resist a thousand of our enemies; when he shall make us a praise and glory that men shall say of succeeding plantations, "the Lord make it like that of New England." For we must consider that we shall be as a city upon a hill.[13] The eyes of all people are upon us, so that if we shall deal falsely with our God in this work we have undertaken, and so cause him to withdraw his present help from us, we shall be made a story and a by-word through the world. We shall open the mouths of enemies to speak evil of the ways of God, and all professors for God's sake. We shall shame the faces of many of God's worthy servants, and cause their prayers to be turned into curses upon us till we be consumed out of the good land whither we are agoing.

And to shut up this discourse with that exhortation of Moses, that faithful servant of the Lord, in his last farewell to Israel, Deuteronomy 30: Beloved, there is now set before us life and good, death and evil, in that we are commanded this day to love the Lord our God, and to love one another, to walk in his ways and to keep his commandments and his ordinance and his laws, and the articles of our covenant with him, that we may live and be multiplied, and that the Lord our God may bless us in the land whither we go to possess it. But if our hearts shall turn away, so that we will not obey, but shall be seduced, and worship other

13. Matthew 5:14–15.

gods, our pleasures and profits, and serve them; it is propounded unto us this day, we shall surely perish out of the good land whither we pass over this vast sea to possess it.

Therefore let us choose life,
that we and our seed
may live by obeying his
voice and cleaving to him,
for he is our life and
our prosperity.

JOHN COTTON

Letter from New England (1634)

WHEN JOHN COTTON assumed the pulpit of St. Botolph's in 1612, he entered on a parish with a tradition of nonconformity. Within three years he began to move well beyond his predecessor's indifference to stated forms and was briefly silenced and suspended. One of his complaining parishioners, Thomas Leverett (later a New Englander), strangely and unexpectedly recanted, and thereafter Cotton, with powerful lay support, progressively reformed his church to his liking. For nearly two decades he enjoyed, even as his ecclesiastical practices grew more brazenly defiant, the protection of the Bishop of Lincoln. The bishop, under instruction from his superiors to inquire into Cotton's treatment of the sacraments, for instance, would write *pro forma* letters of inquiry, Cotton would respond, denying all, and the good Bishop would happily report that any and all rumors of Cotton's misbehavior were wholly unfounded. What to make of Cotton's dissembling is a fascinating question, not only throughout his English years, but also during the Antinomian crisis and in his subsequent accounts of his role. In his sermon series, *God's Mercy Mixed with His Justice,* there appears a tantalizing justification of Paul's insistence, when questioned as to his religion, that he was a Pharisee: the truly faithful, Cotton explains, would have understood his real meaning ("it is true: he was a *Pharisee* and brought up a *Pharisee*"), and with respect to his inquisitors "he now scapes by this devise." So much, according to Cotton, for the better part of valor: "part of the truth, and part he conceals, and that was his wisdom."

In the autumn of 1630, overcome by illness, Cotton left his pulpit and lived for nearly a year with the Earl of Lincoln. During his absence, at the very time the Church of England came under Laud's control, Cotton's enemies in Old Boston—they seem to have been few in number, for even those excluded from full church membership appear to have accepted Cotton's judgment—began to inform on him. Hearing that a summons to the High Commission was about to be served, Cotton went into hiding and, for a moment, seems to have planned to go to Holland. But he was persuaded to visit London (in disguise), and there took place one of the more significant conferences of Puritan divines, during which Thomas Goodwin and John Davenport, among others, sought to persuade Cotton to conform ceremonially, since forms were finally of little importance. Instead, according to legend at least, Cotton persuaded them of the rectitude of his course, thus setting Goodwin on the road to Independency and Davenport thereafter to New England. Cotton himself sailed in June 1633. Within two weeks of his arrival in Boston he was installed as "teacher" in the First Church.

Yet either Cotton felt that he had not wholly satisfied his fellow conferees in London, or else he remained troubled in his own mind about his decision. For in December 1634 (more than a year after his arrival in Boston) he wrote a lengthy letter (probably to Davenport) rehearsing, clarifying, and elaborating on the reasons for his decision. Like Shepard (who wrote a similar explanation), he concluded with the argument that for him there was no further opportunity to be heard in Old England. But his emphases differ from Shepard's, possibly because Cotton was no recent graduate looking vainly for a pulpit but one on whom John Preston's mantle as pre-eminent Puritan intellectual had recently fallen. Not that Cotton was necessarily filled with notions of his unique importance (though this surely was the belief of many who, in New England, sought during the rest of his life to drag him from his "papal" throne). But in confronting the question of why he did not choose the martyr's role—imprisonment or worse—by staying in Old England, Cotton reveals the degree to which he saw himself in direct succession from the worthiest of Puritan worthies.

The text of the *Letter* is from Alexander Young, *Chronicles of the First Planters of Massachusetts Bay* (Boston, 1846), pp. 438–444.

Mr. Cotton's Letter Giving the Reasons of His and Mr. Hooker's Removal to New England

Reverend and beloved brother in our blessed Savior,

. . . The questions you demand, I had rather answer by word of mouth than by letter. Yet I will not refuse to give you account of my brother Hooker's removal and mine own, since you require a reason thereof from us both. We both of us concur in a three-fold ground of removal. 1. God having shut a door against both of us from ministering to him and his people in our wonted congregations, and calling us by a remnant of our people, and by others of this country to minister to them here, and opening a door to us this way, who are we that we should strive against God and refuse to follow the concurrence of his ordinance and providence together, calling us forth to minister here? If we may and ought to follow God's calling three hundred miles, why not three thousand? 2. Our Savior's warrant is in our case, that when we are distressed in our course in one country (*nequid dicam gravius*)[1] we should flee to another. To choose rather to bear witness to the truth by imprisonment than by banishment is indeed sometimes God's way, but not in case men have ability of body and opportunity to remove, and no necessary engagement for to stay. Whilst Peter was young he might gird himself and go whither he would, John 21:8, but when he was old and unfit for travel, then indeed God called him rather to suffer himself to be girt of others, and led along to prison and to death. Nevertheless in this point I conferred with the chief of our people, and offered them to bear witness to the truth I had preached and practiced amongst them even unto bonds, if they conceived it might be any confirmation to their faith and patience. But they dissuaded me that course, as thinking it better for themselves, and for me, and for the church of God, to withdraw myself from the present storm and to minister in this country to such of their town as they had sent before hither, and such others as were willing to go along with me or to follow after me . . . What service myself and brother Hooker might do to our people or other brethren in prison (especially in close prison which was feared) I supposed we both of us (by God's help) do the same, and much more, and with more freedom, from hence, as occasion is offered: besides all our other service to the people here, which yet is enough, and more than enough to fill both our hands, yea and the hands of many brethren more, such as yourself, should God be pleased to make way for your comfortable passage to us. To have tarried in England for the end you mention, to appear in defense of that cause for which we were questioned, had been (as we conceive it in our case) to limit witness-bearing to the cause (which may be done more ways than one) to one only way, and that such a way as we do not see God calling us unto. Did not Paul bear witness against the Levitical ceremonies and yet choose rather to depart quickly out of Jerusalem, because the most of the Jews would not receive his testimony concerning Christ in that question (Acts 22:18) than to stay at Jerusalem to bear witness to that cause unto prison and death? Not that we came hither to strive against ceremonies (or to fight against shadows); there is no need of our further labor in that course. Our people here desire to worship God in spirit and in truth, and our people left in

1. Lest I say anything more serious.

England know as well the grounds and reasons of our suffering against these things, as our sufferings themselves, which we beseech the Lord to accept and bless in our blessed Savior. How far our testimony there hath prevailed with any others to search more seriously into the cause, we do rather observe in thankfulness and silence, than speak of to the prejudice of our brethren.

3. It hath been no small inducement to us to choose rather to remove hither than to stay there, that we might enjoy the liberty, not of some ordinances of God, but of all, and all in purity. For though we bless the Lord with you for the gracious means of salvation which many of your congregations do enjoy (whereof our own souls have found the blessing, and which we desire may be forever continued and enlarged to you), yet seeing Christ hath instituted no ordinance in vain (but all to the offering of the body of Christ), and we know that our souls stand in need of all to the utmost, we durst not so far be wanting to the grace of Christ, and to the necessity of our own souls, as to set down somewhere else, under the shadow of some ordinances, when by two months' travail we might come to enjoy the liberty of all . . .

So I rest,

your very loving brother in our blessed savior,
Boston, December 3, 1634
J.C.

JOHN WINTHROP
Journal (1642)

WITHIN FIVE YEARS of the landing of the *Arbella* nearly all those whom Samuel Eliot Morison styled "Builders of the Bay Colony" were settled in Massachusetts. Hooker who, writing to Cotton from Rotterdam, had come to bemoan the formalism of the Low Country churches—the disappearance of "heart religion" from the center of Continental Reform—himself decided to sail with Cotton in June 1633. Thomas Shepard (later to become, after the death of his first wife, Hooker's son-in-law), subsequently recalled how deeply affected he had been by the departure of these two eminent men: "I saw the Lord departed from England, when Mr. Hooker and Mr. Cotton were gone; . . . and I did think I should feel many miseries if I stayed behind." Once in New England, however, both the public expression and the private correspondence of the Massachusetts spokesmen assumed a more positive tone, as for instance in a letter from Hooker to Richard Mather: "If I speak my own thoughts freely and fully, though there are many places where men may expect and obtain greater worldly advantages; yet I do believe there is not a place upon the face of the earth where a person of a judicious head and a generous heart may receive greater spiritual good to himself, and do more spiritual and temporal good to others." Mather arrived in Boston in 1635, when it still seemed the great good place of Hooker's description—as it seemed to many others, if only briefly, in the middle years of the decade. But within two years, when John Davenport landed in Boston, Massachusetts not only was no longer knit together in its work as one man but was a house divided against itself even on the all-important question of what constituted the "spiritual good." Davenport himself was immediately drawn into the vortex of the Antinomian crisis, with which began the Bay's redefinition of itself and, eventually, its reconception of its original errand.

Not that Massachusetts Bay had been totally free of divisions until then. Thomas Dudley, writing in 1630 to the Countess of Lincoln about the proper "motives for other men's coming to this place," tried to discourage any who might "come hither to plant for worldly ends that can live well at home." Not long after, Governor Winthrop had Dudley formally admonished for erecting a house inappropriately lavish in an infant plantation. Some "honest men," Dudley had allowed in his letter, "out of a desire to draw over others to them, wrote somewhat hyperbolically of many things here." But what correspondence from New England to Old survives from these early years seems generally matter-of-fact in its descriptions of the difficulties of the new plantations. The letters of John Winthrop are often despondent in tone, yet they do not seem overdrawn; it does not appear that Winthrop was bent primarily on proving that the way of the planters was not an "easy" escape from the torments of their native land. Nearly all the same troubles and travails—lack of good water, illness and epidemic, the deaths of leading citizens—are recorded with the same unembellished accuracy in Winthrop's private journal. It may well be that Winthrop and his cohorts unconsciously wanted the wilderness to be a trial, and even that they half-consciously created difficulties for themselves. Yet their earliest utterances seem quite guileless, surely artless, by comparison to what emerged in the second decade of Massachusetts experience.

Winthrop's *Journal* is akin in form to the diaries of spiritual life kept by many Puritans. Yet it differs markedly from them, and from other records of internal experience such as Anne Bradstreet's "Meditations." Winthrop focuses on public events, on the health of the whole plantation—a viewpoint consistent both with the theme of his Arbella sermon and with his role as governor. Yet as the *Journal* progresses through the 1630s, the reader senses that Winthrop's record and interpretation of social and political life in Massachusetts have become his means of assessing his own progress in his particular calling as governor. With Dudley's election to the governorship (for one year in 1634), and even more conspicuously thereafter, Winthrop increasingly looks on "particular providences" as confirmation of the rectitude of his own policies. The *Journal* expands from brief entries to lengthy commentary, as though he were planning one day to produce a full-dress history of Massachusetts Bay, the counterpart of Bradford's—save that Bradford seldom calls attention to himself and that Winthrop's more vigorous entries are often pieces of forensic eloquence directed against his enemies or detractors.

What Bradford and Winthrop had in common was a fear of the centrifugal tendencies that were quickly let loose in both their societies.

Bradford bewailed the pulling up of stakes from the common lands of Plymouth and movement inland to private holdings: these "shaking a-pieces," he predicted, would bring divine judgment on the plantation. In Massachusetts Bay, migration westward became almost inevitable as the population increased over the first half-decade. Efforts were made to control such movement: permission of the General Court was required; only group migrations, with a minister ready to form a proper church, were permitted.

Among the most traumatic, and enduringly significant, of these migrations was the departure of Thomas Hooker and his congregation for the Connecticut Valley in June 1636. Hooker, after all, had been offered the pastorate of the First Church by Cotton; he had declined and settled instead in Cambridge (then Newtowne) with a flock of his own, many of whom had come to New England in anticipation of his arrival. Soon the Cambridge community was demanding more land, and the court sought to satisfy them with a large grant in what is now Watertown, but unavailingly. Perry Miller was possibly right in accepting the traditional explanation of Hooker's trek to Hartford—that the Bay was simply not big enough to contain both him and Cotton. Hooker does seem to have raised the issue of "preparation" and its implications for church membership well before Anne Hutchinson espied its specter: "the rest of the ministers do not concur with him," it was reported back to England while Hooker was still in the Bay; "Cotton and the rest of the contrary opinion are against him and his party in all."

Unhappily, Winthrop's *Journal* offers no insight into this rupture. He reports the event in two brief sentences (following an entry noting the election of Harry Vane as governor: "he was son and heir to a privy counsellor in England"): "Mr. Hooker, pastor of the church of Newtown, and the most of his congregation, went to Connecticut. His wife was carried in a horse litter; and they drove one hundred and sixty cattle, and fed of their milk by the way."

Hooker, to be sure, returned to Boston as one of the inquisitors in the synod that examined Anne Hutchinson. The synodical format was one of the devices whereby the notion of a unity of the brethren was preserved, although clearly Hooker's polity in Connecticut—both civil and ecclesiastical—differed from that of Massachusetts. The ideal of a united New England (some might have said "an imperial Massachusetts") had survived, but Winthrop was now straining to identify providential events that could reassure him of God's continuing favor toward New England.

The text is from the edition of the *Journal* by James Savage (Boston, 1825), II, 85.

Journal

[September 22, 1642]

The court, with advice of the elders, ordered a general fast. The occasions were, 1. The ill news we had out of England concerning the breach between the king and parliament.[1] 2. The danger of the Indians. 3. The unseasonable weather, the rain having continued so long, viz. near a fortnight together, scarce one fair day, and much corn and hay spoiled, though indeed it proved a blessing to us, for it being with warm easterly winds, it brought the Indian corn to maturity, which otherwise would not have been ripe, and it pleased God, that so soon as the fast was agreed upon, the weather changed, and proved fair after.

At this court, the propositions sent from Connecticut, about a combination, etc., were read, and referred to a committee to consider of after the court, who meeting, added some few cautions and new articles, and for the taking in of Plimouth, (who were now willing,) and Sir Ferdinando Gorges' province, and so returned them back to Connecticut, to be considered upon against the spring, for winter was now approaching, and there could be no meeting before, etc.[2]

The sudden fall of land and cattle, and the scarcity of foreign commodities, and money, etc., with the thin access of people from England, put many into an unsettled frame of spirit, so as they concluded there would be no subsisting here, and accordingly they began to hasten away, some to the West Indies, others to the Dutch, at Long Island, etc., (for the governour there invited them by fair offers,) and others back for England. Among others who returned thither, there was one of the magistrates, Mr. Humfrey, and four ministers, and a schoolmaster. These would needs go against all advice, and had a fair and speedy voyage, till they came near England, all which time, three of the ministers, with the schoolmaster, spake reproachfully of the people and of the country, but the wind coming up against them, they were tossed up and down, (being in 10ber,)[3] so long till their provisions and other necessaries were near

1. The first engagement of the civil wars was not fought until October, but all the signs were ominous at this time, and news from England was eagerly anticipated with every ship.

2. This was the first step toward what would be ratified the next year as the New England Confederation, a combination that retained the independence of Massachusetts Bay, Plymouth, New Haven, and Connecticut but provided for management of the common defense, legal disputes, and foreign relations.

3. December (for Winthrop the first month of the year was March).

spent, and they were forced to strait allowance, yet at length the wind coming fair again, they got into the Sleeve, but then there arose so great a tempest at S.E. as they could bear no sail, and so were out of hope of being saved (being in the night also). Then they humbled themselves before the Lord, and acknowledged God's hand to be justly out against them for speaking evil of this good land and the Lord's people here, etc.

WILLIAM HOOKE (1600–1677)
New England's Tears for Old England's Fears (1640)

THE OUTBREAK of the civil wars in England provoked a radical change in New England's sense of its own history, in its conception of its purpose, and even in its reconceptions of its original purpose. For one thing, the Great Migration began to reverse itself: in the early 1640s more people returned to Old England than arrived from there. (Already, after the Antinomian crisis, immigration had slowed, and many had returned, out of disgust with the resolution of the crisis or in anticipation of great things about to be done in Old England.) Those who remained did not immediately celebrate the Puritan insurgency: the more common response of New Englanders was that of Thomas Hooker's Hartford flock, who, on hearing of the outbreak of the rebellion, came running to ask if this was the apocalyptic judgment Hooker had foretold for England.

The official response of New England—of Governor Winthrop and his fellow magistrates—was for many years a studied neutrality. Whatever their private sympathies, New Englanders generally tended to view the warfare in Old England as a calamity and a judgment, to offer muted explanations of how they, as New Englanders, were to some degree responsible, and to offer condolences, but little more, for England's plight. A public day of fasting and humiliation was called for July 23, 1640, but as the sermon delivered by William Hooke on that occasion attests, it became instead something of a day of thanksgiving, even of self-congratulation. Almost as Hooker had once rejoiced in Old England's immunity from the continental wars, so now did New Englanders take comfort in having found refuge from the death and desolation they so extravagantly imagined.

The text of *New England's Tears* is from Samuel Hopkins Emery, *The Ministry of Taunton* (Boston, 1853), I, 85–93.

New England's Tears for Old England's Fears

. . . The use that I do principally intend is of exhortation to you all, as you desire to approve yourselves the true friend and brethren of your dear countrymen in old England, to condole with them this day in their afflictions. Job's friends, you see, did it for him seven days and seven nights, i.e. many days. O let us do it then this one day; at least, for these.

Indeed when we look upon ourselves at this time in this land, the Lord hath given us great cause of rejoicing, both in respect of civil and spiritual peace. God hath at once subdued the proud Pequots[1] and the proud opinions that rose up in this land: and for plenty, never had the land the like. Yea, which is much better, the Word of God grows and multiplieth; the Churches have rest throughout the whole land, and are edified, and walking in the fear of the Lord and in the comfort of the Holy Ghost, are multiplied. This is much, and more it would be, if the edge of these and other our comforts were not this day turned by the fear of civil strifes and combustions in the land of our nativity, which do not a little abate the sweetness of all other our happiness to us, and call for lamentation and sackcloth at our hands . . .

Let us therefore, I beseech you, lay aside the thoughts of all our comforts this day, and let us fasten our eyes upon the calamities of our brethren in old England, calamities, at least, imminent calamities dropping, swords that have hung a long time over their heads by a twine thread, judgments long since threatened as foreseen by many of God's messengers in the causes, though not foretold by a spirit prophetically guided; heavy judgments in all probability, when they fall, if they are not fallen already. And not to look upon the occasions given on the one side or the other, between the two sister nations (sister nations? ah, the word woundeth), let us look this day simply on the event, a sad event in all likelihood, the dividing of a king from his subjects, and him from them, their mutual taking up of arms in opposition and defense; the consequences, even the gloomy and dark consequences thereof, are killing and slaying, and sacking and burning, and robbing, and rifling, cursing and blaspheming, &c.

If you should but see war described to you in a map, especially in a country well known to you, nay dearly beloved of you, where you drew your first breath, where once, yea where lately you dwelt, where you have received ten thousand mercies, and have many a dear friend and countryman and kinsman abiding, how could you but lament and mourn?

1. An Indian tribe that the Puritans had essentially exterminated in the 1637 war.

War is the conflict of enemies enraged with bloody revenge, wherein the parties opposite carry their lives in their hands, every man turning prodigal of his very heart blood, and willing to be killed to kill. The instruments are clashing swords, rattling spears, skull-dividing holberds, murthering pieces, and thundering cannons, from whose mouths proceed the fire, and smell, and smoke, and terror, death, as it were, of the very bottomless pit. We wonder now and then at the sudden death of a man: alas, you might there see a thousand men not only healthy, but stout and strong, struck dead in the twinkling of an eye, their breath exhales without so much as, *Lord have mercy upon us.* Death heweth its way thorow a wood of men in a minute of time from the mouth of a murderer, turning a forest into a champion[2] suddenly; and when it hath used these to slay their opposites, they are recompenced with the like death themselves. O, *the shrill ear-piercing clangs of the trumpets, noise of drums, the animating voices of horse captains, and commanders, learned and learning to destroy! There is the undaunted horse whose neck is clothed with thunder, and the glory of whose nostrils is terrible; how doth he lie pawing and praunsing in the valley, going forth to meet the armed men? He mocks at fear, swallowing the ground with fierceness and rage, and saying among the trumpets, Ha, Ha, he smells the battle afar off, the thunder of the captains and the shouting.* Here ride some dead men swagging in their deep saddles; there fall others alive upon their dead horses; death sends a message to those from the mouth of the muskets, these it talks with face to face, and stabs them in the fift rib: in yonder file there is a man hath his arm struck off from his shoulder, another by him hath lost his leg; here stands a soldier with half a face, there fights another upon his stumps, and at once both kills and is killed; not far off lies a company wallowing in their sweat and gore; such a man whilst he chargeth his musket is discharged of his life, and falls upon his dead fellow. Every battle of the warrior is with confused noise and garments rouled in blood. Death reigns in the field, and is sure to have the day which side soever falls. In the meanwhile (O formidable!) the infernal fiends follow the camp to catch after the souls of rude nefarous soldiers (such as are commonly men of that calling) who fight themselves fearlessly into the mouth of hell for revenge, a booty or a little revenue. How thick and three-fole do they speed one another to destruction? A day of battle is a day of harvest for the devil.

All this while, the poor wife and tender children sit weeping together at home, having taken their late farewell of the harnessed husband and father (O it was a sad parting if you had seen it!) never looking to see

2. That is, a champaign: a treeless field.

his face again, as indeed many and the most of them never do; for anon comes Ely's messenger from the camp saying, *There is a great slaughter among the people, and your husband is dead, your father is dead, he was slain in an hot fight, he was shot dead in the place and never spake a word more.* Then the poor widow who fed yet upon a crumb of hope, tears her hair from her head, rends her cloths, wrings her hands, lifts up her voice to heaven, and weeps like Rachel that would not be comforted. Her children hang about her crying and saying, O my father is slain, my father is dead, I shall never see my father more; and so they cry and sob and sigh out their afflicted souls, and break their hearts together. Alas, alas! this is yet but war thorow a crevice. Beloved, do but consider; there is many times fire without war, and famine and pestilence without war, but war is never without them; and there are many times robberies without war, and murthering of passengers, ravishing of matrons, deflowering of virgins, cruelties and torments, and sometimes barbarous and inhumane practices without war, but war goes seldom or never without them . . .

No wars so cruel, so unnatural, so desolating, as civil wars. You have heard, Beloved, of the dreadful German wars; why if there be any in our own country this day, I may call them German wars, because they are the wars of Germans, even the bloody contentions of brethren; and when relations turn opposites, nothing more opposite. A kingdom at wars with a foreign enemy may stand, but a kingdom divided against itself, can never . . .

To this end, you may think a while upon these particulars.

Of our civil relation to that land, and the inhabitants therein. There is no land that claims our name, but England; we are distinguished from all the nations in the world by the name of *English*. There is no potentate breathing, that we call our dread sovereign, but King Charles, nor laws of any land have civilized us but England's; there is no nation that calls us countrymen but the English. Brethren! Did we not there draw in our first breath? Did not the sun first shine there upon our heads? Did not that land first bear us, even that pleasant island, but for sin, I would say, that garden of the Lord, that paradise? . . .

Or is it not meet that we should bear a part with them in their sorrows, who have borne a part with them in their sins? Have we conferred so many sins as we have done to speed on their confusion, and shall we bestow no sorrow on them? Shall we not help to quench the fire with our tears, that we have kindled with our sins? O cruel! How know we but that the Lord is at this instant visiting our transgressions there acted, which polluted the land? Beloved, did we not commit there ten thousand millions of sins and more amongst us during our abode there? There, O there, we played the ungodly atheists, there it was we halted between God and Baal, sware by the Lord and by Malchom,[3] were neither hot nor cold; there some of us blasphemed the dreadful name of the ever blessed God, polluted his sabbaths, despised his messengers, contemned his holy ways, profaned and abused his mercies, and his good creatures, ran with others to the same excess of riot, &c. And how ever some may say they have repented hereof, yet little do they know what evil examples they have left there behind to fill up the measure both of sin and wrath. If thy sins committed there be pardoned, yet thy sins may be punished, like as a father may be spared, and yet his children executed . . .

Neither let this be forgotten, that of all the Christian people this day in the world, we in this land enjoy the greatest measure of peace and tranquility. We have beaten our swords into ploughshares and our spears into pruning hooks, when others have beaten their pruning hooks into spears, and their ploughshares into swords . . .

3. The god of the Ammonites.

JOHN COTTON

Foreword to John Norton, *The Answer to . . . Mr. William Apollonius* (1648)

In 1645 William Hooke's wife returned to England; eventually he himself sailed, to be appointed chaplain in Cromwell's New Model Army. From England he wrote to Winthrop of his concerns about "levellers" and other troublesome elements in the latter days of the Protectorate. But by far the majority of New England's spokesmen remained and each sought in his own way to resatisfy himself, and all true Christians, that both the decision to come to New England and the decision to stay were right ones. Although we now know that even in the 1630s New Englanders were in correspondence with Puritans back home, outlining their evolving church polity, it was not until the mid-1640s that they began to proclaim "reformation of churches" as their chief reason for crossing the sea. Defending themselves against both the aspersions of English Presbyterians (who pointed to New England's abounding schisms and heresies as evidence of the weaknesses of the Congregational Way) and the queries of the Independents, to whom they had once been allied but who now wondered aloud at such curiosities as New England's synods, they slowly developed the argument that God had dispatched them into the wilderness so that Cromwell, once victorious, might be properly tutored.

In the early 1640s John Cotton had written *The Way of the Churches of Christ in New England* (not published until 1645), in which he depicted the New England Way as the "middle way" between Separatism and Presbyterianism and thus a model rightly to be followed by Old England. *The Keys of the Kingdom of Heaven* (1644) was also a description of New England's practices; it had seven printings and was regularly answered and denounced by English Presbyterians, one of whom described Cotton as the "prime man of them all in New England." In fact few in Old England acknowledged that Cotton had been chastened, even brought down, by the Antinomian controversy. It was perhaps in recognition of his continuing reputation abroad that Cotton was charged with the task of writing Cromwell to reassure him with the good news that all New England was "satisfied" that he had "all along" been fighting the Lord's battles.

In 1648 there were published three major defenses of the New England Way: Hooker's *Survey of the Sum of Church Discipline;* Cotton's *The Way of the Congregational Churches Cleared,* a defense of New England (and himself personally) against the Presbyterian charge that they were Separatists, even raging Anabaptists; and John Norton's *Answer to Mr. Apollonius.* The latter was a Dutch Calvinist who had addressed a series of comparatively nonaccusatory questions to the Independents of England, who in turn referred them to New England for reply. The decision to answer him probably reflected New England's desire to circumvent internecine English polemics by placing the issue of ecclesiastical polity once again in an international context. Latin was therefore the language of exchange, and Norton was given the assignment because he was deemed the most accomplished Latinist in New England. Cotton composed a preface, also in Latin, which he described as "apologetical."

Although in the 1640s "apology" did not carry today's implication of regretfulness (the English Independents had issued their *Apologetical Narration* as an assertion of their ecclesiastical views), Cotton's preface is extraordinarily defensive in tone and theme. Tormented by his fellow ministers in the 1630s, assailed soon thereafter by English Presbyterians and by Roger Williams—perhaps because Williams, like Cotton's critics on the right, deemed him the "greatest divine" in New England and thus the largest target—Cotton had ample reason to defend himself against personal attack. Yet the particular aspersion from which he sought to vindicate himself is one that was seldom, if ever, publicly raised in the ecclesiastical debates of the 1640s: that he and others who had fled to the New World were, quite simply, cowards who had delighted in avoiding the possibility of Christian martyrdom on fields of English battle.

Cotton's preface is nearly a verbatim rehearsal of a letter he had written in 1634, and it seems remarkable that he felt the need to restate his earlier justification for leaving Old England. His sonorous Latin somewhat disguises (even in translation) the intensity of feeling: the reader cannot help wondering whether his prose was not informed by twinges of regret or remorse. It surely reflects an interest to which he had turned in his own embattled years, whether for consolation or inspiration we cannot tell. He never fulfilled his announced intention of writing a continuation of Foxe's *Book of Martyrs* (which, as William Haller has shown, had been a particular inspiration of Puritanism's vision of England as God's "elect nation"), but it is safe to assume that he had hoped to detail the persecution of succeeding generations of nonconformists, down to and through his own. His other writings of the 1640s are sprinkled with references to the severities suffered by the Puritans (as contrasted particularly with the Separatists, of whom, he insisted, the authorities took little note.) Unquestionably, Cotton had sacrificed a great deal in coming to New England and had been, over the years, forced to sacrifice even more—including perhaps his sense of self-respect. But he did not, however provoked, either point to those sacrifices or dramatically redraw the nature of his original decision. With this exception: in 1634 he had not even hinted at the opportunities offered in New England for ecclesiastical reform, whereas the later public declaration invokes the example of John, who entered the wilderness in order to gain further revelation of the perfected church.

The text is from the edition of *The Answer* translated by Douglas Horton (Cambridge, Mass.: Harvard University Press, 1958), pp. 10–12, 14–16.

The Foreword Written in New England
An Apologetical Preface for the Reader of Mr. Norton's Book

. . . It is a serious misrepresentation, unworthy of the spirit of Christian truth, to say that our brethren, either those returned from the Netherlands or those exiled in New England, fled from England like mice from a crumbling house, anticipating its ruin, prudently looking to their own safety, and treacherously giving up the defence of the common cause of the Reformation. Blame was not attached to Elijah that once for fear of Jezebel he fled into the wilderness (I Kings 19), nor to those pious witnesses who in the days of Mary betook themselves to foreign parts in Germany or at Geneva . . . These good men withdrew with the good will of their brethren. With their good will?—with their approval! Nor were they ill spoken of as deserters of their brethren or traitors to their cause. But with us in these recent days no one has been so dull as not to know, no observer of affairs so naive as not to recognize, that action has become far more difficult. If any one set forth our cause before a tribunal, they would instantly say, "You there, are you willing to take the oath we impose on you *ex officio*?" If you took it, they would have a thousand ways of injuring you. They would present accusations against you and your brethren and lead you, in spite of any resistance you could put up, into the trackless labyrinths laid out by pettifogging and mischievous lawyers. And if you refused the oath, it was "Get out of here!"—and off to prison you went instanter. There would be left to you no chance to discuss the matter or make a witness, but only the unavoidable necessity of wasting away in the unbroken silence of a dark and filthy dungeon. Since this was the situation—that we either had to perish uselessly in prison or leave the country—under the leadership of Christ and not by ourselves alone, and only after we had called our brethren into council, we made the decision to leave the country . . .

When (God being good) we reached these shores and when, without the disfavor of any (God being perfect in his mercy), we came to enjoy that liberty of conscience and those pure institutions of Christ which we had eagerly been seeking, we soon and first of all learned from the practice of the church government we began to exercise here that it can most beautifully accord with civil government. Like Hippocrates' twins the two laugh and cry together. Weighty testimony was given to the thoughtful that the discipline we profess could be correlated with public authority, without any note of schism in the church or any danger of sedition in the state. So another obstacle which in the public assemblies of England had persistently been thrown in the path of those who were eager for a purer discipline was easily removed . . .

Some one may say here: "These brethren are farthest of all from deserving well of the churches of Christ. They (with the Apologetical brethren) were the leading factors in retarding and seriously confusing the establishment of the Reformation. If it had not been for them, the other elders all over England would have wholly agreed on the one form of Presbyterian government. Those brethren whom you wish to exonerate from the crime of deserting the cause of the Reformation are actually not only deserters but traitors and enemies of the civil peace. They justly deserve to be severely indicted and severely punished."

Alas that the spirit should be ravished and blinded by so much partisan zeal! It shames and it hurts one, it grieves and it pains one, to recall that those two forms of church government have been prosecuted and promoted with such contention of minds, such bitterness of pens . . .

Consider again what the great chasm is, which has separated the two groups as effectively as a party wall. You contend that all church government should be fixed in the hands of elders. We agree on the subject of church government at this point. We also agree that the rule for government is that all should be administered not according to papal or hierarchical canons but according to the canon of Holy Scriptures. We agree also on the end of government, that everything should be done for the edification of the church and not for secular pomp and circumstance. Like you we recognize and honor synods when there may be need for them. What small thing is it that remains to keep us apart? The acts of government which you wish to have performed by synods, these we seek to have given over by the synods to the churches and performed by the churches with synodal correction. We seek also (and this according to the mind of Christ, as we believe) to have the government of each church administered by the elders of that church in full view of the church and not without the knowledge and consent of the church . . . Since we so beautifully agree in all these matters, which are of the greatest importance, what, I ask, keeps you from regarding us not as traitors or deserters in a common cause, but, in our measure, as defenders and supporters of our joint cause against the enemies of our common faith and our common church? . . .

EDWARD JOHNSON (1598–1672)
Wonder-Working Providence of Sion's Savior in New England (c. 1650)

LATER IN 1648, when Thomas Shepard (in collaboration with John Allin, minister of Dedham), undertook *A Defense of the Answer,* he too felt called on to deal with the charge "that the Godly ministers and Christians that fled to New England, were the most timorous and faint-hearted of all their brethren." In reply, he cited the example of the Marian exiles, but he argued also, *inter alia,* that New Englanders had proven as valuable servants of the Lord as those who had remained to fight in England: had they not come that the Lord's Name might "be known to the heathen"? In point of fact, since 1628, when Matthew Craddock (then governor of the Massachusetts Bay Company) had defined "the main end of our plantation" as that of "indeavoring to bring the Indians to the knowledge of the gospel," little had been heard of the goal of Indian conversion. (It was in October 1646 that John Eliot first preached to an assembly of Indians in their own language.) In the 1630s writers referred chiefly to the "Indian danger," to the "Pequot hornet" sent as divine judgment on a people grown cold in grace (or, alternately, too madly warm), or to the united New England army that defeated ("massacred" would be the better word) them. But when Eliot and Shepard began in the late 1640s to appeal to England for help in the task of evangelizing the heathen, two of their English editors published the happy thought that this might have been all along God's reason for dispatching saints into the wilderness in order thus to expand the kingdom of Christ. Not surprisingly, Eliot and Shepard eagerly grasped at and expanded on the hint, until "Come over and help us" became not merely a part of Massachusetts' official iconography, but, in some tellings, the very head and font of the reasons for the first migrations—a raison d'être equal to, if not surpassing in importance, the exemplary New England Way and its resistance to the novelties so appealing to England's "gospel wantons."

Shepard and Allin pointed also to "the wilderness sorrows we expected to have met withal," but, unlike Bradford, who was reconceiving Plymouth's past in almost the same year, they confessed that Massachusetts, at least, had "sweetly prospered beyond our thoughts, and utmost expectations of prudent men." All these themes were echoed and amplified in Edward Johnson's *History of New England,* published in London in 1654 (though written in 1650–1651) and generally known by its running headline, *Wonder-Working Providence of Sion's Savior in New England.* Johnson first came to New England in 1630, as a trader, and in 1636 returned to England to bring his family to the New World. He settled in what is now Woburn, the settlement of which introduces Chapter 22 of his *History,* a chapter that sets forth the care with which new communities were founded and their church-covenants devised, with the resultant orderly (and unified) expansion of the kingdom of Christ in New England. Johnson also treats of the efforts to convert the Indians, but among his more vivid passages are those concerning the Pequot War, a subject to which he turns, anachronistically but understandably, after noting the outbreak of the Civil Wars (which, he observes, caused some with "resolute courage and boldness to return again to their native land"). Johnson's *History* is throughout an artful work. Indeed, rather than the naive expression of an unlettered layman, which it is often styled, it is perhaps the literary masterpiece of first-generation New England. For *Wonder-Working Providence* is controlled throughout by what Johnson unabashedly calls his "metaphor" of soldiering: from his depiction, in its earliest pages, of the first emigrants as enlistees in the Church Militant about to embark on their "wilderness-work," through his concluding chapter in which he envisions New England as one of the Lord's divisions, equal in import if not in strength to Cromwell's, smashing heretics even as it crushes the last vestiges of prelacy.

Toward the close of *Wonder-Working Providence* Johnson appended a brief note disclosing that his "metaphor" was in fact merely a metaphor, that his history of New England was less a sustained defense and celebration of God's wilderness-people than a desperate effort, through imagination alone, to get the country moving again: "An over-eager desire after the world hath so seized on the spirits of many, that the chief end of our coming hither is forgotten; and notwithstanding all the powerful means used, we stand at a stay, as if the Lord had no farther work for his people to do, but every bird to feather his own nest."

The text is from the edition of 1654, pp. 1–3, 14–15, 23, 34, 230–231.

Wonder-Working Providence of Sion's Savior in New England

When England began to decline in religion, like lukewarm Laodicea,[1] . . . [and] irreligious lascivious and Popish affected persons spread the whole land like grasshoppers, in this very time Christ, the glorious king of his churches, raises an army out of our English nation for freeing his people from their long servitude under usurping prelacy; and because every corner of England was filled with the fury of malignant adversaries, Christ creates a New England to muster up the first of his forces in; whose low condition, little number, and remoteness of place made these adversaries triumph, despising this day of small things, but in this height of their pride the Lord Christ brought sudden and unexpected destruction upon them. Thus have you a touch of the time when this work began . . .

And therefore in the year 1628, [Christ] stirs up his servants as the heralds of a king to make this proclamation for volunteers, as followeth: "Oh yes! oh yes! oh yes! All you the people of Christ that are here oppressed, imprisoned and scurrilously derided, gather yourselves together, your wives and little ones, and answer to your several names as you shall be shipped for his service, in the western world, and more especially for planting the united colonies of New England, where you are to attend the service of the King of Kings." Upon the divulging of this proclamation by his heralds at arms, many (although otherwise willing for this service) began to object as followeth: "Can it possible be the mind of Christ (who formerly inabled so many soldiers of his to keep their station unto the death here) that now so many brave soldiers disciplined by Christ himself, the captain of our salvation, should turn their backs to the disheartening of their fellow-soldiers, and loss of further opportunity in gaining a greater number of subjects to Christ's kingdom?" Notwithstanding this objection, it was further proclaimed as followeth: "What, Creature, wilt not know that Christ thy king crusheth with a rod of iron, the pomp and pride of man . . . [and] causeth [his adversaries] to be cast down suddenly forever, and we find in stories reported, earth's princes have passed their armies at need over seas and deep torrents. Could Caesar so suddenly fetch over fresh forces from Europe to Asia, Pompey to foil? How much more shall Christ who createth all power, call over this 900-league ocean at his pleasure, such instruments as he thinks meet to make use of in this place, from whence you are now to depart, but further that you may not delay the voyage intended, for your

1. A prosperous city excoriated for its decline in faith: Revelation 3:14–22.

full satisfaction, know this is the place where the Lord will create a new heaven and new earth in, new churches, and a new commonwealth together . . . Verily, if the Lord be pleased to open your eyes, you may see the beginning of the fight, and what success the armies of our Lord Christ have hitherto had: the forlorn hopes of Antichrist's army were the proud prelates of England; the forlorn of Christ's armies were these New England people who are the subject of this history, which encountering each other for some space of time, ours being overpowered with multitude, were forced to retreat to a place of greater safety, where they waited for a fresh opportunity to ingage with the main battle of Antichrist, so soon as the Lord shall be pleased to give a word of command . . .

Now let all men know the admirable acts of Christ for his churches and chosen are universally over the whole earth at one and the same time, but sorry man cannot so discourse of them; and therefore let us leave our English nation in way of preparation for this voyage intended, and tell of the marvelous doings of Christ preparing for his people's arrival in the western world, whereas the Indians report they beheld to their great wonderment that perspicuous bright blazing comet (which was so famously noted in Europe); anon after sunset it appeared as they say in the southwest, about three hours, continuing in their horizon for the space of thirty sleeps (for so they reckon their days) after which uncouth sight they expected some strange things to follow, and the rather, because not long before the whole nation of the Mattachusetts were so affrighted with a ship that arrived in their bay, having never seen any before; thus they report some persons among them discerning a great thing to move toward them upon the waters.[2] Wondering what creature it should be, they run with their light cannowes (which are a kind of boats made of birch rinds and sewed together with the roots of white cedar trees) from place to place, stirring up all their countrymen to come forth and behold this monstrous thing; at this sudden news the shores for many miles were filled with this naked nation, gazing at this wonder, till some of the stoutest among them manned out these cannowes. Being armed with bow and arrows, they approached within shot of the ship, being becalmed. They let fly their long shafts at her, which being headed with bone some stuck fast, and others dropped into the water, they wondering it did not cry, but kept quietly on toward them, till all of a sudden the master caused a piece of ordnance to be fired, which stroke such fear into the poor Indians that they hasted to shore, having their wonders exceedingly increased; but being gotten among their great mul-

2. The comet of 1618. The ship was possibly that of Captain John Smith, who had explored New England in 1614.

titude, they waited to see the sequel with much amazement, till the seamen furling up their sails came to an anchor, manned out their long boat, and went on shore, at whose approach the Indians fled . . .

Further know these are but the beginnings of Christ's glorious reformation and restoration of his churches to a more glorious splendor than ever. He hath therefore caused their dazzling brightness of his presence to be contracted in the burning-glass of these his people's zeal, from whence it begins to be left upon many parts of the world with such hot reflection of that burning light, which hath fired many places already, the which shall never be quenched till it hath burnt up Babylon root and branch . . .

Then judge all you (whom the Lord Christ hath given a discerning spirit) whether these poor New England people be not the forerunners of Christ's army, and the marvelous providences which you shall now hear be not the very finger of God, and whether the Lord hath not sent this people to preach in this wilderness, and to proclaim to all nations the near approach of the most wonderful works that ever the sons of men saw. Will not you believe that a nation can be born in a day? Here is a work come very near it . . .

And for a word of terror to the enemy, let them know, Christ will never give over the raising of fresh forces till they are overthrown root and branch. And now you ancient people of Israel look out of your prison grates, let these armies of the Lord Christ Jesus provoke you to acknowledge he is certainly come, aye and speedily he doth come to put life into your dry bones: here is a people not only praying but fighting for you, that the great block may be removed out of the way (which hath hindered hitherto), that they with you may enjoy that glorious resurrection-day, the glorious nuptials of the Lamb: when not only the bridegroom shall appear to his churches both of Jews and Gentiles (which are his spouse) in a more brighter array than ever heretofore, but also his bride shall be clothed by him in the richest garments that ever the sons of men put on, even the glorious graces of Christ Jesus, in such a glorious splendor to the eyes of man, that they shall see and glorify the father of both bridegroom and bride.

PETER BULKELEY (1583–1659)
The Gospel-Covenant (c. 1639–1640)

JOHNSON WAS NOT ALONE in his sense that New England was falling short of its original promise. Nearly all who in the 1640s defended New England by celebrating (in tracts meant for England) its abounding grace and glories were, at the same time, bemoaning from their own pulpits the frightening spiritual silence that had overcome the plantations.

Thus it was probably no mere happenstance that Thomas Shepard, among the first to decry New England's forgetfulness of its original errand (see his *Ten Virgins* below) also wrote the preface to the second and enlarged version of Peter Bulkeley's *The Gospel-Covenant*. For it was in *The Gospel-Covenant* that New England's American-born orthodoxy was fully displayed—the covenant no longer a metaphor making explicable the perseverance of the saints, but a contract more legally binding than any even Hooker had envisioned in Old England. Like Shepard in his own treatise on *Subjection to Christ*, Bulkeley stresses the covenant-duties of both saints and would-be saints, and his treatise culminates with what was soon to become the all-pervading New England self-image, that of a whole people (and not its saints merely) in "national" covenant with God: "Thou shouldst be a special people, an only people—none like thee in all the earth." For Bulkeley, New England, far from being a Johannine Church Militant as Johnson strove to imagine it, was a rigidly circumscribed tribe, each and every member obliged to walk as Abraham walked: "The old way is the good way."

But the first and thinner edition of *The Gospel-Covenant* (1646) was not so filled with the shrill certainties and severe orthodoxies that were soon to control New England's expression and conception of itself. Bulkeley, having been silenced by Laud, had come to New England in 1635, and his people formed one of the first inland settlements, naming it Concord. (A direct ancestor of Ralph Waldo Emerson, he was father of Gershom Bulkeley and grandfather of John, neither of them precisely celebrants of the New England Way.) Thus he could not have heard Winthrop's *Arbella* sermon, however much he seems to echo it in responding to the question that was to continue to plague New England's conscience: not simply "Why came we here?" but "Why do we stay here?" By 1651 Bulkeley would be dismissing even such questions as evidence of God-provoking ungratefulness: "Take heed lest . . . God remove thy candlestick out of the midst of thee; lest being now as a city upon a hill, which many seek unto, thou be left like a beacon upon the top of a mountain, desolate and forsaken . . . Be instructed, and take heed." It had taken twenty years for Winthrop's fears of contempt and scorn to be translated by his contemporaries into an even modestly attractive vision of New England's purpose. At what price, and to what point, it remained for later generations to discover.

The text of *The Gospel-Covenant* is from the second edition (London, 1651), pp. 208–211, 431–432.

The Gospel-Covenant

. . . It is also for the further comfort and consolation of the people of God, when they shall see from whence their help cometh, how God by his immediate hand hath wrought for their good. A gift from the prince's own hand is far more grateful than that which comes another way. So when the Lord casteth in kindness and favors upon his people from himself, this is more comfortable than to have it by another means. Indeed during the time of the trials of God's people, their faith is put to sore plunges, that they begin to question, as they said, Exodus 17:7, *Is the Lord amongst us or not?* And are ready to say, as Isaiah 49:14, *The Lord hath forgotten me, &c.*

But when they see what he hath done, how he hath *ridden on the heavens for their help,* and on the clouds in his glory, and all for their succor and good, when they see the Lord himself supplying their wants from himself, then they change their mind, and say, as Exodus 15:11, *Who is like unto thee, O Lord, amongst the Gods? who is like unto thee, glorious in holiness, fearful in praises, doing wonders?* There is no God like our God, who hath done marvelously for us, and *we who have such a God shall never be ashamed.*

Use 1. This may serve to help our faith against the discouragements which we are apt to fall into, the straits into which the Lord hath brought us. God hath dealt with us as with his people Israel; we are brought out of a fat land into a wilderness, and here we meet with necessities. God hath now set us besides our hopes and expectations; our props which we leaned upon are broken; our money is spent; our states are wasted, and our necessities begin to increase upon us, and now we know not how to be supplied. The waters of the river are cut off, and now we begin to be full of cares and fears, what we shall do. When our means fails us, then our hearts begin to fail us; yea, and our faith also; we begin to be out of hope, and so we do as the Israelites did, who though (when they heard of deliverance) at first they bowed down their heads and worshipped, yet when they met with straits, then they quarrelled with Moses, *Why hast thou brought us hither?* So we begin to quarrel with God's providence, and with ourselves, and to question whether we have done well to come hither or no. But against this discouragement learn we to live by faith in this doctrine now delivered: that God will be all things to his people from himself alone. Therefore, though means fail, yet let not our hearts fail. For the faithful God will not fail us; he hath tied us to means so that we may not neglect them, neither can we maintain the comfort of our lives without them, but the Lord stands in no need of them. He needs not silver or gold, wool or flax, nor houses full of store, he needs not a fruitful land to provide for the necessities of his people; he can without them provide for our good. If we were left to provide for ourselves, then we might despair when means are cut off; but the Lord has said, *Cast your care upon me, I will care for you.* As Joseph said to Pharaoh, *Without me God will provide an answer for Pharaoh*—so may silver and gold, and such things, say to us, "Without us God will provide for the wealth of his people." Though our means be gone, yet God is the same, and if our faith were before fixed upon the Lord, then show it now when means fail us. If we cannot now trust him, our former faith was in the means, not in the Lord. The more our straits be, the more look after the Lord himself, that he should from himself minister needful things unto us. When the stream fails and runs no more, then go to the fountain, where the waters are sweeter and more sure. See the speech of faith, Habakkuk 3:17–18, *Though the figtree does not blossom, nor fruit be in the vines, and the fields yield no fruit, &c., yet I will rejoice in the Lord, I will joy in the God of my salvation.* Though all means fail, yet will I rejoice, *In the mount will the Lord be seen,* Genesis 22:14. If we could but grow up to more dependence upon him, to live by faith in him alone, it would be our great advantage: for though means do prove as a broken reed, or as a false-hearted friend, yet the Lord is faithful, and they that trust in him are blessed. He will by himself create peace and comfort to his people.

Use 2. To settle our hearts against the wavering disposition which we are subject unto in this land. Sometimes the places we live in are hard and barren, and this unsettles us; we know not how to subsist. I deny not but that one place may be better than another, more desirable, more fruitful in itself. But yet the Lord promiseth, Exodus 20:24, that in every place where he sets the remembrance of his name, thither he will come and bless his people, and what is wanting from the place shall be made up from the Lord himself. He turneth a barren land into fruitfulness for his people, Psalms 107. If the places be barren wherein we live, let us be the more humble, the more fruitful in well-doing, the more diligent in prayer, the more strong in faith: and then we shall see, that we abiding with him in the places he hath set us in, he will be with us and bless us, so as we shall want nothing that is good . . .

And for ourselves here, the people of New England, we should in a special manner labor to shine forth in holiness above other people; we have that plenty and abundance of ordinances and means of grace, as few people enjoy the like. We are as a city set upon an hill, in the open view of all the earth; the eyes of the world are upon us because we profess ourselves to be a people in covenant with God, and therefore not only the Lord our God, with whom we have made covenant, but heaven and earth, angels and men, that are witnesses of our profession, will cry shame upon us, if we walk contrary to the covenant which we have professed and promised to walk in. If we open the mouths of men against our profession by reason of the scandal of our lives, we (of all men) shall have the greater sin.

To conclude, let us study so to walk, that this may be our excellency and dignity among the nations of the world, among which we live: That they may be constrained to say of us, "Only this people is wise, an holy and blessed people," that all that see us may see and know that the name of the Lord is called upon us, and that we are the seed which the Lord hath blessed, Deuteronomy 28:10, Isaiah 61:9. There is no people but will strive to excel in some thing; what can we excel in, if not in holiness? If we look to number, we are the fewest; if to strength, we are the weakest; if to wealth and riches, we are the poorest of all the people of God through the whole world. We cannot excel (nor so much as equal) other people in these things, and if we come short in grace and holiness too, we are the most despicable people under heaven; our worldly dignity is gone. If we lose the glory of grace too, then is the glory wholly departed from our Israel, and we are become vile. Strive we therefore herein to excel, and suffer not this crown to be taken away from us: be we an holy people, so shall we be honorable before God, and precious in the eyes of his saints.

And thus also of the properties of the covenant.

Now the God of peace that brought again the Lord Jesus, the great shepherd of the sheep, through the blood of the everlasting covenant, make us perfect in all good works to do his will, working in us that which is pleasing in his sight through Jesus Christ, to whom be praise for ever and ever, Amen.

THREE

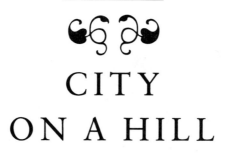

CITY ON A HILL

"THE CHURCHES are here in peace," wrote Thomas Shepard to an English correspondent in 1645, "the commonwealth in peace; the ministry in most sweet peace; the magistrates (I should have named first) in peace." Four announcements of harmony in as many clauses is perhaps sufficient ground to suspect a writer of protesting too much. Shepard was writing after a decade of turmoil—settlements fractured by the Antinomian disputes, Indian war, economic hardship (especially in the forties), arguments over the legitimacy of contact with noncongregational churches, merchant discontent over price regulation, consumer anger at rich men taking advantage of scarcity, whole churches moving south and west away from what Winthrop had hoped would be a close community "knit together . . . as one man." There is no reason to doubt the sincerity of Shepard's report to his embattled friends in England—the noise of the 1630s in Massachusetts had indeed died down. But the question—which Anne Hutchinson and Roger Williams had most eloquently asked, and for which they had been silenced—was whether this was really the quiet of peace, or the quiet that comes when one's first excitement has passed and given way to uncertainty and the feeling of being alone.

THOMAS TILLAM (?–c. 1676)
"Upon the First Sight of New England" (1638)

Thomas Tillam, who was probably born Catholic and who later became a Baptist, wrote this touching poem soon after his first sight of America, where he sought refuge as the civil wars drew near. What Harold Jantz called its "high religious idealism and enthusiasm" have often been remarked; sometimes, perhaps, at the cost of discounting the note of foreboding that breaks into the poem toward its close. For reasons we shall possibly never know with certainty, Tillam did not remain in New England; he was back in England during the years of the Commonwealth and Protectorate, where he wrote several millenarian works—and, upon the Restoration, was imprisoned. Echoing Thomas Hooker's sentiments of thirty years before, he left in 1661 for his final exile "because the sins of this kingdom are so great, that the Lord will destroy it." Tillam settled in Germany as leader of a small devout community, where he died in 1676.

The text is from the *Proceedings of the American Antiquarian Society*, vol. 53, p. 331, ed. Harold Jantz. Reprinted by permission.

Uppon the first sight of New-England
June 29, 1638

Hayle holy-land wherin our holy lord
Hath planted his most true and holy word
Hayle happye people who have dispossest
Your selves of friends, and meanes, to find some rest
For your poore wearied soules, opprest of late
For Jesus-sake, with Envye, spight, and hate
To yow that blessed promise truly's given
Of sure reward, which you'l receve in heaven

Methinks I heare the Lambe of God thus speake
Come my deare little flocke, who for my sake
Have lefte your Country, dearest friends, and goods
And hazarded your lives o'th raginge floods
Posses this Country; free from all anoye
Heare I'le bee with you, heare you shall Injoye
My sabbaths, sacraments, my minestrye
And ordinances in their puritye
But yet beware of Sathans wylye baites
Hee lurkes amongs yow, Cunningly hee waites
To Catch yow from mee; live not then secure
But fight 'gainst sinne, and let your lives be pure
Prepare to heare your sentence thus expressed
Come yee my servants of my father Blessed

ANNE BRADSTREET (1612–1672)
Poems and Prose (c. 1635–1670)

WHEN ANNE BRADSTREET arrived in New England in 1630 at the age of eighteen, she came as the household partner of two established men of affairs: her father, Thomas Dudley, was deputy governor; her husband, Simon Bradstreet, governor-to-be. Among her domestic obligations had been to accept their termination of her comfortable life in the Earl of Lincoln's household, where Dudley had been steward. Their choice of destination did not please her: "I changed my condition and was married," she later told her children, "and came into this country, where I found a new world and new manners, at which my heart rose. But after I was convinced it was the way of God, I submitted to it and joined to the church at Boston." One recent scholar, Robert Daly, has suggested that Bradstreet's dismay had a specific occasion: as a churchgoing Englishwoman, she resented being required publicly to "own" the covenant before being admitted to a new congregation. Whether or not it was this New World innovation at which she balked (just what was required of communicants at this early date remains unclear), her initial American emotion was more retrospective than prospective. John Berryman, in his celebratory poem "Homage to Mistress Bradstreet," puts it in an appropriately staccato phrase: "surely, the English heart quails, stunned."

In the early New England years Bradstreet was troubled too by her failure to bear children. "It pleased God to keep me a long time without a child," she wrote, "which was a great grief to me." When her son Samuel was born in 1633, he came as "The Son of Prayers of vowes, of teares, / The child I stay'd for many years." Some scholars (until recently, mostly male) have seen her turn to poetry as a kind of therapeutic substitute for biological production. This idea, of course, is beyond substantiation, as is the common assumption that she had written no poems in England. In short, much of what we are told about Anne Bradstreet, apart from what she tells us herself, is pure speculation. What may be fairly said of her own published words is that they begin in a curatorial mood. They withhold themselves from the land and people to which she had been committed.

Bradstreet's first surviving poems—such as the "Quaternions," "The Four Monarchies," "A Dialogue Between Old England and New"—center on far-away political events and imitate Renaissance models, chiefly the French poet Guillaume du Bartas, whose somewhat cloying tropes leave their mark on her apprentice work. Writing in the declamatory voice of the public poet, she produced a tribute to Queen Elizabeth that is an implicit attack on Elizabeth's Stuart successors. She composed as well an elegy on Sir Philip Sidney, who was distantly related to the Dudley family and a symbol of aristocratic responsibility in contrast to Charles's entourage. Except for such implied political morals, there is nothing especially Puritan or American about these poems of praise, although, as Ann Stanford has pointed out, they do show flickers of millenarian expectancy. Perhaps the clearest mark of their New World composition is their urge to conserve Old World standards and memories.

There is no reason to believe that Anne Bradstreet kept her creative efforts a strict secret. There are hints, however, that she did feel actual or potential disapproval from a culture that considered women's time ill-spent on scribbling:

> I am obnoxious to each carping tongue
> Who says my hand a needle better fits,
> A Poet's pen all scorn I should thus wrong,
> For such despite they cast on Female wits.

Bradstreet's apprehension of scorn and despite needs to be understood not only in the light of centuries-old distinctions between male and female "gifts," but also in the more immediate context of the Antinomian crisis. The Antinomian subversives, wrote Governor Winthrop, "labored to work first upon women, believing [them] (as they conceived) the weaker to resist; the more flexible, tender, and ready to yield . . . and if once they could wind in them, they hoped by them, as by an *Eve,* to catch their husbands also, which indeed often proved too true amongst us." After the events of 1637, the spiritual volatility of women became a periodic New England complaint.

In 1647 Bradstreet's brother-in-law, an ingenuous admirer, took a copy of her manuscript on a trip to London and offered it for publication. *The Tenth Muse, Lately Sprung up in America,* appeared in 1650—a book garnished with prefatory verses, one of which, by Nathaniel Ward, introduced the exotic author as a "right Du Bartas girle." Samuel Eliot Morison long ago suggested that the publication of *The Tenth Muse*—unsanctioned and unedited by its author—"cured her of the Du Bartas disease, and of writing imitative poetry." Bradstreet did later disclaim this "ill-formed offspring of my feeble brain . . . snatched from [her] friends, less wise than true," and her later work (from which most of the following selections are taken), including some meditative and autobiographical prose found after her death, abandons the gestures of public poetry in favor of a quieter voice. It is this later writer who has taken her place as the first authentic poetic artist in America's history.

The lyrics of Bradstreet's maturity have sometimes been read as a poetry of subversion, expressing a carnal devotion to the things of this world, rhyming out a pagan heat in forced solitude. Bradstreet, so the theory goes, shuts off this authentic self by reverting at the ends of her passionate lyrics to what Berryman calls "pieties that seem / the weary drizzle of an unremembered dream." It is true that there can be an excessively tidy feeling to Bradstreet's endings, not unlike the closing couplets of Shakespeare's sonnets. One of her touching poems on the death of a grandchild, for example, ends this way: "Mean time my throbbing heart's cheered up with this: / Thou with thy saviour art in endless bliss." Such truncated sorrow, along with her lavish desire for the return of her traveling husband, for the splendor of nature, for the furnishings in her burning house—should not be construed as somehow unfaithful to a piety that should have stifled such appetites. The myth of the Puritan as black-frocked prude has lasted too long, and one of its pernicious effects has been to authorize a view of Anne Bradstreet as a sensate woman lonely amid a stony people. She was, in fact, devout and orthodox—afflicted with doubt about her future and with anguish at the passing of her present—exactly the fears that such preachers as Cotton had been contending with for years. Her poetry does not merely evoke the trials and pleasures of living but turns them to figurative and disciplining use. She does not covet earthly pleasures but employs them in a logic of ascension which she probably derived from Plato. This is the effect of her classicism—it is not a heathen subversion of Christian faith but a part of it. There is, of course, tension between her logic and her emotion; and it is precisely in this tension that Bradstreet's poetry resides. Indeed it was in her savoring of earthly faces, sights, touch, that she achieved the honesty requisite for enduring art. She refused the pretense—so tempting to every Christian poet—of describing the surrender of this life as natural or easy. But she never confounded that refusal with the blasphemy of worshipping the creature before the creator.

The texts of the poems are from John Harvard Ellis, ed., *The Works of Anne Bradstreet in Prose and Verse* (Charlestown, Mass., 1867); the texts of "To My Dear Children" and "Meditations Divine and Moral" are from Jeannine Hensley, ed., *The Works of Anne Bradstreet* (Cambridge, Mass.: Harvard University Press, 1967).

The Prologue

1
To sing of Wars, of Captains, and of Kings,
Of Cities founded, Common-wealths begun,
For my mean pen are too superiour things:
Or how they all, or each their dates have run
Let Poets and Historians set these forth,
My obscure Lines shall not so dim their worth.

2
But when my wondring eyes and envious heart
Great *Bartas*[1] sugar'd lines, do but read o're
Fool I do grudg the Muses did not part
'Twixt him and me that overfluent store;
A *Bartas* can, do what a *Bartas* will
But simple I according to my skill.

3
From school-boyes tongue no rhet'rick we expect
Nor yet a sweet Consort[2] from broken strings,
Nor perfect beauty, where's a main defect:
My foolish, broken, blemish'd Muse so sings
And this to mend, alas, no Art is able,
'Cause nature, made it so irreparable.

1. Among Du Bartas' works, the most influential on Bradstreet was probably his epic account of creation (translated into English by Joshua Sylvester as *Divine Weekes and Workes*, 1608).

2. Harmony.

4
Nor can I, like that fluent sweet tongu'd Greek,[3]
Who lisp'd at first, in future times speak plain
By Art he gladly found what he did seek
A full requital of his, striving pain
Art can do much, but this maxime's most sure
A weak or wounded brain admits no cure.

5
I am obnoxious to each carping tongue
Who says my hand a needle better fits,
A Poets pen all scorn I should thus wrong,
For such despite they cast on Female wits:
If what I do prove well, it won't advance,
They'l say it's stoln, or else it was by chance.

6
But sure the Antique Greeks were far more mild
Else of our Sexe, why feigned they those Nine
And poesy made, *Calliope's* own Child;[4]
So 'mongst the rest they placed the Arts Divine,
But this weak knot, they will full soon untie,
The Greeks did nought, but play the fools & lye.

7
Let Greeks be Greeks, and women what they are
Men have precedency and still excell,
It is but vain unjustly to wage warre;
Men can do best, and women know it well
Preheminence in all and each is yours;
Yet grant some small acknowledgement of ours.

8
And oh ye high flown quills that soar the Skies,
And ever with your prey still catch your praise,
If e're you daigne these lowly lines your eyes

3. Demosthenes, an Athenian orator of the fourth century B.C., who, according to legend, conquered his lisp by speaking with a mouthful of pebbles above the roar of the sea.

4. Calliope, mother of Orpheus, was the muse of epic poetry and chief among the muses.

Give Thyme or Parsley wreath, I ask no bayes,[5]
This mean and unrefined ure[6] of mine
Will make you glistring gold, but more to shine.

Contemplations

1
Some time now past in the Autumnal Tide,
When *Phoebus* wanted but one hour to bed,
The trees all richly clad, yet void of pride,
Where gilded o're by his rich golden head.
Their leaves & fruits seem'd painted, but was true
Of green, of red, of yellow, mixed hew,
Rapt were my sences at this delectable view.

2
I wist not what to wish, yet sure thought I,
If so much excellence abide below;
How excellent is he that dwells on high?
Whose power and beauty by his works we know.
Sure he is goodness, wisdome, glory, light,
That hath this under world so richly dight:
More Heaven then Earth was here no winter & no night.

3
Then on a stately Oak I cast mine Eye,
Whose ruffling top the Clouds seem'd to aspire;
How long since thou wast in thine Infancy?
Thy strength, and stature, more thy years admire,
Hath hundred winters past since thou wast born?
Or thou and since thou brakest thy shell of horn,
If so, all these as nought, Eternity doth scorn.

4
Then higher on the glistering Sun I gaz'd,
Whose beams was shaded by the leavie Tree,
The more I look'd, the more I grew amaz'd,
And softly said, what glory's like to thee?

5. The fruit of the bay laurel tree signified honor.
6. Ore.

Soul of this world, this Universes Eye,
No wonder, some made thee a Deity:
Had I not better known, (alas) the same had I.

5
Thou as a Bridegroom from thy Chamber rushes,
And as a strong man, joyes to run a race,
The morn doth usher thee, with smiles & blushes,
The Earth reflects her glances in thy face.
Birds, insects, Animals with Vegative,
Thy heart from death and dulness doth revive:
And in the darksome womb of fruitful nature dive.

6
Thy swift Annual, and diurnal Course,
Thy daily streight, and yearly oblique path,
Thy pleasing fervor, and thy scorching force,
All mortals here the feeling knowledg hath.
Thy presence makes it day, thy absence night,
Quaternal Seasons caused by thy might:
Hail Creature, full of sweetness, beauty & delight.

7
Art thou so full of glory, that no Eye
Hath strength, thy shining Rayes once to behold?
And is thy splendid Throne erect so high?
As to approach it, can no earthly mould.
How full of glory then must thy Creator be?
Who gave this bright light luster unto thee:
Admir'd, ador'd for ever, be that Majesty.

8
Silent alone, where none or saw, or heard,
In pathless paths I lead my wandring feet,
My humble Eyes to lofty Skyes I rear'd
To sing some Song, my mazed Muse thought meet.
My great Creator I would magnifie,
That nature had, thus decked liberally:
But Ah, and Ah, again, my imbecility!

9
I heard the merry grashopper then sing,
The black clad Cricket, bear a second part,
They kept one tune, and plaid on the same string,
Seeming to glory in their little Art.
Shall Creatures abject, thus their voices raise?
And in their kind resound their makers praise:
Whilst I as mute, can warble forth no higher layes.
. . . . .

18
When I behold the heavens as in their prime,
And then the earth (though old) stil clad in green,
The stones and trees, insensible of time,
Nor age nor wrinkle on their front are seen;
If winter come, and greeness then do fade,
A Spring returns, and they more youthfull made;
But Man grows old, lies down, remains where once he's laid.

19
By birth more noble then those creatures all,
Yet seems by nature and by custome curs'd,
No sooner born, but grief and care makes fall
That state obliterate he had at first:
Nor youth, nor strength, nor wisdom spring again
Nor habitations long their names retain,
But in oblivion to the final day remain.

20
Shall I then praise the heavens, the trees, the earth
Because their beauty and their strength last longer
Shall I wish there, or never to had birth,
Because they're bigger, & their bodyes stronger?
Nay, they shall darken, perish, fade and dye,
And when unmade, so ever shall they lye,
But man was made for endless immortality.
. . . . .

29
Man at the best a creature frail and vain,
In knowledg ignorant, in strength but weak,
Subject to sorrows, losses, sickness, pain,

Each storm his state, his mind, his body break,
From some of these he never finds cessation,
But day or night, within, without, vexation,
Troubles from foes, from friends, from dearest, near'st Relation.

30
And yet this sinfull creature, frail and vain,
This lump of wretchedness, of sin and sorrow,
This weather-beaten vessel wrackt with pain,
Joyes not in hope of an eternal morrow;
Nor all his losses, crosses and vexation,
In weight, in frequency and long duration
Can make him deeply groan for that divine Translation.

31
The Mariner that on smooth waves doth glide,
Sings merrily, and steers his Barque with ease,
As if he had command of wind and tide,
And now become great Master of the seas;
But suddenly a storm spoiles all the sport,
And makes him long for a more quiet port,
Which 'gainst all adverse winds may serve for fort.

32
So he that faileth in this world of pleasure,
Feeding on sweets, that never bit of th' sowre,
That's full of friends, of honour and of treasure,
Fond fool, he takes this earth ev'n for heav'ns bower.
But sad affliction comes & makes him see
Here's neither honour, wealth, nor safety;
Only above is found all with security.

33
O Time the fatal wrack of mortal things,
That draws oblivions curtains over kings,
Their sumptuous monuments, men know them not,
Their names without a Record are forgot,
Their parts, their ports, their pomp's all laid in th' dust
Nor wit nor gold, nor buildings scape times rust;
But he whose name is grav'd in the white stone
Shall last and shine when all of these are gone.

Before the Birth of one of her Children

All things within this fading world hath end,
Adversity doth still our joyes attend;
No tyes so strong, no friends so dear and sweet,
But with deaths parting blow is sure to meet.
The sentence past is most irrevocable,
A common thing, yet oh inevitable;
How soon, my Dear, death may my steps attend,
How soon't may be thy Lot to lose thy friend,
We both are ignorant, yet love bids me
These farewell lines to recommend to thee,
That when that knot's unty'd that made us one,
I may seem thine, who in effect am none.
And if I see not half my dayes that's due,
What nature would, God grant to yours and you;
The many faults that well you know I have,
Let be interr'd in my oblivions grave;
If any worth or virtue were in me,
Let that live freshly in thy memory
And when thou feel'st no grief, as I no harms,
Yet love thy dead, who long lay in thine arms:
And when thy loss shall be repaid with gains
Look to my little babes my dear remains.
And if thou love thy self, or loved'st me
These O protect from step Dames injury.
And if chance to thine eyes shall bring this verse,
With some sad sighs honour my absent Herse;[7]
And kiss this paper for thy loves dear sake,
Who with salt tears this last Farewel did take.

To My Dear Children

This book by any yet unread,
I leave for you when I am dead,
That being gone, here you may find
What was your living mother's mind.

7. Grave.

Make use of what I leave in love,
And God shall bless you from above.

My dear children,

I, knowing by experience that the exhortations of parents take most effect when the speakers leave to speak, and those especially sink deepest which are spoke latest, and being ignorant whether on my death bed I shall have opportunity to speak to any of you, much less to all, thought it the best, whilst I was able, to compose some short matters (for what else to call them I know not) and bequeath to you, that when I am no more with you, yet I may be daily in your remembrance (although that is the least in my aim in what I now do), but that you may gain some spiritual advantage by my experience. I have not studied in this you read to show my skill, but to declare the truth, not to set forth myself, but the glory of God. If I had minded the former, it had been perhaps better pleasing to you, but seeing the last is the best, let it be best pleasing to you.

The method I will observe shall be this: I will begin with God's dealing with me from my childhood to this day.

In my young years, about 6 or 7 as I take it, I began to make conscience of my ways, and what I knew was sinful, as lying, disobedience to parents, etc., I avoided it. If at any time I was overtaken with the like evils, it was as a great trouble, and I could not be at rest 'till by prayer I had confessed it unto God. I was also troubled at the neglect of private duties though too often tardy that way. I also found much comfort in reading the Scriptures, especially those places I thought most concerned my condition, and as I grew to have more understanding, so the more solace I took in them.

In a long fit of sickness which I had on my bed I often communed with my heart and made my supplication to the most High who set me free from that affliction.

But as I grew up to be about 14 or 15, I found my heart more carnal, and sitting loose from God, vanity and the follies of youth take hold of me.

About 16, the Lord laid His hand sore upon me and smote me with the smallpox. When I was in my affliction, I besought the Lord and confessed my pride and vanity, and He was entreated of me and again restored me. But I rendered not to Him according to the benefit received.

After a short time I changed my condition and was married, and came into this country, where I found a new world and new manners, at which my heart rose. But after I was convinced it was the way of God, I submitted to it and joined to the church at Boston.

After some time I fell into a lingering sickness like a consumption together with a lameness, which correction I saw the Lord sent to humble and try me and do me good, and it was not altogether ineffectual.

It pleased God to keep me a long time without a child, which was a great grief to me and cost me many prayers and tears before I obtained one, and after him gave me many more of whom I now take the care, that as I have brought you into the world, and with great pains, weakness, cares, and fears brought you to this, I now travail in birth again of you till Christ be formed in you.

Among all my experiences of God's gracious dealings with me, I have constantly observed this, that He hath never suffered me long to sit loose from Him, but by one affliction or other hath made me look home, and search what was amiss; so usually thus it hath been with me that I have no sooner felt my heart out of order, but I have expected correction for it, which most commonly hath been upon my own person in sickness, weakness, pains, sometimes on my soul, in doubts and fears of God's displeasure and my sincerity towards Him; sometimes He hath smote a child with a sickness, sometimes chastened by losses in estate, and these times (through His great mercy) have been the times of my greatest getting and advantage; yea, I have found them the times when the Lord hath manifested the most love to me. Then have I gone to searching and have said with David, "Lord, search me and try me, see what ways of wickedness are in me, and lead me in the way everlasting," and seldom or never but I have found either some sin I lay under which God would have reformed, or some duty neglected which He would have performed, and by His help I have laid vows and bonds upon my soul to perform His righteous commands.

If at any time you are chastened of God, take it as thankfully and joyfully as in greatest mercies, for if ye be His, ye shall reap the greatest benefit by it. It hath been no small support to me in times of darkness when the Almighty hath hid His face from me that yet I have had abundance of sweetness and refreshment after affliction and more circumspection in my walking after I have been afflicted. I have been with God like an untoward child, that no longer than the rod has been on my back (or at least in sight) but I have been apt to forget Him and myself, too. Before I was afflicted, I went astray, but now I keep Thy statutes.

I have had great experience of God's hearing my prayers and returning comfortable answers to me, either in granting the thing I prayed for, or else in satisfying my mind without it, and I have been confident it hath been from Him, because I have found my heart through His goodness enlarged in thankfulness to Him.

I have often been perplexed that I have not found that constant joy in my pilgrimage and refreshing which I supposed most of the servants of God have, although He hath not left me altogether without the witness of His holy spirit, who hath oft given me His word and set to His seal that it shall be well with me. I have sometimes tasted of that hidden manna that the world knows not, and have set up my Ebenezer,[8] and have resolved with myself that against such a promise, such tastes of sweetness, the gates of hell shall never prevail; yet have I many times sinkings and droopings, and not enjoyed that felicity that sometimes I have done. But when I have been in darkness and seen no light, yet have I desired to stay myself upon the Lord, and when I have been in sickness and pain, I have thought if the Lord would but lift up the light of His countenance upon me, although He ground me to powder, it would be but light to me; yea, oft have I thought were I in hell itself and could there find the love of God toward me, it would be a heaven. And could I have been in heaven without the love of God, it would have been a hell to me, for in truth it is the absence and presence of God that makes heaven or hell.

Many times hath Satan troubled me concerning the verity of the Scriptures, many times by atheism how I could know whether there was a God; I never saw any miracles to confirm me, and those which I read of, how did I know but they were feigned? That there is a God my reason would soon tell me by the wondrous works that I see, the vast frame of the heaven and the earth, the order of all things, night and day, summer and winter, spring and autumn, the daily providing for this great household upon the earth, the preserving and directing of all to its proper end. The consideration of these things would with amazement certainly resolve me that there is an Eternal Being. But how should I know He is such a God as I worship in Trinity, and such a Saviour as I rely upon? Though this hath thousands of times been suggested to me, yet God hath helped me over. I have argued thus with myself. That there is a God, I see. If ever this God hath revealed himself, it must be in His word, and this must be it or none. Have I not found that operation by it that no human invention can work upon the soul, hath not judgments befallen divers who have scorned and contemned it, hath it not been preserved through

8. I Samuel 7:12: a stone monument erected by Samuel to commemorate the defeat of the Philistines by the Israelites.

all ages maugre[9] all the heathen tyrants and all of the enemies who have opposed it? Is there any story but that which shows the beginnings of times, and how the world came to be as we see? Do we not know the prophecies in it fulfilled which could not have been so long foretold by any but God Himself?

When I have got over this block, then have I another put in my way, that admit this be the true God whom we worship, and that be his word, yet why may not the Popish religion be the right? They have the same God, the same Christ, the same word. They only enterpret it one way, we another.

This hath sometimes stuck with me, and more it would, but the vain fooleries that are in their religion together with their lying miracles and cruel persecutions of the saints, which admit were they as they term them, yet not so to be dealt withal.

The consideration of these things and many the like would soon turn me to my own religion again.

But some new troubles I have had since the world has been filled with blasphemy and sectaries, and some who have been accounted sincere Christians have been carried away with them, that sometimes I have said, "Is there faith upon the earth?" and I have not known what to think; but then I have remembered the works of Christ that so it must be, and if it were possible, the very elect should be deceived. "Behold," saith our Saviour, "I have told you before." That hath stayed my heart, and I can now say, "Return, O my Soul, to thy rest, upon this rock Christ Jesus will I build my faith, and if I perish, I perish"; but I know all the Powers of Hell shall never prevail against it. I know whom I have trusted, and whom I have believed, and that He is able to keep that I have committed to His charge.

Now to the King, immortal, eternal and invisible, the only wise God, be honour, and glory for ever and ever, Amen.

This was written in much sickness and weakness, and is very weakly and imperfectly done, but if you can pick any benefit out of it, it is the mark which I aimed at.

Meditations Divine and Moral

I

There is no object that we see, no action that we do, no good that we enjoy, no evil that we feel or fear, but we may make some spiritual

9. Despite.

advantage of all; and he that makes such improvement is wise as well as pious.

5
It is reported of the peacock that, priding himself in his gay feathers, he ruffles them up, but spying his black feet, he soon lets fall his plumes; so he that glories in his gifts and adornings should look upon his corruptions, and that will damp his high thoughts.

9
Sweet words are like honey: a little may refresh, but too much gluts the stomach.

14
If we had no winter, the spring would not be so pleasant; if we did not sometimes taste of adversity, prosperity would not be so welcome.

38
Some children are hardly weaned; although the teat be rubbed with wormwood or mustard, they will either wipe it off, or else suck down sweet and bitter together. So is it with some Christians: let God embitter all the sweets of this life, that so they might feed upon more substantial food, yet they are so childishly sottish that they are still hugging and sucking these empty breasts that God is forced to hedge up their way with thorns or lay affliction on their loins that so they might shake hands with the world, before it bid them farewell.

40
The spring is a lively emblem of the resurrection: after a long winter we see the leafless trees and dry stocks (at the approach of the sun) to resume their former vigor and beauty in a more ample manner than what they lost in the autumn; so shall it be at that great day after a long vacation, when the Sun of righteousness shall appear; those dry bones shall arise in far more glory than that which they lost at their creation, and in this transcends the spring that their leaf shall never fail nor their sap decline.

45
We often see stones hang with drops not from any innate moisture, but from a thick air about them; so may we sometime see marble-hearted sinners seem full of contrition, but it is not from any dew of grace within but from some black clouds that impends them, which produces these sweating effects.

50
Sometimes the sun is only shadowed by a cloud that we cannot see his luster although we may walk by his light, but when he is set, we are in darkness till he arise again. So God doth sometime veil His face but for a moment that we cannot behold the light of His countenance as at some other time, yet He affords so much light as may direct our way, that we may go forwards to the city of habitation, but when He seems to set and be quite gone out of sight, then must we needs walk in darkness and see no light; yet then must we trust in the Lord and stay upon our God, and when the morning (which is the appointed time) is come, the Sun of righteousness will arise with healing in His wings.

51
The eyes and the ears are the inlets or doors of the soul, through which innumerable objects enter; yet is not that spacious room filled, neither doth it ever say it is enough, but like the daughters of the horseleach, cries, "Give, give"; and which is most strange, the more it receives, the more empty it finds itself and sees an impossibility ever to be filled but by Him in whom all fullness dwells.

65
We see in the firmament there is but one sun among a multitude of stars and those stars also to differ much one from the other in regard of bigness and brightness, yet all receive their light from that one sun; so is it in the church both militant and triumphant: there is but one Christ, who is the sun of righteousness, in the midst of an unnumerable company of saints and angels; those saints have their degrees, even in this life: some are stars of the first magnitude, and some of a less degree, and others (and they indeed the most in number) but small and obscure, yet all receive their luster (be it more or less) from that glorious sun that enlightens all in all, and if some of them shine so bright while they move on earth, how transcendently splendid shall they be when they are fixt in their heavenly spheres!

70
All men are truly said to be tenants at will, and it may as truly be said that all have a lease of their lives, some longer, some shorter, as it pleases our great Landlord to let. All have their bounds set, over which they cannot pass, and till the expiration of that time, no dangers, no sickness, no pains, nor troubles shall put a period to our days. The certainty that that time will come, together with the uncertainty, how, where, and when, should make us so to number our days as to apply our hearts to wisdom,

that when we are put out of these houses of clay we may be sure of an everlasting habitation that fades not away.

71
All weak and diseased bodies have hourly mementos of their mortality, but the soundest of men, have likewise their nightly monitor by the emblem of death, which is their sleep (for so is death often called), and not only their death, but their grave is lively represented before their eyes by beholding their bed, the morning may mind them of the resurrection, and the sun approaching of the appearing of the Sun of righteousness, at whose coming they shall all rise out of their beds, the long night shall fly away, and the day of eternity shall never end. Seeing these things must be, what manner of persons ought we to be, in all good conversation?

75
It is admirable to consider the power of faith, by which all things are (almost) possible to be done; it can remove mountains (if need were); it hath stayed the course of the sun, raised the dead, cast out devils, reversed the order of nature, quenched the violence of the fire, made the water become firm footing for Peter to walk on; nay, more than all these, it hath overcome the omnipotent Himself, as when Moses intercedes for the people, God saith to him, "Let me alone, that I may destroy them," as if Moses had been able by the hand of faith to hold the everlasting arms of the mighty God of Jacob. Yea Jacob himself when he wrestled with God face to face in Penuel, "Let me go," saith that Angel. "I will not let thee go," replies Jacob, "till thou bless me." Faith is not only thus potent but it is so necessary that without faith there is no salvation; therefore with all our seekings and gettings, let us above all seek to obtain this pearl of price.

Here followes some verses upon the burning of our house, July 10th, 1666. Copyed out of a loose Paper.

In silent night when rest I took,
For sorrow neer I did not look,
I waken'd was with thundring nois
And Piteous shreiks of dreadfull voice.
That fearfull sound of fire and fire,
Let no man know is my Desire.

I, starting up, the light did spye,
And to my God my heart did cry
To strengthen me in my Distresse
And not to leave me succourlesse.
Then coming out beheld a space,
The flame consume my dwelling place.

And, when I could no longer look,
I blest his Name that gave and took,
That layd my goods now in the dust:
Yea so it was, and so 'twas just.
It was his own: it was not mine;
ffar be it that I should repine.

He might of All justly bereft,
But yet sufficient for us left.
When by the Ruines oft I past,
My sorrowing eyes aside did cast,
And here and there the places spye
Where oft I sate, and long did lye.

Here stood that Trunk, and there that chest;
There lay that store I counted best:
My pleasant things in ashes lye,
And them behold no more shall I.
Under thy roof no guest shall sitt,
Nor at thy Table eat a bitt.

No pleasant tale shall 'ere be told,
Nor things recounted done of old.
No Candle 'ere shall shine in Thee,
Nor bridegroom's voice ere heard shall bee.
In silence ever shalt thou lye;
Adeiu, Adeiu; All's vanity.

Then streight I gin my heart to chide,
And did thy wealth on earth abide?
Didst fix thy hope on mouldring dust,
The arm of flesh didst make thy trust?

Raise up thy thoughts above the skye
That dunghill mists away may flie.

Thou hast a house on high erect
Fram'd by that mighty Architect,
With glory richly furnished,
Stands permanent tho: this bee fled.
'Its purchased, and paid for too
By him who hath enough to doe.

A Prise so vast as is unknown,
Yet, by his Gift, is made thine own.
Ther's wealth enough, I need no more;
Farewell my Pelf,[10] farewell my Store.
The world no longer let me Love,
My hope and Treasure lyes Above.

To my Dear and loving Husband

If ever two were one, then surely we.
If ever man were lov'd by wife, then thee;
If ever wife was happy in a man,
Compare with me ye women if you can.
I prize thy love more then whole Mines of gold,
Or all the riches that the East doth hold.
My love is such that Rivers cannot quench,
Nor ought but love from thee, give recompence.
Thy love is such I can no way repay,
The heavens reward thee manifold I pray.
Then while we live, in love lets so persever,
That when we live no more, we may live ever.

A Letter to her Husband, absent upon Publick employment

My head, my heart, mine Eyes, my life, nay more,
My joy, my Magazine of earthly store,

10. Riches.

If two be one, as surely thou and I,
How stayest thou there, whilst I at *Ipswich* lye?
So many steps, head from the heart to sever
If but a neck, soon should we be together:
I like the earth this season, mourn in black,
My Sun is gone so far in's Zodiack,
Whom whilst I 'joy'd, nor storms, nor frosts I felt,
His warmth such frigid colds did cause to melt.
My chilled limbs now nummed lye forlorn;
Return, return sweet *Sol* from *Capricorn;*
In this dead time, alas, what can I more
Then view those fruits which through thy heat I bore?
Which sweet contentment yield me for a space,
True living Pictures of their Fathers face.
O strange effect! now thou art *Southward* gone,
I weary grow, the tedious day so long;
But when thou *Northward* to me shalt return,
I wish my Sun may never set, but burn
Within the Cancer of my glowing breast,
The welcome house of him my dearest guest.
Where ever, ever stay, and go not thence,
Till natures sad decree shall call thee hence;
Flesh of thy flesh, bone of thy bone,
I here, thou there, yet both but one.

In memory of my dear grand-child Elizabeth Bradstreet, who deceased August, 1665, being a year and half old.

Farewel dear babe, my hearts too much content,
Farewel sweet babe, the pleasure of mine eye,
Farewel fair flower that for a space was lent,
Then ta'en away unto Eternity.
Blest babe why should I once bewail thy fate,
Or sigh the dayes so soon were terminate;
Sith thou art setled in an Everlasting state.

2
By nature Trees do rot when they are grown.
And Plumbs and Apples throughly ripe do fall,

And Corn and grass are in their season mown,
And time brings down what is both strong and tall.
But plants new set to be eradicate,
And buds new blown, to have so short a date,
Is by his hand alone that guides nature and fate.

JOHN COTTON
A Treatise of the Covenant of Grace (c. 1636)

WITHIN THREE YEARS of his arrival in Massachusetts Bay, John Cotton was preaching, with a remarkable sense of urgency, a series of passionate sermons on the new covenant—the promise of free grace that God made to Abraham and his seed (Genesis 17) after the old covenant of works had been broken by Adam in Eden. These sermons are filled with the insistent implication that the distinctions between true and counterfeit faith were being lost in New England. They are addressed to a people whom Cotton judges to be far from the Christian consensus for which they came: "to distinguish in men between that sanctification which floweth from the law, and that which is of the gospel, is a matter so narrow, that the angels in heaven have much ado to discern who differ." This distinction, the sermons go on to suggest, is a matter of which New Englanders are losing sight. If Cotton in England had been chiefly concerned to teach the connection between faith and "Christian carriage"—between grace and gracious actions—in New England he has become quickly alarmed by the adoption of behavioral standards for identifying sainthood: "so glorious may . . . common sanctification be, that it may dazzle the eyes of the best of God's children." By common sanctification Cotton means the kind of upright citizenship that involves a taste for decorum, the kind of man who likes to be well thought of, who values his reputation and believes in his own merit. Through the perspective of these sermons, New England appears to be in the grip of a childish conformity; something in the transit to America, Cotton suggests, has authorized undue respect for the safe and proper. These, he insists, have nothing to do with gospel faith, and it is the shame of New England that the renovating experience of grace has so quickly given way to religious routine. The sheer miracle of God's free promise to his children has been forgotten.

With Anne Hutchinson saying much the same thing less obliquely and with less claim to the privilege of judgment, Cotton clearly understood that there was risk in associating himself with her: "if any therefore shall accuse the doctrine of the covenant of free grace of *Antinomianism,* and say, it teacheth men freedom from the law of Moses; and if they commit any sin, they plead they are not bound unto the law; we see how false such an aspersion would be." Exactly that accusation soon came.

The text of *A Treatise of the Covenant of Grace* is from the edition of 1671, pp. 171–179.

A Treatise of the Covenant of Grace

. . . It is the spirit . . . that beareth witness unto all things . . . that are needful for us to know in our times. The annointing teacheth you all things: the comforter shall teach you all things. Great is the power of the spirit to beget and encrease faith. By the word of God and by the works of his providence, he causeth the soul to trust in God, and to say, He that hath delivered me out of six troubles, will not he deliver me out of the seventh? Otherwise if the spirit do not set in, though judgment be convinced, yet the heart is not enlarged to believe. David could not gainsay Nathan when he told him from the Lord that God *had put away his sin, he should not die,* yet still he prayed for mercy, Psalms 51:1, and for establishment with God's free spirit.[1] *Make me to hear the voice of joy and gladness.* Why? Had he not heard it already? It was a most gracious word that Nathan spake; true, but he is not yet clear in it; it is that Holy Ghost, that must make him to hear the voice of joy and gladness. Otherwise, though a man hath much experience of God's goodness to him, and sits and talks of the wonderful things that God hath done for him, to the warming of the hearts of all that hear him; yet the soul cannot reach that abundant satisfaction which he doth desire, till at length the Lord comes in some ordinance of his, and beareth witness freely of love bestowed upon us; and such a testimony will marvelously settle and establish any soul in the world. So that it is the spirit that beareth witness unto faith, and nothing can do it but the spirit only; and yet if the spirit should breathe out of the word, it were but a delusion . . . and therefore the Lord couples his word and his spirit together . . .

Thus the spirit of God in the word is mighty to begin, and mighty to carry [to] an end spiritual work in the soul. Now the ordinary manner of the revelation of the spirit is, if he reveal God's free justification of

1. Nathan prophesies that David, who has married the widow of a slain Hittite, will be spared, but that his child will die in recompense for his father's sin (2 Samuel 12:13).

us, it is by revealing his free grace in a promise not made to works, no not to faith itself, but rather as a thing to be created by the word of a free promise unto sanctification. Indeed he doth bear witness in any promise; as, if the question be about Abraham's sanctification, how the Lord did reveal it? We may see, Genesis 22:12, *By this I know that thou fearest me, seeing thou has not withheld thy son, thine only son from me.*[2] But for his justification, the Lord had revealed that in another promise, Genesis 15:5–6, wherein God brought him forth and bids him, Look now towards heaven, and tell the stars, if thou be able to number them. And he said unto him, so shall thy seed be, and among them he shows him that seed, that shall be a blessing unto all nations. This is a thing beyond his capacity, but this he believed, and it was counted unto him for righteousness. Now in this the Lord reveals nothing but his free grace, without any respect unto any goodness in Abraham: faith was in him before, and had put forth itself; by faith when he was called, he went out, not knowing whither he went, Hebrews 11:8 . . . For it is nothing that God seeth in Abraham, for which he doth reveal his justification to him; but this he doth freely of his grace; and so Abraham receives it, Romans 4:5–6, &c . . . So it is free blessedness that the Lord reveals unto the soul, and lest you should think that these things were peculiar to Abraham and David &c., he tells us (verse 23, 24) that it was not written for his sake alone, that it was imputed to him, but for us also, &c. As it was with the father of the faithful, so it is also with all believers, which are his children: that as he *considered not his own body that was dead, nor the deadness of Sarah's womb,* so neither should we consider this or that in our bodies, or souls. For if we were thus and thus fitted for justification, then the reward would be of works, and so a debt unto us: now though works be there, when justification is again and again revealed, yet it comes not into sight, for a double reason.

Reason 1: First, because when the Lord appears as justifying the soul, he sits upon a throne of justice, and a throne of grace together, not accepting any righteousness but that which is complete and adequate . . . It is not justice for God to pronounce a man just upon any other righteousness, besides the righteousness of his son, for *if God should mark what we have done, no flesh living should be justified in his sight,* Psalms 143:2. But through the righteousness of Christ, which is perfect, the Lord justifies every one that believeth in him. And that act of faith whereby a man taketh hold on Christ and receiveth Christ, that is it which quieteth the soul. For it is not meet that the Lord should justify any simple work of mine: for if the Lord should justify me so, *mine own*

2. Abraham's obedience in preparing to sacrifice Isaac.

clothes would defile me,[3] and if I should come before him with any work, which he hath wrought in me, to be accepted for it, this would be preposterous, and out of place. For he will have a full righteousness to accept me, before he will pronounce me righteous, and therefore I am first called to his son; for as there is no more required to make me a sinful man, but that I be found in Adam, so there is no more required to my justification, but that I should have union with the second Adam.

Reason 2: Secondly, as the Lord doth sit upon a throne of justice when he justifies a soul, so he doth also upon a throne of grace . . . and therefore you shall find it to be true that if the Lord be to declare his acceptance of the sanctification of his people, he will not do it in respect of the worth of their works, but according to the grace of his promise . . .

It is usual with the faithful, when the Lord pronounceth any mercy to them, they see no reason in themselves why the Lord should vouchsafe it. As you see when the light of the sun shineth upon a candle, it damps the light thereof, so it is in this case; when the riches of God's mercy shineth upon the soul, he is not so taken up in the consideration of his own works and holiness, because his heart is lifted up higher in the consideration of the grace of God . . .

Use 1: Now for the use of this: let me apply it to teach Christians not to be afraid of the word revelation. You have heard of many that have attended to revelations, that have been deceived. It is true; for the devil himself will transform himself into an angel of light: he will be foisting in delusions, yea, many times when the soul waiteth for the revelation of God's mercy, the devil will be apt to foist in such revelations, from whence many delusions may grow. But yet on the other side, let not men be afraid, and say that we have no revelation but the word; for I do believe, and dare confidently affirm, that if there were no revelation but the word, there would be no spiritual grace revealed to the soul. For it is more than the letter of the word that is required to it—not that I look for any other matter besides the word. But there is need of greater light than the word of itself is able to give; for it is not all the promises in scripture that have at any time wrought any gracious change in any soul, or are able to beget the faith of God's elect. True it is indeed, whether the father, son, or spirit reveal anything, it is in and according to the word, but without the work of the spirit there is no faith begotten by any promise. The word of God, and all his works, may beget you some knowledge, if you be not mistaken in them, but to beget the faith of God's elect, that may be able to stand against all the powers of darkness, and to crush all the temptations of that wicked one, it is not all the works

3. Job 9:31.

of God, nor all the word of God, of itself, that is able to beget such faith. If there be any, it is but an historical faith, a dead faith that is not able to bring the soul nearer to God.

I beseech you therefore consider of it, as a mystery of God indeed, yet marvelous plain in scripture, as I conceive: that neither the word of grace, nor all the works of grace, are able to clear up the grace of God unto the soul. It is the spirit of God that must do it; he must reveal the grace of God, if ever we see it; otherwise it is not possible that we should believe. For though we should attain unto fullness of knowledge, we shall not attain unto fullness of faith. As for our works in justification, the Lord will dash them to pieces and cast them out of his sight: and though faith comes by hearing, yet it is the spirit in the word that maketh the New Testament a lively letter . . .

ANNE HUTCHINSON (1591–1643)

The Examination of Mrs. Anne Hutchinson (1637)

ANNE MARBURY was born in 1591, the daughter of a minister who preached in Alford, a small Lincolnshire town not far from Boston, England. At twenty she met a London merchant, William Hutchinson, and settled with him in her childhood home, from which she made frequent trips to St. Botolph's Church in Boston to hear its young vicar, John Cotton. Cotton's teaching lifted her out of the spiritual anxiety that had plagued her much of her life, and his ministry became indispensable: "[when] our teacher Mr. Cotton . . . [was] put down," she later wrote, "there was none in *England* that I durst hear." After brief hesitation, she sailed with her husband to Massachusetts Bay to join Cotton's transplanted congregation.

Once settled in her new Boston, and reconciled to what she called "the meanness of the place," she resumed a practice she had begun in England, of paying calls on women in childbed or other distress, as a kind of semiprofessional advisor. Soon she was convening groups of lay people who came together to discuss their religious experiences. From these gatherings a murmur of discontent began to be heard concerning the spiritual guardians of the colony. "I bless the Lord," Hutchinson eventually declared, "he hath let me see which was the clear ministry and which the wrong." It was very plain that she placed most of the Massachusetts clergy (except for Cotton, John Wheelwright, and possibly Thomas Shepard) in the second category.

By 1637, with remarkable speed and partisan ferocity, a cleavage in the entire colony was beginning to form around Hutchinson's leadership. The majority of the First Church was supporting her assertion that only Cotton preached the true gospel of grace while his colleagues preached a covenant of works. "Here is a great stir about graces and looking to hearts," she declared, "but give me Christ; I seek not for graces, but for Christ; I seek not for promises, but for Christ; I seek not for sanctification, but for Christ; tell not me of meditation and duties, but tell me of Christ."

Hutchinson's indictment of New England's ministers was complex and advanced by a brilliant wit that often reduced her opponents to flustered silence—as can be witnessed in the transcript of her trial. Above all, she objected that "sanctification"—Christian behavior—was being substituted for the inner seal of the Holy Spirit as the ultimate test for grace. External propriety was taking the place of internal transformation as the sign of God's favor. This critique of New England's spiritual condition raised many specters in the minds of those she attacked—images of licentious "antinomians" (from the Greek *anti-nomos,* against the law) carrying on in orgiastic ecstasy as they scoffed at the "legal" ministers who preached the commandments as requisite for salvation. There does not seem to have been much basis for such fears, since Hutchinson's followers were mostly sober citizens, including a heavy representation of disciplined merchants. She never denied, moreover, a link between grace and Christian "carriage"; what she did deny was that sanctification was a cause or proof of justification (God's uncoerced act of infusing the sinner with grace).

Hutchinson was no fringe-group fanatic; her adherents included Governor Henry Vane, and the outcome of her struggle for the colony's spiritual allegiance was by no means certain until late in the crisis. At one point John Winthrop fumed that he was denied an honor guard after narrowly regaining his office from Vane, and there seems to have been resistance in Hutchinson's party to fighting the war against the Pequot Indians. In January 1637, on the fast-day called in hopes that harmony could be restored, Hutchinson's brother-in-law, John Wheelwright, was invited by Cotton to step forward from the congregation of the First Church and preach a sermon. It was an incendiary, not a conciliatory performance—one that, according to Winthrop, "stirred up the people against [the magistrates and ministers] with much bitterness and vehemency." Wheelwright was later accused and convicted of sedition.

But the heart of Hutchinson's protest was not civil insurrection or insult to authority. It was her sense that something was going out of New England, that piety had grown chill in the hearts of the ministry, and thereby in the people. Preaching and devotion were becoming mechanical, she thought: a series of obligations with social rewards. In August 1637 a synod of leading ministers was convened to expose and refute the "errors" of the Antinomians. Less than three months later Hutchinson herself was called before the General Court on a variety of civil charges, mostly stemming from her involvement with a petition defending Wheelwright. At her "examination" before the court, Hutchinson's opponents finally forced her into declaring that the Holy Spirit had spoken to her with an "immediate voice"—a claim they leapt upon as proof of her heretical delusion. In fact that dramatic moment has the sound of a fatigued concession, of her telling them what they want to hear. Stamped as unrepentant, abandoned even by Cotton, she was expelled from her church and sent into Rhode Island, where she lived with family and loyal followers until the death of her husband in 1642. Hutchinson died in New York in 1643, at the hands of Indians during the Dutch-Indian war. She had never given her prosecutors the satisfaction of seeing her spirit broken: "Her *Repentance* is in a paper," complained Deputy Governor Dudley, "but . . . not in her countenance." The defeat of Anne Hutchinson sent one strain of Puritan piety underground, but it did not kill it.

The text is excerpted (with slight changes) from David D. Hall, *The Antinomian Controversy 1636–1638: A Documentary History* (Middletown, Conn.: Wesleyan University Press, 1968). Reprinted by permission of David D. Hall.

November 1637
The Examination of Mrs. Anne Hutchinson at the court at Newtown

Mr. Winthrop, governor. Mrs. Hutchinson, you are called here as one of those that have troubled the peace of the commonwealth and the churches here; you are known to be a woman that hath had a great share in the promoting and divulging of those opinions that are causes of this trouble . . . you have maintained a meeting and an assembly in your house that hath been condemned by the general assembly as a thing not tolerable nor comely in the sight of God nor fitting for your sex, and notwithstanding that was cried down you have continued the same. Therefore we have thought good to send for you to understand how things are, that if you be in an erroneous way we may reduce you that so you may become a profitable member here among us, otherwise if you be obstinate in your course that then the court may take such course that you may trouble us no further. Therefore I would intreat you to express whether you do not hold and assent in practice to those opinions and factions that have been handled in court already, that is to say, whether you do not justify Mr. Wheelwright's sermon and the petition.

Mrs. Hutchinson. I am called here to answer before you but I hear no things laid to my charge.

Gov. I have told you some already and more I can tell you.

Mrs. H. Name one Sir.

Gov. Have I not named some already?

Mrs. H. What have I said or done?

Gov. Why for your doings, this you did harbor and countenance those that are parties in this faction that you have heard of.

Mrs. H. That's matter of conscience, Sir.

Gov. Your conscience you must keep or it must be kept for you.

. . . . .

Gov. Let us state the case and then we may know what to do. That which is laid to Mrs. Hutchinson's charge is this, that she hath traduced the magistrates and ministers of this jurisdiction, that she hath said the ministers preached a covenant of works and Mr. Cotton a covenant of grace, and that they were not able ministers of the gospel, and she excuses it that she made it a private conference and with a promise of secrecy, &c. Now this is charged upon her, and they therefore sent for her seeing she made it her table talk, and then she said the fear of man was a snare and therefore she would not be affeared of them.

Mrs. H. This that yourself hath spoken, I desire that they may take their oaths upon.

Gov. That that we should put the reverend elders unto is this, that they would deliver upon oath that which they can remember themselves.

Mr. Shepard. I know no reason of the oath but the importunity of this gentlewoman.

. . . . .

Mr. Eliot.
Mr. Shepard. } We desire to see light why we should take an oath.

Mr. Stoughton. Why it is an end of all strife and I think you ought to swear and put an end to the matter.

Mr. Peters. Our oath is not to satisfy Mrs. Hutchinson but the court.

. . . . .

Dep. Gov. Let her witnesses be called.

Gov. Who be they?

Mrs. H. Mr. Leveret and our teacher and Mr. Coggeshall.

Gov. Mr. Coggeshall was not present.

Mr. Coggeshall. Yes but I was, only I desired to be silent till I should be called.

Gov. Will you Mr. Coggeshall say that she did not say so?

Mr. Coggeshall. Yes I dare say that she did not say all that which they lay against her.

Mr. Peters. How dare you look into the court to say such a word?

Mr. Coggeshall. Mr. Peters takes upon him to forbid me. I shall be silent.

Mr. Stoughton. Ey, but she intended this that they say.

Gov. Well, Mr. Leveret, what were the words? I pray speak.

Mr. Leveret. To my best remembrance when the elders did send for her, Mr. Peters did with much vehemency and intreaty urge her to tell what difference there was between Mr. Cotton and them, and upon his urging of her she said, *The fear of man is a snare, but they that trust upon the Lord shall be safe.* And being asked wherein the difference was, she answered that they did not preach a covenant of grace so clearly as Mr. Cotton did, and she gave this reason of it because that as the apostles were for a time without the spirit so until they had received the witness of the spirit they could not preach a covenant of grace so clearly.[1]

Gov. Don't you remember that she said they were not able ministers of the new testament?

Mrs. H. Mr. Weld and I had an hour's discourse at the window and then I spake that, if I spake it.

. . . . .

Mr. Cotton. I did not think I should be called to bear witness in this cause and therefore did not labor to call to remembrance what was done; but the greatest passage that took impression upon me was to this purpose. The elders spake that they had heard that she had spoken some condemning words of their ministry, and among other things they did first pray her to answer wherein she thought their ministry did differ from mine, how the comparison sprang I am ignorant, but sorry I was that any comparison should be between me and my brethren and uncomfortable it was, she told them to this purpose that they did not hold forth a covenant of grace as I did, but wherein did we differ? why she said that they did not hold forth the seal of the spirit as he doth. Where is the difference there? say they. Why, saith she speaking to one or other of them, I know not to whom, you preach of the seal of the spirit upon a work and he upon free grace without a work or without respect to a work, he preaches the seal of the spirit upon free grace and you upon a work. I told her I was very sorry that she put comparisons between my ministry and theirs, for she had said more than I could myself, and rather I had that she had put us in fellowship with them and not have made that discrepancy . . . I must say that I did not find her saying they were under a covenant of works, nor that she said they did preach a covenant of works.

Gov. You say you do not remember, but can you say she did not speak so——

1. Acts 1:8.

Mr. Cotton. I do remember that she looked at them as the apostles before the ascension.

Mr. Peters. I humbly desire to remember[2] our reverend teacher. May it please you to remember how this came in. Whether do you not remember that she said we were not sealed with the spirit of grace, therefore could not preach a covenant of grace, and she said further you may do it in your judgment but not in experience, but she spake plump that we were not sealed.

Mr. Cotton. You do put me in remembrance that it was asked her why cannot we preach a covenant of grace? Why, saith she, because you can preach no more than you know, or to that purpose, she spake. Now that she said you could not preach a covenant of grace I do not remember such a thing. I remember well that she said you were not sealed with the seal of the spirit.

. . . . .

Mr. Nowell. The witnesses do not answer that which you require.

Gov. I do not see that we need their testimony any further. Mr. Cotton hath expressed what he remembered, and what took impression upon him, and so I think the other elders also did remember that which took impression upon them.

. . . . .

Dep. Gov. They affirm that Mrs. Hutchinson did say they were not able ministers of the new testament.

Mr. Cotton. I do not remember it.

Mrs. H. If you please to give me leave I shall give you the ground of what I know to be true. Being much troubled to see the falseness of the constitution of the church of England, I had like to have turned Separatist; whereupon I kept a day of solemn humiliation and pondering of the thing; this scripture was brought unto me—he that denies Jesus Christ to be come in the flesh is antichrist[3]—This I considered of and in considering found that the papists did not deny him to be come in the flesh, nor we did not deny him—who then was antichrist? Was the Turk antichrist only? The Lord knows that I could not open scripture; he must by his prophetical office open it unto me. So after that being unsatisfied in the thing, the Lord was pleased to bring this scripture out of the Hebrews.[4] He that denies the testament denies the testator, and in this did open unto me and give me to see that those which did not teach the

2. Remind.
3. I John 2:18.
4. Hebrews 9:16.

new covenant had the spirit of antichrist, and upon this he did discover the ministry unto me and ever since. I bless the Lord, he hath let me see which was the clear ministry and which the wrong. Since that time I confess I have been more choice and he hath let me to distinguish between the voice of my beloved and the voice of Moses, the voice of John Baptist and the voice of antichrist, for all those voices are spoken of in scripture. Now if you do condemn me for speaking what in my conscience I know to be truth I must commit myself unto the Lord.

Mr. Nowell. How do you know that that was the spirit?

Mrs. H. How did Abraham know that it was God that bid him offer his son, being a breach of the sixth commandment?

Dep. Gov. By an immediate voice.

Mrs. H. So to me by an immediate revelation.

Dep. Gov. How! an immediate revelation.

Mrs. H. By the voice of his own spirit to my soul. I will give you another scripture, Jeremiah 46:27–28—out of which the Lord showed me what he would do for me and the rest of his servants.[5]—But after he was pleased to reveal himself to me I did presently like Abraham run to Hagar. And after that he did let me see the atheism of my own heart, for which I begged of the Lord that it might not remain in my heart, and being thus, he did shew me this (a twelvemonth after) which I told you of before. Ever since that time I have been confident of what he hath revealed unto me . . . When our teacher came to New England it was a great trouble unto me, my brother Wheelwright being put by also. I was then much troubled concerning the ministry under which I lived, and then that place in the 30th of Isaiah[6] was brought to my mind. *Though the Lord give thee bread of adversity and water of affliction yet shall not thy teachers be removed into corners any more, but thine eyes shall see thy teachers.* The Lord giving me this promise and they being gone there was none then left that I was able to hear, and I could not be at rest but I must come hither. Yet that place of Isaiah did much follow me, though the Lord give thee the bread of adversity and water of affliction. This place lying I say upon me then this place in Daniel[7] was brought unto me and did shew me that though I should meet with affliction yet I am the same God that delivered Daniel out of the lion's den, I will also deliver thee.—Therefore I desire you to look to it, for you see this scripture fulfilled this day and therefore I desire you that as you tender the

5. "I will not make a full end of thee, but correct thee in measure; yet will I not leave thee wholly unpunished."

6. Isaiah 30:20.

7. Daniel 6:4–5.

Lord and the church and commonwealth to consider and look what you do. You have power over my body but the Lord Jesus hath power over my body and soul, and assure yourselves thus much, you do as much as in you lies to put the Lord Jesus Christ from you, and if you go on in this course you begin you will bring a curse upon you and your posterity, and the mouth of the Lord hath spoken it.

Dep. Gov. What is the scripture she brings?

Mr. Stoughton. Behold I turn away from you.

. . . . .

Dep. Gov. I desire Mr. Cotton to tell us whether you do approve of Mrs. Hutchinson's revelations as she hath laid them down.

Mr. Cotton. I know not whether I do understand her, but this I say, if she doth expect a deliverance in a way of providence—then I cannot deny it.

Dep. Gov. No Sir we did not speak of that.

Mr. Cotton. If it be by way of miracle then I would suspect it.

Dep. Gov. Do you believe that her revelations are true?

Mr. Cotton. That she may have some special providence of God to help her is a thing that I cannot bear witness against.

Dep. Gov. Good Sir I do ask whether this revelation be of God or no?

Mr. Cotton. I should desire to know whether the sentence of the court will bring her to any calamity, and then I would know of her whether she expects to be delivered from that calamity by a miracle or a providence of God.

Mrs. H. By a providence of God I say I expect to be delivered from some calamity that shall come to me.

Gov. The case is altered and will not stand with us now, but I see a marvellous providence of God to bring things to this pass that they are. We have been hearkening about the trial of this thing and now the mercy of God by a providence hath answered our desires and made her to lay open her self and the ground of all these disturbances to be by revelations . . . The ground work of her revelations is the immediate revelation of the spirit and not by the ministry of the word. And that is the means by which she hath very much abused the country that they shall look for revelations and are not bound to the ministry of the word, but God will teach them by immediate revelations and this hath been the ground of all these tumults and troubles. And I would that those were all cut off from us that trouble us, for this is the thing that hath been the root of all the mischief.

Court. We all consent with you.

. . . . .

Mr. Endicot. I speak in reference to Mr. Cotton. I am tender of you Sir and there lies much upon you in this particular, for the answer of Mr. Cotton doth not free him from that way which his last answer did bring upon him, therefore I beseech you that you'd be pleased to speak a word to that which Mrs. Hutchinson hath spoken of her revelations as you have heard the manner of it. Whether do you witness for her or against her.

Mr. Cotton. This is that I said Sir, and my answer is plain: that if she doth look for deliverance from the hand of God by his providence, and the revelation be in a word or according to a word, that I cannot deny.

Mr. Endicot. You give me satisfaction.

Dep. Gov. No, no, he gives me none at all.

Mr. Cotton. But if it be in a way of miracle or a revelation without the word that I do not assent to, but look at it as a delusion, and I think so doth she too as I understand her.

Dep. Gov. Sir, you weary me and do not satisfy me.

Mr. Cotton. I pray Sir give me leave to express my self. In that sense that she speaks I dare not bear witness against it.

. . . . .

Dep. Gov. These disturbances that have come among the Germans have been all grounded upon revelations[8], and so they that have vented them have stirred up their hearers to take up arms against their prince and to cut the throats one of another, and these have been the fruits of them, and whether the devil may inspire the same into their hearts here I know not, for I am fully persuaded that Mrs. Hutchinson is deluded by the devil, because the spirit of God speaks truth in all his servants.

Gov. I am persuaded that the revelation she brings forth is delusion.

All the court but some two or three ministers cry out, we all believe it—we all believe it. *Mr. Endicot.* I suppose all the world may see where the foundation of all these troubles among us lies.

Mr. Eliot. I say there is an expectation of things promised, but to have a particular revelation of things that shall fall out, there is no such thing in the scripture.

Gov. We will not limit the word of God.

8. Dudley is referring to the notorious John of Leyden, who led a violent Anabaptist revolt at Munster in 1535, after which Anabaptism became synonymous with fanaticism in the minds of many Protestants.

Mr. Collicut. It is a great burden to us that we differ from Mr. Cotton and that he should justify these revelations. I would intreat him to answer concerning that about the destruction of England.

Gov. Mr. Cotton is not called to answer to any thing but we are to deal with the party here standing before us.

. . . . .

Gov. Seeing the court hath thus declared itself and hearing what hath been laid to the charge of Mrs. Hutchinson and especially what she by the providence of God hath declared freely without being asked, if therefore it be the mind of the court, looking at her as the principal cause of all our trouble, that they would now consider what is to be done to her.—

Mr. Coddington. I do think that you are going to censure therefore I desire to speak a word.

Gov. I pray you speak.

Mr. Coddington. There is one thing objected against the meetings. What if she designed to edify her own family in her own meetings may none else be present?

Gov. If you have nothing else to say but that, it is pity Mr. Coddington that you should interrupt us in proceeding to censure.

Mr. Coddington. I would say more Sir, another thing you lay to her charge is her speech to the elders. Now I do not see any clear witness against her, and you know it is a rule of the court that no man may be a judge and an accuser too. I do not speak to disparage our elders and their callings, but I do not see any thing that they accuse her of witnessed against her, and therefore I do not see how she should be censured for that. And for the other thing which hath fallen from her occasionally by the spirit of God, you know the spirit of God witnesses with our spirits, and there is no truth in scripture but God bears witness to it by his spirit, therefore I would entreat you to consider whether those things you have alleged against her deserve such censure as you are about to pass . . .

JOHN WINTHROP
A Defense of an Order of Court (1637)

WHILE DEALING WITH the immediate threat from the Antinomians, Winthrop and the Court took steps to prevent their reinforcement. In May 1637 the court issued an order "that none should be received to inhabit within this jurisdiction but such as should be allowed by some of the magistrates," and enforced it "by imposing a penalty upon all such as should retain any, &c., above three weeks." Although in his public defense of America's first alien and sedition act Winthrop was less than candid about his reasons, in his journal he was frank: "it was very probable that [the Antinomians] expected many of their opinion to come out of England."

The strategy was clear, but the principle required an explanation. In providing one, Winthrop made his appeal to the conventional analogy of society and body: "the intent of the law is to preserve the welfare of the body; and for this end to have none received into any fellowship with it who are likely to disturb the same." There is, as critics in England were to suggest, something here of the separatist resort to quarantine in time of trouble. Such an instinct for withdrawal had already been present in Winthrop's *Arbella* sermon, and it was now becoming dominant in an emerging conception of New England as an immaculate fortress. If Winthrop had once urged his fellow emigrants to strive for a society built on grace, indeed on love, he now found himself measuring the result according to the criteria of security and order.

The text is from Thomas Hutchinson, *A Collection of Papers Relating to the History of Massachusetts Bay* (Boston, 1769), pp. 67–71.

A Defense of an Order of Court Made in the Year 1637

A declaration of the intent and equity of the order made at the last court, to this effect, that none should be received to inhabit within this jurisdiction but such as should be allowed by some of the magistrates.

For clearing of such scruples as have arisen about this order, it is to be considered, first, what is the essential form of a commonwealth or body politic such as this is, which I conceive to be this—the consent of a certain company of people, to cohabit together under one government for their mutual safety and welfare.

In this description all these things do concur to the well being of such a body: (1) persons, (2) place, (3) consent, (4) government or order, (5) welfare.

It is clearly agreed by all that the care of safety and welfare was the original cause or occasion of commonwealths' and of many families' subjecting themselves to rulers and laws; for no man hath lawful power over another, but by birth or consent, so likewise, by the law of propriety, no man can have just interest in that which belongeth to another, without his consent.

From the premises will arise these conclusions:

1. No commonwealth can be founded but by free consent.

2. The persons so incorporating have a public and relative interest in each other, and in the place of their cohabitation and goods, and laws, &c., and in all the means of their welfare so as none other can claim privilege with them but by free consent.

3. The nature of such an incorporation ties every member thereof to seek out and entertain all means that may conduce to the welfare of the body, and to keep off whatsoever doth appear to tend to their damage.

4. The welfare of the whole is not to be put to apparent hazard for the advantage of any particular members.

From these conclusions I thus reason:

1. If we here be a corporation established by free consent, if the place of our cohabitation be our own, then no man hath right to come into us &c. without our consent.

2. If no man hath right to our lands, our government privileges, &c. but by our consent, then it is reason we should take notice of before we confer any such upon them.

3. If we are bound to keep off whatsoever appears to tend to our ruin or damage, then may we lawfully refuse to receive such whose dispositions suit not with ours and whose society (we know) will be hurtful to us, and therefore it is lawful to take knowledge of all men before we receive them.

4. The churches take liberty (as lawfully they may) to receive or reject at their discretion; yea particular towns make orders to the like effect; why then should the commonweal be denied the like liberty and the whole more restrained than any part?

5. If it be sin in us to deny some men place &c. among us, then it is

because of some right they have to this place &c., for to deny a man that which he hath no right unto is neither sin nor injury.

6. If strangers have right to our houses or lands, &c., then it is either of justice or of mercy. If of justice let them plead it, and we shall know what to answer. But if it be only in way of mercy, or by the rule of hospitality, &c., then I answer first, a man is not a fit object of mercy except he be in misery. Second, we are not bound to exercise mercy to others to the ruin of ourselves. Third, there are few that stand in needs of mercy at their first coming hither. As for hospitality, that rule doth not bind further than for some present occasion, not for continual residence.

7. A family is a little commonwealth, and a commonwealth is a great family. Now as a family is not bound to entertain all comers, no not every good man (otherwise than by way of hospitality) no more is a commonwealth.

8. It is a general received rule, *turpis ejicitur quam non admititur hospes,* it is worse to receive a man whom we must cast out again, than to deny him admittance.

9. The rule of the Apostle, John 2:10,[1] is that such as come and bring not the true doctrine with them should not be received to house, and by the same reason not into the commonweal.

10. . . . The intent of the law is to preserve the welfare of the body; and for this end to have none received into any fellowship with it who are likely to disturb the same . . . Now then, if such to whom the keeping of this law is committed be persuaded in their judgments that such a man is likely to disturb and hinder the public weal, but some others who are not in the same trust, judge otherwise, yet they are to follow their own judgments rather than the judgments of others who are not alike interested. As in trial of an offender by a jury; the twelve men are satisfied in their consciences, upon the evidence given, that the party deserves death: but there are 20 or 40 standers by who conceive otherwise—yet is the jury bound to condemn him according to their own consciences, and not to acquit him upon the different opinion of other men, except their reasons can convince them of the error of their consciences, and this is according to the rule of the Apostle, Romans 14:5, *Let every man be fully persuaded in his own mind . . .*

Whereas it is objected that by this law we reject good Christians and so consequently Christ himself: I answer first, it is not known that any Christian man hath been rejected. Second, a man that is a true Christian,

1. "If there come any unto you, and bring not this doctrine, receive him not into *your* house, neither bid him God speed."

may be denied residence among us in some cases, without rejecting Christ, as admit a true Christian should come over, and should maintain community of goods, or that magistrates ought not to punish the breakers of the first table,[2] or the members of churches, for criminal offenses: or that no man were bound to be subject to those laws or magistrates to which they should not give an explicit consent, &c. I hope no man will say that not to receive such an one were to reject Christ; for such opinions (though being maintained in simple ignorance, they might stand with a state of grace yet), they may be so dangerous to the public weal in many respects, as it would be our sin and unfaithfulness to receive such among us, except it were for trial of their reformation. I would demand then in the case in question . . . whereas it is said that this law was made of purpose to keep away such as are of Mr. Wheelwright his judgment (admit it were so which yet I cannot confess), where is the evil of it? If we conceive and find by sad experience that his opinions [are] such as will cause divisions, and make people look at their magistrates, ministers and brethren as enemies to Christ and Antichrists, &c. were it not sin and unfaithfulness in us to receive more of those opinions, which we already find the evil fruit of: Nay, why do not those who now complain join with us in keeping out of such, as well as formerly they did in expelling Mr. Williams for the like, though less dangerous? Where this change of their judgments should arise I leave to themselves to examine, and I earnestly entreat them so to do, and for this law let the equally minded judge, what evil they find in it, or in the practice of those who are betrusted with the execution of it.

2. The first four commandments. Winthrop has Roger Williams in mind here.

HENRY VANE (1613–1662)
A Brief Answer (1637)

HENRY VANE, well thought of in his early years by King Charles and son of a gentleman prominent at court, was regarded upon his arrival in New England as an increment to the colony's prestige. Winthrop judged the twenty-two-year-old Vane to be a "gentleman of excellent parts, [who] being called to the obedience of the gospel, forsook the honors and preferments of the court, to enjoy the ordinances of Christ in their purity here." That was in 1635. In 1637, after Vane (as Hutchinson's ally) was defeated in his bid to remain as governor, and as he was preparing to sail for England, Winthrop declined to "come from court" and merely left a curt order "with the captain for their honorable dismission." Vane, on whose "firm hand," according to Milton, "religion leans," went on to an illustrious career under Cromwell—for which he paid with his life in 1662.

In his response to Winthrop's *Defense of an Order,* which was also his valediction to America (where he had remained a scant two years), Vane dwelt on the absence of a vocabulary that had once been indispensably present in Winthrop's public utterance: "The churches [says the governor] take liberty (as lawfully they may) to receive or reject at their discretion . . . why then should the commonwealth be denied the like liberty? . . . Churches, [however,] have no liberty to receive or reject at their discretions, but at the discretions of Christ . . . In one word, there is no liberty to be taken neither in church nor commonwealth but that which Christ gives and is according to him." New England, according to Vane, had forgotten its obligations to both King and God.

The text of *A Brief Answer* is from Thomas Hutchinson, *A Collection of Papers Relating to the History of Massachusetts Bay* (Boston, 1769), pp. 72–73, 82–83.

A Brief Answer to a Certain Declaration, Made of the Intent and Equity of the Order of the Court, That None Should Be Received to Inhabit within This Jurisdiction but Such As Should Be Allowed by Some of the Magistrates . . .

. . . The description which is set down in effect [in Winthrop's *Defense of an Order of Court*] is this: A commonwealth is a certain company of people consenting to cohabit together under one government, for their mutual safety and welfare. In which description this main fault is found. At the best it is but a description of a commonwealth at large, and not of such a commonwealth as this (as is said), which is not only Christian, but dependent upon the grant also of our sovereign; for so are the express words of that order of court to which the whole country was required to subscribe . . .

The commonwealth here described may be a company of Turkish pirates as well as Christian professors, unless the consent and government be better limited than it is in this definition; for sure it is, all pagans and infidels, even the Indians here amongst us, may come within this compass. And is this such a body politic as ours, as you say? God forbid. Our commonwealth we fear would be twice miserable, if Christ and the king should be shut out so. Reasons taken from the nature of a commonwealth not founded upon Christ, nor by his majesty's charters, must needs fall to the ground, and fail those that rely upon them . . .

This law we judge to be most wicked and sinful, and that for these reasons.

1. Because this law doth leave these weighty matters of the commonwealth, of receiving or rejecting such as come over, to the approbation of magistrates, and suspends these things upon the judgment of man, whereas the judgment is God's (Deuteronomy 1:17) . . .

2. Because here is liberty given by this law to expel and reject those which are most eminent Christians, if they suit not with the disposition of the magistrates, whereby it will come to pass, that Christ and his members will find worse entertainment amongst us than the Israelites did amongst the Egyptians and Babylonians . . .

3. This law doth cross many laws of Christ. Christ would have us render unto Caesar the things that are Caesar's (Matthew 22:21). But

this law will not give unto the king's majesty his right of planting some of his subjects amongst us, except they please them. Christ bids us not to forget to entertain strangers (Hebrews 13:2). But here by this law we must not entertain, for any continuance of time, such strangers as the magistrates like not, though they be never so gracious, allowed of both by God and good men . . .

THOMAS SHEPARD
The Parable of the Ten Virgins (1636–1640)

THOMAS SHEPARD has been described as "one of Mistress Hutchinson's most vindictive prosecutors," a characterization borne out by his tone during her trials. And yet a fascinating remark of John Cotton's seems to throw Shepard's role in the Antinomian affair into confusion: Mrs. Hutchinson, Cotton declared after the turmoil had died down, "disesteem[ed] generally the elders of the churches (though of them she esteemed best of Mr. Shepard)." The great sermon series Shepard delivered between 1636 and 1640 holds a clue to this strange concession. In its published form, *The Parable of the Ten Virgins* is dramatically split down the middle; it takes up where *The Sound Believer* had left off. "Is it enough," Shepard demands near the start, "to have ordinances?" "No," he answers, and goes on to excoriate those who rest in "dead prayers, dry sermons, sapless sacraments." "He that performs any duty ultimately to ease his conscience . . . is married yet unto the law." These are sentiments to which Anne Hutchinson took no exception; and Shepard's first American sermons are driven by a rapt intimacy with the Holy Spirit that seems no less deeply felt than her own. And yet there comes a moment of sudden self-chastisement, of stepping back to ask, "Have we not fallen a-dreaming here . . . golden dreams of grace? . . . Who would think that ever any should so fall by a simple woman?" The transit Shepard made from the exhilaration of the early sermons to the cautions of the late is one of the most poignant retrenchments in the experience of settlement. Anne Hutchinson knew that he had once been with her. His pulling away—away from his own youthful dream that the holy spirit might actually be incarnate in their new land—is an exemplary version of what so many New Englanders experienced: the relinquishment of fervor in favor of realism. In the *Ten Virgins* we can hear the tragic theme of America's first immigrant literature.

The text of the *Ten Virgins* is based on volume 2 of John Albro's edition of Shepard's *Works* (1853), pp. 169–171, 197–198, 375, 377–378, 406–407.

The Parable of the Ten Virgins

This, if I may have leave to speak plainly, is the great sin, one of them, of New England. Men come over hither for ordinances, and when they have them, neglect them . . . When men had enough by them to live comfortably upon, then God and his ordinances were desired by them; but here, men's removing begetting want, want of the creature, joined with fear and distrust of God's providence to provide for them and theirs . . . sink their hearts . . .

When men are persecuted by enemies, driven into corners, or to towns six miles off, to find a sacrament or hear a sermon, then the gospel of peace, and them that brought the glad tidings of peace, their feet were beautiful; and then men thought, if one Sabbath here so sweet, where ordinances are much corrupted, if some of them be so comfortable in the midst of enemies, O, how sweet to enjoy them all among saints, among friends! And so I know they be to some, and, I hope, to more than I know; but New England's peace and plenty of means breeds strange security; and hence prayer is neglected here. There are no enemies to hunt you to heaven, nor chains to make you cry; hence the gospel and Christ in it is slighted. Why? Here are no sour herbs to make the lamb sweet. And if I get no good this Sabbath, this sermon, this sacrament, this prayer, I hope I shall some other time, when my heart is better and my business is over; not considering that the days of trouble may be near, or God's final farewell may be quickly taken . . .

There is no place in all the world where there is such expectation to find the Lord as here; and hence men bless the Lord for our rising sun when it is setting everywhere else. Here, therefore, they come and find it not; hence not considering the great and last temptation of this place, whereby God tries his friends before he will trust them with more of himself, viz., deep and frequent desertions; they give in, and therefore care not for, nor desire after, those plasters which they feel heal them not, nor that food which they find nourisheth them not. It is strange to see what a faith some men have that can close with Christ as their end, and comfort themselves there. It is not means (say they), but Christ; not duties, but Christ; and by this faith can comfort and quiet themselves in the neglect and contempt of Christ in means—as infallible a brand of God's eternal reprobation of such a soul as any I know. So that this is New England's sin. Is not prayer neglected, wanting place and heart? If not in family, is it not in secret? Yet doth it not die? Didst thou ever find thy spirit so straitened? Where are the mighty groans? What is become of meditation? Dost thou not let Sabbaths, sermons pass over, which shall be preached over again at the last day, and find no Christ, no spirit in them; and thus lie famishing, and yet not cry for bread? . . .

Take not up, therefore, every opinion and doctrine, from men or angel, that bears a fair show of advancing Christ; for they may be but the fruits of evangelical hypocrisy and deceit . . . Do not think, beloved, that Satan will not seek to send delusions among us; and do you think these delusions will come out of the popish place, whose inventions smell above ground here? No; he must come, and will come, with more evangelical fine-spun devices. It is a rule observed among Jesuits at this day, if they would conquer religion by subtlety, never oppose religion with a cross religion, but set it against itself; so oppose the gospel by the gospel; and look, as churches pleading for works had new invented devised works, so when faith is preached, men will have their new inventions of faith. I speak not this against the doctrine of faith where it is preached, but am glad of it; nor that I would have men content themselves with every form of faith; for I believe that most men's faith needs confirming or trying, but I speak to prevent danger on that hand.[1] For it was that which Christ did foretell (Matthew 24), *Many false Christs should arise,* i.e., such as should misapply Christ, that had a spirit for Christ, which was a spirit against Christ, and would deceive, if it were possible, the very elect; for coming with Christ's spirit, they dare not oppose them, lest they oppose the spirit of Christ. The only remedy is to hold to Christ's word, and not to depart one hair's breadth from it (Revelation 10), and to a word well understood, and then dispute no more. Satan comes to Eve, and bids her eat; no, God forbid; yet eat to be like gods; he dazzled her with that which was not; now she fell. Take the truth from what the word saith, and depart not from it . . .

Let us therefore now examine whether this sin be not our sin in this country, if it be not begun among us: if we be not sleeping, yet are we not slumbering? If we are not virgin churches, why have we the name of it? If we be virgin churches, then make search if this be not our sin: we have all our beds and lodgings provided, the Lord hath made them easy to us; we never looked for such days in New England; the Lord hath freed us from the pain and anguish of our consciences; we have ordinances to the full, sermons too long, and lectures too many, and private meetings too frequent; a large profession many have made; but are you not yet weary? If weary, not sleepy, not slumbering? It may be

1. This remark is an act of deference to Cotton.

on you before you are aware, and you not know it; and when so it is, it may be so sweet that you may be loath to see it, that so you may forsake it. Let me knock again: is it not so? Let me come to every man's bedside, and ask your consciences . . .

Have we not fallen a-dreaming here? What meaneth else the delusion of men's brains? What a swarm of strange opinions, which (like flies) have gone to the sores of men's heads and hearts, and these are believed also; and more dreams men have that are never spoken; every man hath some drunken conceit that rocks him asleep: dreams are quite contrary to the truth. What meaneth these, if men are not sleeping? First, drunken dreams of the world. Secondly, golden dreams of grace; that these things advance grace which indeed destroy grace; that there is no grace in the saints, no grace in Christ, no human nature, no promise to evidence grace, no law to be a rule to them that have received grace: who would think that ever any should so fall by a simple woman? But if this be not general, yet look how do men begin to dream concerning the world? Scarce a man but finds want, or is well; if he wants, O, then, if I had such a lot about me, such an estate, how well then were I! . . .

Doth not the Lord often awaken us, yet we fall to sleep again? The Lord awakened us by the Pequot hornet, yet what use is there made of it? Doth not the Lord often meet us in an ordinance, but he is soon lost and gone again? Is there a man that hath not had his cross since he came hither, as loss in cattle and estate, a dear husband, child, wife dead? A sore and sharp sickness, etc., he hath been exercised with, etc., but do you not sleep still? . . .

Make the coming of the Lord real, see it real, and set it really (as it shall be) before your eyes (Hebrews 9:28), *To them that look for him,* etc.[2] Why do not men look for him? Truly, very few do look for him really; it is only a report, a noise . . . If a man that is to make a sea voyage did know that whatever he brought to shore, besides gold and pearls, should be consumed as soon as he comes to shore, he would not freight his ship with those things: if men were assured, here is a house where you and yours shall be burned, they would set it elsewhere; men come from one country to another, because sin will consume . . .

Consider the fierce wrath upon reprobates, who shall rise like toads coming out of their holes in winter time, standing before Christ's tribunal, crying out of the day that ever they were born, and receiving their final doom; imagine the silence while the Lord is pronouncing the sentence, and, when past, a cry; and then Christ to depart, and shut up himself in

2. "Unto them that look for him shall he appear the second time without sin unto salvation."

heaven with his saints, the reprobate never to see him nor his face any more: are these things tales, fables, notions? If they be, blot out the scripture; but if real, O, then, who can but awake? If God intends mercy to you, the thoughts of these things will awake you, you shall see them really; if not, they shall awaken you by feeling of them.

Consider how many will be found to light at that day.

Make this day present: optic glasses will take within them the present image of things afar off; a mud wall cannot give the form of them; so, by faith, look at these things that be to come as near; for if we see really the Lord's coming, but we look upon it as a thing that is afar off, it will not affect: now a thing may be present to faith which is not to sense; it may be the last and great coming of the Lord is not very nigh (although we are doubtless in the last times), but the beginnings of this, thy petty sessions[3] before the general assize, may be nigh. O, therefore, make it present.

3. A local court with jurisdiction limited to minor crimes.

THOMAS HOOKER
The Application of Redemption (c. 1640)

WHETHER OR NOT Thomas Hooker, as William Hubbard suggested in the 1670s, took his flock and family to Hartford because "two such eminent stars [as he and Cotton] . . . could not well continue in the same orb," his American sermons do make a striking contrast with those of the man who had inspired the Hutchinsonians. At Hartford, Hooker gave to the subject of preparation what Cotton Mather called a "third concoction." In these sermons, he placed an even greater premium upon self-examination than he had in England: "there is no greater hindrance to be found on earth to holy meditation than froathy company and companions; while a man is in the crowd amongst such wretches there is no possibility in reason that one should search his own heart and examine his own way." Just which distracting multitude Hooker has in mind he does not say, but much of the *Application* is filled with this appetite for solitude, for the right conditions for introspection. It is hard to dismiss the feeling that Anne Hutchinson's celebration of the regenerate soul has something to do with Hooker's relentless search for sin within the satisfied self. The idea of evil as a palpable, entrenched thing has become his American theme. Cotton's promise of an invasion by grace has been postponed until the work of preparation can be completed.

The text is from the ninth book of *The Application of Redemption* (1656), pp. 5–13.

The Application of Redemption by the Effectual Work of the Word and Spirit of Christ for the Bringing Home of Lost Sinners to God

The heart must be broken and humbled before the Lord will own it as his, take up his abode with it, and rule in it.

There must be contrition and humiliation before the Lord comes to take possession; the house must be aired and fitted before it comes to be inhabited, swept by brokenness and emptiness of spirit, before the Lord will come to set up his abode in it. This was typified in the passage of the children of Israel towards the promised land; they must come into, and go through a vast and a roaring wilderness, where they must be bruised with many pressures, humbled under many overbearing difficulties they were to meet withal before they could possess that good land which abounded with all prosperity, flowed with milk and honey. The truth of this type, the prophet Hosea explains and expresseth at large in the Lord's dealing with his people in regard of their spiritual condition, Hosea 2:14–15, *I will lead her into the wilderness,* and break her heart with many bruising miseries, and *then I will speak kindly to her heart, and will give her the Valley of Achor for a door of hope . . .*

As we say of grounds before we cast in seed; there is two things to be attended there, it must be a fit ground, and a fat ground; the ground is fit when the weeds and green sward are plowed up, and the soil there, and made mold. And this is done in contrition and humiliation; then it must be a fat ground, the soil must have heart. We say the ground is plowed well, and lies well, but it's worn out, it's out of heart. Now faith fats the soil, furnisheth the soul with ability to fatten upon Christ, and so to receive the seed of the word, and the graces of sanctification, and thence it produceth good fruit in obedience. Upon this condition God's favor is promised, Psalms 34:18, *The Lord is nigh to them that be of a contrite spirit, and saveth them that be of a broken heart.* Isaiah 61:3, *He gives the garment of praise to those that have had the spirit of heaviness;* it will fit none, fit none, it's prepared for none but such, it's their livery only . . .

Be it granted that the soul finds sin as a plague, and therefore would be preserved from the evil of it, the second impediment which wholly keeps out faith is this: when the sinner expects supply and succor from its own sufficiency, either outward excellence, abilities of nature, or common graces, or the beauty of some performances which issue from any of these . . .

A word of terror to dash the hopes and sink the hearts of all haughty and hard-hearted sinners: God owns not such, will never vouchsafe his gracious presence with them or his blessing upon them for good . . . Hear and fear then all you stout-hearted, stubborn, and rebellious creatures, whose consciences can evidence that the day is yet to dawn, the hour yet to come, that ever you found your sins a pressure to you—they have been your pastime and your delight in which you have pleased yourselves . . . The great God of heaven and earth is up in arms against thee, he is upon the march to work thy destruction, James 4:6, *The Lord resists the proud, but he gives grace to the humble.* All grace is in his gift, and he doles it only to the bruised and abased; but there is no thought nor expectation that thou shalt receive any grace. Nay, that grace that thy rebellious and proud heart hath opposed and resisted, will work thy own ruin. Thou art the mark of God's direful indignation and vengeance. He plants all his forces against thee; if all the wisdom in heaven can contrive thy confusion, all the power in heaven work it, all the justice there determine it, it shall be done. God is nigh to them that are of a contrite heart, he saveth such as be of a broken spirit, Psalms 34:18. True, and mark it, of such, but such thou art not, such thou deridest, scornest, whose hearts fail them under the weight of their abominations. Thou lookest at them as mopish, silly, despicable men. Well, such you shall see saved forever, when such untamed, presumptuous, proud wretches as thou art shall be turned into hell . . .

Pharaoh is the pattern of all proud hearts. He hardened himself in his wickedness against the word of the Lord. But a broken and humble heart either lies right, or will come right. It will come to that bent of the rule that is revealed: hard things make that which is most soft to assimilate to them; easy and yielding things assimilate to whatever they close: so water in a round vessel takes that form, in a threesquare vessel, takes that. So here.

NATHANIEL WARD (c. 1578–1652)
The Simple Cobbler of Aggawam (c. 1646)

Most of Nathaniel Ward's life was behind him when he came to New England in 1634 at the age of fifty-five. He had taken his degree at Emmanuel College in 1603, nurtured by teachers who may be better called Elizabethan reformers than Puritans—men like Laurence Chaderton, who were steering the English church in a more pastoral direction but without clear denominational allegiance. In the second decade of the century Ward lived on the continent, mostly at Heidelberg, where he attended Frederick, the Elector Palatine, and his wife, the daughter of King James. Ward thus had a personal attachment to the beleaguered Protestant family whose defeat by Spanish armies meant nothing less to many Englishmen than blood-treason by their king. Later, as chaplain to an English merchant colony in Prussia, he had his first taste of preaching to an English community in an alien land.

Ward was regarded, when he came to Massachusetts, as something of a veteran, a man who had been on the front lines. During the early 1630s he became a member of the Massachusetts Bay Company, and when Laud forbade him to carry on his Essex ministry, the company furnished an escape route. He settled at Ipswich, where Anne and Simon Bradstreet lived for a time, and was chosen in 1641 to draw up what became the Massachusetts Body of Liberties, a codification of the colony's laws that drew heavily upon, but somewhat softened, Cotton's earlier draft of 1636.

In the mid-1640s, with his attention again fixed upon England, Ward wrote *The Simple Cobbler of Aggawam* (the Indian name for Ipswich). His book was a tour de force that devastated the fashions on the other side of the ocean, by which he meant everything from daring ladies' clothing to the newfangled idea of religious toleration. The latter he called "poly-piety," and the connection between the two was one shared quality—decadence.

The Simple Cobbler provides the best reply to the common charge that early New England writing has no humor. If not exactly raucous, it does attain a splendid sarcasm toward the "young spaniels" of revolutionary England, and it is probably the closest thing to Puritan satire since the anti-Episcopal Marprelate tracts of the sixteenth century. Rightly insisting that he is neither "nigard nor cinick," Ward shakes his head at rising hemlines and falling vigilance against religious heresy. In fact, his animus—in keeping with his early training—was not so much against this or that form of church government as against the idea of religious variety itself. It struck him as absurd that a Christian commonwealth could be indifferent to the church practices of its subjects.

Ward returned to England in 1647 and delivered a zesty rebuke to Parliament for its collusion in the abduction of King Charles. We have no record of his reaction to the king's execution, but regicide had no place in his imagination. Though he was left behind by the pace of revolution, *The Simple Cobbler* made him a celebrity. He died, probably in 1652, ministering to a small town near his childhood home. He may have been fortunate not to live to see his literary judgment confirmed by widened practice—for within ten years of his death, the kind of satire he had pioneered would, under the Restoration, become a weapon against the cause to which he had devoted his life.

The text is reprinted from the standard edition, ed. Paul M. Zall, pp. 5–6, 8, 10–12, 14–15, 23–25, 28–29, by permission of the University of Nebraska Press. Copyright © 1969 by the University of Nebraska Press.

The Simple Cobbler of Aggawam

Sutor Ultra Crepidam[1]

Either I am in an Appoplexie, or that man is in a Lethargie, who doth not now sensibly feele God shaking the heavens over his head, and the earth under his feet: The Heavens so, as the Sun begins to turne into darknesse, the Moon into blood, the Starres to fall down to the ground;[2] So that little Light of Comfort or Counsell is left to the sonnes of men . . .

Sathan is now in his passions, he feeles his passion approaching; hee loves to fish in royled waters. Though that Dragon cannot sting the vitals of the Elect mortally, yet that Beelzebub can fly-blow their Intellectuals miserably: The finer Religion grows, the finer hee spins his Cobwebs, hee will hold pace with Christ so long as his wits will serve him. Hee sees

1. A Latin proverb, usually *sutor ne supra crepidam:* "cobbler, stick to thy last."
2. Revelation 6:12–13.

himselfe beaten out of grosse Idolatries, Heresies, Ceremonies, where the Light breakes forth with power; he will therefore bestirre him to prevaricate Evangelicall Truths, and Ordinances, that if they will needs be walking, yet they shall *laborare varicibus*,[3] and not keep their path, he will put them out of time and place . . .

Such as have given or taken any unfriendly reports of us New-English, should doe well to recollect themselves. Wee have beene reputed a Colluvies[4] of wild Opinionists, swarmed into a remote wildernes to find elbowroome for our phanatick Doctrines and practises: I trust our diligence past, and constant sedulity against such persons and courses, will plead better things for us. I dare take upon me, to bee the Herauld of *New-England* so farre, as to proclaime to the world, in the name of our Colony, that all Familists, Antinomians, Anabaptists, and other Enthusiasts shall have free Liberty to keepe away from us, and such as will come to be gone as fast as they can, the sooner the better . . .

The power of all Religion and Ordinances, lies in their purity: their purity in their simplicity: then are mixtures pernicious. I lived in a City, where a Papist preached in one Church, a Lutheran in another, a Calvinist in a third; a Lutheran one part of the day, a Calvinist the other, in the same Pulpit: the Religion of that place was but motley and meagre, their affections Leopard-like . . .

Concerning Tolerations I may further assert . . .

He that is willing to tolerate any Religion, or discrepant way of Religion, besides his own, unlesse it be in matters meerly indifferent, either doubts of his own, or is not sincere in it.

I am not altogether ignorant of the eight Rules given by Orthodox divines about giving Tolerations, yet with their favour I dare affirme,

That there is no Rule given by God for any State to give an affirmative Toleration to any false Religion, or Opinion whatsoever; they must connive in some Cases, but may not concede in any.

That the State of *England* (so farre as my Intelligence serves) might in time have prevented with ease and may yet without any great difficultie deny both Toleration, and irregular connivences *salva Republica*.[5]

That if the State of *England* shall either willingly Tolerate, or weakly connive at such Courses, the Church of that Kingdome will sooner become the Devils dancing-Schoole, then Gods Temple: The Civill State a Beare-garden, then an Exchange: The whole Realme a Pais base[6] then

3. Fritter away their time.
4. Junk-heap.
5. To save the state.
6. An ordinary country.

an *England*. And what pity it is, that that Country which hath been the Staple of Truth to all Christendome, should now become the Aviary of Errors to the whole world, let every fearing heart judge.

I take Liberty of Conscience to be nothing but a freedome from sinne, and error. *Conscientia in tantum libera, in quantum ab errore liberata.*[7] And Liberty of Errour nothing but a Prison for Conscience. Then small will be the kindnesse of a State to build such Prisons for their Subjects . . .

It is said, That Men ought to have Liberty of their Conscience, and that it is persecution to debarre them of it: I can rather stand amazed then reply to this: it is an astonishment to think that the braines of men should be parboyl'd in such impious ignorance; Let all the wits under the Heavens lay their heads together and finde an Assertion worse then this (one excepted) I will petition to be chosen the universall Ideot of the world . . .

But why dwell I so intolerable long about Tolerations, I hope my fears are but panick, against which I have a double cordiall. First, that the Parliament will not though they could: Secondly, that they cannot though they would grant such Tolerations. God who hath so honoured them with eminent wisdome in all other things, will not suffer them to cast both his, and their Honour in the dust of perpetuall Infamy, doe what they can; nor shall those who have spent so great a part of their substance in redeeming their Civil Liberties from Usurpation, lose all that remaines in enthralling their spirituall Liberty by Toleration . . .

If all be true we heare, Never was any people under the Sun, so sick of new opinions as *English-men;* nor of new fashions as *English-women:* If God helpe not the one, and the devill leave not helping the other, a blind man may easily foresee what will become of both. I have spoken what I intend for the present to men; I shall speake a word to the women anon: in the mean time I intreat them to prepare patience.

. . . that godly humble Christians ought not to wonder impatiently at the wonderfull workes of God in these times; it is full Season for him to worke Soveraign worke, to vindicate un-stated, Rulers growne Over-rulers, Subjects worse then men, Churches-decayed. Tofts,[8] Professors, empty casks filled with unholy humours; I speake not of all, but too many; I condemne not the generation of the just [:] God hath his remnant, whom he will carefully preserve. If it bee time for men to take up Defensive Arms against such as are called Gods, upon the point of *Salus populi,*[9] it is high time for him that is God indeed, to draw his Sword

7. Conscience is free only to the extent that it is free from error.
8. Dandies.
9. Welfare of the people.

against wormes and no men, upon the point of *Majestas imperii:*[10] The piercing of his Sword shall discover the thoughts of many hearts.

Lastly, I dare averre, that it ill becomes Christians any thing well-shod with the preparation of the Gospel, to meditate flight from their deare Countrey upon these disturbances. Stand your grounds ye *Eleazars* and *Shammahs,*[11] stir not a foot so long as you have halfe a foot of ground to stand upon: after one or two such Worthies, a great Victory may be regained, and flying *Israel* may returne to a rich spoile. *Englishmen,* be advised to love *England,* with your hearts and to preserve it by your Prayers. I am bold to say that since the pure Primitive time, the Gospel never thrived so well in any soile on earth, as in the *Brittish,* nor is the like goodnesse of nature, or Cornucopian plenty else-where to be found: if ye lose that Country and finde a better before ye come to Heaven, my Cosmography failes me. I am farre from discouraging any, whom necessity of Conscience or condition thrusts out by head and shoulders: if God calls any into a Wildernesse, Hee will bee no wildernesse to them, *Jeremiah* 2.31. witnesse his large beneficence to us here beyond expectation.

Ye say, why come not we over to helpe the Lord against the Mighty, in these Sacred battailes?

I answer, many here are diligently observing the counsell of the same Prophet, 22.10. *Weepe not for him that is dead, neither bemoan him; but weep for him that is gone away and shall returne no more to see his Native Country.* Divers make it an Article of our *American* Creed, which a celebrate Divine of *England* hath observed upon *Hebrews* 11.9.[12] That no man ought to forsake his owne countrey, but upon extraordinary cause, and when that cause ceaseth, he is bound in conscience to returne if he can: We are looking to him who hath our hopes and seasons in his only wise hand . . .

I have often heard divers Ladies vent loud feminine complaints of the wearisome varieties and chargable changes of fashions: I marvell themselves preferre not a Bill of redresse. I would *Essex* Ladies would lead the *Chore,*[13] for the honour of their County and persons; or rather the thrice honorable Ladies of the Court, whom it best beesemes: who may wel presume of a *Le Roy le veult* from our sober King, a *Les Seigneurs ont assentus*[14] from our prudent Peers, and the like *Assentus,* from our considerate, I dare not say wife-worne Commons: who I beleeve had

10. Majesty of the empire.
11. Nehemiah 12:42.
12. "By faith he removed into the land of promise, as into a strange country."
13. Choir or company.
14. "The King so wills it . . . the Lords have assented."

much rather passe one such Bill, than pay so many Taylors Bills as they are forced to doe.

Most deare and unparallel'd Ladies, be pleased to attempt it: as you have the precellency of the women of the world for beauty and feature; so assume the honour to give, and not take Law from any, in matter of attire: if ye can transact so faire a motion among your selves unanimously, I dare say, they that most renite,[15] will least repent. What greater honour can your Honors desire, then to build a Promontory president to all foraigne Ladies, to deserve so eminently at the hands of all the English Gentry present and to come: and to confute the opinion of all the wise men in the world; who never thought it possible for women to doe so good a work?

If any man think I have spoken rather merrily than seriously he is much mistaken, I have written what I write with all the indignation I can, and no more then I ought . . .

15. Resist.

ROBERT KEAYNE (1595–1656)
Last Will and Testament (1653)

To say that the early settlements of New England included or tolerated merchant activity is badly to understate the case. It is more accurate to say that the first English settlements *were* merchant activities. Beginning in the first decade of the seventeenth century with the competing efforts of two groups of English investors—one dominated by men from the west country of Devonshire and Bristol, the other by a group of London entrepreneurs—New England had been the scene of one abortive trading mission after another. The expense and difficulty of buying and outfitting ships, providing supplies and materials for shelter that could withstand a New England winter, securing Indian cooperation in bringing marketable skins and furs to the coast—all combined to make profitable import expeditions to America rare. By the second decade of the century, the New England coast was penetrated only here and there by small-scale operators hoping to find a protected harbor and a cooperative tribe that would provide enough marketable goods to pay off their backers—and perhaps allow a last laugh at those at home who had declined a share of the risk.

By the late 1620s the climate for such adventures had improved. Sir Ferdinando Gorges, a nobleman with dreams of establishing a kind of feudal fiefdom in Northeast America, had acquired a patent for most of what would become modern New England and part of New York and Pennsylvania. But Gorges's plans never got off the ground. He was unable to prevent others from encroaching on "his" lands, and he failed to collect the percentage of profits his patent authorized him to demand from those who did. At the same time it was becoming clear that the old technique of sending a band of traders to exchange trinkets to please the "savage" eye for goods saleable to the "civilized" European would have to give way to different methods, such as the establishment of more durable settlements that could carry on longer-term trade, send a steadier return back home, and multiply the original investment. It was this kind of enterprise that was attempted in 1628 by a group called the New England Company. These entrepreneurs secured a patent from Gorges and dispatched John Endecott to Salem with a group of fishermen, planters, traders, and two ministers named Higginson and Skelton. The backers of Endecott's group, cannier than their predecessors, managed to secure a royal charter for their colony and became the Massachusetts Bay Company. Within a year, under worsening economic conditions in England, the growing fury of Archbishop Laud against Puritan sympathizers, and the approach of national conflict between Parliament and king, New England came to be seen as a place of exile as well as a potential supply house. As Bernard Bailyn has persuasively argued, it was at this juncture that the settlement of Massachusetts became more an affair of Puritan-minded country gentlemen—men like Winthrop, Dudley, Isaac Johnson, and the Harlakendens—and less one of urban merchants. The Great Migration that brought about twenty thousand immigrants to New England between 1630 and 1640 included representatives of both these social groups. But the official political ideology was enunciated by rural gentry like Winthrop, not by the businessmen who had, in effect, been there first.

As Winthrop declared in his *Arbella* sermon and Cotton restated in *Moses His Judicials* (1636), Massachusetts was to be a place where the instinct for profit would be reined in—where "the Governor . . . [shall] appoint a reasonable rate of prices." This sanction of governmental control over private business was in some respects more Lutheran than Calvinist, even perhaps more medieval than modern—an attempt to check what Max Weber was to identify as the partnership of Protestantism and capitalism. It was also a highly ironic repetition of one of the English monarch's practices that most enraged certain English Puritans—namely the granting of monopolies—such as that to the Merchant Adventurers for the Flemish cloth trade. This kind of royal monopoly had added to the Puritan ranks frustrated businessmen forced to stay out of lucrative trade (or to pay for the privilege of joining in), and such exclusions proved ultimately as unenforceable in New England as in Old. Though the magistrates tried, it was impossible to assign merchants from certain towns to specific incoming ships and to keep other customers away. The laws about lending, buying, and selling were clear, but their application was a murky matter indeed. A "combination of virtues," Cotton had called this ideal of civic responsibility, "strangely mixed in every lively holy Christian . . . diligence in worldly business, and yet deadness to the world."

This delicate balance, which Cotton called "such a mystery as none can read, but they that know it," proved to be an idea of rare incarnation. Yet in 1639 one prominent merchant, a man who had loyally attended

John Davenport's sermons at St. Stephen's in London, was summoned to court for violating it. Robert Keayne was charged with overpricing a bag of nails. Soon others who had bought such items as buttons and thread from Keayne joined in what was becoming a chorus of recrimination against him. As Bailyn has stressed, Keayne thought of himself as a thorough Christian, with nothing casual or shallow about his religious commitment. He was now a member of Cotton's church, and he felt proud of meeting one of Cotton's criteria for the Christian life: following a "warrantable calling." It is precisely this circumstance that explains the poignant bewilderment—sometimes as prickly self-defense, sometimes as exasperated penance—that Keayne's *Last Will and Testament* reveals. The case of Keayne may be seen as a stand-off setting clergy and rural gentlemen against the law of supply and demand and against city-bred tradesmen who understood that law. But despite Keayne's personal humiliation, the ultimate outcome of this confrontation was a foregone conclusion: Keayne's party would prevail in the life of the colony; Cotton's would not. More than a skirmish of personalities or social factions, this was perhaps the last time in American history that there existed a governmental authority as well as a private conscience to hold every individual accountable for what we now believe to be the "natural" thing—the desire, as our jargon puts it, to maximize profit.

The text is from Bernard Bailyn's edition of *The Apologia of Robert Keayne,* in *Colonial Society of Massachusetts Transactions,* 42 (1952–1956), 294, 296, 300, 308.

Last Will and Testament

[These attacks came] together with that deep and sharp censure that was laid upon me in the country and carried on with so much bitterness and indignation of some, contrary both to law or any foregoing precedent if I mistake not, and, I am sure, contrary or beyond the quality and desert of the complaints that came against me, which indeed were rather shadows of offense, out of a desire of revenge made great by the aggravations of some to make them heinous and odious than that they were so indeed, and this not in my own judgments only (which may be looked at as partial) but in the judgments of hundreds that have expressed themselves, both then and especially since. Yet by some it was carried on with such violence and pretended zeal as if they had had some of the greatest sins in the world to censure . . .

I paid the fine to the uttermost, which is not nor hath been done by many (nor so earnestly required as mine was) though for certain and not supposed offenses of far higher nature, which I can make good not by hearsay only but in my own knowledge, yea offenses of the same kind. [My own offense] was so greatly aggravated and with such indignation pursued by some, as if no censure could be too great or too severe, as if I had not been worthy to have lived upon the earth. [Such offenses] are not only now common almost in every shop and warehouse but even then and ever since with a higher measure of excess, yea even by some of them that were most zealous and had their hands and tongues deepest in my censure . . .

I did not then nor dare not now go about to justify all my actions. I know God is righteous and doth all upon just grounds, though men may mistake in their grounds and proceedings, counsel have erred and courts may err and a faction may be too hard and outvote the better or more discerning part. I know the errors of my life. The failings in my trade and otherwise have been many. Therefore from God [the censure] was most just. Though it had been much more severe I dare not so open my mouth against it, nor never did as I remember [except to] justify him. Yet I dare not say nor did I ever think (as far as I can call to mind) that the censure was just and righteous from men. Was the price of a bridle, not for taking but only asking, 2s. for [what] cost here 20d. such a heinous sin? [Such bridles] have since been commonly sold and still are for 2s. 6d. and 3s. or more, though worse in kind. Was it such a heinous sin to sell 2 or 3 dozen of great gold buttons for 2s. 10d. per dozen that cost 2s. 2d. ready money in London, bought at the best hand, as I showed to many by my invoice (though I could not find it at the instant when the court desired to see it) and since was confirmed by special testimony from London? . . . Was the selling of 6d. nails for 8d. per lb. and 8d. nails for 10d. per lb. such a crying and oppressing sin? . . .

It is true that in anything wherein I might justly take shame or sorrow to myself God inclined my heart not to withstand it, for he that hides his sins shall not prosper, but he that confesseth and forsaketh them shall find mercy. In many [ways] we all sin in this. And who can say his heart is clean? Yet for the chief of the things that was most urged against me in court and for which the sentence was passed against me, as the gold buttons, the bridle, the nails, the falsifying of my book, I did justify and stand to maintain that they was evident mistakes and that I was wronged about them . . . I had no cause of penitency or confession of guilt [unless] it was for having been so used and reproached about them against all equity. But if they should have cast me out of the church 20 times for this I should have chosen it rather than to have confessed myself guilty for [anyone's] satisfaction wherein I knew myself (better than any else did) to be innocent . . .

FOUR

O NEW ENGLAND!

THE OUTBREAK of the civil wars in England, the rise of the Commonwealth and the Protectorate, the emergence of "toleration" as the guiding principle of an English Puritanism liberated by the New Model Army; all had their impact on New England's own conception of itself, its definition of its special character and destiny. So too, of course, did the Restoration of the British monarchy and Episcopacy in 1660, which left New England seemingly a last and isolated redoubt of pure religion in a Christendom restored to darkness. Until 1660, however, New England increasingly imagined itself a "model" for the Old World, issuing progressively more strident instructions to its former Independent allies and proffering gratuitous and even impudent advice to Cromwell himself, as in Thomas Cobbett's *The Civil Magistrate's Power* (1653).

During these same years, however, New England was disposed both to the testiest of responses to English critics and to quieter, though by no means secret, self-criticism. In 1657, for instance, Richard Mather, feeling death approaching (actually he lived for another dozen years), issued a "Farewell" to his Dorchester congregation. He admonished them to remain faithful to *The Westminster Confession* (which he, the principal author of the Cambridge Platform in 1648, had persuaded the synod to endorse). But he went on to observe that creeds and forms were not enough: "experience shows that it is an easy thing in the middest of worldly business to lose the life and power of religion, that nothing thereof should be left but only the external form, as it were the carcass or shell, worldliness having eaten out the kernel, and having consumed the very soul and life of godliness." Possibly the crucial word in Mather's fearful vision was "experience," for warnings of the same order had been emitted from New England pulpits for at least two decades, though few before Mather had pronounced so generally on New England's declension from its primitive spirit. For the same two decades, however, the very preachers who discerned a waning of New England piety had taken the lead in proclaiming to the world its extraordinary achievements in perfecting due forms of government, both civil and ecclesiastical.

The New England Way, during these years, was not immune to criticism from New Englanders disaffected from the emerging orthodoxy. Public assaults on the establishment were issued by those who were exiled from the Bay or left it voluntarily in the aftermath of the Antinomian crisis. In 1645, for instance, John Wheelwright, having taken refuge in what is now New Hampshire, arranged for the publication in London of his *Mercurius Americanus,* which apprised England of the doctrinal and ecclesiastical "oppression" of himself and his kin. A decade later the General Court thought it appropriate to certify Wheelwright as restored to soundness—possibly because it was known he was about to return to England to visit his friend and classmate the Lord Protector. ("I remember the time when I was more afraid to meet Wheelwright at football," Cromwell is said to have announced after a friendly bout of wrestling with Wheelwright during his visit, "than I have been of meeting any army since in the field.") Another banished during the crisis of the 1630s was Samuel Gorton, who set about, in Rhode Island, building his own peculiar faith and church. Denounced by Edward Winslow in *Hypocrisy Unmasked* (1646), Gorton immediately arranged to have published in London his *Simplicity's Defense Against Seven-Headed Policy.* Winthrop professed to find the book's doctrines incomprehensible, but Gorton's writings clearly reveal him as a "familist" and perfectionist, a denier of all outward ordinances and even of the Trinity. To appreciate fully New England's intellectual life, one must understand that the Gortonists survived as a group for nearly a century and that, over the same years, there emerged as well in New England Quakers, Baptists, Rogerenes, and a host of other persuasions for whom the New England Way was far from sacrosanct.

In 1660 John Norton published a lengthy treatise evincing the degree to which the standing order felt threatened by the proliferation of "enthusiasms." To read *The Heart of New England Rent at the Blasphemies of the Present Generation* is to sense that "popular errors" seemed almost as rampant in New England as they had grown to be in Old England in the latter days of the Protectorate. Norton's chief target was Quakerism, which was already gaining adherents among the New England populace, and which he believed ought to be outlawed and suppressed, even as a decade later the established clergy called for similar action against a handful of Baptists. Even Roger Williams despaired of the Quakers, but he challenged them to debate, alleging that they denied the "historical Christ" in favor of one that was wholly inward—thus typologizing, as it were, the New Testament itself. (Williams also allowed, however, in a letter to John Winthrop's son, that the Quakers may have had more of the original Puritan spirit in them than the descendants of New England's founders.) Norton was not interested in debate: "madmen acting according to their frantic passions are to be restrained with chains, when they cannot be restrained otherwise." The usually equable Norton's impassioned response to Quakerism may well have been, as Kai Erikson has argued, another attempt, like the trial of Anne Hutchinson, to give to a fragmenting New England a sense of its unity by exorcising a definably "criminal" frame of mind.

Also published in 1660 was John Eliot's *The Christian Commonwealth,* the ultimate in prescriptions gratuitously offered to Puritan Old England. Eliot's volume, imbued with a confidence in the imminent dawning of the Kingdom of God on earth, was a monument to the belief of many in New England that it was their obligation to set out in advance the institutional framework for the millennial years. Eliot's curious political structure—a symmetrical hierarchy of tens, fifties, hundreds, and so forth—may have owed as much to Cromwell's order of battle (and to the New England yearning to share somehow in the tangible victories of the English Church Militant) as to scripture. It also appears to have reflected Eliot's experience among the Indians of New England, who, he observed, once converted to Christianity were impatient "to leave their wild and scattered manner of life, and come under" such "government, both civil and ecclesiastical, as the Lord hath commanded in the holy scriptures." Unhappily there was, in the New England of 1660, no absolute unanimity as to the details of church government commanded in scripture, but even more unhappily for Eliot and his tract, he had chosen the most unpropitious of moments to publish his political theorizing in London.

Eliot had written *The Christian Commonwealth* in the early 1650s, intending it even then for "the chosen, and holy and faithful, who manage the wars of the Lord against Antichrist in Great Britain." But, perhaps because he felt under compulsion to publish only when news of England's debacle under Richard Cromwell became known, he suddenly rushed it into print at the end of the decade. By the time it appeared, many of the faithful had already been beheaded, and the presumed Antichrist, in the person of Charles II, had been restored to the British throne. Curiously, the English authorities seem to have ignored Eliot's book, but in Massachusetts the General Court, more cautious than ever, immediately condemned it as "full of seditious principles and notions in relation to all established governments in the Christian world, especially against the government established in their native country." When the court ordered all copies in New England to be confiscated or effaced, Eliot meekly admitted the justice of their judgment and recanted by calling Cromwell and his party "the late innovators" and by acknowledging the restored monarchy to be "not only a lawful but eminent form of government." Later in 1661 Eliot published his Indian translation of the New Testament, and thereafter he labored quietly among the Indians, outliving his generation so well that his last years were devoted to preaching zealously against the novel fashion of long hair.

Eliot's career—his "discovery" of the Indian mission in the 1640s, the grandiose political expectations and pronouncements of the 1650s, his tractability in the wake of the Restoration, and his subsequent turning inward and even to seeming trivia—could stand as something of an epitome of the New England mind in the middle years of the seventeenth century. Yet it could also be said that the mind of New England during these years was at no point single: ironies and contradictions, even confrontations, abounded. Some who lived long enough to despair of their children began to argue among themselves over the question of whether those without an experience of saving grace could present *their* children for baptism: this debate over the so-called Half-Way Covenant, smoothed over in the Cambridge synod, surfaced publicly almost immediately after the Restoration. Many New Englanders who had been born in the early years of the colony and were now coming of age had never stepped forward to make the profession of faith required for full church membership. According to established congregational practice, the children of such half-way members could not be granted the privilege of baptism. It was this exclusion that the synod of 1662 struck down. The synod gave impetus to the evolving New England conception of itself as modeled on Old Testament Israel, a nation whose original covenant with God was handed down through generations. By contrast, those who opposed the concessions of the synod—John Davenport, for instance—remained faithful to the Pauline ideal that grace was a transcendent and identifiable experience that had nothing to do with inheritance. Davenport, almost alone among the survivors of the first settlers, insisted that all ecclesiastical arguments "must be drawn expressly, or by good consequence, from the New Testament . . . or the primitive churches, planted or approved by the Apostles, for our patterns."

To a considerable degree the struggle over the Half-Way Covenant was an intergenerational one; it was Jonathan Mitchell, Shepard's student and successor to the Cambridge pulpit, who argued (from Exodus 20) that the "mercy and grace of the covenant is extended to the faithful and their seed unto a *thousand* generations . . . so as that the Lord will never reject them till they reject him." Ironically Mitchell, who in a few years was to preach one of the most celebrated of New England "jeremiads" lamenting the colony's decline from its primitive purity and principles, argued in 1662 for his notion of inheritable or "federal covenant" on the basis that scriptural warrant must be applied, even though such notions "had not formerly been held or heard of amongst us." Quite correctly, however, Mitchell observed that neither he nor his generation were the first to suggest that New England ought to follow in Abraham's footsteps rather than mindlessly, as it were, following the road taken by Paul. For long before 1660, when the progress of history and the passing of time seemed to conspire to cause New England to reconceive itself as a "peculiar and separate people" like the tribes of Israel, such a possibility had both intrigued and tormented a New England mind that was, from the beginning, divided against itself.

ROGER WILLIAMS (1603–1683)
The Bloody Tenent of Persecution (1643)

THE MOST CELEBRATED of critics of the New England Way—perhaps the most persistent, even in certain respects the noblest, of nay-sayers in all American history—was Roger Williams. He is remembered chiefly for his long and bitter debate with John Cotton, who in turn has suffered, in the eyes of history, as Williams' tormentor, particularly to those who see Williams (quite wrongly) as a forerunner of Jeffersonian religious "toleration." It is clear that Williams considered himself hounded by Cotton and that Williams, who had arrived in the Bay in 1631 and had been installed as minister of Salem in 1633, was quite unprepared for Cotton's visit to Salem, much less for Cotton's denunciation of the doctrines and notions of church purity Williams was espousing there. Quite simply, Williams was one of those who believed that the churches of New England ought to forswear *all* communion with the Church of England—thus flagrantly challenging not merely Cotton's exhortations at Southampton but, even more to the point, what Cotton himself wanted to believe the faithful were doing in New England.

Soon Williams was banished from the Bay, not merely for his Separatist leanings but for his insistence that the crown had no power to grant Indian lands to the Massachusetts Bay Company. (Even in Separatist Plymouth Williams quickly wore out his welcome; he then moved beyond all known jurisdictions to establish what came to be Rhode Island.) Out of his Rhode Island experience and his communion with the Indians emerged *A Key into the Language of America,* published in London in 1643, which can be read as the subtlest, and thus perhaps the most telling, of his criticisms of Massachusetts Bay. An exercise in linguistic analysis (preceding by several years Eliot's first sermon in the Indian tongue), it reads also as a study in comparative cultural anthropology. Often incidentally, as in his characterization of the "wilderness" as a "type" of a world in which the weak are oppressed by the strong, and even more often only by implication, in suggestions of the superiority of Indian institutions to those of "civilized" New England, Williams adroitly discharges some of his grievances against the Bay. Not all of them, however, for in the same year he also published the first of his diatribes against Cotton.

The long interchange between Cotton and Williams began in the summer of 1636, when Cotton dispatched a letter, imperious in tone, listing all the charges against Williams. Insisting that Separatism was the head and font of Williams' offending, Cotton condescendingly urged Williams to repent. He went a step beyond the doctrines of *God's Promise,* however, to make the point that would be his most telling throughout the long debate with Williams: for a church, or even one saint, to separate from the world or from worldlings would and could have but one consequence: leaving the world under the unchecked control of the reprobate. Already in 1633 Cotton sensed that Williams' views could lead (as they eventually did) to a wholly noninstitutional individualism.

Cotton's letter was not published until 1643, when Williams was in London seeking a charter for Rhode Island. Williams, noting that Cotton's letter had somehow "providentially" found its way into print, hastily prepared a public reply (he had never responded privately). He strove to blame Cotton personally for his banishment and for the fact that he, Williams, had almost "perished in that sorrowful winter's flight." Although he did profess an enduring love for Cotton, he could not hide his bitterness and disappointment, even quite possibly his envy; he charged Cotton with defending the Massachusetts establishment in order to rise to eminence on the shoulders of the magistrates. Williams was well aware of how Cotton had been chastened through the trials of Anne Hutchinson, but it was not this episode to which he pointed in implying that Cotton had abandoned his earlier ideals in a desire for precedence and respectability.

Williams also presumably knew by 1643 that Cotton had warned his Boston congregation that, though they might take pride in having wrought "reformation of churches," they were unlikely, given their spiritual declension, to take part in "the resurrection of Christ." Even before Nathaniel Ward had sensed a relationship between perfection of church forms and decay of individual piety, Williams drew the connection directly. Incessantly he belittled Cotton's argument that non-Separating churches were more conducive to their members' "growth in grace." But the most significant of Williams' arguments—one first broached in the *Answer*—was that any and all relevance of the Old Testament, its forms, ceremonies, and institutions, was abrogated with the coming of Christ. Thereafter all men, as individuals, were free to seek their own salvation, unencumbered by any government, that of the church or of the world. It was not the authority of the Massachusetts ministry simply that Williams denied; indeed he had resigned, as it were, from their church without ever joining it. Nor was the issue, at bottom, one of the "separation of church and state." His demurral from the New England Way was the ultimate one: no power on earth was entitled to prevent any individual from seeking Christ in his own way.

No sooner had Williams answered Cotton's letter than he turned to composing his more majestic affirmation of the principles of religious freedom: *The Bloody Tenent of Persecution*. Once again he cast his treatise as a refutation of Cotton, who, Williams sensed, was already struggling against the mainstream of history. This despite the fact that in 1644 the Presbyterians still controlled Parliament (and, according to Williams, consigned *The Bloody Tenent* to the flames). But by this time many English Puritans, including Williams' newfound friend John Milton (who was busy writing his *Areopagitica*) were broaching proposals for full and unrestrained freedom of Protestant conscience. Half of *The Bloody Tenent* was a reply to an unpublished essay by Cotton on freedom of conscience, another half a critique of the "Model of Church and Civil Power" drawn up by the Massachusetts clergy in 1635, for which Williams wrongly held Cotton responsible.

But the central issue raised in *The Bloody Tenent* transcended the outmoded political theory of the 1630s and probably even the ecclesiastical debates of revolutionary England. Although Williams was hampered by his point-by-point adherence to the positions of the "Model," and although he was often so carried away by his convictions as to forget which of his two characters, Truth or Peace, was carrying the burden of his argument, the message of his "dialogue" and its eloquence emerged with abundant clarity:

> *Truth*. There is a civil sword, called the sword of civil justice, which, being of a material civil nature, for the defense of persons, estates, families, liberties of a city or civil state, and the suppressing of uncivil or injurious persons or actions by such civil punishments—it cannot, according to its utmost reach and capacity (now under Christ, when all nations are merely civil, without any such typical, holy respect upon them as was upon Israel, a national church), I say, cannot extend to spiritual and soul causes, spiritual and soul punishment, which belongs to that spiritual sword with two edges, the soul-piercing (in soul-saving or soul-killing), the Word of God.

Williams' differences with Cotton (and with New England) were indeed over that issue which would later come to be known as "the relationship of church and state." But *The Bloody Tenent* is hardly to be read as a forerunner of Jefferson, or even of Madison. *The* issue for Williams was, as Perry Miller has demonstrated, a right reading of scripture. In Williams' mind the whole of the Old Testament was to be read as "types," and none of its exemplary character persisted into the Christian era. History began, in effect, wholly anew with the coming of Christ, and neither history nor nature embodied any pattern discernible or relevant to the saints. Williams' disappointment with Cotton was more than merely personal; indeed, he seems to have persisted in his arguments in the hope that Cotton, if anyone in New England, could be brought to realize the implications of his own hermeneutics.

The text of *The Bloody Tenent* is from the Narragansett edition of Williams' *Complete Writings,* III, 361–363, 398–399, 416–417.

☙ *The Bloody Tenent of Persecution*

. . . Such enemies, such armies, no history, no experience proves ever to have come against one poor nation as against Israel in the type; and never was nor shall be known to come against any state or country now, but the Israel of God the spiritual Jews, Christ's true followers in all parts and quarters of the world . . .

The Israel of God now, men and women, fight under the great Lord General, the Lord Jesus Christ: their weapons, armor, and artillery, is like themselves spiritual, set forth from top to toe, Ephesians 6. So mighty and so potent that they break down the strongest holds and castles, yea in the very souls of men and carry into captivity the very thoughts of men, subjecting them to Christ Jesus: they are spiritual conquerors . . .

Their victories and conquests in this are contrary to those of this world, for when they are slain and slaughtered, yet then they conquer: so overcame they the devil in the Roman emperors, Revelation 12. By the blood of the lamb: 2. By the word of their testimony: 3. The cheerful spilling of their own blood for Christ; for they loved not their lives unto the death . . .

This glorious army of white troopers, horses and harness (Christ Jesus and his true Israel), Revelation 19, gloriously conquer and overcome the beast, the false prophet and the kings of the earth up in arms against them, and lastly, reigning with Christ a thousand years they conquer the devil himself and the numberless armies (like the sand on the seashore) of Gog and Magog,[1] and yet not a tittle of mention of any sword, helmet,

1. The names given to Antichrist in Revelation 20:8–15 .

breastplate, shield or horse, but what is spiritual and of a heavenly nature: all which wars of Israel have been, may be, and shall be fulfilled mystically and spiritually.

But (to wind all up) as it is most true that magistracy in general is of God (Romans 13) for the preservation of mankind in civil order and peace (the world otherwise would be like the sea, wherein men, like fishes, would hunt and devour each other, and the greater devour the less), so also it is true, that magistracy in special for the several kinds of it is of man, I Peter 2:13. Now what kind of magistrate soever the people shall agree to set up, whether he receive Christianity before he be set in office, or whether he receive Christianity after, he receives no more power of magistracy than a magistrate that hath received no Christianity. For neither of them both can receive more than the commonweal, the body of people and civil state, as men, communicate unto them and betrust with them.

All lawful magistrates in the world, both before the coming of Christ Jesus and since (excepting those unparalleled typical magistrates of the church of Israel), are but derivatives and agents immediately derived and employed as eyes and hands, serving for the good of the whole: hence they have and can have no more power than fundamentally lies in the bodies or fountains themselves, which power, might, or authority is not religious, Christian, &c., but natural, humane and civil.

And hence it is true, that a Christian captain, Christian merchant, physician, lawyer, pilot, father, master, and (so consequently) magistrate, etc., is no more a captain, merchant, physician, lawyer, pilot, father, master, magistrate, &c., than a captain, merchant, &c. of any other conscience or religion . . .

The want of discerning the true parallel, between Israel in the type then, and Israel the antitype now, is that rock whereon (through the Lord's righteous jealousy, punishing the world and chastising his people) thousands dash and make woeful shipwreck . . . O that it may please the father of lights to discover this to all that fear his name! Then would they not sin to save a kingdom, nor run into the lamentable breach of civil peace and order in the world, nor be guilty of forcing thousands to hypocrisy, in a state worship, nor of profaning the holy name of God and Christ, by putting their names and ordinances upon unclean and unholy persons; nor of shedding the blood of such heretics, &c., whom Christ would have enjoy longer patience and permission until the harvest; nor of the blood of the Lord Jesus himself, in his faithful witnesses of truth; nor lastly, of the blood of so many hundred thousands slaughtered men, women, and children, by such uncivil and unchristian wars and combustions about the Christian faith and religion . . .

JOHN COTTON

The Bloody Tenent, Washed and Made White in the Blood of the Lamb (1646)

THE INTELLECTUAL predicament in which Williams had placed Cotton is suggested by the latter's seemingly instinctive adoption of the persona of "Defender" in his effort to cleanse Williams' *Bloody Tenent* of what seemed to him its pollutions. *The Bloody Tenent Washed* is one of the weakest of Cotton's performances, rhetorically if not intellectually. There is little in it of Cotton's "ancient vigor," for Cotton seldom takes the initiative, adhering instead to the points of Williams' argument and, in an often tired manner, reminding Williams that his own views were not absolutely identical with the New England Way Williams was deriding. It was a "middle way" that Cotton was defending against both Presbyterianism and those of New England's erstwhile Independent allies—many of them now Williams' friends—who, Cotton knew, were beginning to question the once-unassailable postulate of the need for religious uniformity.

Throughout *The Bloody Tenent Washed* Cotton seems to have been reduced to a thesis neither intellectually respectable nor historically demonstrable: that in Massachusetts the relationship of church and state had proven itself workable and efficient, and that therefore the experiment was worthy of being enforced as an establishment. Yet Cotton seems uncertain whether such arrangements are demanded for the glory of God or, as Winthrop had argued a decade earlier, for the security of the state. His call for "more light" at the conclusion of the treatise was more than a pious invocation, for he knew that the orthodoxy of Massachusetts was not in fact wholly a triumph. Writing in the year of the Cambridge synod, Cotton defended (against Williams' insistence that "tares" must be purged from the wheatfields of the Church) the value of "hypocrites": they "follow their callings, and are so far from being burthensome to others by their idleness, that they are even choked with the cares and businesses of this world, and yet are not behind in liberal contributions to pious uses." Such an argument (almost a retroactive exculpation of Robert Keayne) showed how far Cotton had come, or been taken, since his years in Old Boston: by 1647 he seemed reduced to the hope of salvaging New England's errand by harnessing carnal energies to the purposes of God.

The most poignant section of *The Bloody Tenent Washed* is that in which Cotton answers Williams' charge that the New England clergy gave power to the magistrates in order that their own nests might be feathered. If ever the case were more wholly the opposite, Cotton replied, "let him that can discern it, make it appear." The lesson of all history (and Williams, as well as Cotton, knew precisely *which* history) was abundantly clear: "To allow them power over ourselves in case of heretical delinquency is not to make them stairs or stirrups of our advancement, but swords and staves (if need be) for our punishment." Cotton, whose internal exile was perhaps more pitiable than that endured by Williams in Rhode Island, nonetheless refused to let Christians and their ministry resign from active engagement in the battles of this world. A muted prophet in the New England whose destiny he had once hoped to control, Cotton would not give up what gains New England had achieved in perfection of its institutions. New England must contend earnestly, he announced with some finality, not to replicate the patterns of the Old Testament but to fulfill the revelation once vouchsafed to St. John in his wilderness.

Whatever the many issues raised in the Cotton-Williams debate, their differences hinged finally on the question of whether the Kingdom of God would be brought to earth through the salvation of individuals merely or by way of institutional development. This question New England was to continue to debate, without resolution, long after both combatants had left the field of battle.

The text of *The Bloody Tenent Washed* is from the edition of 1647, pp. 12–13, 92–93, 146, 161–162.

The Bloody Tenent Washed and Made White in the Blood of the Lamb

Wherein the great questions of this present time are handled, viz., how far liberty of conscience ought to be given to those that truly fear God? And how far restrained to turbulent and pestilent persons, that not only raze the foundation of godliness, but disturb the civil peace where they lie? Also how far the magistrate may proceed in the duties of the first table?[1] . . .

It is true, where the church is not, cities and towns may enjoy some measure of civil peace, yea and flourish in outward prosperity for a time through the patience and bounty and long-sufferance of God . . . But when the church cometh to be planted amongst them, if then civil states do neglect them and suffer the churches to corrupt and annoy themselves by pollutions in religion, the staff of the peace of the commonwealth will soon be broken . . . The commonwealth of Rome flourished five hundred years before the kingdom of God in his church came amongst them; and the decays of the commonwealth occasioned by the persecutions of the church were repaired by the public establishment of the church's peace in Christian emperors. But when the churches begun to pollute themselves by the idolatrous worship of images, and the Christian emperors took no care to reform this abuse in churches, the Lord sent in (amongst other barbarous nations) the Turks to punish, not only degenerate churches, but also the civil state for this wickedness . . .

Civil peace (to speak properly) is not only a peace in civil things, for the object; but a peace of all the persons of the city, for the subject. The church is one society in the city, as well as is the society of merchants, or drapers, fishmongers, and haberdashers . . .

Discusser. It is a most bloody doctrine, the wolves (heretics) are to be driven away, their brains knocked out and killed, the poor sheep to be persecuted for whom Christ died.

Defender. Belike[2] it is a milky and peaceable and gospel-like doctrine the wolves (heretics) are to be tolerated, not an hair to be struck off from their heads. But for the poor sheep, for whom Christ died, let them perish unless Christ mean to preserve them himself alone, with his own immediate hand: no care of preserving them belongeth to the civil magistrate.

Discusser. Is not this to take Christ, and to make him a temporal king by force? (John 6:15) Is not this to make his kingdom of this world? To set up a civil and temporal Israel? To bound out new earthly holy lands of Canaan? Yea and to set up a Spanish Inquisition in all parts of the world, to the speedy destruction of millions of souls and to the frustrating of the sweet end of the coming of the Lord Jesus, which was to save men's souls (and to that end, not to destroy their bodies) by his own blood?

1. The first four commandments.
2. Perhaps. Cotton here adopts a tone of mockery in summarizing William's position.

Defender. Now of all these: when the kingdoms of the earth become the kingdoms of the Lord (Revelation 11:15) it is not by making Christ a temporal king, but by making temporal kingdoms nursing fathers to his church. In the days of Christ's flesh it was incompatible to his ministry to make him a king (as they went about to do, John 6:15). Christ hath enjoyed (even as mediator) an everlasting kingdom, not only in the church, but in the government of all the kingdoms of the earth, by his glorious power and righteousness. But the kingdoms of the earth are then said to be the kingdoms of our Lord, when they submit their laws to the laws of his word. But that neither maketh him a temporal king, nor his kingdom in the church to be a kingdom of this world. The church and commonwealth are still distinct kingdoms, the one of this world, the other of heaven, and yet both of them from Christ; unto whom the father hath committed all judgment (Job 5:22).

Neither will this set up a civil and temporal Israel, an holy Canaan, unless all the members of the commonwealth were called to be members of the church, and subject to all the ceremonial and all the judicial laws of Moses (not only those of moral and perpetual equity) but peculiar to that state, as the brother to marry his deceased brother's wife.[3]

Nor is it a Spanish Inquisition to preserve the sheep of Christ from the raven of wolves; but this rather (such is the practice of the Discusser) to promote the principal end of the Spanish Inquisition, to advance the Romish tyranny, idolatry, and apostasy, by proclaiming impunity to all their whorish and wolvish emissaries.

Nor is it a frustrating of the sweet end of Christ's coming which was to save souls, but rather a direct advancing of it to destroy (if need be) the bodies of those wolves who seek to destroy the souls of those for whom Christ died and whom he bought with his own blood . . .

Discusser. That answer . . . implieth two things.

1. That the civil magistrate, who is to constrain, must judge of all the consciences of their subjects, whether they be convinced or not.[4]

2. That when the civil magistrate discerneth that his subjects' consciences are convinced, then he may constrain them *vi & armis*[5] hostilely . . .

Defender. Neither of both these things are implied in that answer.

3. Deuteronomy 25:5–10 requires a man to marry his brother's widow and stipulates that any children of this marriage shall be considered those of the first husband.

4. Williams, according to Cotton, is objecting that persecution by the magistrate for *religious* error requires that the civil authority must decide, in each case, whether the subject is acting contrary to a "convinced conscience," or is genuinely unaware of the truth which he has contravened. For Williams, it was futile and destructive to force an erring conscience into conformity with right religious practice, or failing that, into punishment or exile. For Cotton, such authority was required to maintain a Christian commonwealth.

5. By strength and arms.

Not the first (that the civil magistrate must then judge of all of the consciences of their subjects, whether they be convinced, or no). For it implieth no more than that he is not to constrain them till he see they be convinced. If he never see them convinced, he is to see they be never constrained. But how far the magistrate may discern and judge in matters of religion hath been spoken above. Nor the second: For the constraint I spake of, was not by positive means *vi & armis*, but negative, withholding such trust and employment from such as he seeth are not faithful and trusty to their God of whose truth they are convinced and yet withhold it in unrighteousness. I know no constraint at all that lieth upon the consciences of any in New England to come to church; neither do I know that any scruple lieth upon any conscience in New England, that withholdeth any from hearing the word amongst us. But least of all do I know that any are constrained to pay church duties in New England[6] . . . What they pay, they give voluntarily, each one with his own hand, without any constraint at all, but their own will as the Lord directs them . . .

A man that is willing to open his eyes may easily see that though the government of the civil magistrate do extend no further than over the bodies and goods of his subjects, yet he may, and ought to, improve that power over their bodies and goods, to the good of their souls . . . The bodies and goods and outward estates of men may expect a blessing when their souls prosper . . . If it seem a monstrous thing in the eyes of the Discusser to imagine that the good estate of the church, and the well-ordering of the ordinances of God therein, should concern the civil good of the commonwealth, it may well seem monstrous to him to imagine that the flourishing of religion is the flourishing of the civil state, and the decay of religion is the decay and ruin of the civil state . . .

And therefore the magistrate need not to fear that he should exceed the bounds of his office if he should meddle with the spiritual affairs of the church in God's way. It is true, if he shall meddle with the execution of a minister's office as Uzziah did; or if he shall set up humane inventions in doctrine, worship, government, instead of Christ's institutions, as David brought the ark of God upon oxen, instead of the shoulders of the Levites; or if he shall thrust in Jeroboam's priests upon the church, and cast out faithful ministers;[7] or if he shall make laws to bind conscience, in all these, or any such like, he exceedeth the bounds of his office. But if he

6. Officially, the earliest Massachusetts ministers were supported by voluntary contributions. In practice, however, this was a matter of some ambiguity; by 1639 the General Court found it necessary to pass a law assessing those who did not voluntarily contribute.

7. Uzziah tolerated worship of gods other than Yaweh (II Kings 15). David feared God's displeasure at his handling of the ark (I Chronicles 13:9–12). The defiance of Moses by the Jews in their worship of the golden calf (Exodus 32:4) was later resumed by Jeroboam, who installed two calves at Dan and Bethel (I Kings 12:28).

shall diligently seek after the Lord, and read in the word of the Lord all the days of his life (Deuteronomy 17:19) that he may both live as a Christian, and rule as a Christian; if he shall seek to establish and advance the kingdom of Christ more than his own; if he shall encourage the good in a Christian course, and discourage such as have evil will to Sion, and punish none for matter of religion, but such as subvert the principles of saving truth (which no good Christian, much less good magistrate, can be ignorant of) or at least such as disturb the order of the gospel in a turbulent way, verily the Lord will build up and establish the house and kingdom of such princes as do thus build up his.

ROGER WILLIAMS
Experiments of Spiritual Life and Health (c. 1650)

IN 1652, the year of Cotton's death, Williams published his final "reply" to Cotton, *The Bloody Tenent Yet More Bloody*. But this was less a continuation of fifteen years of argument than a long farewell to the premises that had sustained not only Cotton's Massachusetts but Cromwell's England as well. Williams offered a relentless demonstration, from the facts of history, that the saints should *never* entrust magistrates with the keys of the kingdom for the simple reason that very few magistrates, if any—indeed very few of any of the powers and potentates of earth—were true Christians. Where hope and trust were to be placed emerged in a volume Williams had published shortly before *The Bloody Tenent Yet More Bloody*, entitled *Experiments of Spiritual Life and Health*. In dedicating this work to the wife of Sir Henry Vane, Williams turned from the collective "flock of Jesus"—an army that, according to Williams, had for many a century "been scattered, routed, and laid waste and desolate"—to Christ's "personal and particular sheep." In so focusing on the souls of individual Christians, Williams was joining with many Puritans of the 1650s who were coming to emphasize personal devotion and meditation.

As for the kingdom of God, Williams argued, it could and would come only in and through the minds and hearts of men—"by the breath of His mouth in His prophets and witnesses"—and could not be hurried into being by institutions or coercion. Williams was already anticipating a post-Restoration piety, the more private religion of, say, Richard Baxter's *The Saint's Everlasting Rest*. In 1660 the so-called fifth-monarchy men would elect Williams' friend Vane their "king" in anticipation of the coming kingdom, but Williams had all along argued that only through the personal intervention of Christ—a second shattering of the continuity of history, rather than its progressive unfolding—could that kingdom be brought to earth. Williams' Christ would come, moreover, to rain pain and judgment on those who had tormented his "meek and humble" servants, more than to bring ultimate joy to his faithful saints. The seeming contradiction between Williams' compassionate defense of the victims of earthly persecution and his prospective delight in Christ's brandishing a body-destroying sword was another of those "riddles or mysteries" which lay at the center of his thought. For Williams had brazenly articulated all along what other New Englanders, even Cotton, barely hinted at: that the spirit of Christ filled men in times and places of persecution and that it ebbed as men were given the opportunity to incarnate, in comparative freedom, their visions of the New Jerusalem.

The text is from Winthrop S. Hudson's edition of *Experiments of Spiritual Life and Health* (Philadelphia: Westminster Press, 1951), pp. 39–41.

Experiments of Spiritual Life and Health

Preface
Wherein the Nature of This Discourse Is Set Forth

To Every Truly Christian Reader:

As it is in the earthly, so it is in the heavenly marriage of a poor sinner to his Maker. There is first a private kindling of love and a private consent and promise (which sometimes are long) before the open solemnity and the public profession of a married life together. This is my present design, not to controvert the matters of public order and worship, but to present some poor experiments of those personal excellencies of each true believing soul and spirit . . .

My scope is to fill each truly Christian soul with triumphing and rejoicing. I speak peace and joy to the weakest lamb and child in Christianity that is so low, so weak, so little, so poor in its own eyes, that it sometimes saith it hath no Christ, no Spirit, no faith, no love, no, nor true desire in itself. To this poor weak one I speak peace and joy, and say that this spiritual poverty is blessed and is the first step or round of that spiritual ladder, *Blessed are the poor in spirit, for theirs is the kingdom of heaven* (Matthew 5:3). Secondly, I sound joyful alarms of encouragement to the strong to grow (as Peter exhorteth) in the grace and knowledge of the Lord Jesus.

'Tis true, the communion of saints is sweet and joyful, strong and powerful, eternally gainful and profitable; and holy and blessed is that spirit that makes the saints (who are the excellent of the earth) its delight. And let all that love Christ Jesus mourn and lament, breathe and pant, after that blessed hour of the saints uniting in one heart, one spirit, one worship. And yet the weakest and the faintest lamb that comes but stealing in the crowd to touch the hem of the Lord Jesus, his garment; that is content to be esteemed a dog and to wait for crumbs of mercy under the table of the Son of God; let them, I say, rejoice also, for he that hath begun that blessed work by his own free and eternal spirit, will by the same, his own holy arm, gloriously finish it.

I end, dear Christian, with the proposal of two Christian knots or riddles, not unsuitable to these present times and spirits. First, why is the heart of a David himself (Psalm 30) more apt to decline from God upon the mountain of joy, deliverance, victory, prosperity, than in the dark vale of the shadow of death, persecution, sickness, adversity, etc.? Secondly, why is it, since God worketh freely in us to do and to will of his own good pleasure, that yet he is pleased to command us to work out our own salvation with fear and trembling? Let us all humbly beg the finger (the spirit) of the Lord to untie these knots for us.

I desire to be thine unfeigned in Christ Jesus,

R.W.

JOHN NORTON (1606–1663)
Abel Being Dead Yet Speaketh (c. 1655)

THE LAST of John Cotton's writings was an introduction to John Norton's *The Orthodox Evangelist,* the most valiant of efforts to heal New England's differences over the doctrine of preparation. Written just before Cotton's death (though not published until 1654) but well after those of Hooker and Shepard, Norton's book was also in part a response to those English Puritans who had begun to query New England's apparent commitment to crypto-Arminian notions of the order of salvation. Norton's formulas probably would not have satisfied either Hooker or Shepard, and they were not embraced by other survivors of the crises of the 1630s such as Peter Bulkeley. For Norton argued that sin was privative, not positive, and that the darkness Hooker had insisted man must labor to remove was none other than the absence of the light, which would be dispersed only at the moment when the illumination of saving grace entered the soul.

In Old England Norton, something of a protégé of Richard Sibbes, had achieved considerable renown for his opposition to Arminianism and the inroads it had made in the Church of England. He was soon confined to a private chaplaincy, and in 1634 he resolved to sail for Massachusetts. In 1635 Norton arrived in New England, not in Massachusetts but in Plymouth, brought there through the efforts of Edward Winslow, who had been in England seeking a teaching elder for the church at Plymouth. A year later Norton moved to Boston, and soon thereafter to Ipswich, first as assistant to Nathaniel Ward and then as installed pastor.

A legend of early Massachusetts has Cotton, on his deathbed, dreaming of Norton riding into Boston on a white horse to succeed him. When Cotton recommended that Norton be invited to the Boston pulpit, Ipswich at first resisted, and two years after Norton accepted Boston's call in 1653 they implored him to return. Councils and controversies followed, and Norton was about ready to return to England when a council of twelve churches, summoned by the General Court, decided that he should be installed as Boston's pastor.

Norton may have spent part of these three years of commuting and controversy preparing his biography of John Cotton. He had been close to Cotton in the profoundest sense, but he had also spent much of his New England career at a distance from Boston. So it is not surprising that Norton acknowledges his indebtedness to two other treatments of Cotton, one of them the most sadly "lost" of any early New England manuscript: John Davenport's biography. Biographies of New England's founding worthies were something of a flourishing genre in the 1650s, the Puritans being disposed to serve as the "Lord's Remembrancers" by way of personal eulogy as well as through historical writing. The members of the second generation were inclined to dwell on the heroic acts, the public services, even the "principles" of their fathers, especially as the issue began to be joined over the Half-Way Covenant and its consonance with the ecclesiastical aims of the founders. What distinguishes Norton's biography is that it seeks to convey those internal qualities that made Cotton preeminent among his generation. It is not, therefore, an "exemplary" biography, tracing footsteps to be followed. It stands rather in the long tradition stretching from Foxe's *Book of Martyrs* through Jonathan Edwards' *Life of Brainerd,* portraying Cotton as something of an "image of Christ," seeking less to instruct than to inspire, as a beatific vision in miniature that might induce the faithful to a fuller growth in grace. Norton defends Cotton from his enemies and detractors, to be sure, but his ultimate tribute to Cotton lies in his having imbibed and found new expression for the true lesson of the master: that what one does matters less than the spirit in which one does it.

The text of *Abel Being Dead Yet Speaketh* is from the edition of 1658, pp. 5–6, 12–14, 20–24, 27–28, 39–42, 46–47, 49–50.

Abel Being Dead Yet Speaketh
Or, the Life and Death of That Deservedly Famous Man of God
Mr. John Cotton

Hebrews 13:7. Remember them which have the rule over you, who have spoken unto you the word of God, whose faith follow, considering the end of their conversation.

. . . The mystery of God, concerning all the transactions of his eternal purpose upon the theater of this world, throughout the whole time of time, being fully accomplished and revealed (that of Jesus Christ himself excepted)—in none of all the work which he hath gloriously done, will he be admired so much in that day, as in what he hath wrought in the lives and deaths of believers, as believers. The same object is as admirable now as then. That it is not so much admired, is because it is not seen now so much as it shall be then. The greatest object out of heaven is the life and death of such upon earth, who are now in heaven. You may believe it—what God hath done for the soul of the least saint of some few years' continuance, were it digested into order, would make a volume full of temptations, signs and wonders, a wonderful history, because a history of such experiences, each one whereof is more than a wonder. No greater acts than their obedience, both active and passive unto the death. The sufferings of the Apostles may well be reckoned amongst the acts of the Apostles. No greater monuments than their register: to live and die in the faith of Jesus; to do things worthy to be written, and to write things worthy to be done, both is good, and doth good. 'Tis better with William Hunter[1] than with William the Conqueror. 'Tis better to have a name in the Book of Martyrs than in the Book of Chronicles. Martial conquerors conquer bodies, by destroying. Confessors conquer souls by saving . . . Divine providence otherwise disposing, it remains that they who have known His doctrine, manner of life, purpose, faith, long-suffering, love, patience, persecutions, and affliction, do not suffer such a light to be hid under a bushel, but put it on a candlestick, that it may give light to them that are in the house . . .

The manner of his conversion take in his own words (as near as can be remembered) thus. During his residence in the university, God began to work upon him under the ministry of Mr. Perkins of blessed memory. But the motions and stirrings of his heart which then were, he suppressed; thinking that if he should trouble himself with matters of religion, according to the light he had received, it would be an hindrance to him in his studies, which then he had addicted himself unto. Therefore he was willing to silence those suggestions and callings he had from the spirit inwardly, and did wittingly defer the prosecution of that work until afterwards. At length, walking in the field, and hearing the bell toll for Mr. Perkins who then lay dying, he was secretly glad in his heart that he should now be rid of him who had (as he said) laid siege to and beleaguered his heart. This became a cause of much affliction to him, God keeping it upon his spirit, with the aggravation of it, and making it an effectual means of convincing and humbling him in the sight and sense of the natural enmity that is man's nature against God. Afterwards, hearing Doctor Sibbes (then Mr. Sibbes) preaching a sermon about re-

1. A boy of nineteen, celebrated in *Foxe's Book of Martyrs* for refusing to attend communion mass as ordered by Queen Mary; he was burned for persisting in reading his Bible and for his unrepented doubt concerning the corporeal presence.

generation, where he first showed what regeneration was not, when opening the state of a civil man, he saw his own condition fully discovered, which through mercy did drive him to a stand—as plainly seeing himself to have no true grace, all his false hopes and grounds now failing him. And so he lay a long time in an uncomfortable despairing way; and of all things this was his heaviest burthen, that he had wittingly withstood the means and offers of grace and mercy which he found had been tendered to him, till it pleased God to let in some word of faith into his heart, to cause him to look unto Christ for healing, which word (if memory faileth not) was dispensed unto him by Doctor Sibbes, which begat in him a singular and constant love of Doctor Sibbes, of whom he was also answerably beloved.

That which first made him famous in Cambridge was his funeral oration for Doctor Some, Master of Peterhouse—so accurately performed, in respect of invention, elegancy, purity of style, ornaments of rhetoric, elocution, and oratorious beauty of the whole, as that he was thenceforth looked at as another Xenophon, or Musa Attica, throughout the university. Some space of time intervening, he was called to preach at St. Mary's, where he preached an university-sermon, with high applause of academical wits, so that the fame of his learning grew greater and greater. Afterwards being called to preach in the same place (as one oration of Pericles left the hearer with an appetite of another), for the memory of his former accurate exercises filled the colleges, especially the young students, with a fresh expectation of such elegancies of learning, that the curious and Corinthian wits, who prefer the Muses before Moses, who taste Plato more than Paul, and relish the orator of Athens far above the preacher of the Cross (like Quintilian's numerous auditory, sufficient to tempt the abilities of the speaker), flock to the sermon with an Athenian itch after some new thing, as to the ornaments of rhetoric and abstruser notions of philosophy. But his spirit now savoring of the cross of Christ more than of humane literature, and being taught of God to distinguish between the word of wisdom, and the wisdom of words, his speech and preaching was not with the enticing words of man's wisdom, but in the demonstration of the spirit and of power.

The disappointed expectation of the auditory soon appeared in their countenances; and the discouragement of their nonacceptance returned him unto his chamber not without some sadder thoughts of heart—where he had not been long alone, but lo, Doctor Preston (then Master Preston) knocks at his door, and coming in, acquaints him with his spiritual condition, and how it had pleased God to speak effectually unto his heart by that sermon, after which Doctor Preston ever highly prized him, and both fully and strongly closed with him . . .

The cause of his departure was this: the corruption of the times being such, as would not endure his officiating any longer in his station without sin; and the envy of his maligners having procured letters missive to convent him before the high commission, which a debauched inhabitant of the town (who not long after died of the plague) undertook to deliver to him, according as he had already done to some others. Mr. Cotton having intelligence thereof, and well knowing that nothing but scorns and imprisonment were to be expected; conformably to the advice of many able heads and upright hearts . . . he kept himself close for a time in and about London, as Luther sometimes at Wittenberg, and Pareus afterwards at Anvilla.[2] Neither was that season of his recess unprofitable: but as Jerome retired to his den at Bethlehem was an oracle unto many in his time, so addresses during that interim were made unto him privately by divers persons of worth and piety, who received from him satisfaction unto their consciences in cases of greatest concernment.[3] His flight was not like that of Pliny's mice, that forsake a house foreseeing the ruin of it, or of mercenaries, who fly from duty in time of danger, but providence divine shutting up the door of service in England, and on the other hand opening it in New England . . . *When they persecute you in one city, fly unto another.* Cyprian implieth, that a tempestive flight is a kind of confession of our faith; it being an open profession, that our faith is dearer to us than all that we fly from, for the defense thereof.[4] It was not a flight from duty, but from evident, and regularly evitable, danger; not from the evil of persecution, but from the evil of obstruction unto serviceableness. It was not a flight from duty, but unto duty; not from the profession of the truth, but unto a more opportune place for the profession of it.

Thus this infant and small commonwealth being now capacitated both in respect of civil and church estate, to walk with God according to the prescript of his word; it was the good hand of the Lord unto his servants who had afflicted their souls to seek of him a right way for themselves, their little ones, and their substance, to send unto them (amongst many others) this man of understanding, that might be unto them as eyes in this wilderness. His manner of entrance unto them was with much blessing. For at his first coming, he found them not without some troubles about settling the matter of the church and commonwealth . . .

Those arts which the university requireth such a proficiency from her

2. David Pareus, a German Reformer whose *Commentary on Romans* (1617) was burned by James I for its authorization of rebellion against ill-governing monarchs.

3. St. Jerome, one of the leading church fathers, a contemporary of Augustine.

4. Cyprian, a third-century Bishop of Carthage who ruled his church in forced absentia.

graduates in, he both digested and refined by his more accurate knowledge of them. He was a good Hebrician, in Greek a critic, and could with great facility both speak and write Latin in a pure and elegant Ciceronian style; a good historian, no stranger to the Fathers, Councils, or Schoolmen; abundantly exercised in commentators of all sorts. His library was great, his reading and learning answerable, himself a living and better library. Though he was a constant student, yet he had communion with God, and acquaintance with his own heart, observing the daily passages of his life. He had a deep sight into the mystery of God's grace, and man's corruption, and large apprehensions of these things. It was wont to be said *Bonus texturius est bonus theologus;* a good text-man is a good divine. If you look upon him in that notion, he was an expositor (without offense be it spoken) not inferior to any of this more sublimated age; that great motto so much wondered at, *Labore & constantia,* Labor and constancy, containing nothing more than the duty which God hath laid upon every man. Learning (saith Jerome) is not to be purchased with silver; it is the companion of sweat and painfulness, of abstemiousness, not of fullness, of continency, not of wantonness. The earth continueth barren or worse, except industry be its midwife. The hen which brings not forth without uncessant sitting night and day is an apt emblem of students . . .

In his study he neither sat down unto, nor arose from his meditations without prayer. Whilst his eyes were upon his book, his expectation was from God. He had learned to study, because he had learned to pray; an able student, a gospel-student, because unable to study without Jesus Christ . . .

As any weighty cause presented itself either in the church, commonwealth, or family, he would set days apart to seek the face of God in secret. Such were the bowels of this spiritual father, the horsemen and chariots of this Israel. He might say with Paul, he was in fastings often. His conversation upon earth was a trading in heaven; a demonstration of the praises of him who had called him; a practical and exemplary ministry of grace unto the hearer and beholder, a temperature of that holiness, sweetness and love, which continually gained upon the hearts of many spectators. The habitual gracious scope of his heart in his whole ministry is not illegible in that usual subscription of his at the end of all his sermons, *Tibi Domine,* Unto thy honor, O Lord! . . .

Whilst he was in England, his eminent piety, success of his labors, interest in the hearts of both superiors, inferiors and equals, drew much envy upon him; and his nonconformity, added thereunto, delivered him in a great degree unto the will of his adversaries, whose hour, and the power of darkness being come, spared not to shoot at him, and grieve him; not giving over until they had bereaved him of much of his livelihood, his liberty, country, and therewith of the sweet society of lovers, friends, and many ways endeared acquaintance, much more precious to him than life itself . . .

As concerning any tenet wherein he may seem singular, remember, he was a man, and therefore to be heard and read with judgment, and happily sometimes with favor. Jerome makes a difference between reading the writings of the Apostles, and the tractates of other authors: they (saith he) always spake the truth; these, as men, in some things err. Let him but receive with some proportion to the measure that he gave, and he will be found no debtor upon that account. No man did more placidly bear a dissentient.[5] The Jews unto their own question—why Asa and Jehoshaphat removing the idols in high places took not also away the brazen serpent—give this answer: *The fathers left a place for Hezekiah to exercise his zeal.*[6] That great conqueror vainly feared, that his father Philip's victories would deprive the son of an opportunity to improve his magnanimity. Much of the wisdom of God, both in the scripture and creature, is still unseen; and it hath been judged but meet that each age should contribute somewhat toward the fuller discovery of truth. But this cannot be, except men of a larger acumen, and greater industry, may be permitted to communicate their notions; especially whilst (as Austin in his time) they use this liberty by way of disquisition, not of position; rather as indicators of scripture-light, than as dictators of private opinions. A prophet may be heard whilst he speaks with a spirit subject to the prophets . . .

He quietly breathed out his spirit into the hands of him that gave it, December 23, 1652, between eleven and twelve (after the bell had called to the lecture, thus preventing the assembly in going to see what they were but going to hear), being entered into the sixty and eighth year of his age. So ceased this silver-trumpet, waiting for the sound of the last trump. The eyes of his dead body were soon closed, but before that, the eye of his ever-living soul beholds the face of Jesus Christ.

Upon the twenty-ninth day the body was interred within a tomb of brick, a numerous confluence of all degrees, from all parts, as the season would permit, orderly accompanying the corpse, borne upon the shoulders of his fellow ministers unto the chambers of death, not only with sighs and tears, and funeral poems, all in abundance, but with the sol-

5. Dispute.

6. Asa "removed all the idols that his fathers had made . . . but the high places were not removed" (I Kings 15:12, 14); his son, Jehoshaphat, also "did not seek the Baals" but did permit idolatrous sacrifice (I Kings 22:43). It was Hezekiah who "removed the high places . . . and brake in pieces the brazen serpent" (II Kings 18:4).

emnity of sorrow of heart itself—alas! too manifest in the carriage and countenance of those, whose visage was as the visage of them which are bereaved of the breath of their nostrils. The inhabitants of the land might have said, "This was a great mourning." Such were New England's tears for the man of their desires; of whom they (and especially his own congregation) cannot speak without lamentation unto this day—*Fuimus Troes, fuit Ilium: New England was, and flourished.*

Now our candlesticks cannot but lament in darkness, when their lights are gone; and the thrones of David mourn, that so many of our late worthies can be seen there no more. Our desiderable[7] men that remain, remove from us, and few they are who return again . . .

Sure we are that Josiah was gathered unto his fathers, that he might not see the evil that was to come upon Jerusalem. Augustine is taken out of the world, before Hippo is taken by the Vandals. Pareus is gotten to his better country, before Heidelberg and the Palatinate are delivered into the power of the enemies. Whatsoever it be, we may not here silence that monitory apparition in the heavens that appeared about fourteen days before, and according to the report of some observers thereof was not seen here after this man of God was taken from amongst us[8] . . .

Times are in the hands of God, and to discern the times is the gift of God. Being designed to suffer is not so great an evil, as grace to suffer for the designer's sake is good . . .

The best of the servants of God have lived in the worst times. Noah was not so unhappy that he lived in an unrighteous generation, as he was happy in being righteous in that generation. Though the captivity took up so much of Daniel's life, yet when he shall stand in his lot, at the end of days, it shall be no grief of heart unto him that he was both to spend and end his days in Babylon. It will be as well with those at that day who fulfilled their course upon earth, prophesying in sackcloth, as with those who are reserved to live in the glorious times of the gospel. It is not material in what age we live, but that we live as we ought, in that age wherein we live.

7. Desirable.
8. The comet of 1652.

JOHN DAVENPORT (1597–1670)
The Saint's Anchor-Hold (1661)

ONE LATTER-DAY SURVIVOR of the early settlements who refused to capitulate either to the Restoration or to the Half-Way Covenant was John Davenport. Among the few graduates of Oxford involved in the founding of New England, Davenport had been one of the most ardent and energetic organizers of the Feofees of Impropriation (a committee that raised funds for Puritan lecturers). For this he was arraigned before the Court of Exchequer and a year later was summoned before Laud himself. Legend has it that when Davenport joined in the efforts to dissuade Cotton from moving to New England, he was instead himself persuaded to withdraw from the established church. Under increasing suspicion, he gained release from his London congregation and in 1633 moved to Holland, where he quickly became a leading opponent of the "promiscuous" baptism of children. Within two years he was forced to resign his pastorate.

In 1631 Davenport and his friend and mentor Richard Sibbes had introduced their edition of Preston's *Breastplate of Faith and Love* with an admonition to the "Christian Reader" to "be resolute in a good cause. A type whereof were the *Israelites,* whose servitude was redoubled when they turned themselves to forsake Egypt: Wherefore we have much need of Christian fortitude, according to that direction; *Watch ye, stand fast, quit your selves like men.*" Six years later, however, presumably after reading Cotton's letter reaffirming his own reasons for migration, Davenport embarked for Boston. There he was immediately engaged in the synodical inquisition of Anne Hutchinson. In 1638 he and a number of the families who had sailed with him moved to a place they called New Haven. The following year he was installed as pastor of the New Haven church.

After the Restoration, several members of the court that had condemned Charles I fled to New England. They were quickly hurried out of Boston, but Davenport risked arrest by hiding them in and around

New Haven, for at least a month in his own home. One of the most eloquent, as well as courageous, sections of *The Saint's Anchor-Hold* is that which not only justifies protection of the regicides but makes of it a Christian obligation. But the sermon is, in the larger sense, a recapitulation of the doctrine of Preston's *Breastplate:* a sustained argument for contending earnestly for the faith. According to Increase Mather (John Cotton's son-in-law), who fought alongside Davenport against the Half-Way Covenant, Davenport, known in his early years as a preacher for his "fervent and vehement" delivery, came by the 1660s to "very much imitate Mr. Cotton" in the gravity of his manner. The doctrinal portions of *The Saint's Anchor-Hold* are Cottonian, for Davenport insists, as did Norton, that sainthood is not a matter of performance of duties or of preparatory obligations, but of an exalting indwelling of the Holy Spirit, illuminating the soul.

Davenport and his New Haven church of course refused to adopt the Half-Way Covenant, which Davenport saw as a regression to the very promiscuity he had fought in Holland thirty years earlier. But in 1662 Connecticut Colony (Hartford) obtained a charter from Charles II that added New Haven to its jurisdiction. Davenport and his congregation rightly feared for the purity of their civil and religious order, and there soon began the migration to Long Island and New Jersey that was to make New England, by the early eighteenth century, a far larger entity than could be defined by any cartographer. But Davenport withheld himself from any such further exile; instead he returned to the fount of New England's declension. Tendered an invitation to Cotton's church in Boston, whose members were embattled over the Half-Way Covenant, he accepted, though it took him several years to overcome the pleas of his New Haven congregation that he remain with them. When he was finally installed in Boston's First Church in 1668, disaffected pro-synod members of the congregation bolted to form what became known as Old South Church.

The issues raised by this secession were eventually taken before the General Court, where Davenport's party was, for the moment, triumphant. In 1669 the lower house chose Davenport as the election preacher, and he delivered a sermon quite unlike any of the preceding decade or that which followed. His sermon was a prolonged indictment of Massachusetts for sacrificing God's truth to worldly policy. Pressure was already being exerted, he noted, to go even beyond the Half-Way Covenant to give the franchise to non-churchmembers. This extension of the synod's result, he observed, was being argued as necessary to prevent the disaffected from carrying their complaints to the crown. The king, it was thought, might revoke the charter, thus toppling what remained of the establishment, if Massachusetts persisted in its obstinate and outmoded ways. Davenport's scorn for such sailing with the wind was undisguised: "Take heed of a various management of matters of religion, to the advantage of the present postures and conditions of your civil affairs. The things of Christ should be as Joseph's sheaf, to which all others should bow. When they are made to cringe and bend to men's policies, they are no longer the things of Christ." Davenport used the occasion to remind the rising generation of just what *were* the "first principles" of New England—nearly all of which had been corrupted, both from New England's pulpits and in its practices, the remainder endangered by its politicians. Having personally experienced the truth contained in Roger Williams' reading of history—that magistrates (such as those of Connecticut) were not to be trusted with the preservation of the faith—he knew also, out of the experience of 1662, that the ministry was possibly an even thinner reed. Two of Davenport's fast-day sermons, published in 1670, pronounced what was to be for half a century the wilderness-cry of New England's nearly silenced spiritual minority: that what God's people ought to pray for, in the midst of suffering and difficulty, was not a renewal of outward blessings but a fresh outpouring of the spirit. Like Cotton in Old Boston, and like Master Preston, Davenport here, as in the majestic sermons of 1661, insisted that the faith once delivered to the saints was safe only when it not merely lived, but thrived, in the bosoms of a whole people.

The text of *The Saint's Anchor-Hold* is from the edition of 1682, pp. 181–199, 228–230.

The Saint's Anchor-Hold In All Storms and Tempests

> *Hebrews 6:18–19. Lay hold upon the hopes set before us, which hope we have, as an anchor of the soul, both sure and steadfast . . .*

. . . I shall give you a true narrative of the Protestant churches in Europe, singly and severally considered, as I have received it from a faithful and unquestionable hand. 1. The churches in Poland, Bohemia, Moravia, Austria, and Silesia, which were, not long since, many and flourishing, are now wholly dissipated and wasted. 2. Though some churches remain in Transylvania and Hungary, yet they are in danger to be ruined by any advantage of power which the house of Austria may get against them. 3. In Germany, the churches are so divided, and the Protestant states are so distracted, that not only all concurrences in a common way for their mutual edification and preservation are hindered; but also, as the Lutheran party, by their contentious ministry, hath set itself to destroy the rest; so God hath suffered their chief protectors, the kings of Sweden and Denmark, to destroy each other . . . 4. In the low countries, their present actings tend rather to serve the enemy's design against the Protestant interest, than for it. 5. In France, the Protestant churches are deprived of their former privileges, so that their standing is a mere toleration, at pleasure . . . How it is with our native country, England, and those conjoined with it, in Scotland and Ireland, you have formerly heard, in part, and may have more hereafter. If we add hereunto the great advantages which the Popish party hath against the Protestant; and what posture the Protestant churches are in, in respect of their mutual relation each to other, to oppose this combination of their enemies so strongly and universally laid, it will be manifest that the antichristian party had never so great advantage against the churches of Christ since the reformation began, as now they have . . . In France, where the popish Inquisition was not formerly admitted, it is now of late introduced under a new name of the *Congregation de propaganda fide,*[1] which is an Inquisition in effect, and hath begun to act there with public authority, prohibiting all commerce from abroad, for the vent[2] of divinity books, in so much that they do not suffer Bibles brought from Geneva to be sold anywhere, but do confiscate them . . . It is intended that this design shall be prosecuted universally against all Protestant churches in other places, so soon as the Protestant states shall be sufficiently weakened by divisions among themselves . . . And while the enemies have agents everywhere, and an universal correspondency to weaken us by division, and then to ruin us; no such way of agency or correspondency is set on foot by public authority among us, to engage the godly-wise and peaceable to join with us to lay the common gospel interest to heart, and to communicate counsel and assistance each to other—at least, to pray for one another suitably to the exigencies of things, that when help faileth on earth, it may be procured from the mighty God immediately. For which the Lord may justly dash us into pieces, one against another, as vessels unfit for his honor and service . . .

God looks upon every man . . . with a jealous eye, observing with what workings of bowels they read or speak of the concernments of his church. You see, in Amos 6:6, how his wrath was incensed against those who solaced themselves with their private prosperity but were not sick: their

1. Originating in the late sixteenth century, this was the commission of cardinals charged with propagating the faith in "heathen" nations.

2. Sale.

hearts ached not for the affliction of Joseph . . . They know that if they withdraw from being helpful to the church, God will do good to his church without them; but he will be avenged upon them that desert or neglect his cause and people . . . Meroz was cursed by the angel of the Lord *because he came not to the help of the Lord against the mighty,* Judges 5:23 . . . Though the Lord needs not men's help in such cases; for *when he saw that there was no man, no intercessor, his own arm brought salvation unto him,* Isaiah 51:16, yet it is our duty to show on whose side we stand. For Christ will look on them as his enemies that disown his cause and people, at such times, as he saith, *He that is not with me, is against me* . . .

I have spoken thee more largely unto this, because the present temptation of this time, in the other afflictions of the churches, is the reproachful titles put upon the people of God, whom profane men call fanatics. But, if he is a fool that will be laughed out of his coat, much more is he a fool, and a mad man, that will suffer himself to be laughed out of heaven, that will hazard the loss of his soul and salvation to free himself from the mocks and scoffs of a profane and sinful world. If Christ had not, for our sakes, *endured the cross, despising the shame,* we could never have been redeemed and saved . . . Let us . . . own the reproached and persecuted people and cause of Christ in suffering times. Withhold not countenance, entertainment, protection, from such, if they come to us from other countries, as from France or England, or any other place. *Be not forgetful to entertain strangers* for thereby some have *entertained angels unawares. Remember them that are in bonds, as bound with them, and them which suffer adversity, as being yourselves also in the body,* Hebrews 13:2–3 . . . *Hide the outcasts, bewray*[3] *not him that wandereth: Let mine outcasts dwell with thee Moab, be thou a covert to them from the face of the spoiler,* Isaiah 16:3–4 . . .

Therefore let this hope strengthen you, first, *to cleave unto God with purpose of heart,* Acts 11:23. It is good cleaving to him who will never leave nor forsake his people in their distress . . . When the people of God are in distress, wicked men will insult against them, and say, *Where is now their God?,* Psalms 115:2. But their answer is ready, *Our God is in the Heavens, he hath done whatsoever he pleased* . . . Only be sure, if you would cleave to God, that you cleave to his word, and every truth in it, when it is opposed by a sinful and unbelieving generation: *contend for the faith which was once given to the saints,* Jude 3 . . . The thing to be contended for is the faith, not a fancy, but the truths received with

3. Malign.

faith, upon God's authority in his word, the least jot and tittle whereof God values at a higher rate than heaven and earth . . . This faith was once delivered once for all. If it be lost, or exchanged for error, there is danger that it will be lost forever . . . This faith was delivered, deposited, committed to our trust, of which a strict account must be given how we have kept and used it . . .

JOHN NORTON

Election Sermon: *Sion the Outcast Healed of Her Wounds* (1661)

THREE YEARS after the publication of his elegiac biography of Cotton, when news of the Restoration had reached New England, Norton was called on to deliver the annual election sermon. Such sermons, given on the day deputies were to be selected who would in turn elect the governor, had been delivered for decades; Norton himself had spoken before, in 1657. But Norton's sermon of 1661 was among the first to be published, possibly because the advice and comfort it offered were less political than psychological and even rhetorical. In *Sion the Outcast* Norton sketched the New Englanders as in many ways comparable to the Children of Israel in their days of wandering—hinting at New England's status as a "peculiar people" especially covenanted with the Lord. Norton stopped far short of the doctrines that were to dominate election sermons for two decades and more; he did not threaten a backsliding New England but rather offered solace to a people fearful in their isolation. Like his mentor Richard Sibbes, Norton to the end read the message of both Testaments as one of comfort. Most important, perhaps, he proposed the language of the Old Testament as a code in which they might discuss their own affairs without offending the newly reestablished English authorities.

In 1662 Norton and Governor Bradstreet (husband of the poet) were sent as official delegates of Massachusetts to London, where they persuaded Charles II to reaffirm the Bay's charter. The king, however, also insisted that the courts of Massachusetts thereafter act only in his name, and he demanded that all but the openly dissolute be accorded the privileges of the sacraments. Norton's apparent acquiescence struck many New Englanders as a betrayal of their rights and an unholy compromise of their ecclesiastical vision. That Norton came under increasing attack in 1662 was not surprising, for New England was then debating the right of unregenerate children of the original saints to present their children for baptism. Within a year of the adoption of the Half-Way Covenant, Norton was stricken by apoplexy and died suddenly; his funeral sermon was preached by one of the few survivors from the 1630s, Richard Mather. Norton's admirers quickly arranged to publish his 1661 election sermon, along with a sabbath sermon appropriately entitled "The Believer's Consolation" and one of his Thursday lectures, preached on Hebrews 8:5: "See that thou make all things according to the pattern showed thee in the mount." With Norton's death, few if any remained to insist that New England must continue to pattern itself on what was to be found in the New Testament alone.

The text of *Sion the Outcast* is from *Three Choice and Profitable Sermons* (Cambridge, 1664), pp. 3–5, 11–12, 14–15.

Sion the Outcast Healed of Her Wounds

> *Jeremiah 30:17. For I will restore health unto thee, and I will heal thee of thy wounds, saith the Lord; because they called thee an outcast, saying, this is Sion, whom no man seeketh after . . .*

Doctrine. When Sion for its sin is become an outcast (a subject of contempt) God takes occasion from her calamity to give her repentance, that so he may bring upon her the blessing of his own people.

I will not more than intimate to you the paradoxes that the text doth abound with. Sion, and acknowledged, and yet no man careth for her. A people, none neglected like them; a people, none beloved like them: neglected, if you look at men; beloved, if you look at God. A people, whose very adversaries are instrumental to their prosperity. These are such riddles as we may truly say God's grace only makes . . . *Therefore, saith the Lord, although I have cast them far off, &c., though I have scattered them, &c., yet will I be a little sanctuary unto them* . . . They had been in the furnace long enough. As the Lord dealeth thus with his people, so David maketh use of the like in his personal case, II Samuel 16:12: *It may be the Lord will look upon mine affliction, and requite me good [and] bless me because of his cursing.*

The reasons of the point are: Reason 1. From the sympathy that there is between the head and the members, Christ is sensible of the sufferings of his outcast. It is true that the outcast doth suffer; it is a greater truth that the God of the outcast suffereth. Isaiah 63:9: *In all their affliction, he was afflicted;* it relateth to Israel in Egypt. Zachariah 2:8: *He that toucheth you, toucheth the apple of his eye;* it relateth to the good figs in exile.[1] . . .

Reason 2. Because that God's name suffereth, while his outcasts do thus suffer . . . You remember the argument which Joshua useth, chapter 7–9: *When Israel falleth before the enemy, what wilt thou do to thy great name?* The destruction of Israel would raise a scandal to religion and the God of Israel.

Reason 3. To capacitate the outcast to receive the benediction of a father, the actual blessing of his people. To be God's people is one thing; but to be made meet to receive the blessing of his people is another thing . . .

Use. Hence learn that Sion is subject to sad apostasy, or defections . . . But as the orator solemnizing a sad funeral desired to have learned mortality from another instance rather than that of Scaliger,[2] so I would God would learn us this truth from some other instances, rather than from these churches . . .

To differ from our orthodox, pious, and learned brethren, is such an affliction to a Christian and ingenuous spirit as nothing but love to the truth could arm a man of peace against. Our profession being in a way differing from these and those, it doth the more concern us that our walking be very cautelous,[3] and that it be without giving any just offense . . . And give me leave to speak freely: let us see that we walk without offense toward civil authority. Suffer not your minds to be prejudiced against the present and ancient government of our nation: Isaiah 49:23, *Kings shall be thy nursing fathers, and queens thy nursing mothers;* 'tis spoken of gospel times. It is not a gospel spirit to be against kings; 'tis neither gospel nor English spirit for any of us to be against the government by King, Lords, and Commons. It was the usual stratagem anciently of the adversary, to calumniate the Christians as disaffected to the state, and such as were for reformation, as enemies to Caesar. But Jewel could testify in his time *Gratias agimus Deo,*[4] . . . *That there could be no instance given wherein they in that state of reformation had offered any violence to princes,* &c. So said that famous apologist. God make

1. Jeremiah 24:5–6: "Thus saith the Lord, the God of Israel: Like these good figs, so will I acknowledge them that are carried away captive of Judah, whom I have sent out of this place into the land of the Chaldeans for their good. For I will set mine eyes upon them for good, and I will bring them again to this land: and I will build them, and not pull them down; and I will plant them, and not pluck them up."

2. Joseph Justus Scaliger, sixteenth-century French Protestant classical scholar.

3. Cautious.

4. We give thanks to God. Bishop Jewel served Queen Elizabeth in the early years of her reign. His *An Apology of the Church of England*, published in 1564, was the first important statement of the principles of the Elizabethan settlement.

us more wise and religious then so to carry it, that they should no sooner see a congregational-man, than to have cause to say *they see an enemy to the crown* . . . In matters of the state-civil, and of the church, let it be shown that we are his disciples, who (Matthew 22:21) said, *Give unto Caesar the things that are Caesar's and unto God the things that are God's.* And in matters of religion, let it be known that we are for Reformation and not for separation . . .

Do not betray liberty under the pretense of liberty. You that are in the honored magistracy, remember David's troubles, Psalms 132:1, 5. He could not rest till the ark had rest. And those that are in the ministry, remember Paul's troubles, and what his cares were, I Corinthians 11:28. Let us all mind what were the troubles and thoughts of heart that were in them that lived in the days of Malachi, chapter 3:16. But are there not many that mind only their cieled houses, &c?[5] And how much doth the work of the outcast lie unattempted, witness the sick estate of the churches; and how can it be remedied, if we will not acknowledge order? And shall I say that we are real therein? You have brought upon yourselves real troubles, and likewise upon your relations and friends in England, and those here that suffer with you in this exile. See then that you be not hypocritical, but real to the truth which you have professed. I could tell you, and you must not forget it, that there have been men of renown, as they are called, Numbers 16:2, *famous in the congregation of Israel,* that did go out of Egypt, but yet could not endure the order of God in the wilderness. Let us show it, that we mistook not ourselves, pretending to come into this wilderness to live under the order of the gospel. We are outcasts indeed, and reproached, but let us be such outcasts as are caring for the truth, and therefore not to neglect an apology, it doth become and greatly concern God's outcasts to mind it. You know there are those who represent you as disaffected to government, and as sectaries, and schismatics, and as fanatics: you see cause to apologize therein. And for that term of fanatic, you must remember it is not of yesterday, however it be now used or abused. You may learn the original use of it from that distribution of professors in relation to church government, in former times, into four sorts, viz., *Orthodoxi, Pontificii, Rationales, and Fanatici.*[6] But I trust that God doth and angels and men shall know that we are orthodox. God's outcasts are not fanatics. The woman in the wilderness may have the vomit of the dragon cast in her

5. Haggai 1:4: "Is it time for you, O ye, to dwell in your cieled [roofed] houses, and this house [God's temple] lie waste?" The reference to Malachi implies a time of corruption and greed.

6. The orthodox, bishops, schoolmen, and enthusiasts.

face; if you let it lie on you, you will suffer; wash it off therefore by an apology. Thus did Justin Martyr, Tertullian,[7] Jewel, and others in their time. Give not the advantage of interpreting silence as consent, nor think it labor lost if an apology will wash your face. And though we may be cast out by men, yet may we hope that God will look after his outcasts, and care for us, being outcasts for the truth. Let it appear that we are such outcasts to whom the calamity and temptations of outcasts are sanctified, outcasts healed, outcasts that care for the truth, and then outcasts on which God will bring the blessing of his own people. If this plaister findeth acceptance with you, you shall find esteem, and acceptance, and favor from God and man. Let us all labor so to carry it, as that we may have this *rejoicing of a good conscience* to sweeten that bottle full of tears shed in your outcast condition in this wilderness, viz., that we came into it, not only with a spirit testifying, according to the scriptures, against the inventions of men, but also that we do come up unto the institutions of Christ; that as we have departed from inventions humane, so we may not be found to be, or here continue, opposers against institutions divine; that we are not negligent of, but faithful to, that order of the gospel which we are outcasts for.

7. Justin Martyr and Tertullian were defenders of Christianity during the second and third centuries; like Jewel, they wrote well-known apologies for the church.

MICHAEL WIGGLESWORTH (1631–1705)

"God's Controversy with New England" (1662)

THE YEAR of the Half-Way Covenant, 1662, can be seen as the moment when New England's second generation of intellectual spokesmen, some of them born in the New World, began their dominance of the region's thought and discourse. Shepard's student and protégé Jonathan Mitchell emerged as *the* advocate of the ecclesiastical modifications adopted by the synod, and for a while Increase Mather was Davenport's chief ally in opposing them. Although Davenport made the task difficult, one younger New Englander after another strove to claim the fathers as their very own: the younger Shepard, for instance, apostrophized Norton in verse as above all "zealous for *order*." But the most celebrated utterance of 1662 was Michael Wigglesworth's versified *The Day of Doom,* which, until the publication nearly a century later of Benjamin Franklin's *The Way to Wealth,* was the best-selling of all colonial writings.

Wigglesworth arrived in the New World at the age of seven, when his parents settled in New Haven. Soon thereafter he was dispatched to Boston for study with Ezekiel Cheever, Master of Boston Latin School, but he returned to New Haven to assist the family when his father became lame. At the age of fourteen he returned to Boston and remained to enter Harvard, from which he was graduated in 1651. Until his final year there he seemed committed to a medical career, but in his last months at college he learned "to study with God, and for God." In 1653 he was invited to preach at Malden, and soon thereafter he was installed as pastor. In 1653 he began a diary, a most remarkable document, filled with hints of anxiety about his relationship with his father—indeed with *all* fathers, surrogate, human, and divine—and the torments of one who could not bring his spiritual life into exact conformity with the *ordo salutis* prescribed by Harvard's intellectual father, Thomas Shepard, and embalmed in its curriculum during all of Wigglesworth's years as a student. He was probably also affected by the fact that Jonathan Mitchell had been invited to Hartford to succeed Hooker at the age of twenty-five and in the following year—as Wigglesworth remained at Harvard for further study while awaiting a "call"—installed in Shepard's prestigious Cambridge pulpit.

In these years Wigglesworth was also overcome with a mysterious (and to him shameful) disease; this, together with his earlier disposition toward medicine, may account for the insights into what we today might call psychosomatic illness that seem to leap from the pages of the *Diary* and from what is surely his most sensitive and evocative poetry, the meditative *Meat out of the Eater* (1670). His health was such that in 1663 he spent more than six months in Bermuda seeking recuperation, and for more than two decades, though remaining officially pastor at Malden, he performed none of his expected duties, devoting himself instead to medical practice. In 1685, suddenly and "miraculously," he was restored to full health. Thereafter he preached for two more decades, sometimes two or three times a week, serving his flock "not only as a pastor but a physician too." Neither the nature of his long illness nor the reasons for his recuperation are known, for Wigglesworth, in both his private and his public writings, dwelled not on bodily malaise, but spiritual. He was preoccupied with sin: his own as well as that of his students and his parishioners. As a tutor at Harvard he detected, already in the early 1650s, a "spirit of unbridled licentiousness" and in himself ("a poor sinful worm") an inability to exercise authority successfully: "Lord in mercy heal, or I know not what will become of New England."

In the same year *The Day of Doom* was published, Wigglesworth expressed in verse his thoughts on what, in all likelihood, lay in store for New England should it not be healed of its sins. "God's Controversy with New England," discovered in manuscript in the nineteenth century, may well be the first sustained New England jeremiad. Indeed, it may stand as the classic jeremiad of the second generation, because here, for the first time, a whole people is addressed, and not the saints merely, as in Hooker's *Danger of Desertion,* Shepard's lamentations for the saints' forgetting their original errand, or Cotton's regretful reminders that even the best of Bostonians had fixed their eyes on earth rather than on heaven. The assumptions underlying "God's Controversy" are consistent with those that sustained the Half-Way Covenant: that God had established a covenant with his New World people not unlike that once vouchsafed not just to Abraham but all his seed. Wigglesworth's diagnosis is comparatively general, lacking the precise catalogue of "procuring sins" that was to emerge in subsequent utterances by his contemporaries and to be codified, eventually, by the Reforming Synod of 1679. But there was little to be added to Wigglesworth's prognosis: New England, mightily the subject of divine favor for thirty and more years, was threatened—by its back-sliding and ingratitude—with far worse than the temporary drought of 1662. The remnant of the faithful was now too few to save New England, and the once-glorious prospects of the New World were translated into a vision of impending judgment that only heroic collective efforts at repentance could forestall.

The text of "God's Controversy" is excerpted from *Proceedings of the Massachusetts Historical Society,* 12 (1873).

God's Controversy with New England
Written in the Time of the Great Drought Anno 1662

. . . . .

Are these the men that erst at my command
  Forsook their ancient seats and native soile,
To follow me into a desart land,
  Contemning all the travell and the toile,
Whose love was such to purest ordinances
  As made them set at nought their fair inheritances?

Are these the men that prized libertee
  To walk with God according to their light,
To be as good as he would have them bee,
  To serve and worship him with all their might,
Before the pleasures which a fruitfull field,
  And country flowing-full of all good things, could yield,

Are these the folk whom from the brittish Iles,
  Through the stern billows of the watry main,
I safely led so many thousand miles,
  As if their journey had been through a plain?
Whom having from all enemies protected,
  And through so many deaths and dangers well directed,

I brought and planted on the western shore,
  Where nought but bruits and salvage wights[1] did swarm
(Untaught, untrain'd, untam'd by vertue's lore)
  That sought their blood, yet could not do them harm?

1. Savage men.

My fury's flaile them thresht, my fatall broom
  Did sweep them hence, to make my people elbow-room.

Are these the men whose gates with peace I crown'd,
  To whom for bulwarks I salvation gave,
Whilst all things else with rattling tumults sound,
  And mortall frayes send thousands to the grave?
Whilest their own brethren bloody hands embrewed
  In brothers blood, and fields with carcases bestrewed?

Is this the people blest with bounteous store,
  By land and sea full richly clad and fed,
Whom plenty's self stands waiting still before,
  And powreth out their cups well tempered?
For whose dear sake an howling wildernes
  I lately turned into a fruitfull paradeis?

. . . . .

With whom I made a Covenant of peace,
  And unto whom I did most firmly plight
My faithfulness, If whilst I live I cease
  To be their Guide, their God, their full delight;
Since them with cords of love to me I drew,
  Enwrapping in my grace such as should them ensew.

Are these the men, that now mine eyes behold,
  Concerning whom I thought, and whilome spake,
First Heaven shall pass away together scrold,
  Ere they my lawes and righteous wayes forsake,
Or that they slack to runn their heavenly race?
  Are these the same? or are some others come in place?

If these be they, how is it that I find
  In stead of holiness Carnality,
In stead of heavenly frames an Earthly mind,
  For burning zeal luke-warm Indifferency,
For flaming love, key-cold Dead-heartedness,
  For temperance (in meat, and drinke, and cloaths) excess?

Whence cometh it, that Pride, and Luxurie
  Debate, Deceit, Contention, and Strife,
False-dealing, Covetousness, Hypocrisie

(With such like Crimes) amongst them are so rife,
That one of them doth over-reach another?
And that an honest man can hardly trust his Brother?

How is it, that Security, and Sloth,
Amongst the best are Common to be found?
That grosser sins, in stead of Graces growth,
Amongst the many more and more abound?
I hate dissembling shews of Holiness.
Or practise as you talk, or never more profess.

Judge not, vain world, that all are hypocrites
That do profess more holiness then thou:
All foster not dissembling, guilefull sprites,
Nor love their lusts, though very many do.
Some sin through want of care and constant watch,
Some with the sick converse, till they the sickness catch.

Some, that maintain a reall root of grace,
Are overgrown with many noysome weeds,
Whose heart, that those no longer may take place,
The benefit of due correction needs.
And such as these however gone astray
I shall by stripes reduce into a better way.

Moreover some there be that still retain
Their ancient vigour and sincerity;
Whom both their own, and others sins, constrain
To sigh, and mourn, and weep, and wail, & cry:
And for their sakes I have forborn to powre
My wrath upon Revolters to this present houre.

To praying Saints I always have respect,
And tender love, and pittifull regard:
Nor will I now in any wise neglect
Their love and faithfull service to reward;
Although I deal with others for their folly,
And turn their mirth to tears that have been too jolly.

For thinke not, O Backsliders, in your heart,
That I shall still your evill manners beare:

Your sinns me press as sheaves do load a cart,
  And therefore I will plague you for this geare
Except you seriously, and soon, repent,
  Ile not delay your pain and heavy punishment.

. . . . .

One wave another followeth,
  And one disease begins
Before another cease, becaus
  We turn not from our sins.
We stopp our ear against reproof,
  And hearken not to God:
God stops his ear against o^{r} prayer,
  And takes not off his rod.

Our fruitful seasons have been turnd
  Of late to barrenness,
Sometimes through great & parching drought,
  Sometimes through rain's excess.
Yea now the pastures & corn fields
  For want of rain do languish:
The cattell mourn, & hearts of men
  Are fill'd with fear & anguish.

The clouds are often gathered,
  As if we should have rain:
But for o^{r} great unworthiness
  Are scattered again.
We pray & fast, & make fair shewes,
  As if we meant to turn:
But whilst we turn not, God goes on
  Our field, & fruits to burn.

And burnt are all things in such sort,
  That nothing now appears,
But what may wound our hearts with grief,
  And draw foorth floods of teares.
All things a famine do presage
  In that extremity,
As if both men, and also beasts,
  Should soon be done to dy.

This O New-England hast thou got
  By riot, & excess:
This hast thou brought upon thy self
  By pride & wantonness.
Thus must thy worldlyness be whipt.
  They, that too much do crave,
Provoke the Lord to take away
  Such blessings as they have.

We have been also threatened
  With worser things then these:
And God can bring them on us still,
  To morrow if he please.
For if his mercy be abus'd,
  Which holpe us at our need
And mov'd his heart to pitty us,
  We shall be plagu'd indeed.

Beware, O sinful Land, beware;
  And do not think it strange
That sorer judgements are at hand,
  Unless thou quickly change.
Or God, or thou, must quickly change;
  Or else thou art undon:
Wrath cannot cease, if sin remain,
  Where judgement is begun.

Ah dear New England! dearest land to me;
  Which unto God hast hitherto been dear,
And mayst be still more dear than formerlie,
  If to his voice thou wilt incline thine ear.

Consider wel & wisely what the rod,
  Wherewith thou art from yeer to yeer chastized,
Instructeth thee. Repent, & turn to God,
  Who wil not have his nurture be despized.

Thou still hast in thee many praying saints,
  Of great account, and precious with the Lord,

Who dayly powre out unto him their plaints,
   And strive to please him both in deed & word.

Cheer on, sweet souls, my heart is with you all,
   And shall be with you, maugre Sathan's might:
And whereso'ere this body be a Thrall,
   Still in New-England shall be my delight.

INCREASE MATHER (1639–1723)
The Mystery of Israel's Salvation (1667)

DURING the two decades of Wigglesworth's silence as a preacher, the ideas expressed in "God's Controversy" were served up by election preacher after election preacher as nearly the staple literary and intellectual diet of New England. Among the handful of exceptions was Increase Mather's *Mystery of Israel's Salvation,* a singularly lonely effort, in these years, to rekindle an interest in millenarianism. How far New England had come since Cotton's *The Pouring Out of the Seven Vials* (or even since Eliot's *Christian Commonwealth*) is suggested by Mather's felt need to apologize, in his epistle to the reader, for his "novelism." The tract, first delivered as sermons and ready for printing as early as 1667, was Mather's effort, by amplifying the Scripture prophecies concerning the conversion of the Jews, to reestablish a common platform for international Calvinism. More important, he seems to have been seeking to draw New England out of its provincial self-obsession and to restore its hope in the dark days following the Restoration and the bitter struggles of the synod of 1662 and its aftermath.

Mather had been spared participation in New England's internecine arguments of the late 1650s, having left almost immediately after graduating from Harvard in 1656. In 1657 he was awarded an M.A. from Trinity College, Dublin, and from 1658 on he preached at various Puritan garrisons and conventicles in Britain until the Restoration. Almost alone among his generation of New Englanders, he experienced the Restoration personally and directly rather than indirectly as did those New Englanders who were stunned when the news arrived. In 1662 he returned to Boston, married a daughter of John Cotton, and was installed as pastor of Boston's Second Church. His first publication—a preface to John Davenport's denunciation of the result of the synod of 1662—bespoke his effort to assume the fallen mantle of the first generation, especially the man he often referred to as his "father Cotton." (Increase's own father, Richard Mather, was an advocate of the Half-Way Covenant.) Increase had, to be sure, received instruction from John Cotton, but his more formal mentor was Cotton's friend, colleague, and biographer, John Norton. After Norton's death he identified ever more closely with Davenport, to whom he turned, when *Israel's Salvation* was ready for publication, for an introductory imprimatur.

Throughout the 1660s, Increase Mather remained out of tune with the thinking of his own generation, and yet often challenged Jonathan Mitchell for its intellectual leadership. Later he was persuaded by his father (presumably in a deathbed plea) to change his stance on the Half-Way Covenant, but in upholding "the doctrine of Christ's glorious kingdom on Earth" Mather uttered thoughts generally absent from the standard sermons of his time. Notions of the coming kingdom were privately held by such refugees as the regicide judges and by not a few of New England's citizens. But Mitchell, the younger Shepard, and other members of Mather's generation who preached and published from 1660 through 1690 were disposed both to a tribal self-obsession with New England's internal troubles and to a judgmentally pessimistic vision of the coming era.

Not that Mather's tract of 1669 was wholly optative in tone; its doctrines marked an important step toward the chiliasm he and his son Cotton were to popularize in the last decade of the century. Increase's "father Cotton" had once gone so far as to predict flatly that Christ's earthly kingdom would begin in 1655 and would come about solely through the saints' perfection of their own institutions. Edward Johnson's church militant had marched under a postmillenarian banner: in confidence that the saints could establish and enjoy the kingdom for a thousand years before it became necessary for Christ to appear personally in judgment. By the late 1660s, however, this appeared inconceivable even to Increase Mather (or, for that matter, to Davenport). The anti-Christian forces having been restored to power, it would be necessary for Christ to reverse the course of history personally by coming in judgment *before* the thousand-year reign of the saints. Thus Mather (like the preachers of the jeremiads) assumed that history—all history, not merely that of New England—was tending toward darkness, but he could also predict that a personally intervening Christ would restore the world to the light. Such a view of history was, in Mather's words, "marvelously refreshing," and could, if properly understood, rouse even the drowsiest of Christ's people from their spiritual slumbers.

In the 1670s and 1680s Mather, now one with his fellow clergy on the issue of church discipline, conveyed his sense of history through the formula codified in the synod of 1679; like others he seemed obsessed (in the words of the title of one of his jeremiads) with "the great concernment of a covenant people." But he never wholly abandoned his millenarianism, and in 1702 he was speaking with considerable confidence of "the glorious times which are expected, and will certainly be accomplished." As for New England, however, Mather, aggrieved by his removal from the Harvard presidency when the college came under the control of men tired of the old Puritan stringencies, left the darkest of thoughts as his legacy to his people: "in the glorious times promised to the Church on earth, *America* will be hell." When in the 1740s Charles Chauncy sought to undo what he considered Jonathan Edwards' mad prophecies of a millennial light dawning in the New World, he seized upon and emphasized this latter-day utterance of Mather's. Chauncy did not, however, recall that in 1669 Mather had announced—at one of New England's most despairing moments—that God's New World saints might be the first to discern the full meaning of the prophecies and to share in the blessings of their fulfillment.

The text of *The Mystery of Israel's Salvation* is from the edition of 1669, pp. 145–164, 180–181.

The Mystery of Israel's Salvation

> *Hear the word of the Lord, O ye nations, and declare it in the isles afar off, and say, he that scattered Israel will gather him, and keep him as a shepherd doth his flock, Jeremiah 31:10. And then shall appear the sign of the Son of Man, and then shall all the tribes of the land mourn, and they shall see the Son of Man coming in the clouds of heaven with power and great glory, Matthew 24:30. In the days of the voice of the seventh angel, when he shall begin to sound, the mystery of God shall be finished, as he hath declared to his servants the prophets, Revelation 10:7.*

Is it so that the time will surely come when all Israel shall partake of such a salvation as that which hath been spoken of? Hence then it followeth that we should labor to be acquainted with these truths which do concern the mystery of God in Israel's salvation . . . concerning the kingdom of Jesus Christ, first, as a little stone by the power of his word and spirit subduing the world; and after that as a great mountain filling the whole earth. So that there will a time come when the kingdom of Christ shall be established all the earth over, the thing is certain and sure. And therefore John (or Christ by John) speaking concerning that new heaven and new earth which shall be when part of heaven shall come down upon the earth, when New Jerusalem shall come down from God out of heaven . . .

Consider . . . the divine excellency which is in these mysterious truths. Indeed all truth is of a divine original. God is the author of all truth because he is the author of all being, and truth and being are the same . . . Especially is this true concerning those truths that cannot be known by the book of the creature but only by the book of scripture; and most of all is this true concerning prophetical scripture. All scripture is given by inspiration of God; but this is eminently to be affirmed of the prophesies contained in the scriptures of truth, II Peter 1:20–21. Hence the prophetical book of the New Testament is called by the name of Revelation . . . Why revelation? But because the things contained in that book had never been known amongst the sons of men, had it not been for the extraordinary revelation of the spirit of Christ . . .

Besides, it is evident that there is some peculiar excellency in these mysteries which concerns the glory of Christ's kingdom upon earth, because it hath been the great design of Satan to obscure and darken and hide these truths from the world. From the great subtlety of Satan it hath come to pass that some men of very corrupt minds have asserted that Messiah shall have a glorious kingdom upon the earth. Some say that Cerinthus[1] (adding to this opinion carnal and heretical delusions) did so maintain; to be sure he was a very desperate heretic, and maybe one of those Antichrists which the Apostle speaketh of when he saith, that many Antichrists were then come, I John 2:18. Likewise the Jews in their Talmud have many gross and carnal conceits about the temporal glory of Messiah his kingdom. So have many that are of the fifth-monarchy persuasion.[2] So had those monstrous German Anabaptists which were stirred up by the Devil to oppose the reformation in Luther's days.[3] And there is a popish sect at this present, which doth maintain that there will be a glorious restitution of all things here below. Now by this means Satan hath greatly prevailed to keep the world in ignorance of the true glory of these mysteries; for many good men are apt to think with themselves, what? Shall we believe that the saints shall have a glorious reign upon earth? That's an opinion which heretics have held, which savors of Judaism, which such and such disorderly persons have been taken with, and so Satan hath his design in keeping many godly souls from

1. An Ephesian religious leader of the second century who taught a form of Gnosticism, a religion of personal revelation.

2. Fifth-Monarchism flourished in England during and after the years of civil war. Based on Daniel 2:36–45, it was essentially the belief, authorizing radical antiroyalism, that the personal reign of Christ was imminent.

3. See *The Examination of Mrs. Anne Hutchinson,* note 8.

enjoying the comfort of these truths. This then showeth that there is some divine excellency in these mysteries, otherwise the wicked one would not so envy God's children the knowledge of these things . . .

Consider . . . that a gracious soul may have much spiritual delight and comfort in diving into these mysterious truths. John had experience of this, Revelations 10:10, *when I ate the book, it was in my mouth sweet as honey.* It is true, that when the book was in his belly, it was bitter, the meaning of which may be that bitter afflictions should befall the church during the reign of Antichrist, and in respect of those calamitous events the book is said to be bitter in his belly. But in his mouth it was sweet as honey, to signify to us that the understanding of prophecies is a most sweet and comfortable thing. And thus also the prophet Jeremiah, chapter 31:26, *upon this I awaked, and beheld, and my sleep was sweet unto me,* i.e., he had newly had a vision concerning the salvation of all the tribes of Israel, and upon this, his sleep was sweet unto him . . . The truth is, that whilst a man is dwelling upon these meditations, he is as it were in heaven upon earth; he hath fellowship with the angels in heaven, whence the angel said unto John, *I am thy fellow servant, and of thy brethren the prophets* . . . When the servants of the Lord are reading or writing or meditating or praying concerning these mysteries to the great God of heaven and earth, the blessed angels are standing by them all the time . . . But there is that which is better than fellowship with angels—even communion with the blessed holy God is to be enjoyed in these meditations . . . God dwelleth in the dark prophecies of his word. *There* he is to be seen; *there* are the breathings of his spirit; *there* is a presence of God that is unutterable.

And this I may affirm to you, that if there be any man which hath not had communion with God in looking into these mysteries (which angels love to pry into) either it is because he hath no grace in his soul—and these mysteries indeed are such things as an unregenerate heart can find no sap, nor savor in them; they are the deep things of the spirit of God, which being spiritually discerned, the natural man cannot see any beauty in them; nay, his heart secretly riseth against them—or else it is because of ignorance and unacquaintedness with the truth of these mysteries that a man seeth not much of God in them . . . There are [those] that look upon the things that concern the first resurrection as dreams not to be believed. As if these things were only the airy, empty speculations of some men with notions above the clouds. But as for those whose understandings God hath opened to conceive and receive these truths, they see a glory in them above the world, that eye hath not seen, nor tongue can express.

Consider . . . that the time wherein the mystery of God shall be finished draweth on apace. The salvation of all Israel, it is now near to be revealed. And this is a marvelous incouragement to look into this mystery of Israel's salvation. For inasmuch as the time of fulfilling prophecies is at hand, we may hope that they shall be unsealed unto those whose hearts are set upon them, Revelation 22:10 and chapter 10, verse 11. It was said to John, *Thou must prophesy again:* what is the meaning of that? Is it (as some have thought) that John should be again sent into the world before the last day? I do not think so. Though something may be said to prove that John Baptist shall be raised from the dead a little before the day of judgment, to be an instrument of converting the Jewish nation, yet there's no reason to believe so concerning John the Apostle. The meaning then of those words, *thou shalt prophesy again,* may be that there will a time come when the gift of interpreting prophetical scripture shall be wonderfully revived in the church, that the Book of Revelation shall be interpreted and understood as clearly, almost, as if John himself were here to preach of these things. And when should this time be, if not when the prophecies are come to their birth? Well, but how doth it appear that the mystery of God will shortly be finished? This is manifest, because the signs forerunning the accomplishment of the mystery of God in the glorious salvation of all Israel are already working. What sign? What token of this day can you think of, but that it is even now appearing? I'll mention (by the help of Christ) two things unto you, that are signs of this great and notable day of the Lord being near. 1. *When the virgins, not only foolish, but wise also, are asleep, this is a sign that the mystery of God shall be finished ere long,* Matthew 25:5–6. *Whilst the bridegroom tarried, they all slumbered and slept, and at midnight there was a cry made, behold, the bridegroom cometh.* So then, when the wise virgins are asleep amongst the rest, this is a sign that Jesus Christ is coming (not to the ultimate judgment), but as a bridegroom. This is a sign that the great and blessed nuptials draw on apace, concerning which Christ spake at the institution of the Lord's Supper, saying, *I will drink no more of the fruit of the vine until that day that I drink it new,* i.e., not corporally, but after a spiritual and new kind of manner, *in the kingdom of God.* Mark 14:25. Consider also Revelation 19:6–7, *There was the voice of a great multitude, saying Allelujah, the Lord God omnipotent reigneth, the marriage of the Lamb is come, and his wife hath made herself ready.* When once the Jews are converted, then will this voice be heard; then will the Lamb's wife be made ready for the marriage. Now, I say, the foregoing sign of this is sleeping amongst the virgins. And alas, is it not so now? Are not all the virgins asleep? What else meaneth that strange spirit of worldliness that possesseth and prevaileth upon great professors? . . .

Secondly. The present tumults and shaking of the *nations are a sign that the mystery of God shall be finished ere long, and that the kingdom shall become the Lord's all the world over.* Certainly I do believe that this earthquake which the Lord of heaven and earth hath now begun will not be over until Babylon fall and rise no more.[4] A few years ago there was a strange calm upon the world; what was that a sign of? Truly, that calm which was on the earth six or seven years ago was a prognostic of the earthquake wherein the witnesses shall be raised and a tenth part of the city shall fall. Consider the scriptures, see Psalm 46 (which some are wont to call Luther's psalm, because Luther was much delighted in the reading and singing thereof) . . . From the title of the psalm we may gather that when the things therein spoken do come to pass, it is a sign that the . . . *mystery which hath been hid in God,* as the Apostle speaketh, is fulfilling and finishing. Now see verse 8, *Behold the works of God, what desolations he hath made in the earth.* Is not this scripture fulfilling? Is not the Lord making desolations in the earth? We may gather thence, that the *hidden things of the mystery of God* are finishing apace. Consider also verse 9, *He maketh wars to cease unto the end of the earth, he breaketh the bow, and cutteth the spear in sunder, he burneth the chariot in fire.* There shall such a day as this come upon the earth, even a day wherein the nations shall learn war no more, but before this day there must be terrible doings and desolations made upon the earth as a sign of that glorious tranquillity which the most high (whose method of divine providence is to bring light out of darkness, good out of evil, order out of confusion, peace out of war) will establish on the earth. I may tell you therefore, that dreadful wars, confused noise, and garments rolled in blood, are a sign of Christ's appearing to establish his kingdom on the earth . . . Now this is come to pass at this day. There is a sword fallen from heaven to the earth; the God of heaven and earth hath put all the world into a bloody frame of revenge and war one against another. Therefore let the saints lift up their heads, and let them know that the Lord *is coming, is coming, is coming.* The great and terrible day of the Lord, it is near, it is near, wherein the mighty man shall cry bitterly.

I might also tell you that direful and astonishing desolations by fire are a sign that the time is at hand wherein the mystery of God shall be finished. Consider Revelation 16:8, *The angel of the fourth vial hath power given him to scorch men with fire . . .*

4. Mather is referring to the earthquake of April, 1668, and doubtless has in mind Revelation 16:18, which notes as one consequence of the pouring out of the seventh vial "a great earthquake, such as was not since men were upon the earth, so mighty an earthquake, and so great."

Now is it not so at this day, that the world seemeth to be all on fire? Did not providence a few days since bring unto our ears doleful and exanimating[5] tidings that a fire is broke forth in God's anger which hath burnt to the foundations of the mountains?[6] That now we may say unto God, how terrible art thou in thy works? The uttermost parts are afraid at thy tokens! The voice of the Lord is calling upon us, saying, *Come and see the works of God, he is terrible in his doings toward the children of men*. But though this calamity be heavy, yet be comforted, in that these awful tremendous dispensations are such as that by the light of this fire we may see the vial full of the wrath of God is ready to be poured upon the head of Rome. Yea, such things as these, they are a sign not only of Christ's providential coming to destroy Rome, but also (which will follow not long after that) of his personal coming to begin that long, and last, and great day, when the saints shall judge the world. Acts 2:19–20, *There must be wonders in heaven above, and signs in the earth beneath, blood and fire, and vapor of smoke, before that great and notable day of the Lord cometh*. What's the meaning of all this? Part of the meaning of it may be that there shall be strange and terrible prodigies in heaven and earth, to signify that Christ's coming to judgment draweth on apace.

Blood may note the turning of water into blood; fire, that there shall be strange fiery meteors, flashes of fire in a fearful manner seen in the heavens; vapor of smoke may signify terrible comets, which (some say) the Hebrews of old were wont to call by the name of a *pillar of smoke*. But besides this, blood may note a bloody sword; and fire, terrible devastations by burning, and (possibly) vapor of smoke may signify burnings by fire also. Now then, is this the day of blood and fire? The Lord then is roaring from on high to give us warning that the great and notable day is coming. One scripture more let me mention before I pass off from this, viz., Haggai 2:6–7, *Thus saith the Lord of hosts, yet once it is a little while, and I will shake the heaven and the earth, and the sea and the dry land, and I will shake all nations and the desire of all nations shall come*. The words are true concerning the second coming of the Messiah, as well as concerning his first coming. Observe now, *I will shake heaven and earth*, i.e., the whole world. Particularly consider what is said. *I will shake the heaven*, saith God. Is not this come to pass? Are not the powers of heaven shaking? I am persuaded that whoever liveth a while longer will hear that the stars are falling down from heaven, like

5. Killing.

6. Probably the great London fire of September 1666, which virtually destroyed the city.

untimely figs from a shaken tree. *And the earth,* is not this fulfilling also? Do you not feel an earthquake at this day? Is not the Lord arising to shake terribly the earth? The earth is moved exceedingly, the earth reeleth to and fro, the earth is clean dissolved, the transgression thereof is heavy upon it, the windows from on high are open, and the foundations of the earth do shake. *And the sea.* Is not this sign also fulfilling? What roarings have there been upon the sea of late? Is not the day of the Lord upon the ships of Tarshish?[7] How are men afraid to venture upon the sea? Because God is shaking not only the dry land but the sea? *I will shake all nations.* Is not this also fulfilling? God hath alarumed all the nations, do you not hear the rushing of the nations? When were all the nations in such a posture? Europe, Asia, Africa, America, all are in a tumult. The Lord hath alarmed them all. Men know not where now to go; they cannot think of what nation to transport themselves unto, but the *shaking of God* will take hold on them in that nation. Now, these are signs that he who is the desire of the elect amongst all nations will come ere long. *Amen, even so, come, come, come Lord Jesus!*

Consider . . . that some of us are under special advantage to understand these mysterious truths of God; that is to say, such of us as are in an exiled condition in this wilderness. Indeed some came hither upon worldly accounts, but others there are that came into this wilderness purely upon spiritual accounts (yea, and that continue here upon no other account) that so they might bear witness not only against the name of the beast, and against his character, but also against his number . . . [and] against all humane inventions in the worship of God . . . Now such of you (I speak to some such this day) may hope that God will discover much of his counsel to you, if in his fear you search into what he hath declared by his servants the Prophets. Where was John when he had the Revelation of Jesus Christ? He was, by reason of Domitian the king, banished into the Isle of Patmos, Revelation 1:9. So Daniel and Ezekiel were exiles when they saw visions of God. And I have often thought upon that which is said, Revelation 17:3. Namely, *that John was led into the wilderness* to see the destruction of Rome . . . God hath led us into a wilderness, and surely it was not because the Lord hated us but because he loved us that he brought us hither into this Jeshimon.[8] Who knoweth but that he may send down his spirit upon us here if we continue faithful before him? . . .

7. That is, sound ships (II Chronicles 9:21). In 1684 Mather published *An Essay for the Recording of Illustrious Providences,* a compendium of such punishments by nature as earthquakes, fire, and shipwreck.

8. The wilderness (Numbers 21:20).

Prayer may be a means to hasten the coming of this glorious day of Israel's salvation. Would we not have Sion to be delivered, and that speedily? Pour forth earnest and continual prayer, and it will hasten the birth of Sion, that even a nation shall be born in one day. It is prayer that sets the wheels of divine providence a-going. It is prayer that turns the world upside down. Therefore you may observe that seldom doth any great alteration of the state and face of things come to pass in the world but the Lord first sends down a spirit of prayer into the hearts of his saints, "and that shaketh heaven and earth in pieces in a short time." Observe then (my friends and brethren, beloved in the Lord) and be awakened this day, I say. Observe that when the prayers of saints ascend before the throne of God, with the incense of the merits and intercession of the Lord Jesus, there followeth upon it *thunderings, voices, lightnings, and an earthquake,* Revelation 8:4–5 . . . Oh then pray as for your lives all manner of prayer, even public prayer, family prayer, secret prayer, and in all stir up yourselves to call upon the Lord, and say "awake, awake, O arm of the Lord as in the days of old; awake, as in the years of ancient generations, that Sion may return with singing, and everlasting joy upon her head" . . .

If the Lord stir up the hearts of his poor servants to favor the dust of Sion, and to show it by earnest prayer before him at all times, surely the day will not be long before the Lord appear in glory to build up Sion, for he will have regard to the prayer of the destitute, and he will not despise their prayer. Know ye this, you servants of the Lord, to your everlasting encouragement. *But thou, O Lord, how long! how long! how long!*

THOMAS SHEPARD, JR. (1635–1677)

Eye-Salve (1672)

ONE OF Increase Mather's reasons for capitulating on the issue of the Half-Way Covenant may have been his realization that a divided clergy would be no match for an increasingly accommodationist civil government. When the ministers of God announce "with *one* voice" that the day of trouble is near, he proclaimed in a later election sermon, "then the day of trouble *is* near." The election sermons gave the clergy an opportunity to proclaim their views on the state of the colony before the elected deputies and then to circulate them in print among the entire populace. Not surprisingly, as the General Court began to divide into factions (largely over whether to grant greater "toleration" in order to forestall royal revocation of the charter), the civil authorities did not invariably rejoice in what they heard on election day: at one point they prohibited the printing of one of Increase Mather's commentaries on errant behavior in society and state.

Since one of the recurrent themes of the election sermons of the 1660s and the 1670s was a celebration of the virtues of the fathers, from which their children had woefully declined, the sermon delivered in 1672 by Thomas Shepard, Jr., is of particular interest. The younger Shepard, was, along with Increase Mather, among the very few children of the founding fathers accorded the honor of preaching on election day. He was the eldest of Shepard's three sons, the only one born in England. He received his degree from Harvard in 1653 (four years after his father's death), was subsequently appointed Fellow of Harvard College and tutor, and in 1659 was installed as teacher in Charlestown. Like the Mathers, he was well aware of his ancestry, its implications and its obligations. (Cotton Mather pointed to three generations of Shepards as evidence that descent does not invariably bring declension—that indeed piety might grow like a snowball as it rolls, from generation to generation, down the slope of history.) Aside from his election sermon, Shepard's only effort at publication was an edition of his father's *Parable of the Ten Virgins,* for which he and Jonathan Mitchell provided a brief introduction.

Eye-Salve is remarkable for its elaborate exfoliation of the context—physical as well as intellectual—out of which the jeremiad evolved and which so long sustained it as credible utterance. Election preachers poured a variety of meanings into the word "wilderness," nearly always deriving them from Old Testament parallels. Shepard's lengthy sermon—undoubtedly expanded for publication—is diffident by comparison to others in setting forth parallels between the history of the Children of Israel ("a looking-glass," New Englanders were later told, "in which we can see our own face") and that of New England. But the larger significance of New England's wilderness experience for seventeenth-century intellectual development was otherwise almost precisely as Shepard explained it. The first generation had contended against the difficulties and the perils of a wilderness and, through divine blessing, had seen it turn into a pleasant place. The provoking disobedience of their offspring, even while it threatened New England with divine displeasure, proved them to be the children of Abraham indeed.

In his published sermon, Shepard left no doubt as to what he took to be the prevailing sins of his generation—insubordination among the populace, weakness of will in the magistracy. The sermon is largely an elaborate argument on behalf of a single proposition: religion is "best established and flourisheth when there is a concurrence of the magistracy and ministry together to promote the true worship of God, and to suppress what is contrary thereunto." Shepard was speaking on behalf of a clergy still smarting from resistance to the Half-Way Covenant, to open attacks on synods: "the substance," Shepard insisted, of "that good old way." In 1668 Shepard had participated in a council that had ordered a group of Baptists to "remove themselves out of this jurisdiction." He had then helplessly watched them remain, unmolested by a General Court that refused to enforce the orders of the clerical council. Magistrates, Shepard insisted, must use their "*coercive* power in matters of religion." Baptists were one thing, but what about the discernible longing of some New Englanders for the "leeks and onions" of Episcopacy? Unless the magistrates erected and kept intact a "hedge" against such an intrusion, Shepard predicted (drawing quite cautiously on the Book of Revelation), then "this poor woman in this wilderness" might be utterly and totally consumed by the "dragon" from which she had fled.

It was probably in expanding his sermon for publication that Shepard gave emphasis to an apparently newly discovered lever with which to move the magistrates. Although he expressed the hope that God himself would "steel the hearts of our godly leaders" against religious abominations, it might also come to pass that the "generality" of the people of New England might convert their detestation of Episcopacy into wrath against a magistracy inclined to toleration. Take heed, he warned, lest the multitude undergo "an alteration and change of affections," one that would see them not "so affected as formerly to their civil rulers, or their very civil state and constitution." Shepard's language was careful and moderate, but his jeremiad was, at bottom, less a summons to repentance than a threat of rebellion. Ironically, Shepard—in most matters more conservative even than his father—was resurrecting some of the very notions for which John Wheelwright, in the days of the fathers, had been banished from the Bay.

The text of *Eye-Salve* is from the edition of 1672, pp. 1–13, 15–22, 25–27, 30–37, 48–52.

Eye-Salve or a Watch-Word from Our Lord Jesus Christ unto His Churches in New England

Deuteronomy 8:10 &c. When thou hast eaten and art full, then thou shalt bless the Lord thy God, for the good land which he hath given thee. Beware that thou forget not the Lord thy God in not keeping his commandments . . . Chapter 5:32–33. Ye shall observe to do therefore as the Lord your God hath commanded you: you shall not turn aside to the right hand or to the left, you shall walk in the ways which the Lord your God hath commanded you, that ye may live, and that it may be well with you and that ye may prolong your days in the land which ye shall possess. Jeremiah 2:31. O generation, see ye the word of the Lord: Have I been a wilderness unto Israel? A land of darkness? Wherefore say my people, we are lords, we will come no more unto thee.

These words contain the Lord's solemn and affectionate expostulation with his people, both as to the equity and goodness of his way toward them, and the iniquity and perverseness of their ways toward himself; wherein the Lord labors to recover the degenerating back-sliding people, showing, (1) What he had been to them, viz., not a wilderness, nor a land of darkness, (2) What returns they had made unto the Lord . . .

Explication

(O Generation) This word . . . in our text . . . betokens the persons in such an age succeeding their fathers, who were in Jeremiah's time upon

the stage of action, Ecclesiastes 1:4, *One generation passeth away and another generation cometh, but the earth* (the great stage of action, upon which all generations are to act their part) *abideth forever* . . . It is here also a degenerating generation that is taxed; as Calvin notes, into what times are we fallen! What an age is this we live in! . . .

(*Have I been a wilderness to Israel?*) By Israel is meant the people of God in covenant with him, his peculiar people. And this question is to be understood in way of a strong negation: the Lord had not been so to them, and the Lord so speaks as putting it to them themselves to be judge in the case: have I been so? Do you consult your own experience, and let that make the answer, and the true answer must be that assuredly I have not been a wilderness to Israel. Yet the expression doth imply or import at least their tacit and practical accusation of the Lord that he had been so to them . . . The words are metaphorical, *Have I been a wilderness to Israel?* i.e., have I been that to my people which a wilderness is unto men that are made to wilder therein, where they meet with nothing but wants, and terror, and woe, &c. And it may seem to allude to the state and condition of the children of Israel in the wilderness . . . where the Lord led them forty years to humble them and to prove them, &c., called the *great and terrible wilderness, where were fiery serpents, and scorpions, and drought, &c.*, called moreover, a *waste howling wilderness, . . . a land of deserts, and pits, a land of drought and of the shadow of death,* a land that no man passed through, and where no man dwelt, and contradistinguished from . . . a pleasant and fruitful land. There are these five things which we may consider of in a wilderness:

1. A wilderness notes a desolate, solitary place without inhabitant, and where there is nothing but confusion and disorder . . .

2. A wilderness speaks a place uncultivated, a condition destitute of many necessary comforts . . . The wilderness is not only a solitary way where no city is to dwell in, but they want meat and drink, and their soul faints within them. Now have I been so to you, said the Lord! Have I suffered you to want? . . .

3. In a wilderness there is not a beaten path, whence it is that men there are in danger to be lost, and are made to wander about for want of a way before them wherein they might travail . . . Have I not made your way plain before you at all times, and passable, so that you have had direction and conduct from me? . . .

4. Again, in a wilderness there is not only want of many comforts, but there is danger as to many positive evils which such are exposed unto. Hence . . . the wilderness is said to be a land of pits and fiery serpents; *when Christ is in the wilderness he is among the wild beasts* (Mark 1:13) *and there are the briars and thorns of the wilderness* (Judges 8:7). They that are in a wilderness state may look to suffer much, and

thus it becomes a place of temptation. *Christ is therefore led into the wilderness to be tempted* (Matthew 4:1). Thus (may the Lord say) have I been as a wilderness, to sting and vex you? To entrap you, to terrify you and tear you in pieces? . . .

5. A wilderness is not hedged in, nor fenced about. What is in the wilderness hath no defense, but lies open to the injury of those that will break into bark the trees thereof, and root up the same. The wilderness is no inclosure, *Have I then been so to you?* Have I left you without defense, without an hedge of protection? *Have you not been as an inclosed garden to me, and I a wall of fire round about you?* Have not I given you those walls, such defenders, leaders, instruments of safety, whereby you have been hedged about, walled in, and secured? . . .

(A land of darkness) Darkness betokens the privation of light: it is divers times in scripture taken for trouble, ignorance, sorrow, and (in a word) all woeful evil . . . [The Lord] hath not been a wilderness to us, or a land of darkness, but hath granted to us light and salvation. There hath been the light of the gospel, the light of the ministry of the word; the light of his countenance hath been shining upon his people, respecting leaders in the commonwealth that have been guides, and eyes, and light to us in this good land . . . The college (that school of the prophets) hath been a means under God to continue the lamps lighted among us, even the light for the sanctuary, and that not here only but also in other parts of the world.

(*Wherefore say my people we are lords*) Here in these words the defection and revolt of the people of God from the Lord is described . . . As if they had not received any such thing from the hand of God, they now despise the Lord, and in the pride and height of their spirits swell, and grow secure and lofty and cast off the fear of God . . . We have power, and the kingdom is settled in our hands, and we have things at command. We have peace and liberty, and are full, and in prosperity. And thus through their self-confidence and carnal interests they are ready to look at themselves as absolute lords, and so independent . . .

(*We will come no more unto thee*) They had made a defection from God, and now would not return to him . . . as though they might now choose what God they would, a spirit of whoredom in them in revolting from the Lord . . . This greatly aggravates the sin, and so will increase the judgment of such a people as that was.

Doctrine

That the undeniable experience which the covenant-people of God have had of the Lord's being to them not a wilderness nor a land of darkness, but the contrary, should caution them never to incur the guilt of so unreasonable a sin and dangerous folly and provocation, as to revolt from under the Lord, or to be unwilling to return again in case they have begun to decline from him . . . A people once glad to enjoy God, though in a wilderness state, yet it's oft seen that their affections towards God alter with the change of their wilderness into a fruitful field. Deuteronomy 32:10–15, 20: *Jesurun waxing fat with the wine, and the milk, and honey, &c. kicketh against God, forsakes him &c. and becomes a very froward generation* . . .

Reason 1. I might argue by an induction of particulars, whereby the eminency of the Lord's being such an one as the doctrine speaks him to be unto his people will appear, whereby our minds may be induced to assent unto that general truth propounded in the doctrine.

Reason 2 . . . The scripture is furnished with many histories of the observation of God's people in their time this way, and the changes of providence in our own generation will supply us with more, so that now if experience, which is wont to be the mistress even of fools, will not teach and caution these we are speaking of, it argues wonderful sottishness indeed . . .

Reason 3. From the excellency of Israel's God above all other gods of the nations, which gods yet these nations will not ordinarily reject . . . They will not part with their gods though they be such as cannot save them in the day of their distress, they being dunghill gods; but the God of Israel is the true God and our fathers' God (as the covenant relation speaks). And therefore we should never cast him off.

Reason 4. From the covenant relation and obligation of such a people unto God: to cleave forever unto him. As the Lord on his part by performing his promise, fulfills his covenant relation to them . . . so the consideration of the covenant on their part . . . should be such a caution to them as the doctrine intimates . . .

Reason 5. From the certainty and extremity of the woe of such a people as shall so cast off the Lord: wrath comes on them to the uttermost. There's no hiding their sin from God, nor any avoiding the judgment of God . . .

Reason 6. (And in special referring to the last branch of the doctrine) Because of the wonderful unparallel grace of God to re-entertain unto favor penitent ones that do return to him, notwithstanding their greatest backslidings.

Use 1. Hence the people of God should not suffer[1] their experiences of the Lord's being to them not a wilderness or a land of darkness in this good land which he hath given them to die and perish with them,

1. Allow.

but ought to preserve and improve them for this end, that they might be kept thereby from casting off their subjection and obedience unto the Lord their God.

The Lord hath not left things to a wilderness confusion, but there hath been that beauty of order which he hath stamped on this people respecting the doctrine, and way of worship here professed, and in the due subordination of superiors, and inferiors, and fellowship of the servants of God together in the Lord—that order and fellowship in the gospel and communion, both with the Lord and one another. O how sweet hath that communion of saints been! . . . *The Lord filled his servants with a zeal for the house of God* (Ezekiel 43:10–12). Such a zeal had Christ, the zeal whereof did even eat him up; and it was Phineas his zeal which did quench the fire of God's wrath that began to burn against Israel. And so, on the contrary, our coldness, our lukewarmness, will kindle the fire of his displeasure. Hence also was it the care which God put into the hearts of the first generation that planted this wilderness (that so this land might not be a land of darkness and wilderness, as aforesaid) to provide nurseries for church and commonwealth, in their ordering schools of learning, and in particular the college; whence it may be said of our New England Cambridge also, as of old, *Hinc lucem, & pocula sacra!*[2] . . . And we have had experience of the blessing of God upon that endeavor. And O let no hand therefore be suffered to lay the axe of destruction to the root of that tree, by any direct or indirect means, or to draw away those influences from above or beneath, which tend to its flourishing and increasing!

2. As to the provision which the Lord hath made for his people of food and comforts for soul and body; he hath turned a wilderness into a fruitful field, which we have admirable experience of also . . . We have been able to relieve and support other plantations of the English in other parts of the world, and have had the blessings of peace, while others have been wasted with war . . . God hath given it a name like the name of the great nations of the earth, and hath planted his people in a place of their own, and in the place which he hath chosen for them, to set his name in . . . *The Lord hath not left himself without witness, but hath given us rain from heaven &c.* (Acts 14:17).

3. As to direction, making the way of his people plain before them—they have not been left to such a wilderness state as wherein to find no path beaten out for them, but . . . even as by a pillar of fire and cloud hath he showed them the way. Hence it is that God also hath given to his people those that might be as eyes to them in the wilderness, persons

2. From this there shall come illumination and holy refreshment.

eminently furnished with his spirit . . . The Lord sowed this land at first with such precious seed-corn, as was picked out of our whole nation . . .

4. The Lord [did] stir up a spirit of courage, and wisdom and zeal, and faithfulness in our godly leaders to take those foxes so full of subtlety and mischief, that would else have destroyed his vineyard, and that by plucking off its buds and tender grapes. The Lord hath not suffered that brood of the serpent to increase here as otherwise would have been; we should have been filled with poisonful, fiery, stinging serpents . . . By the effectual crushing the same in the very egg—hath not the Lord blessed the coercive power of the civil magistrate for that end? Let our experience give in evidence: In the case of the heresy of the familists, which brake out of old among us; and O to what a height they suddenly grew,[3] working at length woeful disturbance in the civil state as well as in the churches—this is not to be forgotten. As tame as error for a time pretended to be, yet at length it could gird itself with a sword, but the Lord would not suffer it to be drawn. So likewise after this, with reference to the *Gortonists, &c.*, which things should be remembered forever; and the mercy of the Lord acknowledged, in that he preserved us from those hornets also, and that ministerially by our rulers spirited by himself thereunto.[4]

And it is to be hoped that this coercive power of a godly magistracy which we have experienced the benefit of so many ways, being duly managed, shall not be abandoned . . .

I say we have found the Lord (experimentally) blessing his people in this way. Hath it not been so? Will not our experience witness for God? And give in abundant evidence of these things? . . . O call to remembrance those times, you of the old generation; how notably did the Lord, in the way of council of churches, by that famous synod then met at Cambridge, free this wilderness from being a land of darkness by seasonably dispelling that hellish damp, and mist of errors and heresy! Again, when these churches lay under the reproach of schism, or rigid separation from the churches in England, &c., as is to be seen in the preface to the platform of discipline: and when some great ones there had said, *fieri non posse ut Zelotes isti in unam ecclesiasticae politiae formam (ne si optio quidem daretur) communi inter se consensu unquam conspirare velint, &c.*,[5] this

3. See *The Examination of Mrs. Anne Hutchinson.*

4. Samuel Gorton was a religious radical who refused to recognize the jurisdiction of Massachusetts over a tract of land he had purchased from Indians. He was removed by a military force and was eventually banished to Rhode Island. He considered an organized ministry an impediment to the true believer's relation with God.

5. It is impossible that those zealots should ever willingly come together into a single form of church polity (even if the option were given them).

(as reverend and worthy Mr. Cotton of blessed memory speaks in his epistle before Mr. Norton's answer to Apollonius)[6] was presently removed also by means of another synod, which did from the word of God draw up the platform of discipline, characteristical of the way of these churches, with admirable consent and harmony.[7] Other experiences I might instance of the singular smiles of God . . .

O generation, see the word of the Lord! Is there any new way more eligible than that good old way . . . which the Lord's people have . . . experimentally found to be the way of blessing from God? Shall we seek and enquire after any new-found-out way? As the Lord speaks of *new gods* as they are called (Deuteronomy 32:17), upstart gods, which our *fathers knew not,* should some of our fathers that are now asleep in Jesus, and that have with so many prayers and tears, hazards and labors and watchings, and studies, night and day to lay a sound and sure and happy foundation of prosperity for this people, arise out of their graves, and hear the discourses of some, and observe the endeavors of others, as Edomites against their brother Jacob (Psalm 137:7), crying *Raze it, raze it, even to the foundation!* . . . Would they not even rent their garments and weep over this generation? And are there any that think to mend themselves by going back to leeks and onions?[8] Yea to that very *vomit of the dragon,* to lick up that vomit which he hath formerly cast out of his mouth, whereby to cause this poor woman in this wilderness also (if I may so far allude at least to that expression in Revelation 12:15) to be carried away therewith even as by a flood? I hope the good people of the Lord in this wilderness will not do it, for the generality of them; and I trust the Lord will steel the hearts of our godly leaders with courage and holy zeal against all such abomination . . .

Question: Who are those that so revolt? Are there any so foolish or vile that will so do? Wherein doth it appear?

Answer: It is threatened and appears when the sovereignty of God in the matters of instituted worship according to the second commandment is despised and rejected by setting up some false way of worship; . . . herein Christ's lordship is highly opposed . . .

We read how Uzziah smarted for his boldness in vying with the lordship of God herein; though he were a king, yet the Lord would not bear with him (II Chronicles 26), when as he would rise up against God's order to *burn incense,* which pertained not to him but to the priest, *he is smitten*

6. See John Cotton, Foreword to John Norton's *The Answer.*

7. The synod of 1646 that drew up the Cambridge Platform.

8. "And the people cried unto Moses . . . We remember the fish which we did eat in Egypt freely; the cucumbers, and the melons, and the leeks, and the onions" (Numbers 11:2, 5).

with the leprosy. And it is observed, verse 16 (as the cause of his errors therein) *that his heart was lifted up,* i.e., through pride. Proud hearts will sometimes adventure desperately this way, but it will finally prove a losing cast to throw out thus against the Lord's appointment. And this was Korah's sin, *All the Lord's people are holy,* and why may not all take their turns publicly to preach and rule?[9] And why should there be such a distinction of persons &c.? O take heed of this, for this is to say, as in our text they did, *We are lords . . .*

So 'tis here, they will be no more so snibbed and under the yoke as they have been &c. Surely God hath chains for such as will break and cast away Christ's gracious cords from them. Men's lusts are sweet to them, and they would not be disturbed or disquieted in their sin. Hence there be so many, such as cry up toleration boundless, and libertinism, so as (if it were in their power) to order a total and perpetual confinement of the sword of the civil magistrate unto its scabbard (a notion that is evidently destructive to this people, and to the public liberty, peace and prosperity of any instituted churches under heaven). I cannot but heartily approve, notwithstanding of that advice of an old counselor, to one of the kings of France, asking him, "What way should be taken for his own and his people's happiness in his governing of them?" he thereupon presented him with a little book, in the beginning, middle and end whereof there was only written this word: *Moderation! Moderation! Moderation!* We are in danger of extremes; and however some cry up *Toleration, Toleration, Toleration* at present, yet experience will evince that that will quickly in conjunction with others, be changed to persecution . . .

O there was not at first that contempt of the magistrates, or ministers, or churches for their zeal for God herein, as begins to grow up among us in these days . . .

Consider, that a revolt from God is usually graduated, having its more imperceptible beginnings. By degrees the souls of men slide back from God. Satan hath variety of artifices whereby to cast us down, and overthrow the true religion and kingdom of Christ among us, if he could. He makes use of the divisions and scandals of God's people to promote his hellish designs; he will improve the spirit of fear and cowardice in some, the rashness of others, the jealousies of others, the ambition of others, the covetousness of others, the simplicity of others, the passions of others, the sheepishness of others, &c., to advance his own cause in the apostasy of professors. Yea, and mischief (perhaps) shall be laid in, in the very primers for children whereby they may even suck in poison in their tender

9. Korah challenged the authority of Moses and Aaron: "Ye take too much upon you, seeing all the congregation are holy, every one of them" (Numbers 16:3).

years and also in the pictures and images of Christ, of the Virgin Mary, and other canonized popish saints &c., sold in some shops, or brought over among us—things that will take with children, but though they may seem minute, yet will surely prove dangerous consequence at length to those tender years, and may become an introduction to popery itself. I wish such things might be crushed in the egg, and abandoned by every one that professeth the Christian name—*for the Lord thy God, O New England, is a jealous God! He is a jealous husband* especially in the matters of the second commandment. But as to this, or any other way of back-sliding from God, O fear all the graduations thereof and the first steps thereunto: *principiis obsta,*[10] watch against it . . .

If Christians will break one from another, and churches break one from another, and others, in their communion, have we not cause to fear that God will suffer *some wild boar or beast of the forest* to enter in at the breaches *and lay waste this vineyard, and turn it into a wilderness again?* So that when it shall be asked in time to come, *Why hath the Lord done thus to this land! And wherefore is all this great anger of the Lord? Why hath the Lord done thus unto such a people?* . . . then the answer should be "because they have forsaken the covenant of their God, and they would be lords, and would no more come back to the Lord their God . . . because they forgat the main end of their coming into this wilderness; because they forsook their first love to God, and so to his ordinances, and so to his people, their brethren." Witness their strifes while alive, and witness the many tearless funerals in many places (a sign they were not so beloved while alive) and because of their spiritual wantonness under ordinances. Their church covenant grew to be with many but a form, brotherly watch came to be neglected, the house of God despised, and their own preferred before the same . . . And for that they grew a worldly people, and so neglect of communion with God in secret grew upon them. There was a form of godliness, but the power thereof denied. Hypocrisy, divisors, carnal mixtures, despising God's Sabbaths, loosewalking, temporizing, sensuality, pride and idleness, fullness of bread, and not strengthening the hand of the poor and needy (those Sodom sins) found in New England—oppression of the poor, and oppression of the rich, unmercifulness, self-seeking, growing heady and high minded, and running deep upon the score of those sins of the last times, which make those times perilous . . . And they grew spiritually proud, and conceited, and censorious, and reviling (not sparing therein their very rulers in church and commonwealth) and lukewarm in the things of God and full of the sins of the tongue, in respect of lying (loss of moral truth), dissi-

10. Stand by your principles.

mulation, equivocations, and such sins as those which loosen all the bonds of even humane society, that there should be no trust or confidence put in one another . . . When God hath a purpose to destroy a people he is wont to give them a vertiginous spirit—But therefore *O generation, see the word of the Lord!* Let the sound Christians of the first good old generation that do yet remain *see the word of the Lord,* viz., in order to thankfulness unto God for all experiences that he hath given them of his being not a *wilderness or land of darkness;* and they should declare that they do so *by showing to the generation to come the praises of the Lord and his strength, and his wonderful works that he hath done* (Psalm 78:4–6). They should leave behind them registers of God's mighty acts, that their children after them might learn *to set their hope in God, and not forget his works.* And let those of the second generation, that are entered, or upon the point of entering upon the stage of action in the service of their generation, *see the word of the Lord also . . .*

Remember that a main design of God's people's adventuring into this wilderness was for progress in the work of Reformation, and that in the way of brotherly communion with the reformed churches of Christ in other parts of the world. O forsake not, deny not, condemn not, that fundamental design! And otherwise indeed what needed they to have removed from England? (This cannot justly be denied). There were then in the place from whence they came, mixtures in the worship of God, and the blessed Sabbath of God struck at &c., which they were grieved with and *vexed their righteous souls from day to day.* But here they hoped they might enjoy freedom from those pollutions, and *freedom to follow the Lord fully in all his ordinances and appointments*—I say to follow the Lord (not by halves; not still in way of mixtures in religion to have a medley of all sorts of religion, but) fully—with what purity the Lord would give them light for, and power to enjoy without molestation: and therefore as not in a way of separation from the churches of Christ in Old England, which the printed books of our New England divines do abundantly show. It was for Reformation, then, not for toleration of all religions: and awful are the words that fell from the pen of our famous Cotton in his *Bloody Tenent Washed.* It was toleration that made the world antichristian and (said he) the church never took hurt by the punishment of heretics . . .

O Generation (therefore) *see the word of the Lord,* and know that here is encouragement for God's people in the worst times—for the Lord being our God he will not be a wilderness or land of darkness to us if we sincerely rely upon him. Can there be a wilderness where the glory of the God of heaven dwells? Can there be darkness where there is the sun? There are influences of light, and life and refreshing, and fruitfulness and blessedness from this sun of righteousness to them that fear his name. Christ hath imbarked himself in this our state; and therefore as Caesar encouraged the boatman in time of danger by a dark tempest, i.e., *confide nauta Caesarem vehis,* [11] so here . : . O let him *never leave us, nor forsake us, but be with us as he was with our fathers* (I Kings 8:57). and that the shining brightness of the favor of the glorious God of Israel . . . may be still the vision of the God of New England, not dark and cloudy, but light and glorious . . . O generation, see the way of Israel unto God, and our own ways in special—Have there been no beginnings of revolt from under the Lordship of our God? May not the Lord expostulate with us . . . *Why have you not obeyed my voice?* Why have you not come up fully to the practice of my will held forth to you by my servants? Why are there these and those images of jealousy among you? What is this noise that I hear in so many churches? The noise of the axes and hammers of those that would cut and beat down the carved work? Why is there such neglect of your church-work of the house of God? And hath that been diligently done which is commanded by the God of heaven? For why should there be wrath against the colony of the Massachusetts? Why is family-duties in many houses laid aside—that in multitudes of families there is (it may be) no prayer from the one end of the week to the other? No family catechizing, no repetition of the word preached, nor calling children and servants to an account of what they do or should hear? No reading of the scripture? Maybe no Bible, or only a torn Bible to be found, so that the whole scripture is never read throughout in some families? . . .

To conclude: The Lord help our leaders in the commonwealth and in the churches also, not to faint or be discouraged though they meet with opposition, difficulties, and ill requitals from some. *Bene facere, & male audire regium est,*[12] said Seneca, and a good speech was it . . . Though there be the murmuring and strife of the congregation in some times of temptation, yet Moses must remember he is a nursing father (Numbers 11:12) *and Paul as a nurse must be gentle.* And the child must not be thrown away because it is unquiet. Though there be a storm, yet betray not the ship. *In naufragio* (saith Seneca) *rector laudandus quem obruit mare clavum tenentem,* i.e., that steersman or master of the vessel is indeed to be commended, that will not shrink from duty through fear or self-interest, though he be washed, and raked over and over with the sea, or whatever the event be. I beseech our honored leaders and steersmen not to desert us, or the cause of God imbarked in the vessel of this

11. Have faith, sailor, you are carrying Caesar in your vessel.
12. To do good and to hear evil is the lot of kings.

commonwealth, and of these churches. You are as David to serve as rowers under Christ; let it never be said of you that you did let go your hold by being false to your precious betrustments this way. Yea should a wrack come (which the Lord in mercy prevent), yet also may you so manage yourselves as to be seen to the last . . . serving Jesus Christ faithfully here . . . and that without being biased with a spirit of men-pleasing, temporizing, humorizing, faction, popularity, &c. It is by Christ that you rule, and as you are by him, so you are to be for him; and if we all cleave to the Lord, we need not then fear but God will be with us, so that we shall be able with Luther in greatest shakings to sing the Forty-Sixth Psalm.[13] And though all the earth should be gathered against this Jerusalem, yet the Lord our God can make it a *burdensome stone, and a cup of trembling*. So that when these and those of the nations shall enquire about the state of such a people, *what shall one then answer the messengers of the nations?* Truly, as Isaiah 14:32, *That the Lord hath founded this Sion and the poor of his people shall trust in it.*

13. "God is our refuge and strength, a very present help in trouble."

MARY ROWLANDSON (c. 1635–c. 1678)

Narrative of Captivity and Restoration (c. 1677)

THE NOTION that the New England wilderness was a "waste place," void of profitable servants of God, had been a staple of Massachusetts thinking almost from the beginning. Except for Roger Williams, few challenged the right of English-born saints to occupy Indian lands: whether through negotiation or warfare mattered little. For a third of a century after the defeat of the Pequots, New England's expansion went unchallenged by the Indians. In 1670 John Eliot, who had spent the 1660s translating the Bible into "the Indian tongue," produced one of the most optative of any of his "Indian tracts," *A Brief Narrative of the Progress of the Gospel among the Indians in New England*. By mid-decade, however, war had broken out between the English and the Wampanoag Indians under the leadership of King Philip, the brilliant sachem Metacomet whom the English had renamed for Philip of Macedon. During the war, which obliterated twelve New England towns and cost a great number of lives on both sides, Eliot, with the help of Daniel Gookin, strove with little success to protect his "praying Indians." King Philip's War, however, was becoming an effort to devastate not merely King Philip's armies, who had risen up to resist New England's expansion, but all the native Americans who seemed to stand in the way of the region's manifest destiny.

King Philip's War marked a watershed in several respects, not the least of them being the opening of divisions among New England's intellectual leadership that would persist and grow through the next century. Increase Mather and most of the clergy, who saw the war as one of the divine judgments predicted for a backsliding New England, attributed the eventual triumph of white arms to the practice of "owning the covenant" and thus testifying to the form, at least, of repentance. William Hubbard, however, in his history of the war, all but abandoned the providential view of history and explained New England's victories by its superior strength of mind and will. In 1677, on the occasion of the election of artillery company officers, Urian Oakes preached his celebrated sermon *The Sovereign Efficacy of Divine Providence*. His text was Ecclesiastes 9:11 ("the race is not to the swift, nor the battle to the strong"), and his doctrine—that the prime mover of all events is God, men being mere "second causes"—has often been termed the classic Puritan formulation of the doctrine of Providence. In Puritanism's classical age, however, the doctrine never had to be stated—so much was it taken for granted.

Though he spoke directly of the war, Oakes's larger purpose was to "check the confidence of men" in their own endeavors, which he had watched growing in all aspects of their worldly affairs. His sermon was, in effect, an archaic rejoinder to Hubbard, whose election sermon of the previous year had not been a jeremiad but an argument for a more tolerant response to Episcopacy and, above all, a hymn to order and hierarchy in the affairs of men, to the "dignity and power" of those of "the superior rank." Otherwise, Hubbard had asked, "might not the foolish and ignorant be like to lose themselves in the wilderness, if others were not as eyes to them." But even as the rays of an emerging rationalism shone forth from Hubbard's sermon—he turned to nature and its Chain of Being to argue against "parity" in "the rational and political world"—so too did the fires of Philip's War rekindle, in more than one respect, a piety far more intense than any pleaded for in the years when New England's mind was confined by the jeremiad and its notions of a "national covenant."

Perhaps the most popular piece of writing to emerge from King Philip's War—it was thrice printed in 1682, and it went through nearly a dozen editions in the eighteenth century and even more in the nineteenth—was *A Narrative of Captivity and Restoration* by Mary Rowlandson. This tale of Mrs. Rowlandson's wanderings and torments after she was taken captive by Indians in February 1676 served, along with John Williams' *The Redeemed Captive Returning to Zion* (1707) to inaugurate a genre that owed its appeal among later generations to its titillating melodrama. But the original point and purpose of Mrs. Rowlandson's *Narrative* was anything but entertainment or excitement. Hers is rather a tale of spiritual experience, of "trials and afflictions" that shattered her earlier complacency and brought her not only to a realization of God's "love and goodness" but to that taste sweeter than honey which multitudes, not only in New England but throughout America, were soon to long for.

The text is from the Lancaster Edition (Boston: Houghton Mifflin, 1930), pp. 5–9, 70–79.

The Sovereignty and Goodness of God A Narrative of Captivity and Restoration

. . . Now is the dreadful hour come, that I have often heard of (in time of war, as was the case with others) but now mine eyes see it. Some in our house were fighting for their lives, others wallowing in their blood, the house on fire over our heads, and the bloody heathen ready to knock us on the head if we stirred out. Now might we hear mothers and children crying out for themselves, and one another, *Lord, what shall we do?* Then I took my children (and one of my sisters hers) to go forth and leave the house: but as soon as we came to the door, and appeared, the Indians shot so thick, that the bullets rattled against the house, as if one had taken an handful of stones and threw them, so that we were fain to give back. We had six stout dogs belonging to our garrison, but none of them would stir, though [at] another time, if an Indian had come to the door, they were ready to fly upon him and tear him down. The Lord hereby would make us the more to acknowledge his hand, and to see that our help is always in him. But out we must go, the fire increasing, and coming along behind us, roaring, and the Indians gaping before us with their guns, spears, and hatchets, to devour us. No sooner were we out of the house, but my brother-in-law (being before wounded, in defending the house, in or near the throat) fell down dead, whereat the Indians scornfully shouted, and hallooed, and were presently upon him, stripping off his clothes. The bullets flying thick, one went through my side, and the same (as would seem) through the bowels and hand of my dear child in my arms. One of my elder sister's children, named William, had then his leg broken, which the Indians perceiving, they knocked him on the head. Thus were we butchered by those merciless heathens, standing amazed, with the blood running down to our heels. My elder sister being yet in the house, and seeing those woeful sights, the infidels hauling mothers one way, and children another, and some wallowing in their blood, and her eldest son telling her that her son William was dead, and myself was wounded, she said, And, *Lord let me die with them:* which was no sooner said, but she was struck with a bullet, and fell down dead over the threshold. I hope she is reaping the fruit of her good labors, being faithful to the service of God in her place. In her younger years she lay under much trouble upon spiritual accounts, till it pleased God to make that precious scripture take hold of her heart, II Corinthians 12:9, *And he said unto me, my grace is sufficient for thee.* More than twenty years after, I have heard her tell how sweet and comfortable that place was to her. But to return: the Indians laid hold of us, pulling me one way, and the children another, and said, "Come, go along with us." I told them they would kill me. They answered, if I were willing to go along with them, they would not hurt me . . .

I had often before this said, that if the Indians should come, I should choose rather to be killed by them, than taken alive; but when it came to the trial, my mind changed; their glittering weapons so daunted my spirit, that I chose rather to go along with those (as I may say) ravenous bears, than that moment to end my days. And that I may the better declare what happened to me during that grievous captivity, I shall particularly speak of the several removes we had up and down the wilderness . . .

When the Lord had brought his people to this, that they saw no help in anything but himself, then he takes the quarrel into his own hand, and though they [the Indians] had made a pit (in their own imaginations) as deep as hell for the Christians that summer, yet the Lord hurled themselves into it. And the Lord had not so many ways before to preserve them but now he hath as many to destroy them.

But to return again to my going home, where we may see a remarkable change of providence . . . In my travels an Indian came to me and told me if I were willing he and his squaw would run away and go home along with me. I told him no; I was not willing to run away but desired to wait God's time that I might go home quietly and without fear. And now God hath granted me my desire. O the wonderful power of God that I have seen and the experience that I have had. I have been in the midst of those roaring lions and savage bears that feared neither God nor man nor the devil, by night and day, alone and in company, sleeping all sorts together, and yet not one of them ever offered me the least abuse of unchastity to me in word or action. Though some are ready to say, I speak it for my own credit; but I speak it in the presence of God, and to his glory . . . So I took my leave of them and in coming along my heart melted into tears more than all the while I was with them and I was almost swallowed up with the thoughts that ever I should go home again. About the sun going down, Mr. Hoar and myself and the two Indians came to Lancaster and a solemn sight it was to me. There had I lived many comfortable years amongst my relations and neighbors, and now not one Christian to be seen nor one house left standing. We went on to a farm-house that was yet standing, where we lay all night; and a comfortable lodging we had, though nothing but straw to lie on. The Lord preserved us in safety that night and raised us up again in the morning and carried us along; thus before noon we came to Concord.

Now was I full of joy and yet not without sorrow; joy to see such a lovely sight, so many Christians together and some of my neighbors . . . Yet I was not without sorrow to think how many were looking and longing, and my own children among the rest, to enjoy that deliverance that I had now received, and I did not know whether ever I should see them again . . .

The twenty pounds, the price of my redemption, was raised by some Boston gentlemen, and Mr. Usher, whose bounty and religious charity, I would not forget to make mention of. Then Mr. Thomas Shepard of Charlestown received us into his house where we continued eleven weeks; and a father and mother they were to us. And many more tender-hearted friends we met with in that place. We were now in the midst of love, yet not without much and frequent heaviness of heart for our poor children and other relations who were still in affliction. The week following, after my coming in, the governor and the council sent forth to the Indians again, and that not without success, for they brought in my sister and good-wife Kettle. Their not knowing where our children were, was a sore trial to us still, and yet we were not without secret hopes that we should see them again. That which was dead lay heavier upon my spirit than those which were living and amongst the heathen, thinking how it suffered with its wounds and I was no way able to relieve it, and how it was buried by the heathens in the wilderness from among all Christians. We were hurried up and down in our thoughts, sometimes we should hear a report that they had gone this way, and sometimes that. We kept inquiring and listening to hear concerning them, but no certain news as yet. About this time the council had ordered a day of public thanksgiving, though I thought I still had cause for mourning, and being unsettled in our minds, we thought we would ride toward the eastward to see if we could hear anything concerning our children. And as we were riding along (God is the wise disposer of all things) between Ipswich and Rowley we met with Mr. William Hubbard who told us that our son Joseph was come in to Major Waldron's and another with him, which was my sister's son . . . Now hath God fulfilled that precious scripture which was such a comfort to me in my distressed condition. When my heart was ready to sink into the earth (my children being gone I could not tell whither) and my knees trembled under me, and I was walking *through the valley of the shadow of death,* then the Lord brought, and now has fulfilled, that reviving word unto me: Thus saith the Lord, *Refrain thy voice from weeping and thine eyes from tears, for thy work shall be rewarded, saith the Lord, and they shall come again from the land of the enemy . . .*

I can remember the time when I used to sleep quietly without working in my thoughts, whole nights together, but now it is otherwise with me.

When all are fast about me and no eye open but his who ever waketh, my thoughts are upon things past, upon the awful dispensation of the Lord towards us, upon his wonderful power and might in carrying us through so many difficulties, in returning us to safety and suffering none to hurt us. I remember in the night season, how the other day I was in the midst of thousands of enemies and nothing but death before me. It was then hard work to persuade myself that ever I should be satisfied with bread again. But now we are fed with the finest of the wheat, and (as I may say) with *honey out of the rock*.[1] Instead of the husk, we have the fatted calf.[2] The thoughts of these things in the particulars of them, and of the love and goodness of God towards us, make it true of me, what David said to himself, Psalm 6:5, *I watered my couch with my tears*. O the wonderful power of God that mine eyes have seen, affording matter enough for my thoughts to run in, that when others are sleeping mine eyes are weeping.

I have seen the extreme vanity of this world. One hour I have been in health, and wealth, wanting nothing, but the next hour in sickness, and wounds, and death, having nothing but sorrow and affliction.

Before I knew what affliction meant, I was ready sometimes to wish for it. When I lived in prosperity, having the comforts of the world about me, my relations by me, my heart cheerful, and taking little care for anything, and yet seeing many (whom I preferred before myself) under many trials and afflictions, in sickness, weakness, poverty, losses, crosses, and cares of the world, I should be sometimes jealous lest I should have my portion in this life, and that scripture would come to my mind, Hebrews 12:6, *For whom the Lord loveth he chasteneth, and scourgeth every son whom he receiveth*. But now I see the Lord had his time to scourge and chasten me. The portion of some is to have their affliction by drops, now one drop and then another, but the dregs of the cup, the wine of astonishment (like a sweeping rain that leaveth no food) did the Lord prepare to be my portion. Affliction I wanted, and affliction I had, full measure (I thought) pressed down and running over. Yet I see when God calls a person to anything, and through never so many difficulties, yet he is fully able to carry them through, and make them see and say they have been gainers thereby. And I hope I can say in some measure, as David did, *It is good for me that I have been afflicted*. The Lord hath showed me the vanity of these outward things; that they are the *Vanity of vanities, and vexation of spirit;* that they are but a shadow, a blast, a bubble, and things of no continuance; that we must rely on God himself,

1. Deuteronomy 32:13.
2. Luke 15:23.

and our whole dependence must be upon him. If trouble with smaller things begin to arise in me, I have something at hand to check myself with, and say, why am I troubled? It was but the other day that if I had had the world, I would have given it for my freedom, or to have been a servant to a Christian. I have learned to look beyond present and smaller troubles, and to be quieted under them, as Moses said, Exodus 14:13, *Stand still and see the salvation of the Lord.*

SOLOMON STODDARD (1634–1729)
The Safety of Appearing at the Day of Judgment (c. 1685)

MARY ROWLANDSON'S narrative of her redemption could be read—and probably was read—as an externalization of notions of redemption stretching back through Hooker and Ames at least to John Downame's *The Christian Warfare* (1605). Grace did not come suddenly or capriciously but only after the individual had been prepared and purged by trial and affliction. In this respect, the implicit doctrine of her narrative was novel only in its individualization of piety, since for years one message of the jeremiads had been that the afflictions witnessed on a degenerate New England might be intended by God as purgatives preparing the colony for future blessings. Hooker, after all, insisting before his Hartford congregation on the need for contrition and humiliation, had long before observed that "This was typified in the passage of the Children of Israel towards the Promised Land; they must come into and go through a vast and roaring wilderness; where they must be bruised with many pressures, humbled under many overbearing difficulties, they were to meet withal before they could possess that good land which abounded with all prosperity, flowed with milk and honey." It could be said that the jeremiad, as it poured forth from New England pulpits, was an application of Hooker's notion of preparation to New England as *history,* rather than as type. What distinguished Mary Rowlandson is that she went through her captivity "with her hands by her sides," a wholly passive recipient of God's mercy and grace, one whose spiritual victory derived not in the least from any active endeavor of her own.

Hooker's notion of "preparation," however embedded in the Harvard curriculum in Shepard's modified formulation, never wholly dominated the mind of seventeenth-century New England. But it was not openly challenged as counterproductive and psychologically absurd until more than a decade after Philip's War. Solomon Stoddard's *The Safety of Appearing at the Day of Judgment* is noteworthy for, among other things, its frontal assault on the doctrine of preparation. By 1687, however,

Stoddard was already notorious for ecclesiastical innovations he had instituted in his Northampton congregation, innovations that perhaps reflected his absence from New England during the critical years of the 1660s. Stoddard was the son of one of the wealthiest first-generation New England merchants and a niece of Governor Winthrop. He was graduated from Harvard in the year of the Half-Way Covenant synod and soon left for Barbados, where he preached for two years to dissenters. He returned to New England in 1669 with the thought of removing again to take up a nonconforming pulpit in England. Suddenly he was called to Northampton, however, to fill the pulpit vacated by the death of Eleazar Mather, whose widow Stoddard married in 1670.

Like his brother Increase, Eleazar Mather had opposed the Half-Way Covenant, but his congregation forced it upon him just a few months before his death. Then Stoddard, within five years of his arrival, took a further step, abolishing the distinction between "half-way" and "full" members, admitting all to the Lord's Supper. In his election sermon of 1677, Increase Mather took indirect notice of these "loose, large principles," and in the synod of 1679 he challenged Stoddard to public debate. The contest was halted without decision or vote, but the synod's "*Confession*" was reworded to call only for "a personal and public profession of faith," not the relation of a saving experience, for admission to the sacrament.

For twenty years—until the founding of Brattle Street Church on similar principles—this issue festered beneath the surface of New England's intellectual life. In 1700 Stoddard, in *The Doctrine of Instituted Churches,* proclaimed the Lord's Supper accessible to all: "it is not only for the strengthening of saints, but a means also to work saving regeneration." It may be that a new geographical mobility, especially on the frontier, had made the old distinctions and the professions of saving faith impossible to assess or perhaps, as in the 1630s, divisive in a community of migrants from all parts of New England. "Being morally sincere," Stoddard simply concluded, "makes a man a visible saint." Stoddard's ecclesiology, which appears to have owed more to Lutheran and other continental traditions than to the Presbyterianism with which it was identified at the time, was, however, not all that different in inspiration or in practice from that of Thomas Hooker. Like Hooker, who deemed all who had experienced the first inkling of preparation admissible to church membership, Stoddard seemed bent on bringing the entire community under his control.

Yet through all these changes Stoddard maintained a high Calvinism that might have troubled Hooker, one that had seldom been clearly spoken in New England for generations: "The only reason why God sets his love on one man and not upon another is, because he pleases." Out of his own anomalous experience outside New England, perhaps, or simply through his own knowledge of human nature (the infinite capacity of the human heart for self-deception, as his grandson was to phrase it), Stoddard was able in 1687 to utter the thought that had only been half-whispered since 1638: "preparation" is designed to humble men, but in fact, by focusing their eyes and thoughts on their own endeavors, it engorges their pride. His argument against preparation was an infinitely practical one; like all "those false doctrines that have been invented by men," it had proven totally ineffectual in bringing "souls to Christ." When Stoddard's grandson Jonathan Edwards entered on his inheritance, almost exactly a century after Winthrop had sketched out his hopes of a saintly New World, he assumed the pulpit of a congregation organized in ways that New England's fathers would have deemed scandalous. But he also inherited the doctrines of *The Safety of Appearing at the Day of Judgment*—a text that was usable and influential during the Great Awakening and that was reprinted well into the nineteenth century as *the* "evangelical tract" of New England's first century.

The text is from the 1804 edition, pp. 170–174, 343–347.

The Safety of Appearing at the Day of Judgment

Take these characters of those men that seek salvation by their own righteousness.

1. *Such men as magnify themselves by their duties and frames.* They count highly of themselves, because of what they do. *Pride* is the very spirit of self-righteousness. The self-righteous man sets a great price upon what he does: he loves to be thinking upon what he has done; how his heart melted in such a duty, how his affections were drawn out and enlarged in such a prayer, what he has done and suffered in the cause of God. He loves to chew over duties again, as things that do commend him to God: while another man is magnifying free grace, and the righteousness of Christ, the self-righteous man is idolizing his own services, falls in love with his own beauty; is taken with his own carriage, and thinks that God and man should be taken with him. He thinks his works do ingratiate him with God, and draw the heart of God towards him . . .

2 . . . A godly man makes his uprightness an argument to hope. The self-righteous man makes his duties the foundation of his faith; in a stormy time he gets under them for shelter, instead of getting under the shadow of Christ, he flies to his own duties; they are his castle, wherein

he fortifies himself against fear, they are his harbor, where he casts anchor; from thence he takes his great encouragement.

. . . The self-righteous man comforts up his heart with this, that surely God will have some respect unto his pains, his affections, his charity, his strict walking: this is his fort that he retires unto in time of danger. He has not been so bad as other men, and he hopes God will not deal in rigor with him. He thinks that his duties do lay some engagements upon the love and compassion of God; he hopes his prayers and tears have some constraining efficacy upon the compassionate heart of God.

Sometimes, he thinks that his duties lay some bonds upon the *justice* of God, he thinks it equal that he should be spared, and that it would be extreme rigor, for God to cast him off at last, when he has done so much for him. Sometimes he thinks his duties have laid a tie upon the *faithfulness* of God: God has made promises to them that seek, and he claims an interest in them: he makes his duties the stay of his soul, and when conscience is pursuing of him, he takes sanctuary here.

3. *Such men take their encouragement from their frames and duties to come to Christ.* Many self-righteous men do draw comfort from Christ, and they think they have their dependence on Christ; count themselves believers: but the comfort they draw from Christ is at the second-hand; their encouragement takes its first rise from some excellency in themselves . . .

[4]. *Such persons labor after some goodness to prepare them for Christ.* They are striving after some in order to their closing with Christ. When they are invited to come to Christ for salvation, they excuse themselves, and think they are not good enough yet to come to Christ. They think it would be presumption to come with such hearts as they have, they think nobody ever came to Christ that had such hearts; but they think if they were better they might come; and so they are laboring after some self-excellency, in order to their closing with Christ. They are purifying themselves, and garnishing themselves, that they may be fit to come to Christ. They think if their hearts were more broken, they might come. If they had more love to Christ, if they did see the real evil of sin; and so they make it their business to get these qualifications . . . So those men are striving against their dullness and hardness; they tug with their own hearts to make them better; for he thinks he must be better before he believes in Christ: whereas a saint, when he finds his heart bad, comes to Christ to make it better.

The next thing to be considered is what course Christians should take, that they may live a life of faith upon Christ's righteousness, and not be discouraged.

Direct. 1. *Diligently attend the ordinances of God unto that end.* The ordinances of God have a tendency to stir up faith, as well as other graces; and it is in that way that God has promised his presence and spirit. God delights to be found in ways appointed by himself . . . God's very prescribing of means is an encouragement unto us to attend upon them, especially when he has annexed his promise to the same. If men be remiss and slighty in attending upon God's ordinances, they are not likely to thrive in faith, or any other grace; it would be no wonder if they should wither away, and live in a dark discouraged condition: but, if Christians be careful to attend ordinances, and improve them for the strengthening of their faith, they are in a hopeful way to thrive . . . You never knew an eminent believer that was not a great prizer of ordinances; in this way, there is hope that faith will increase, therefore diligently attend them.

Particularly,

1. *Read the word of God diligently . . .*

2. *Frequently attend the preaching of the word.* That which God makes use of, especially for the begetting of faith, is very proper for the nourishing of it, Romans 10:17, *Faith cometh by hearing, and hearing by the word of God.* This is an ordinance, as well as the reading of the word. And there is a special usefulness in it several ways. The life and zeal that is in the delivery, is of special use, and a great means to affect the heart. In the preaching of the word, counsels and encouragements are directed more particularly unto them; and that by those that God has set over them, that must give an account of their souls, Acts 20:23. Yea, the very solemnity of the assembly, does help to solemnize the heart, and prepare it to receive what is spoken from the word of God . . .

3. *Attend the sacrament of the Lord's Supper.* The great design of this ordinance is for the strengthening of faith; therein is offered to us special communion with a crucified Savior. Therein is a sacramental representation made before us of the death of Christ. Therein is a special offer made unto us of the blood of Christ, for the remission of sins, Matthew 26:26–28. Herein the hearts of God's people have had peculiar establishment. Some, when in a discouraged condition, are backward to come to this ordinance. The devil has a great hand in it, to keep them from that which is the means of help. They are afraid that they "shall eat and drink judgment to themselves." But God nowhere requires a faith of assurance in those that partake of that ordinance. This ordinance is a special help to those that are in the dark . . .

FIVE

COMING OF AGE

"I SUPPOSE," wrote Perry Miller about the jeremiads of late seventeenth-century New England, "that in the whole literature of the world, including the satirists of imperial Rome, there is hardly such another uninhibited and unrelenting documentation of a people's descent into corruption." The jeremiad, of course, proceeded not only by lavish outrage but also with an exhortative hope for reform: much of the ministry, with Edward Taylor, was pleading that New England "Refine/ Thyselfe from thy Declentions. Tend thy line." In Taylor's case this was a specific language of horror at New England's betrayal of the founders' commitment to limit their churches to visible saints. One of the founders, John Davenport, lived long enough to have his say on the question, and expressed contempt for his successors:

> I shall conclude with a brief reminding you of the first beginning of the colony . . . which I have the better advantage and more special engagement to do, being one of them by whom the patent which you enjoy was procured . . . Churches also were gathered in a Congregational way, and walked therein, according to the rules of the gospel . . . Now therefore take heed and beware, that the Lord may not have just cause to complain of us . . . lest you lose by God's punishing justice, what you received from his free mercy.

The synod of 1679, led by Increase Mather, recorded its conclusion in the same spirit: "There is a great and visible decay of the power of godliness amongst many professors in these churches."

There were many reasons—apart from the ministers' estimate of her spiritual condition—for New England to suspect divine disfavor. King Philip's War, which broke out in 1675, remains proportionally the bloodiest war in American history; nearly one in ten of the male English colonists died before it was over. One November day toward the end of that war, Increase Mather preached on Revelation 3:3, "hold fast and repent," and within a few hours much of the city, including his own house, had burned to the ground. Two years later, something like fifteen percent of Boston's inhabitants contracted the smallpox; as many as seven hundred died and hundreds more were disfigured. And the calamities did not end with the seventies. By 1684 the charter was lost; soon thereafter a royal governor was installed, in Samuel Sewall's words, with "a Red-Coat going on his right hand."

And yet, when the colony had already encountered many of these disasters, the leaders of the synod of 1679 still ranked "the pride that doth abound in New England" high on the list of provoking sins. There is more here than a conventional inveighing against self-love—the times were dark, the wail of lamentation grown loud—and yet New England still presumed a primacy of place in the mind of God. It is upon this paradox that recent scholarship has focused. The jeremiad never lost its enabling premise of God's particular love for his New World children; the pain of their punishment was a measure of their intimacy with the Father who was meting it out. Every chastisement carried the hope, even perhaps the secret conviction, that reconciliation would someday come.

Ever since Alexis de Tocqueville declared that the "whole destiny of America is contained in the first Puritan who landed on these shores," a great deal of ink has been spilled in crediting—or blaming—the Puritans for much of what came later in our culture. This chain of attributions, which in the 1930s, for instance, was headed by such features of American life as prudery and prohibition, today tends to start with the idea of America's historical centrality—America's arrogance. There is no doubt that the jeremiad (which, after all, takes its name from Old Testament prophecy) did conserve the idea of America as a place of special concern to God. But there is often a touch of panic in New England's millenarian hopes: "I humbly crave leave to enter a claim," says Sewall, as he proposes Massachusetts as the site of the New Jerusalem, "that the New-World may no longer be made an Outcast." Again and again, the literature of New England in the later seventeenth century discloses a corrosive fear of exclusion. George Bancroft long ago identified such a fear of estrangement from the divine as the heart of the witchcraft hysteria: "The common mind of Massachusetts was . . . more ready to receive every tale from the invisible world, than to gaze on the universe without acknowledging an Infinite Intelligence." In New England's incessant transcription of God's voice of displeasure, there was a whispered fear of his imminent silence.

SAMUEL SEWALL (1652–1730)
Diary (1675–1727)

SAMUEL SEWALL, Chief Justice of Massachusetts for more than a decade and one of its leading landowners and merchants, was born in England in 1652. As "a poor little School-boy of Nine years and 1/4 old" he emigrated to Newbury, Massachusetts, where his grandfather had settled seventeen years before. There he was tutored by Thomas Parker, a disciple of William Ames, who sent him on to Harvard in 1667. After an M.A. thesis on original sin, the ministry seemed his likely vocation, but in the end he chose "merchandize." That choice was encouraged by his marriage to the daughter of the Boston mint-master, John Hull, who owned exclusive rights to the production of the colony's new currency and pocketed a fee of one in every twenty shillings that he minted. Nathaniel Hawthorne, in *Grandfather's Chair* (1840), imagined that Hull calculated the size of Hannah's dowry by standing her on one side of a great scale and hauling a chest full of silver on to the other until she was balanced. As the expectant groom watched, the lid was raised from the merchant's coffer, and the young Sewall "began to think that his father-in-law had got possession of all the money in the Massachusetts treasury." In Hawthorne's version, at least, Hannah was a hefty bride.

Sewall's now-comfortable life was passed in a rhythm of accumulation and philanthropy. A worldly, well-traveled man, he kept for most of his days an ingenuous diary that gives us the hum of colonial life as does no other document of its time. Through its pages one feels the burden of daily business and family cares. Of Sewall's fourteen children only six lived beyond childhood; only three longer than their father; among these were one cuckolded son and a daughter who suffered explosions of terror that she might be damned. Coping with difficult parenthood, a failing wife, and competing demands for his allegiance from various political and religious factions, Sewall looked to his faith to brace and guide him. As a young man fresh out of college he was "extremely tormented" at the prospect of joining the South Church, apparently because its minister,

Samuel Willard, had diluted the stringencies of the founders: one could, for example, submit one's profession of faith in writing to the church elders. Sewall took religion seriously, and such innovations always troubled him, as did other affronts—from the use of pagan names for the days of the week and names of the months, to the wearing of wigs. He was shocked by the behavior of Quakers, and grimly resigned to the infiltration of Anglicans into Puritan Massachusetts. For much of his life he dabbled in eschatological speculation, nursing a hope that the millennium would begin in New England. With this hope in mind, he was a great promoter of John Eliot's and Thomas Thorowgood's conviction that the Indians were of Jewish origin and that their conversion would be a step toward Christ's second coming.

The *Diary* is in some respects a unique record of a functioning Puritan faith. It coaxes a pious moral out of every circumstance—not just major private or public events such as the death of his wife or the fall of Andros (the unpopular royal governor deposed and imprisoned in the revolt of 1689), but also from a leak in his chamberpot, or a child's ball clogging his gutter. Despite such scrupulous "improvement" of every event, Sewall was finally relaxed on matters of doctrine, and so could move as a kind of genial ambassador between mutually hostile parties—we find him dining, on consecutive evenings, with the Mathers, with Benjamin Colman, with Stoddard. Yet he was more than a follower. In 1700 he published *The Selling of Joseph,* one of the first antislavery tracts written in America. He was captain of the Ancient and Honorable Artillery Company, overseer of Harvard, member of the governor's council, and member of the court of oyer and terminer that hanged nineteen witches in 1692. The *Diary* is relatively spare on the subject of witchcraft, though it does include the famous statement of contrition that Sewall posted on his meeting-house door in 1697. He stood at his pew while his minister read the statement aloud. With head bowed under his own accusation, Judge Sewall was a figure of fallible decency for all of New England. Through the *Diary,* he remains immensely human for us.

Diary

July 31 [1675], at midnight, Tho. Wood, Carpenter of Rowly, had his house and goods burnt, and, *væ malum,*[1] a daughter of about

1. O misfortune.

10 years of age, who directed her brother so that he got out, was herself consumed to ashes.

Novem. 27, 1676, about 5 M. Boston's greatest Fire brake forth at Mr. Moors, through the default of a Taylour Boy, who rising alone and early to work, fell asleep and let his Light fire the House, which gave fire to the next, so that about fifty Landlords were despoyled of their Housing. *N.B.* The House of the Man of God, Mr. Mather, and Gods House were burnt with fire. Yet God mingled mercy, and sent a considerable rain, which gave check in great measure to the (otherwise) masterless flames: lasted all the time of the fire, though fair before and after. Mr. Mather saved his Books and other Goods.

Jan. 13, 1677. Giving my chickens meat, it came to my mind that I gave them nothing save Indian corn and water, and yet they eat it and thrived very well, and that that food was necessary for them, how mean soever, which much affected me and convinced what need I stood in of spiritual food, and that I should not nauseat daily duties of Prayer, &c.

March 21, [*1677*], since I had thoughts of joining to the Church, I have been exceedingly tormented in my mind, sometimes lest the Third church [the South] should not be in God's way in breaking off from the old . . . yet through importunity of friends, and hope that God might communicate himself to me in the ordinance, and because of my child (then hoped for) its being baptised, I offered myself, and was not refused. Besides what I had written, when I was speaking [about admission to the church] I resolved to confess what a great Sinner I had been, but going on in the method of the Paper, it came not to my mind. And now the Scruple of the Church vanished, and I began to be more afraid of myself.

July 8, 1677. New Meeting House. In Sermon time there came in a female Quaker, in a Canvas Frock, her hair disshevelled and loose like a Periwigg, her face as black as ink, led by two other Quakers, and two other followed. It occasioned the greatest and most amazing uproar that I ever saw.

Satterday, Jan^{y} *2*^{d} [*1686*]. Last night had a very unusual Dream; *viz.* That our Saviour in the dayes of his Flesh when upon Earth, came to Boston and abode here sometime, and moreover that He Lodged in that time at Father Hull's; upon which in my Dream had two Reflections,

One was how much more Boston had to say than Rome boasting of Peter's being there. The other a sense of great Respect that I ought to have shewed Father Hull since Christ chose when in Town, to take up His Quarters at his House. Admired the goodness and Wisdom of Christ in coming hither and spending some part of His short Life here. The Chronological absurdity never came into my mind, as I remember.

Sabbath, Jan^r 24 [*1686*]. This day so cold that the Sacramental Bread is frozen pretty hard, and rattles sadly as broken into the Plates.

Sabbath, Febr. 7th, 1686. Mr. Moodey preached from Isaiah 12:1 beginning upon that Scripture this day—In that day thou shalt say, &c. Shewing that 'twas chiefly a Directory of Thanksgiving for the Conversion of the Jews; and that should get our Praises ready before hand.

Friday, May 14 [*1686*]. The Rose-Frigot arrives at Nantasket, Mr. Randolph up at Town about 8 *mane:* takes Coach for Roxbury: Major Pynchon and Mr. Stoughton are sent to the Magistrates to acquaint them with the King's Commands being come . . .[2]

Monday, May 17th 1686. Generall Court Sits at One aclock, I goe thither, about 3. The Old Government draws to the North-side, Mr. Addington, Capt. Smith and I sit at the Table, there not being room: Major Dudley the Præsident, Major Pynchon, Capt. Gedney, Mr. Mason, Randolph, Capt. Winthrop, Mr. Wharton come in on the Left . . . the Room pretty well filled with Spectators in an Instant. Major Dudley made a Speech, that was sorry could treat them no longer as Governour and Company; Produced the Exemplification of the Charter's Condemnation, the Commission under the Broad-Seal of England—both: Letter of the Lords, Commission of Admiralty, openly exhibiting them to the People; when had done, Deputy Governour said suppos'd they expected not the Court's Answer now; which the Præsident took up and said they could not acknowledge them as such, and could no way capitulate with them, to which I think no Reply. When gone, Major Generall, Major Richards, Mr. Russell and Self spake our minds. I chose to say after the Major Generall, adding that the foundations being destroyed what can the Righteous do: speaking against a Protest; which some spake for.

2. Randolph had made his first visit to Massachusetts on a mission of inquiry for Charles II in 1676, reporting that the "Bostoners have no right either to land or government in any part of New England, but are usurpers," and that "they have protected the murtherers of your royal father."

Friday, Augt. 20 [*1686*]. I was and am in great exercise about the Cross to be put into the Colours, and afraid if I should have a hand in 't whether it may not hinder my Entrance into the Holy Land.[3]

Monday, Augt. 23 [*1686*]. At even I wait on the President and shew him that I cannot hold because of the Cross now to be introduc'd, and offer'd him my Commission, which he refus'd, said would not take it but in Council. Receiv'd me very candidly, and told me we might expect Sir Edmund Andros, our Governour, here within six weeks . . .

Sabbath, 26th [*February 1688*]. I sit down with the Church of Newbury at the Lord's Table. The Songs of the 5th of the Revelation were sung. I was ready to burst into tears at that word, *bought with thy blood.* Me thoughts 'twas strange that Christ should *cheapen* us; but that when the bargain came to be driven, he should consent rather to part with his *blood,* than goe without us; 'twas amazing.

Thorsday, May 3 [*1688*]. Fast at the old Church and several other Churches for Rain.

Friday, May 4th 1688. Last night there was a very refreshing Rain; this 4th May, a Print comes out shewing the Lawfullness of Swearing according to the English mode, Laying the hand on the Bible.

Feb. 8 and 9th [*1690*]. Schenectady, a village 20 miles above Albany, destroy'd by the French. 60 Men, Women and Children murder'd. Women with Child rip'd up, Children had their Brains dash'd out. Were surpris'd about 11. or 12 aclock Satterday night, being divided, and secure.[4]

March 19, 1691. Mr. C. Mather preaches the Lecture from Matthew 24, and appoint his portion with the Hypocrites: In his proem said, *Totus mundus agit histrionem.*[5] Said one sign of a hypocrit was for a man to strain at a Gnat and swallow a Camel. Sign in's Throat discovered him; To be zealous against an innocent fashion, taken up and used by the best of men; and yet make no Conscience of being guilty of great

3. Sewall considered it idolatry to display the cross—especially in the flag symbolizing civil authority.

4. English and French traders and fishermen had been fighting sporadically for years from the Great Lakes region to Newfoundland. Upon the accession of William III in 1689 the war intensified and became a matter of English policy.

5. The whole world's a stage.

Immoralities. Tis supposed means wearing of Perriwigs: said would deny themselves in any thing but parting with an opportunity to do God service; that so might not offend good Christians. Meaning, I suppose, was fain to wear a Perriwig for his health. I expected not to hear a vindication of Perriwigs in Boston Pulpit by Mr. Mather; however, not from that Text. The Lord give me a good Heart and help to know, and not only to know but also to doe his Will; that my Heart and Head may be his.

Tuesday, Jan. 26, 1692. News comes to Town by Robin Orchard, of Dolberry's being arrived at Cape Cod; Sir William Phips made Governour of the Province of New England.

April 11th 1692. Went to Salem, where, in the Meeting-house, the persons accused of Witchcraft were examined; was a very great Assembly; 'twas awfull to see how the afflicted persons were agitated. Mr. Noyes pray'd at the beginning, and Mr. Higginson concluded. [In the margin], Væ, Væ, Væ, Witchcraft.[6]

Augt. 19th, 1692. This day [in the margin, Dolefull! Witchcraft] George Burrough, John Willard, Jno Procter, Martha Carrier and George Jacobs were executed at Salem, a very great number of Spectators being present. Mr. Cotton Mather was there, Mr. Sims, Hale, Noyes, Chiever, &c. All of them said they were innocent, Carrier and all. Mr. Mather says they all died by a Righteous Sentence. Mr. Burrough by his Speech, Prayer, protestation of his Innocence, did much move unthinking persons, which occasions their speaking hardly concerning his being executed.

Augt. 25 [1692]. Fast at the old [First] Church, respecting the Witchcraft, Drought, &c.

Monday, Sept. 19, 1692. About noon, at Salem, Giles Corey was press'd to death for standing Mute; much pains was used with him two days, one after another, by the Court and Capt. Gardner of Nantucket who had been of his acquaintance: but all in vain.[7]

6. Nicholas Noyes was an ardent prosecutor of witches, who later repented his actions. John Higginson was now an elder statesmen of the New England ministry; he held aloof from the witchcraft trials, his own daughter being one of the accused.

7. Giles Corey was the only person accused of witchcraft who flatly refused to answer the indictment. He could not, therefore, be legally tried—but he could be, and was, tortured by being pressed to death with stones in an effort to force a confession. He may have made his choice in order to protect his heirs from having their inherited property sequestered, a common practice toward capital offenders.

Sept. 20 [1692]. Now I hear from Salem that about 18 years agoe, he [Corey] was suspected to have stampd and press'd a man to death, but was cleared. Twas not remembered till Anne Putnam was told of it by said Corey's Spectre the Sabbath-day night before Execution.

Oct. 26, 1692. A Bill is sent in about calling a Fast, and Convocation of Ministers, that may be led in the right way as to the Witchcrafts. The season and manner of doing it, is such, that the Court of Oyer and Terminer count themselves thereby dismissed.

Wednesday, March, 22, 1693. Our kitchen chimney fell on fire about noon, and blaz'd out sorely at top, appeared to be very foul: the fire fell on the shingles so that they begun to burn in several places being very dry: but by the good Providence of God, no harm done. Mr. Fisk was with us, and we sat merrily to dinner on the Westfield Pork that was snatch'd from the fire on this Occasion.

Monday, April 29, 1695. Mr. Willard, &c. Mr. Cotton Mather dined with us, and was with me in the new Kitchen when this was; He had just been mentioning that more Ministers Houses than others proportionably had been smitten with Lightening; enquiring what the meaning of God should be in it. Many Hail-Stones broke throw the Glass and flew to the middle of the Room, or farther: People afterward Gazed upon the House to see its Ruins. I got Mr. Mather to pray with us after this awfull Providence; He told God He had broken the brittle part of our house, and prayd that we might be ready for the time when our Clay-Tabernacles should be broken.

Jan. 13, 1696. When I came in, past 7. at night, my wife met me in the Entry and told me Betty had surprised them. I was surprised with the abruptness of the Relation. It seems Betty Sewall had given some signs of dejection and sorrow; but a little after dinner she burst out into an amazing cry, which caus'd all the family to cry too: Her Mother ask'd the reason; she gave none; at last said she was afraid she should goe to Hell, her Sins were not pardon'd. She was first wounded by my reading a Sermon of Mr. Norton's, about the 5th of Jan. Text John 7:34, Ye shall seek me and shall not find me. And those words in the Sermon, John 8:21, Ye shall seek me and shall die in your sins, ran in her mind, and terrified her greatly. And staying at home Jan. 12 she read out of Mr. Cotton Mather—Why hath Satan filled thy heart, which increas'd her Fear. Her Mother ask'd her whether she pray'd. She answer'd, Yes; but feared her prayers were not heard because her Sins not pardon'd.

Sabbath, May 3, 1696. Betty can hardly read her chapter for weeping; tells me she is afraid she is gon back, does not taste that sweetness in reading the Word which once she did; fears that what was once upon her is worn off. I said what I could to her, and in the evening pray'd with her alone.

Fourth-day Augt 12, 1696. Mr. Melyen, upon a slight occasion, spoke to me very smartly about the Salem Witchcraft: in discourse he said, if a man should take Beacon hill on's back, carry it away; and then bring it and set it in its place again, he should not make any thing of that.

Jany 15 [*1697*]. Copy of the Bill I put up on the Fast day; giving it to Mr. Willard as he pass'd by, and standing up at the reading of it, and bowing when finished; in the Afternoon.

Samuel Sewall, sensible of the reiterated strokes of God upon himself and family; and being sensible, that as to the Guilt contracted, upon the opening of the late Commission of Oyer and Terminer at Salem (to which the order for this Day relates) he is, upon many accounts, more concerned than any that he knows of, Desires to take the Blame and Shame of it, Asking pardon of Men, And especially desiring prayers that God, who has an Unlimited Authority, would pardon that Sin and all other his Sins; personal and Relative: And according to his infinite Benignity, and Soveraignty, Not Visit the Sin of him, or of any other, upon himself or any of his, nor upon the Land: But that He would powerfully defend him against all Temptations to Sin, for the future; and vouchsafe him the Efficacious, Saving Conduct of his Word and Spirit.

Decr 9 [*1699*]. Mr. Colman visits me: I Expostulat with him about the 3^{d} Article in the Manifesto,[8] that had shew'd no more Respect to N.E. Churches. I told him Christ was a Bride-Groom, and He lov'd to have his Bride commended.

Dec^{r}21. 1699 Went to lecture, wearing my black cap.

Fourth-day, June, 19. 1700. Having been long and much dissatisfied with the Trade of fetching Negros from Guinea; at last I had a strong Inclination to Write something about it; but it wore off. At last reading Bayne, Ephesians about servants, who mentions Blackamoors; I

8. The third article of the *Manifesto* of the Brattle Street Church. See the headnote to Benjamin Colman's *The Parable of the Ten Virgins.*

began to be uneasy that I had so long neglected doing any thing.[9] When I was thus thinking, in came Bro^r Belknap to shew me a Petition he intended to present to the Genl Court for the freeing a Negro and his wife, who were unjustly held in Bondage. And there is a Motion by a Boston Committee to get a Law that all Importers of Negros shall pay 40^s *per* head, to discourage the bringing of them. And Mr. C. Mather resolves to publish a sheet to exhort Masters to labour their Conversion. Which makes me hope that I was call'd of God to Write this Apology for them; Let his Blessing accompany the same.

Jany 1. 1701. Just about Break-a-day Jacob Amsden and 3 other Trumpeters gave a Blast with the Trumpets on the common near Mr. Alford's [in margin: Entrance of the *18*^th Century]. Then went to the Green Chamber, and sounded there till about sunrise. Bellman said these verses a little before Break-a-day, which I printed and gave them. [In margin: My Verses upon New Century.]

Once more! our God vouchsafe to shine:
Correct the Coldness of our Clime.
Make haste with thy Impartial Light,
And terminate this long dark night.

Give the poor Indians Eyes to see
The Light of Life: and set them free.
So Men shall God in Christ adore,
And worship Idols vain, no more.

So Asia, and Africa,
Eurôpa, with America;
All Four, in Consort join'd, shall Sing
New Songs of Praise to Christ our King.

The Trumpeters cost me five pieces 8/8.

Octr 20 [1701]. Mr. Cotton Mather came to Mr. Wilkins's shop, and there talked very sharply against me as if I had used his father worse than a Neger; spake so loud that people in the street might hear him. Then went and told Sam, That one pleaded much for Negros, and he

9. Paul Baynes, *A Commentarie upon . . . Ephesians* (1618). Ephesians 6:5 has long been invoked by Christian apologists for slavery: "Servants, be obedient to them that are your masters according to the flesh, with fear and trembling, in singleness of heart."

had used his father worse than a Negro, and told him that was his Father.[10]

Octr 9 [*1701*]. I sent Mr. Increase Mather a Hanch of very good Venison; I hope in that I did not treat him as a Negro.

April, 24. 1704. I went to Cambridge to see some Books on the Revelation . . .

Decr 1 [*1705*]. Deputies send in a Bill against fornication, or Marriage of White men with Negros or Indians; with extraordinary penalties; directing the Secretary to draw a Bill accordingly. If it be pass'd, I fear twill be an Oppression provoking to God, and that which will promote Murders and other Abominations. I have got the Indians out of the Bill, and some mitigation for them [the Negroes] left in it, and the clause about their Masters not denying their Marriage.

Jany 12 [*1706*]. Capt. Belchar appears at Council in his new Wigg: Said he needed more than his own Hair for his Journey to Portsmouth; and other provision was not suitable for a Wedding. *Jany 13*^th^ appears at Meeting in his Wigg. He had a good Head of Hair, though twas grown a little thin.

*March, 27th* [*1706*]. I walk in the Meetinghouse. Set out homeward, lodg'd at Cushing's. *Note.* I pray'd not with my Servant, being weary. Seeing no Chamber-pot call'd for one; A little before day I us'd it in the Bed, and the bottom came out, and all the water run upon me. I was amaz'd, not knowing the bottom was out till I felt it in the Bed. The Trouble and Disgrace of it did afflict me. As soon as it was Light, I calld up my man and he made a fire and warm'd me a clean Shirt and I put it on, and was comfortable. How unexpectedly a man may be expos'd! There's no security but in God, who is to be sought by Prayer.

*Jany 26th* [*1707*]. I dream'd last night that I was chosen Lord Maior of London; which much perplex'd me; a strange absurd Dream!

[*Sept. 8, 1708*]. I look'd out at our South-east Window, and fear'd that our Warehouse was a-fire: But it proves a smith's shop, Hubbard's by Mr. Dafforn's, and a Boat-builders Shed: 'Tis thought a Hundred

10. See the headnote to Cotton Mather's General Introduction to the *Magnalia Christi Americana.*

pounds Damage is done. Blessed be GOD it stop'd there. Mr. Pemberton's Maid saw the Light of the Fire reflecting from a Black Cloud, and came crying to him under Consternation; supposing the last Conflagration had begun.

This day, Midweek, Febr. 27 [1712]. Joseph Bailey of Newbury, introduc'd by Mr. Myles, Mr. Harris, and Mr. Bridger, Presented a Petition to the Govr, sign'd by Abraham Merrill, Joshua Brown. Sam Bartlett, John Bartlet, Sam. Sawyer, Joseph Bayley &c., 22. in all, declaring that they were of the pure Episcopal Church of England, would no longer persist with their mistaken dissenting Brethren in the Separation; had sent to their Diocesan, the Bp. of London, for a Minister, and desired Protection.

Fifth-day, Febr. 28 [1712]. Great Storm of Rain: This day the Govr Dates his Letter to the Episcopal church of Newbury. At night the Rain falls vehemently with Thunder and Lightening.

Octob^r^ 16. 1713. I went to see the portentous Birth; it seems to be two fine Girls to whom an unhappy Union has been fatal. The Heads and Necks, as low as a Line drawn from the Arm-pits, are distinct. A little below the Navel, downward again distinct, with distinct Arms and Legs; Four of each. I measured across the perfect Union about the Hips and found it to hold about eight Inches. Oh the Mercies of my Birth, and of the Birth of Mine! *Laus Deo!*[11] Dr. Cotton Mather introduc'd me and Mr. John Winthrop to this rare and awfull Sight.

Octob^r^ 20 [1713]. He [Mr. Winslow of Marshfield] appears with a Flaxen Wigg, I was griev'd to see it, he had so comly a head of black Hair.

Octob^r^ 25 [1713]. In the Night after 12. Susan comes, and knocks at our chamber door, said she could not sleep, was afraid she should dye. Which amaz'd my wife and me. We let her in, blew up the Fire, wrapt her warm, and went to bed again. She sat there till near day, and then return'd; and was well in the morning. *Laus Deo.* I was the more startled because I had spilt a whole Vinyard Cann of water just before we went to Bed: and made that Reflection that our Lives would shortly be spilt.

11. Praise be to God.

July, 6 [*1715*]. This day it is Fifty four years Since I first was brought ashoar to Boston near where Scarlet's wharf now is, July, 6, 1661, Lord's Day. The Lord help me to Redeem the Time which passes so swiftly. I was then a poor little School-boy of Nine years and 1/4 old.

Febr. 16 [*1716*]. Dr. C. Mather preaches Excellently from James 2:5. Poor of this world, rich in Faith. Doctrine, Grace has a Lustre as well in the meanest, as greatest.

I essay'd *June, 22* [*1716*], to prevent Indians and Negros being Rated with Horses and Hogs; but could not prevail. Col. Thaxter brought it back, and gave as a reason of the Non-agreement, They were just going to make a New Valuation.

[*October*] *15* [*1717*]. My Wife got some Relapse by a new Cold and grew very bad; Sent for Mr. Oakes, and he sat up with me all night.

[*October*] *16* [*1717*]. The Distemper increases; yet my Wife speaks to me to goe to Bed.

7th day, [*October*] *19* [*1717*]. Call'd Dr. C. Mather to pray, which he did excellently in the Dining Room, having Suggested good Thoughts to my wife before he went down. After, Mr. Wadsworth pray'd in the Chamber when 'twas suppos'd my wife took little notice. About a quarter of an hour past four, my dear Wife expired in the Afternoon, whereby the Chamber was fill'd with a Flood of Tears. God is teaching me a new Lesson; to live a Widower's Life. Lord help me to Learn; and be a Sun and Shield to me, now so much of my Comfort and Defense are taken away.

Novr 7.5 [*1717*]. Last night died the Excellent Waitstill Winthrop esqr., for Parentage, Piety, Prudence, Philosophy, Love to New England Ways and people very Eminent.

Decr 2 [*1717*]. Serene and Cold. Dr. Cotton Mather dines with us. I visit Madam Winthrop at her own House . . .

Febr. 6 [*1718*]. This morning wandering in my mind whether to live a Single or a Married Life; I had a sweet and very affectionat Meditation Concerning the Lord Jesus; Nothing was to be objected against his Person, Parentage, Relations, Estate, House, Home! Why did I not resolutely, presently close with Him! And I cry'd mightily to God that He would help me so to doe!

[*October*] *10th* [*1720*]. In the Evening I visited Madam Winthrop, who treated me with a great deal of Curtesy; Wine, Marmalade.

[*October*] *12.* [*1720*]. Mrs. Anne Cotton came to door (twas before 8.) said Madam Winthrop was within, directed me into the little Room, where she was full of work behind a Stand; Mrs. Cotton came in and stood. Madam Winthrop pointed to her to set me a Chair. Madam Winthrop's Countenance was much changed from what 'twas on Monday, look'd dark and lowering. At last, the work, (black stuff or Silk) was taken away, I got my Chair in place, had some Converse, but very Cold and indifferent to what 'twas before. Ask'd her to acquit me of Rudeness if I drew off her Glove. Enquiring the reason, I told her twas great odds between handling a dead Goat, and a living Lady. Got it off.

[*October*] *15* [*1720*]. I dine on Fish and Oyle at Mr. Stoddard's. Capt. Hill wish'd me Joy of my proceedings i.e. with M[adam]Winthrop; Sister Cooper applauded it, spake of Visiting her.

[*October*] *20* [*1720*]. At Council, Col. Townsend spake to me of my Hood:[12] Should get a Wigg. I said twas my chief Ornament: I wore it for sake of the Day.

Jany 10 [*1722*]. Overseers of the College, their Meeting at the Council Chamber, to consider of Mr. Hollis's Proposals as to his Professour of Divinity. Debate was had in the fore-noon about that Article, "He shall be a Master of Art, and in Communion with a Church of Congregational, Presbyterian, or Baptists." I objected against it, as chusing rather to lose the Donation than to Accept it. In the Afternoon I finally said, One great end for which the first Planters came over into New England, was to fly from the Cross in Baptisme.[13]

For my part, I had rather have Baptisme administered with the incumbrance of the Cross, than not to have it Administered at all.

This Qualification of the Divinity Professour, is to me, a Bribe to give my Sentence in Disparagement of Infant Baptisme: and I will endeavour to shake my hands from holding it.

12. Sewall was known for wearing a black hood instead of the usual wig.

13. Sewall's objection is to the latitude of these qualifications, which could be met by a Baptist or a Presbyterian.

When it came to the Vote, but very few appear'd in the Negative. I desired to have my Dissent enter'd. The Governour deny'd it with an Air of Displeasure, saying, You *shânt* have it!

Monday, Augt 2 [1725]. Mrs. Katherine Winthrop, Relict of the hon^{ble} Waitstill Winthrop esqr., died, *Ætatis* 61. She was born in September 1664. The Escutcheons on the Hearse bore the Arms of Winthrop and Brattle, The Lion Sable. *Aug^{t}* 5. 1725. Bearers, His Hon^{r} Lt Govr Dummer, Saml Sewall; Col. Byfield, Edw. Bromfield esqr; Simeon Stoddard esqr., Adam Winthrop esqr. Was buried in the South-burying place, in a Tomb near the North-east Corner. Will be much miss'd.

SAMUEL SEWALL

Phaenomena quaedam Apocalyptica (1697)

As early as 1684, Sewall was gathering evidence from scripture and from recent historical events to support his growing conviction that "the heart of America may . . . be the seat of the New Jerusalem." In a number of letters to the Mathers and to his old friend Edward Taylor, he took excited note of such disasters in Spanish America as the Lima earthquake of 1687—and proposed that the prophecy of Revelation 16:12, "the angel poured out his vial upon the great river Euphrates; and the water thereof was dried up," was being fulfilled in the American hemisphere as a prelude to the reign of the saints. Most of those whom he tried to persuade remained skeptical; thus in 1697 Sewall published his *Phaenomena quaedam Apocalyptica* (phenomena concerning the apocalypse) to reiterate and detail his belief in both the temporal and geographical nearness of the millennium.

The *Phaenomena* contains a famous passage on the beauty of Plum Island that has long been read as one of American literature's earliest effusions of love for the breathtaking land. And so it is. But it is also a metaphoric plea for maintenance of the congregational way—"as long as any free and harmless doves . . . shall voluntarily present themselves to perform the office of gleaners . . . as long as nature . . . shall constantly remember to give the rows of Indian corn their education, by pairs . . ." Even as Sewall turned the fact of America's provincial isolation into a vision of solitary majesty, he cautioned his fellow New Englanders that they would have to conserve their heritage if they wished to earn their destiny.

The text of the *Phaenomena quaedam Apocalyptica* is from the edition of 1727, pp. 1, 63.

Phaenomena quaedam Apocalyptica Some Few Lines towards a Description of the New Heaven

Not to begin to be, and so not to be limited by the concernments of time and place, is the prerogative of God alone. But as it is the privilege of creatures that God has given them a beginning, so to deny their actions or them the respect they bear to place and successive duration is, under a pretense of promotion, to take away their very being. Yet notwithstanding, some things have had this to glory of: that they have been time out of mind, and their continuance refuses to be measured by the memory of man. Whereas New England and Boston of the Massachusetts have this to make mention of—that they can tell their age, and account it their honor to have their birth and parentage kept in everlasting remembrance. And in very deed, the families and churches which first ventured to follow Christ through the Atlantic Ocean into a strange land full of wild men were so religious, their end so holy, their self-denial in pursuing of it so extraordinary, that I can't but hope that the plantation has thereby gained a very strong crasis;[1] and that it will not be one, or two, or three centuries only, but by the grace of God it will be very long lasting. Some who peremptorily conclude that Asia must afford situation for New Jerusalem, are of the mind [that] when that divine city comes to be built, the commodities of it will be so inviting as will drain disconsolate America of all its Christian inhabitants, as not able to brook so remote a distance from the beloved city. But if Asia should be again thus highly favored, and the eldest daughter be still made the darling, yet 'tis known there will be a river, the streams whereof shall make glad the city of God (Psalms 46:4). The correspondence and commerce of the little cities and villages in the three kingdoms[2] and plantations do make London glad. And so it will be with New Jerusalem: *The nations of them which are saved, shall walk in the light of it: and the kings of the earth do bring their glory and honor into it* (Revelation 21:24) . . .

As long as Plum Island shall faithfully keep the commanded post, notwithstanding all the hectoring words and hard blows of the proud and boisterous ocean; as long as any salmon or sturgeon shall swim in the streams of Merrimack; or any perch or pickerel in Crane Pond; as long as the sea-fowl shall know the time of their coming, and not neglect

1. Bodily constitution.
2. That is, England, Scotland, Ireland.

seasonably to visit the places of their acquaintance; as long as any cattle shall be fed with the grass growing in the meadows, which do humbly bow down themselves before Turkey Hill; as long as any sheep shall walk upon Old Town Hills, and shall from thence pleasantly look down upon the River Parker, and the fruitful marshes lying beneath; as long as any free and harmless doves shall find a white oak or other tree within the township, to perch, or feed, or build a careless nest upon, and shall voluntarily present themselves to perform the office of gleaners after barley harvest; as long as nature shall not grow old and dote,[3] but shall constantly remember to give the rows of Indian corn their education, by pairs: So long shall Christians be born there; and being first made meet, shall from thence be translated, to be made partakers of the inheritance of the saints in light.

3. Senile.

EDWARD TAYLOR (1642–1729)
Poems (c. 1680–1725)

IN 1937 THOMAS H. JOHNSON made a discovery in the library of Yale University that dealt the final blow to the idea that New England Puritanism was incompatible with poetic art. What Johnson found was a manuscript that had gone unnoticed for fifty years since being donated to Yale by a descendant of Edward Taylor, a seventeenth-century minister in Westfield, Connecticut (now Massachusetts). As the tightly written pages of that book were deciphered and appeared in print, American poetry gained a major artist, to whom we cannot attribute the scholar's favorite virtue—influence—since only a very few of Taylor's verses were printed before this century, but who now stands beside Anne Bradstreet as the earliest American poets of distinctive voice.

Taylor ministered to the frontier village of Westfield from 1671 until his death at the age of eighty-seven in 1729. Over the course of this long service he composed a series of poems he called "Preparatory Meditations before my approach to the Lord's Supper," apparently private meditations on scriptural texts that often provided the basis for the sermon he was about to deliver at the celebration of the sacrament. "I shall not be ashamed to acknowledge," Calvin himself had written about the presence of Christ at the communion supper, "that it is a mystery too sublime for me to be able to express." Although Puritan doctrine had thoroughly banished the Catholic idea of transubstantiation, the sharing of the bread and wine remained an act of high devotion—the holy remembrance of Christ's blessing his disciples at the Last Supper, and thereby the seal of the covenant of grace into which God had summoned his regenerate human children. Breaking the bread and passing the wine at communion was, to Edward Taylor, a rite of high exclusiveness as well as solemnity; especially because after 1662 baptism was no longer even nominally a seal of the covenant. Since the earliest days of New England congregationalism, communion had been a vivid reminder of the division between participants and observers that obtained even within the meetinghouse;

Thomas Lechford, an unsympathetic observer of Puritan practice, described in the 1630s how the elect gathered to receive the sacrament, "all others departing." Like his predecessors, Taylor wished to bring to the Lord's Supper only the fittest participants and the holiest frame of mind. "Not to prepare," he explained, "is a contempt of the invitation."

For decades it was believed that this public guardian of the old Puritan standards left an explicit prohibition against publishing his poetry—a legend that fit well with the notion that he was a heterodox sensualist, under whose official sternness burned a private fire. Both ideas have been pretty well disposed of by recent scholarship, and Taylor has emerged, perhaps through some degree of scholarly overcompensation, as an orthodox Puritan, in particular as a champion of the old way against what Increase Mather called the "loose, large principles" of Solomon Stoddard. In fact, like many of his contemporaries, Taylor took his sensory satisfaction where he could legitimately find it—sometimes from nature but more often from the Bible. He was a conspicuously typological poet; he tapped, as Ursula Brumm and others have disclosed, the whole biblical inventory of types as "a roster of symbolic equivalents of grace," which was the subject of his lifelong celebration. Joseph's many-colored coat, Jonah's entrapment in the belly of the whale, the Feast of Booths—all these are types of Christ's life and beauty and are therefore divinely authorized objects of loving contemplation: "In all those Typick Lumps of Glory I/Spy thee [Christ] the Gem made up of all their shine."

Since the recognition over the last twenty years that typological thinking was a common activity of the New England mind rather than a curious practice of eccentrics like Roger Williams, Taylor's delight in the splendor of Old Testament language (especially the erotic imagery of Solomon's Song) can no longer be regarded as a heretical indulgence. In this, as in his doctrinal attitudes, he was entirely within the Puritan mainstream. It is nevertheless not fanciful to detect in this frontier artist (who spent his youth and early manhood in England) an imaginative hunger within the spare interior existence into which he was pressed by the Westfield winters. He found his aesthetic solace in the one permissible place—the Bible—but he fell upon it with a nearly carnal delight: "I'm but a Flesh and Blood bag: Oh! do thou/Sill, Plate, Ridge, Rib, and Rafter me with Grace."

In Taylor's ecclesiology, by contrast, there is no hint of adventure. His church faithfully observed the established procedures of the Half-Way Covenant. Although baptism had been extended to children of the unprofessed, the Lord's Supper was still restricted to full church-members: that is, to those whose lives were not merely "unscandalous" but who had been judged, through public testimony of their saving experience, to be saints. Knowing something of Taylor's preferred church practice may seem unnecessary for appreciating his poetry, but a large part of his writing is devoted not only to arousing in himself the right spirit for administering the sacrament but also to fierce ecclesiastical controversy. In this respect, most of Taylor's work is what we would call "occasional verse," produced for specific events and purposes, and it is a measure of our distance from him that we tend to think of such writing as somehow inferior to that which arises purely out of the internal pressure of the expressive self. For Taylor, as the unrelieved intensity of his poems confirms, there could be nothing more important, nothing more demanding of self-examination and discipline, than the duties of the minister to his flock. His long poem *God's Determinations Touching His Elect,* for example, centers on the psychological paralysis of those who dared not offer themselves for communion."Half-way membership," as Thomas and Virginia Davis have put it, "thrust sincere believers into a position suspended between two different kinds of exclusion"—between, that is, those who were kept outside the church and those inside who were excluded from the Lord's Supper. It was to people caught in such a limbo that Taylor ministered all his life, and it is in this sense that his poetry was an extension of his ministry—not because he expected it to be read by those in need, but because through it he limbered his sympathetic imagination, and deepened his understanding of their dilemmas and hopes.

Stoddard, in nearby Northampton, had chosen to lure reluctant candidates (and to chasten those who were eager) for full membership by striking down the barriers that had daunted them: by declaring the Lord's Supper to be a "converting ordinance" and the old qualifications for communion to be obsolete. For Taylor, this was treachery—in part to the principles of the founders, but also to the new communicants, who were, in his view, being duped into trusting a false rescue. Stoddard's error, as Taylor saw it, was to deprive the half-way members of their appropriately deferred longing for true church fellowship (an emotion whose prevalence he overestimated) and to replace it with a counterfeit comfort. Seen in this way, the "Preparatory Meditations" are revealed as a scheduled spiritual regimen that, in Barbara Lewalski's phrase, "deliberately enact[ed] failure, as a means to glorify God." They were, in effect, a demonstration—for Taylor himself, but also as a rehearsal for what he would soon give to his waiting congregation—of the necessary coexistence in the saint of self-loathing and a desire for God.

In such an account of Taylor's achievement, however, there is a problem as well as an explanation. Reading through the meditations, one has to imagine (a task that a brief anthologized selection makes difficult) his subjecting himself to these assaults roughly once a month for more than forty years. The poetry does have an almost metronomic uniformity that can suggest dutifulness more than emotion. We must be careful not to impose post-Romantic standards of spontaneity and sincerity upon a writer steeped in religious, and to some extent poetic, convention. There are many echoes of George Herbert in Taylor's verse, which help to give it a certain apprentice flavor, though Taylor's often-remarked rhythmic awkwardness (in comparison to his English master) may have been less a technical deficiency than a conscious obstruction of what he felt as the profane excitement of singing meters. In any case, the issue of sincerity is quite distinct from the questions of derivativeness and skill. Even as he lacerates himself, the speaker in these poems is, as Lewalski says, "curiously serene." This apparent contradiction can be readily explained doctrinally: Taylor subscribed wholeheartedly to the five points of the Calvinist Synod of Dort, of which the two most important for him were "total depravity" and "irresistible grace." The sexually receptive posture of the speaker in his poems; the imagery of filth, of sluggishness, of obstructive weight—all these are tributes to the eradicating will of God.

In Taylor's imagination, the heinousness of the sinner glorifies the redeemer. And yet the fact remains that the integrity of the poems is threatened by the paradox of what the poet is doing: writing his unworthiness in preparation for a sacrament for which he thinks himself worthy. This is, finally, an inescapable conundrum for the kind of strenuous Protestantism that we call Puritan. It had been a problem for the New England mind since the beginning, and it released itself into a range of solutions: despair, or Antinomian authorization of the self, or (as Stoddard chose) a cessation of preliminary inquiry into the spiritual condition of the soul. Edward Taylor tried to evade all these possible results, and it is no indictment of his art to say that he did not always succeed. He managed often enough, as Albert Gelpi puts it, to render with "words [that] have the lumpish shape and weight of objects on the tongue," the combination of humility and joy that had been the Puritan aspiration all along.

The poems are from the standard edition, Donald Stanford, ed., *The Poems of Edward Taylor* (New Haven: Yale University Press, 1960).

Prologue

Lord, Can a Crumb of Dust the Earth outweigh,
Outmatch all mountains, nay the Chrystall Sky?
Imbosom in't designs that shall Display
And trace into the Boundless Deity?

Yea hand a Pen whose moysture doth guild ore
Eternall Glory with a glorious glore.

If it its Pen had of an Angels Quill,
And Sharpend on a Pretious Stone ground tite,
And dipt in Liquid Gold, and mov'de by Skill
In Christall leaves should golden Letters write
It would but blot and blur yea jag, and jar
Unless thou mak'st the Pen, and Scribener.

I am this Crumb of Dust which is design'd
To make my Pen unto thy Praise alone,
And my dull Phancy I would gladly grinde
Unto an Edge on Zions Pretious Stone.
And Write in Liquid Gold upon thy Name
My Letters till thy glory forth doth flame.

Let not th'attempts breake down my Dust I pray
Nor laugh thou them to scorn but pardon give.
Inspire this Crumb of Dust till it display
Thy Glory through't: and then thy dust shall live.
Its failings then thou'lt overlook I trust,
They being Slips slipt from thy Crumb of Dust.

Thy Crumb of Dust breaths two words from its breast,
That thou wilt guide its pen to write aright
To Prove thou art, and that thou art the best
And shew thy Properties to shine most bright.
And then thy Works will shine as flowers on Stems
Or as in Jewellary Shops, do jems.

Meditations: Series I

1. Meditation

WESTFIELD [JULY] *1682.*

What Love is this of thine, that Cannot bee
In thine Infinity, O Lord, Confinde,
Unless it in thy very Person see,

Infinity, and Finity Conjoyn'd?
What hath thy Godhead, as not satisfide
Marri'de our Manhood, making it its Bride?

Oh, Matchless Love! filling Heaven to the brim!
O're running it: all running o're beside
This World! Nay Overflowing Hell; wherein
For thine Elect, there rose a mighty Tide!
That there our Veans might through thy Person bleed,
To quench those flames, that else would on us feed.

Oh! that thy Love might overflow my Heart!
To fire the same with Love: for Love I would.
But oh! my streight'ned Breast! my Lifeless Sparke!
My Fireless Flame! What Chilly Love, and Cold?
In measure small! In Manner Chilly! See.
Lord blow the Coal: Thy Love Enflame in mee.

4. Meditation. Cant. 2.1 I am the Rose of Sharon.

[APRIL] *1683.*

My Silver Chest a Sparke of Love up locks:
And out will let it when I can't well Use.
The gawdy World me Courts t'unlock the Box,
A motion makes, where Love may pick and choose.
Her Downy Bosom opes, that pedlars Stall,
Of Wealth, Sports, Honours, Beauty, slickt up all.

Love pausing on't, these Clayey Faces she
Disdains to Court; but Pilgrims life designs,
And Walkes in Gilliads Land,[1] and there doth see
The Rose of Sharon which with Beauty shines.
Her Chest Unlocks; the Sparke of Love out breaths
To Court this Rose: and lodgeth in its leaves.

No flower in Garzia Horti shines like this:
No Beauty sweet in all the World so Choice:
It is the Rose of Sharon sweet, that is
The Fairest Rose that Grows in Paradise.

1. Gilead, the land of "spicery, balm, and myrrh" (Genesis 37:25).

Blushes of Beauty bright, Pure White, and Red
In Sweats of Glory on Each Leafe doth bed.

Lord lead me into this sweet Rosy Bower:
Oh! Lodge my Soul in this Sweet Rosy bed:
Array my Soul with this sweet Sharon flower:
Perfume me with the Odours it doth shed.
Wealth, Pleasure, Beauty Spirituall will line
My pretious Soul, if Sharons Rose be mine.

The Blood Red Pretious Syrup of this Rose
Doth all Catholicons[2] excell what ere.
Ill Humours all that do the Soule inclose
When rightly usd, it purgeth out most clear.
Lord purge my Soul with this Choice Syrup, and
Chase all thine Enemies out of my land.

The Rosy Oyle, from Sharons Rose extract
Better than Palma Christi[3] far is found.
Its Gilliads Balm for Conscience when she's wrackt
Unguent Apostolorum[4] for each Wound.
Let me thy Patient, thou my Surgeon bee.
Lord, with thy Oyle of Roses Supple mee.

No Flower there is in Paradise that grows
Whose Virtues Can Consumptive Souls restore
But Shugar of Roses made of Sharons Rose
When Dayly usd, doth never fail to Cure.
Lord let my Dwindling Soul be dayly fed
With Sugar of Sharons Rose, its dayly Bread.

God Chymist is, doth Sharons Rose distill.
Oh! Choice Rose Water! Swim my Soul herein.
Let Conscience bibble in it with her Bill.
Its Cordiall, ease doth Heart burns Causd by Sin.
Oyle, Syrup, Sugar, and Rose Water such.
Lord, give, give, give; I cannot have too much.

2. Universal remedies.

3. The castor-oil plant, whose leaves resemble the shape of hands; possibly a punning reference to the palm, which is an ingredient of Chrism, the oil used in Catholic liturgical ceremony.

4. Unguent of the apostles.

But, oh! alas! that such should be my need
    That this Brave Flower must Pluckt, stampt, squeezed bee,
And boyld up in its Blood, its Spirits sheed,
    To make a Physick sweet, sure, safe for mee.
    But yet this mangled Rose rose up again
    And in its pristine glory, doth remain.

All Sweets, and Beauties of all Flowers appeare
    In Sharons Rose, whose Glorious Leaves out vie
In Vertue, Beauty, Sweetness, Glory Cleare,
    The Spangled Leaves of Heavens cleare Chrystall Sky.
    Thou Rose of Heaven, Glory's Blossom Cleare
    Open thy Rosie Leaves, and lodge mee there.

My Dear-Sweet Lord, shall I thy Glory meet
    Lodg'd in a Rose, that out a sweet Breath breaths.
What is my way to Glory made thus sweet,
    Strewd all along with Sharons Rosy Leaves.
    I'le walk this Rosy Path: World fawn, or frown
    And Sharons Rose shall be my Rose, and Crown.

The Reflexion.

UNDATED.

Lord, art thou at the Table Head above
    Meat, Med'cine, sweetness, sparkling Beautys to
Enamour Souls with Flaming Flakes of Love,
    And not my Trencher, nor my Cup o'reflow?
    Be n't I a bidden Guest? Oh! sweat mine Eye.
    Oreflow with Teares: Oh! draw thy fountains dry.

Shall I not smell thy sweet, oh! Sharons Rose?
    Shall not mine Eye salute thy Beauty? Why?
Shall thy sweet leaves their Beautious sweets upclose?
    As halfe ashamde my sight should on them ly?
    Woe's me! for this my sighs shall be in grain
    Offer'd on Sorrows Altar for the same.

Had not my Soule's thy Conduit, Pipes stopt bin
    With mud, what Ravishment would'st thou Convay?

Let Graces Golden Spade dig till the Spring
    Of tears arise, and cleare this filth away.
    Lord, let thy spirit raise my sightings till
    These Pipes my soule do with thy sweetness fill.

Earth once was Paradise of Heaven below
    Till inkefac'd sin had it with poyson stockt
And Chast this Paradise away into
    Heav'ns upmost Loft, and it in Glory Lockt.
    But thou, sweet Lord, hast with thy golden Key
    Unlockt the Doore, and made, a golden day.

Once at thy Feast, I saw thee Pearle-like stand
    'Tween Heaven, and Earth where Heavens Bright glory all
In streams fell on thee, as a floodgate and,
    Like Sun Beams through thee on the World To Fall.
    Oh! sugar sweet then! my Deare sweet Lord, I see
    Saints Heavens-lost Happiness restor'd by thee.

Shall Heaven, and Earth's bright Glory all up lie
    Like Sun Beams bundled in the sun, in thee?
Dost thou sit Rose at Table Head, where I
    Do sit, and Carv'st no morsell sweet for mee?
    So much before, so little now! Sprindge, Lord,
    Thy Rosie Leaves, and me their Glee afford.

Shall not thy Rose my Garden fresh perfume?
    Shall not thy Beauty my dull Heart assaile?
Shall not thy golden gleams run through this gloom?
    Shall my black Velvet Mask thy fair Face Vaile?
    Pass o're my Faults: shine forth, bright sun: arise
    Enthrone thy Rosy-selfe within mine Eyes.

8. Meditation. Joh. 6.51. I am the Living Bread.

[JUNE] *1684.*

I kening[5] through Astronomy Divine
    The Worlds bright Battlement, wherein I spy

5. Discovering.

A Golden Path my Pensill cannot line,
From that bright Throne unto my Threshold ly.
And while my puzzled thoughts about it pore
I finde the Bread of Life in't at my doore.

When that this Bird of Paradise put in
This Wicker Cage (my Corps) to tweedle praise
Had peckt the Fruite forbad: and so did fling
Away its Food; and lost its golden dayes;
It fell into Celestiall Famine sore:
And never could attain a morsell more.

Alas! alas! Poore Bird, what wilt thou doe?
The Creatures field no food for Souls e're gave.
And if thou knock at Angells dores they show
An Empty Barrell: they no soul bread have.
Alas! Poore Bird, the Worlds White Loafe is done.
And cannot yield thee here the smallest Crumb.

In this sad state, Gods Tender Bowells run
Out streams of Grace: And he to end all strife
The Purest Wheate in Heaven, his deare-dear Son
Grinds, and kneads up into this Bread of Life.
Which Bread of Life from Heaven down came and stands
Disht on thy Table up by Angells Hands.

Did God mould up this Bread in Heaven, and bake,
Which from his Table came, and to thine goeth?
Doth he bespeake thee thus, This Soule Bread take.
Come Eate thy fill of this thy Gods White Loafe?
Its Food too fine for Angells, yet come, take
And Eate thy fill. Its Heavens Sugar Cake.

What Grace is this knead in this Loafe? This thing
Souls are but petty things it to admire.
Yee Angells, help: This fill would to the brim
Heav'ns whelm'd-down Chrystall meele Bowle, yea and higher.
This Bread of Life dropt in thy mouth, doth Cry.
Eate, Eate me, Soul, and thou shalt never dy.

Meditations: Series II

1. Meditation. Col. 2.17. Which are Shaddows of things to come and the body is Christs.

[16]93.

Oh Leaden heeld.[6] Lord, give, forgive I pray.
Infire my Heart: it bedded is in Snow.
I Chide myselfe seing myselfe decay.
In heate and Zeale to thee, I frozen grow.
File my dull Spirits: make them sharp and bright:
Them firbush for thyselfe, and thy delight.

My Stains are such, and sinke so deep, that all
The Excellency in Created Shells
Too low, and little is to make it fall
Out of my leather Coate wherein it dwells.
This Excellence is but a Shade to that
Which is enough to make my Stains go back.

The glory of the world slickt up in types
In all Choise things chosen to typify,
His glory upon whom the worke doth light,
To thine's a Shaddow, or a butterfly.
How glorious then, my Lord, art thou to mee
Seing to cleanse me, 's worke alone for thee.

The glory of all Types doth meet in thee.
Thy glory doth their glory quite excell:
More than the Sun excells in its bright glee
A nat, an Earewig, Weevill, Snaile, or Shell.
Wonders in Crowds start up; your eyes may strut
Viewing his Excellence, and's bleeding cut.

Oh! that I had but halfe an eye to view
This excellence of thine, undazled: so
Therewith to give my heart a touch anew
Untill I quickned am, and made to glow.

6. Heels.

All is too little for thee: but alass
Most of my little all hath other pass.

Then Pardon, Lord, my fault: and let thy beams
Of Holiness pierce through this Heart of mine.
Ope to thy Blood a passage through my veans.
Let thy pure blood my impure blood refine.
Then with new blood and spirits I will dub
My tunes upon thy Excellency good.

7. Meditation. ps. 105.17. He sent a man before them, even Joseph, who was sold etc.

[AUG.] *1694.*

All Dull, my Lord, my Spirits flat, and dead
All water sockt and sapless to the skin.
Oh! Screw mee up and make my Spirits bed
Thy quickening vertue For my inke is dim,
My pensill blunt. Doth Joseph type out thee?
Haraulds of Angells sing out, Bow the Knee.

Is Josephs glorious shine a Type of thee?
How bright art thou? He Envi'de was as well.
And so was thou. He's stript, and pick't, poore hee,
Into the pit. And so was thou. They shell
Thee of thy Kirnell. He by Judah's sold
For twenty Bits, thirty for thee he'd told.

Joseph was tempted by his Mistress vile.
Thou by the Divell, but both shame the foe.
Joseph was cast into the jayle awhile.
And so was thou. Sweet apples mellow so.
Joseph did from his jayle to glory run.
Thou from Death's pallot rose like morning sun.

Joseph layes in against the Famine, and
Thou dost prepare the Bread of Life for thine.
He bought with Corn for Pharaoh th'men and Land.
Thou with thy Bread mak'st such themselves Consign

Over to thee, that eate it. Joseph makes
His brethren bow before him. Thine too quake.

Joseph constrains his Brethren till their sins
Do gall their Soul. Repentance babbles fresh.
Thou treatest sinners till Repentance springs
Then with him sendst a Benjamin like messe.
Joseph doth Cleare his humble brethren. Thou
Dost stud with Joy the mourning Saints that bow.

Josephs bright shine th'Eleven Tribes must preach.
And thing Apostles now Eleven, thine.
They beare his presents to his Friends: thine reach
Thine unto thine, thus now behold a shine.
How hast thou pensild out, my Lord, most bright
Thy glorious Image here, on Josephs Light.

This I bewaile in me under this shine
To see so dull a Colour in my Skin.
Lord, lay thy brightsome Colours on me thine.
Scoure thou my pipes then play thy tunes therein.
I will not hang my Harp in Willows by.
While thy sweet praise, my Tunes doth glorify.

[*When*] *Let*[7] *by rain.*

UNDATED

Ye Flippering Soule,
Why dost between the Nippers[8] dwell?
Not stay, nor goe. Not yea, nor yet Controle.
Doth this doe well?
Rise journy'ng when the skies fall weeping Showers.
Not o're under th'Clouds and Cloudy Powers.

Not yea, nor noe:
On tiptoes thus? Why sit on thorns?
Resolve the matter: Stay thyselfe or goe.

7. Hindered.
8. Pincers.

Be n't both wayes born.
Wager thyselfe against thy surplice, see,
And win thy Coate: or let thy Coate Win thee.

Is this th'Effect,
To leaven thus my Spirits all?
To make my heart a Crabtree Cask direct?
A verjuicte[9] Hall?
As Bottle Ale, whose Spirits prisond nurst
When jog'd, the bung with Violence doth burst?

Shall I be made
A sparkling Wildfire Shop
Where my dull Spirits at the Fireball trade
Do frisk and hop?
And while the Hammer doth the Anvill pay,
The fireball matter sparkles ery way.

One sorry fret,
An anvill Sparke, rose higher
And in thy Temple falling almost set
The house on fire.
Such fireballs droping in the Temple Flame
Burns up the building: Lord forbid the same.

Upon a Wasp Child[10] with Cold.

UNDATED.

The Bare that breaths the Northern blast
Did numb, Torpedo[11] like, a Wasp
Whose stiffend limbs encrampt, lay bathing
In Sol's warm breath and shine as saving,
Which with her hands she chafes and stands
Rubbing her Legs, Shanks, Thighs, and hands.
Her petty toes, and fingers ends
Nipt with this breath, she out extends

9. Soured.
10. Chilled.
11. A fish that emits a slight electric charge.

Unto the Sun, in greate desire
To warm her digits at that fire.
Doth hold her Temples in this state
Where pulse doth beate, and head doth ake.
Doth turn, and stretch her body small,
Doth Comb her velvet Capitall.
As if her little brain pan were
A Volume of Choice precepts cleare.
As if her sattin jacket hot
Contained Apothecaries Shop
Of Natures recepts, that prevails
To remedy all her sad ailes,
As if her velvet helmet high
Did turret rationality.
She fans her wing up to the Winde
As if her Pettycoate were lin'de,
With reasons fleece, and hoises[12] sails
And hu'ming flies in thankfull gails
Unto her dun Curld palace Hall
Her warm thanks offering for all.

Lord cleare my misted sight that I
May hence view thy Divinity.
Some sparkes whereof thou up dost hasp
Within this little downy Wasp
In whose small Corporation wee
A school and a schoolmaster see
Where we may learn, and easily finde
A nimble Spirit bravely minde
Her worke in e'ry limb: and lace
It up neate with a vitall grace,
Acting each part though ne'er so small
Here of this Fustian animall.
Till I enravisht Climb into
The Godhead on this Lather doe.
Where all my pipes inspir'de upraise
An Heavenly musick furrd with praise.

12. Hoists.

Huswifery.

UNDATED.

Make me, O Lord, thy Spining Wheele compleate.
    Thy Holy Worde my Distaff make for mee.
Make mine Affections thy Swift Flyers neate
    And make my Soule thy holy Spoole to bee.
    My Conversation make to be thy Reele
    And reele the yarn thereon spun of thy Wheele.

Make me thy Loome then, knit therein this Twine:
    And make thy Holy Spirit, Lord, winde quills:
Then weave the Web thyselfe. The yarn is fine.
    Thine Ordinances make my Fulling Mills.
    Then dy the same in Heavenly Colours Choice,
    All pinkt with Varnisht Flowers of Paradise.

Then cloath therewith mine Understanding, Will,
    Affections, Judgment, Conscience, Memory
My Words, and Actions, that their shine may fill
    My wayes with glory and thee glorify.
    Then mine apparell shall display before yee
    That I am Cloathd in Holy robes for glory.

The Ebb and Flow.

UNDATED.

When first thou on me Lord wrought'st thy Sweet Print,
    My heart was made thy tinder box.
    My 'ffections were thy tinder in't.
        Where fell thy Sparkes by drops.
Those holy Sparks of Heavenly Fire that came
Did ever catch and often out would flame.

But now my Heart is made thy Censar trim,
    Full of thy golden Altars fire,
    To offer up Sweet Incense in

Unto thyselfe intire:
I finde my tinder scarce thy sparks can feel
That drop out from thy Holy flint and Steel.

Hence doubts out bud for feare thy fire in mee
'S a mocking Ignis Fatuus
Or lest thine Altars fire out bee,
Its hid in ashes thus.
Yet when the bellows of thy Spirit blow
Away mine ashes, then thy fire doth glow.

An Elegy upon the Death of that Holy and Reverend Man of God, Mr. Samuel Hooker,

Pastor of the Church of Christ at Farmington, (*and Son to the Famous Mr. Thomas Hooker, who was a Pastor of, and began with the Church of Christ at Hartford on Connecticut in New England*) *who slept in Christ, the 6th day of November, about one a Clock in the morning in the 64 year of his age entered upon. Annoque Domini 1697 . . .*

2. To New England.

Alas! alas! New England go weep.
Thy loss is greate in him: For he did keep
Within thine Orb as a bright shining Sun
To give thee Light, but now his race is run . . .

Mourn, mourn, New England, alas! alas!
To see thy Freckled Face in Gospell Glass:
To feele thy Pulse, and finde thy Spleen's not well:
Whose Vapors cause thy Pericordium t'swell:
Do suffocat, and Cramp thee, and grow worse
By Hypochondrik Passions of the purse,
Affect thy Brains toucht with the Turn, till thou
Halfe sick of Preachers false, and Gospell Plow.
Such Symptoms say, if nothing else will ease,
Thy Sickness soon will cure thy sad Disease.
For when such Studs, as stop, and scotch the Way
Of thy Declensions are remoov'd thy bay,

Apostasy wherewith thou art thus driven
Unto the tents of Presbyterianism
(Which is refined Prelacy at best)
Will not stay long here in her tents, and rest,
But o're this Bridge will carry thee apace
Into the Realm of Prelates arch, the place
Where open Sinners vile unmaskt indeed
Are Welcom Guests (if they can say the Creed)
Unto Christs Table, While they can their Sins
Atone in Courts by offering Silverlings.
Watch, Watch thou then: Reform thy life: Refine
Thyselfe from thy Declentions. Tend thy line.
Steeples were Weathercocks: but Turrits gain
An Happiness under a Faithfull Vane.
And weep thy Sins away, lest woe be nigh.
For Angells with thy Lots away do high . . .

Part 3. To Connecticut.

. . . . .

And as for you his Buds, and Blossoms blown,
Stems of his Root, his very Flesh and Bone,
You needs must have great droopings, now the Tree
Is fallen down the boughs whereof you bee.
You have a Father lost, and Choice one too.
Weeping for him is honour due from you.
Yet let your Sorrows run in godly wise
As if his Spirits tears fell from your eyes.
Strive for his Spirit: rather Christ's, than His
To dwell, and act his Flesh, yourselves, to bliss.
Its pitty these in him conjoyn'd, up grew
Together, should be parted here in you.
Plants of a Noble Vine, a Right, Right Seed.
Oh! turn not to a Strange Wild vine or Weed.
Your Grand sire were a Chiefe Foundation Stone
In this Blesst Building: Father was well known
To be a Chiefe Good Builder in the Same
And with his might did ever it mentain.
Your Grandsire's Spirit through your Father breathd
In Life, on you, and as his Life he leav'd,
Striving to breath into your hearts his Spirit

As out of him it passed, to inherit.
Be n't like such babes as parents brains out pull
To make a Wassill Bowle then of the Skull.
Then Pick their Parents eyes out, and the holes
Stuff up with folly, as if no braind Souls.
You are of better form than this sad guise
Yet beare this Caution: Some apostatise.
And strive your Sires, and Grandsires Life and Line
Through you their Flesh and blood may brightly shine.
Imminde your Father's Death bed Charge and aime.
You are his Very Flesh, and Blood, and Name . . .

His Epitaph.

A turffe of Glory, Rich Celestiall Dust,
A Bit of Christ here in Death's Cradle husht.
An Orb of Heavenly Sunshine: a bright Star
That never glimmerd: ever shining faire,
A Paradise bespangled all with Grace:
A Curious Web o'relaid with holy lace
A Magazeen of Prudence: Golden Pot
Of Gracious Flowers never to be forgot
Farmingtons Glory, and its Pulpits Grace
Lies here a Chrystallizing till the trace
Of Time is at an end and all out run.
Then shall arise and quite outshine the Sun.

God's Determinations Touching His Elect

The Preface.

UNDATED.

Infinity, when all things it beheld
In Nothing, and of Nothing all did build,
Upon what Base was fixt the Lath, wherein
He turn'd this Globe, and riggalld it so trim?
Who blew the Bellows of his Furnace Vast?
Or held the Mould wherein the world was Cast?
Who laid its Corner Stone? Or whose Command?

Where stand the Pillars upon which it stands?
Who Lac'de and Fillitted the earth so fine,
With Rivers like green Ribbons Smaragdine?
Who made the Sea's its Selvedge, and it locks
Like a Quilt Ball within a Silver Box?
Who Spread its Canopy? Or Curtains Spun?
Who in this Bowling Alley bowld the Sun?
Who made it always when it rises set
To go at once both down, and up to get?
Who th'Curtain rods made for this Tapistry?
Who hung the twinckling Lanthorns in the Sky?
Who? who did this? or who is he? Why, know
Its Onely Might Almighty this did doe.
His hand hath made this noble worke which Stands
His Glorious Handywork not made by hands.
Who spake all things from nothing; and with ease
Can speake all things to nothing, if he please.
Whose Little finger at his pleasure Can
Out mete ten thousand worlds with halfe a Span:
Whose Might Almighty can by half a looks
Root up the rocks and rock the hills by th'roots.
Can take this mighty World up in his hande,
And shake it like a Squitchen or a Wand.
Whose single Frown will make the Heavens shake
Like as an aspen leafe the Winde makes quake.
Oh! what a might is this Whose single frown
Doth shake the world as it would shake it down?
Which All from Nothing fet, from Nothing, All:
Hath All on Nothing set, lets Nothing fall.
Gave All to nothing Man indeed, whereby
Through nothing man all might him Glorify.
In Nothing then imbosst the brightest Gem
More pretious than all pretiousness in them.
But Nothing man did throw down all by Sin:
And darkened that lightsom Gem in him.
　　That now his Brightest Diamond is grown
　　Darker by far than any Coalpit Stone.

The Frowardness of the Elect in the Work of Conversion.

　　Those upon whom Almighty doth intend
His all Eternall Glory to expend,

Lulld in the lap of sinfull Nature snugg,
Like Pearls in Puddles cover'd ore with mudd:
Whom if you search, perhaps some few you'l finde,
That to notorious Sins were ne're inclinde.
Some shunning some, some most, some greate, some small.
Some this, that or the other, some none at all.
But all, or almost all you'st easly finde,
To all, or almost all Defects inclinde
To Revell with the Rabble rout who say
Let's hiss this Piety out of our Day.
And those whose frame is made of finer twine
Stand further off from Grace than Wash from Wine.
Those who suck Grace from th'breast, are nigh as rare
As Black Swans that in milkwhite Rivers are.
Grace therefore calls them all, and sweetly wooes.
Some won come in, the rest as yet refuse,
And run away: Mercy persues apace,
Then some Cast down their arms, Cry Quarter, Grace.
Some Chased out of breath drop down with feare
Perceiving the persuer drawing neer.
The rest persude, divide into two rancks
And this way one, and that the other prancks.

Then in comes Justice with her forces by her,
And doth persue as hot as sparkling fire.
The right wing then begins to fly away.
But in the streights strong Baracadoes lay.
They're therefore forc'd to face about, and have
Their spirits Queld, and therefore Quarter Crave.
These Captivde thus: justice persues the Game
With all her troops to take the other train.
Which being Chast in a Peninsula
And followd close, they finde no other way
To make escape, but t'rally round about:
Which if it faile them that they get not out,
They're forct into the Infernall Gulfe alive
Or hackt in pieces are or took Captive.
But spying Mercy stand with Justice, they
Cast down their Weapons, and for Quarter pray.
Their lives are therefore spar'de, yet they are ta'ne
As th'other band: and prisoners must remain.
And so they must now Justice's Captives bee

On Mercies Quarrell: Mercy sets not free.
    Their former Captain is their Deadly foe.
    And now, poor souls, they know not what to do.

The Joy of Church Fellowship rightly attended.

In Heaven soaring up, I dropt an Eare
    On Earth: and oh! sweet Melody:
And listening, found it was the Saints who were
    Encoacht for Heaven that sang for Joy.
    For in Christs Coach they sweetly sing;
    As they to Glory ride therein.

Oh! joyous hearts! Enfir'de with holy Flame!
    Is speech thus tassled with praise?
Will not your inward fire of Joy contain;
    That it in open flames doth blaze?
For in Christ's Coach Saints sweetly sing,
    As they to Glory ride therein.

And if a string do slip, by Chance, they soon
    Do screw it up again: whereby
They set it in a more melodious Tune
    And a Diviner Harmony.
    For in Christs Coach they sweetly sing
    As they to Glory ride therein.

In all their Acts, publick, and private, nay
    And secret too, they praise impart.
But in their Acts Divine and Worship, they
    With Hymns do offer up their Heart.
    Thus in Christs Coach they sweetly sing
    As they to Glory ride therein.

Some few not in; and some whose Time, and Place
    Block up this Coaches way do goe
As Travellers afoot, and so do trace
    The Road that gives them right thereto
    While in this Coach these sweetly sing
    As they to Glory ride therein.

COTTON MATHER (1663–1728)
Magnalia Christi Americana (1693–1702)

"HAD HE BEEN BORN in Jerusalem under the shadow of the Temple and circumcised in the Synagogue by his uncle the high priest, under the name of Israel Cohen, he would scarcely have been more distinctly branded, and not much more heavily handicapped in the races of the coming century, in running for such stakes as the century was to offer." Those words, with which Henry Adams opened his great memoir about carrying his own New England heritage into the twentieth century, are exactly right for Cotton Mather two hundred years earlier. Grandson of Richard Mather and of John Cotton, this Puritan heir felt the weight of his inheritance from childhood. His first Latin declamation at Harvard (which he entered in 1674 at the age of eleven) addressed the theme that Odysseus' son might one day exceed his father in courage and valor. Even before his college oration, Cotton had reason to regard his filial debt with a mixture of gratitude and regret. As an exceptionally young undergraduate, he was anointed by his father to be the Mathers' scion, and hazed by his peers as a prig. As late as the 1680s, having not quite laid "aside [his] thoughts of being a physician," he was still restless under the Mather mantle, but in 1685 he was duly installed as his father's assistant in the Second Church of Boston.

The story of the Mathers' collaboration is one of fierce family unity. "Most of the time," Robert Middlekauff has written, "the two Mathers looked at the world as if they had but one pair of eyes between them." But not all of the time: there was strain over the witchcraft issue (Cotton never signed the preface to Increase's *Cases of Conscience* (1693), the book that helped to end the persecution). But generally Cotton needed their alliance and gave himself to it fully. "Left alone in the care of a vast congregation," he confessed unseemly panic when Increase thought of settling in England after his negotiations for the new charter. A few years later Cotton flew into a rage against their old family friend Samuel Sewall, accusing him in a Boston bookshop of treating his father like "a

Neger" over the Harvard presidency, while the browsers looked on in amazement. The fortunes of the Mathers and the will of God kept close company in Cotton's mind: "the Lord will do it, the Lord will do it," he wrote in his *Diary;* "my father shall be carried into England [to secure the charter] . . . and the Lord shall have revenues of glory from it."

The *Diary* (Mather called it his *Reserved Memorials*) combines spontaneity and conscious craft into a record of a temperament swinging from ecstasy to something close to despair. In its many rises and falls, it pauses rarely in the region of serenity. Mather drove himself through a regimen of strenuous devotion, setting aside six hours each day for worship, raising that number to seven a few years before his death. "It seemed one of the chief aspirations of his soul," said Benjamin Colman at his funeral, "to honor God by *sacrifices,* and to have his own *will* swallowed up entirely in the will of God."

This volatile spiritual life gave to Mather's public labors an enormous energy. Beginning with a sermon preached at a murderer's hanging in 1686, he embarked on a publishing career that yielded more than 450 works, including one of the masterpieces of American literature, the *Magnalia Christi Americana* (1702). Throughout that career, Mather maintained a position of prominence in the religious life of Boston, but his political power fell far short of what his father and grandfather had achieved. He was never quite the "foremost American Puritan," as his father has been rightly called; indeed he outlived Increase by only five years.

This falling-short has fostered the opinion that Cotton Mather was somehow ill-equipped for power. He did lack his father's cosmopolitanism and gift for diplomacy (he never left New England). He willingly reconciled himself, however, to the fact that the spread of toleration in what he called these "dying times" had killed the old dream of New England as a congregational commonwealth. He did not indulge in fruitless lamentation. Turning the force of toleration to his own use, he pressed for alliance between Congregationalists and Presbyterians to check the High Church upstarts and other "innovators" who presumed a place for themselves in eighteenth-century New England. In this "midnight of confusion" he was able to see the futility of staking New England's future on ecclesiastical uniformity; with his loss of prestige in the witchcraft scandal, followed by his father's expulsion from the Harvard presidency, he turned away from institutional commitment and looked inward. It was the time more than the man that cost him his inherited authority.

Without conceding too much to the historian's taste for breaking past lives into convenient phases, it may be said that Cotton Mather's life, through this process of political withdrawal, became a sustained act of meditation which he shared with his contemporaries in his writing. The *Magnalia,* which he began composing in the 1690s, has an elegiac, almost valedictory tone. Its famous sentence—"whether *New England* may Live any where else or no, it must *Live* in our *History!*"—is more than a reflexive gesture. There is a sense in which Mather, by 1700, expected to live outside of history. When he turned away from Harvard as it fell to Leverett and the Brattles—those "fallacious people"—he looked to Yale to defend the faith, but remained at a benefactor's distance. Successive tragedies in his private life shut off any solace he might have hoped to draw from worldly things: two wives died, a third went mad, and his favorite son, whom he had hopefully named after his father, became a rowdy embarrassment to the family name. Many of his most moving writings, such as the *Early Piety* of 1688 on the death of his brother Nathanael, were composed in response to such losses. He was, in Sacvan Bercovitch's phrase, "using literature as a means of personal redress."

As his sorrows grew, so did his piety. The later entries of the *Diary* are filled with swelling rapture at the imminence of God's kingdom; and he comes closer and closer to claiming direct communication with God. While his relation to the Father became that of a confidant, his relation to the Son moved from intimacy to identification: "Without the imitation of Christ," he told New England in 1702, "all thy Christianity is a meer nonentity." He found his own fervency ratified in the writings of the medieval mystic Thomas à Kempis, and he began a correspondence with the German Pietist August Hermann Francke, with whom he discussed the coming hegemony of the saints throughout the world.

While Mather anticipated a future contagion of faith that would sweep across the earth, he organized watchdog societies designed to maintain a minimum of present decorum. Through these "do-good" groups, he inveighed against such features of contemporary life as alehouses and houses of prostitution—no longer New England rarities. These crusades, and a personal faith that has struck modern commentators as quaint or even pathological, have earned Mather a reputation as a witch-hunting hysteric who raged at change and prayed for the liquidation of his enemies. This caricature has been slow to die. In fact Mather was remarkably open to the new science, through whose instruments he saw both the miniature and majestic works of God. He exclaimed with delight at the turmoil of life disclosed by the microscope in a waterdrop, and at the telescope's revelation of a multitude of stars. (His massive unpublished commentary on scripture, the "Biblia Americana," composed from 1706 to the end of his life, is in part devoted to reconciling the truth of scripture with the truth of science.) Amid all this intellectual and devotional adventure, he remained committed to his pastorate. In the 1720s he once again widened his flock to include all of New England by leading the fight for smallpox vaccination in the face of public ridicule—an episode conveniently ignored by those who prefer the version of Mather as pompous reactionary.

The works reprinted in this volume represent only a tiny fraction of Mather's writing. They nevertheless make it possible to follow him from militancy (he interpreted the witch conspiracy in *The Wonders of the Invisible World* (1693) as a sign that Satan was growing desperate and therefore vulnerable); through the poignant reclamation of the disappearing past in the *Magnalia;* to the reaffirmation of pastoral commitment in the *Agricola,* a work in which he reconceived the preparatory experience and cast it in a nearly post-Puritan language. Through these selections the reader may glimpse what is perhaps the most affecting quality of Mather's work—his struggle to keep redemption in view even as it threatens to fade into the welter of concealing experience.

The text of the General Introduction to the *Magnalia* is from the edition by Kenneth B. Murdock and Elizabeth W. Miller (Cambridge, Mass.: Harvard University Press, 1977), pp. 89–94.

Magnalia Christi Americana

A General Introduction

Dicam hoc propter utilitatem eorum qui Lecturi sunt hoc opus.[1]
Theodoret

1. I WRITE the *Wonders* of the CHRISTIAN RELIGION, flying from the Depravations of *Europe,* to the *American Strand.* And, assisted by the Holy Author of that *Religion,* I do, with all Conscience of *Truth,* required therein by Him, who is the *Truth* itself, Report the *Wonderful Displays* of His Infinite Power, Wisdom, Goodness, and Faithfulness, wherewith His Divine Providence hath *Irradiated* an *Indian Wilderness.*

I Relate the *Considerable Matters,* that produced and attended the First Settlement of COLONIES, which have been Renowned for the Degree of REFORMATION, Professed and Attained by *Evangelical Churches,* erected in those *Ends of the Earth:* And a *Field* being thus prepared, I proceed unto a Relation of the *Considerable Matters* which have been acted thereupon.

1. This I say for the good of those who shall read the book.

I first introduce the *Actors,* that have, in a more exemplary manner served those *Colonies;* and give *Remarkable Occurrences,* in the exemplary LIVES of many *Magistrates,* and of more *Ministers,* who so *Lived,* as to leave unto Posterity, *Examples* worthy of *Everlasting Remembrance.*

I add hereunto, the *Notables* of the only *Protestant University,* that ever *shone* in that Hemisphere of the *New World;* with particular Instances of *Criolians,*[2] in our *Biography,* provoking the *whole World,* with vertuous Objects of Emulation.

I introduce then, the *Actions* of a more Eminent Importance, that have signalized those *Colonies;* Whether the *Establishments,* directed by their *Synods;* with a Rich Variety of *Synodical* and *Ecclesiastical* Determinations; or, the *Disturbances,* with which they have been from all sorts of *Temptations* and *Enemies* Tempestuated; and the *Methods* by which they have still weathered out each *Horrible Tempest.*

And into the midst of these *Actions,* I interpose an entire *Book,* wherein there is, with all possible Veracity, a *Collection* made, of *Memorable Occurrences,* and amazing *Judgments* and *Mercies,* befalling many *particular Persons* among the People of *New-England.*

Let my Readers expect all that I have promised them, in this *Bill of Fare;* and it may be they will find themselves entertained with yet many other Passages, above and beyond their Expectation, deserving likewise a room in *History:* In all which, there will be nothing, but the *Author's* too mean way of preparing so great Entertainments, to Reproach the Invitation . . .

3. It is the History of these PROTESTANTS, that is here attempted: PROTESTANTS that highly honoured and affected *The Church of* ENGLAND, and humbly Petition to be a *Part* of it: But by the Mistake of a few powerful *Brethren,* driven to seek a place for the Exercise of the *Protestant Religion,* according to the Light of their Consciences, in the Desarts of *America.* And in this Attempt I have proposed, not only to preserve and secure the Interest of *Religion,* in the Churches of that little Country *NEW-ENGLAND,* so far as the Lord Jesus Christ may please to Bless it for that End, but also to offer unto the Churches of the *Reformation,* abroad in the World, some small *Memorials,* that may be serviceable unto the Designs of *Reformation,* whereto, I believe, they are quickly to be awakened . . . Tho' the *Reformed Churches* in the *American Regions,* have, by very Injurious Representations of their Brethren (all which they desire to Forget and Forgive!) been many times thrown into a *Dung-Cart;* yet, as they have been a *precious Odour to God in Christ,* so, I hope, they will be a *precious Odour* unto *His People;* and

2. Persons born in America to parents born in Europe.

not only *Precious,* but *Useful* also, when the *History* of them shall come to be considered. A *Reformation of the Church* is coming on, and I cannot but thereupon say, with the dying *Cyrus* to his Children in *Xenophon . . . Learn from the things that have been done already, for this is the best way of Learning.* The Reader hath here an Account of *The Things that have been done already. Bernard* upon that Clause in the *Canticles,* [*O thou fairest among Women*] has this ingenious Gloss, *Pulchram, non omnimodo quidem, sed pulchram inter mulieres cam dicit, videlicet cum Distinctione, quatenus et ex hoc amplius reprimatur, & sciat quid desit sibi.*[3] Thus I do not say, That the Churches of *New-England* are the most *Regular* that can be; yet I do say, and am sure, That they are very like unto those that were in the *First Ages* of Christianity. And if I assert, That in the *Reformation* of the Church, the State of it in those *First Ages,* is to be not a little considered, the Great *Peter Ramus,*[4] among others, has emboldened me . . . In short, The *First Age* was the *Golden Age:* To return unto *That,* will make a Man a *Protestant,* and I may add, a *Puritan.* 'Tis possible, That our Lord Jesus Christ carried some Thousands of *Reformers* into the Retirements of an *American Desart,* on purpose, that, with an opportunity granted unto many of his Faithful Servants, to enjoy the precious *Liberty* of their *Ministry,* tho' in the midst of many *Temptations* all their days, He might there, *To* them first, and then *By* them, give a *Specimen* of many Good Things, which He would have His Churches elsewhere aspire and arise unto: And *This* being done, He knows whether there be not *All done,* that *New-England* was planted for; and whether the Plantation may not, soon after this, *Come to Nothing.* Upon that Expression in the Sacred Scripture, *Cast the unprofitable Servant into Outer Darkness,* it hath been imagined by some, That the *Regiones Exteræ* of *America,* are the *Tenebræ Exteriores,*[5] which the *Unprofitable* are there condemned unto. No doubt, the Authors of those Ecclesiastical Impositions and Severities, which drove the English Christians into the *Dark Regions* of *America,* esteemed those *Christians* to be a very *unprofitable* sort of Creatures. But behold, ye *European* Churches, There are *Golden Candlesticks* [more than *twice Seven times Seven!*][6] in the midst of this *Outer Darkness:* Unto the *upright* Children

3. She is beautiful, he says, not absolutely, but among women—a distinction that qualifies his praise and tells her what she lacks.

4. A French Protestant philosopher who died in the St. Bartholomew's Day massacre of 1570. The Ramean logic attempted to break down the Aristotelian categories into a series of simple dialectic oppositions by which all experience can be mapped out in reflection of God's intentions.

5. Outer regions.

6. See Revelation 1:12; 2:5.

of *Abraham,* here hath arisen *Light in Darkness.* And let us humbly speak it, it shall be *Profitable* for you to consider the *Light,* which from the midst of this *Outer Darkness,* is now to be Darted over unto the other side of the *Atlantick Ocean.* But we must therewithal ask your Prayers, that these *Golden Candlesticks* may not *quickly* be *Removed out of their place!*

4. But whether *New England* may *Live* any where else or no, it must *Live* in our *History!* . . .

COTTON MATHER
Reserved Memorials (1681–1724)

For more than forty years—not daily, but sporadically—Cotton Mather recorded his experiences and thoughts in a large manuscript that he called his *Reserved Memorials,* partly intended as a spiritual guide for his pupils and younger relatives. It was not published until the twentieth century. Although its modern editor gave it the title of *Diary,* it is more a series of crafted meditations (often written down well after the event had passed) than spontaneous jottings like those in Sewall's diary. Despite its craft and care, no work in Mather's vast production gives a more intimate sense of his character and mind. The prose, often fervid, always alive, expresses the urgency with which he tried to put his days to godly use; how he struggled to find meaning—whether rebuke or encouragement from God—in every moment of his life; how he alternately reveled in worldly achievement and deflected his hope to the coming kingdom of Christ. Sometimes moving, sometimes amusing, the *Reserved Memorials* is an extraordinary record, in a time when the old Puritan certitudes were fading, of one man's effort to keep control over himself and to feel and understand the will of God.

The text of the *Reserved Memorials* is from Worthington C. Ford's edition, in the Massachusetts Historical Society *Collections,* ser. 7, vol. 7, pp. 11, 61, 83–84, 89, 186, 207–208, 223–226, 273–274, 327–328, 357, 360, 430–432, 434, 444–449.

Reserved Memorials

[*May 1681.*] Oh! the *Hardness* of my Heart! If Mercies could have softned or quickned mee I should not have been as I am; but there is *desperate Wickedness,* from which I am yett uncleansed. I have sometimes thought I should never come to this Pass, when in secret Places, my filled Soul has been satisfied with the communion of the Blessed God.

But nothing will now work in mee! Oh! I am as fitt for *Sickness,* as ever any poor Creature was. *Fitt,* in the same Sense, that a rotten Stump, is *fitt* for the Fire. And, *Lord,* shall I never bee awakened, until I feel the heavy *Blowes* of thy Hand? However, I have this to say. *First, Lord,* Thou canst *rectify* my Spirit every Way, without such bitter *Corrections,* as I have Reason to expect. *Next, Lord,* yett if thou wilt *afflict* mee, yett if I may bee brought thereby to *see* thee more, and love thee more, I *submitt;* here I am; afflict mee; do what thou wilt with mee; *kill* mee; for thy *Grace* hath made mee willing to dy; *only, only, only,* help mee to delight in thee, and to glorify thy dearest Name.

[*May 1683.*] My highest Acquisition, I will reckon to bee, *a Likeness unto God.* To *love* that which *God* loves, and *hate* that which *God* hates; to bee *holy as God is holy,* and like Him, a *great Forgiver;* and bee His *Child,* as much as may bee like the *just at the Resurrection from the Dead.* This will I seek, as the noblest *Crown,* that ever I can wear; and that which the *Thorns* placed upon the Temples of the greatest earthly Monarchs, were never worthy to bee compared with. O That I may bee conformable unto the *communicable Attributes* of God, and agreeable unto his *Incommunicable.*

[*February 1684.*] . . . when I have been sitting in a Room full of People, at a *Funeral,* where they take not much Liberty for *Talk,* and where yett much *Time* is most unreasonably lost, I have usually sett my Witts a work, to contrive *agreeable Benedictions,* for each Person in the Company.

In passing along the *Street,* I have sett myself to *bless* thousands of persons, who never knew that I did it; with *secret Wishes,* after this manner sent unto Heaven for them.

Upon the Sight of	Ejaculations.
A *tall* Man.	*Lord,* give that Man, *High Attainments* in Christianity: lett him fear God, *above many.*
A *lame* Man.	*Lord,* help that Man, to *walk uprightly.*
A *Negro.*	*Lord, wash* that poor Soul *white* in the *Blood* of thy Son.
Children standing together.	*Lord, lett* the *blessing Hands* of my Lord Jesus Christ, bee putt upon these *Children.*

Children at *Play.*	*Lord,* lett not these Children always forgett the *Work,* which they came into the World upon.
A *Merchant.*	*Lord,* make that man a *wise Merchant.*
A Very *little* Man.	*Lord,* bestow *great Blessings* upon that Man, and above all, thy *Christ,* the *greatest of Blessings.*
A Man carrying a *Burden.*	*Lord,* help this Man, to carry a *burdened Soul,* unto his Lord-Redeemer.
A Man on *Horseback.*	*Lord,* thy *Creatures* do serve that man; help him to serve his *Maker.*
Young People.	*Lord,* help these Persons to *remember their Creator in the Dayes of their Youth.*
Young Gentlewomen.	*Lord,* make 'em *wise Virgins,* as the *polish'd Stones of thy Temple.*
A *Shop-keeper,* busy in the Shop.	*Lord,* lett not the *World,* cause that Person to neglect the *one thing that is needful.*
A Man, who going by mee took *no Notice* of mee.	*Lord,* help that Man, to take a *due Notice* of the Lord Jesus Christ, I pray thee.
One in *mourning.*	*Lord,* give to that Person, the *Comforts,* which thou hast promised for *blessed Mourners.*
A very *old* Man.	*Lord,* make this an *old Disciple.*
One leaning on a *Staff.*	*Lord,* teach this Person to *lean* on a *Christ.*
One whom I *know not:* (and saw no other singular Circumstance about him, to shape any Thoughts upon.)	*Lord,* lett this Person bee so *known* to, as to bee *sav'd* by, the Lord.
One who (as I had heard) had spoken very *reproachfully* and *injuriously* of mee.	*Lord,* bless and spare and save that Person, even as *my own Soul.* May *that Person* share with mee, in all the *Salvations* of the Lord.
One that was reckon'd a very *wicked* Man.	*Lord,* rescue that poor Man, from *Satan,* who *leads him captive.*

It were *endless,* and it is now *needless* to exemplify an hundreth part of the *Ejaculations,* which I find, a Person may, without any *Loss* of his Time or any *Prejudice* and *Obstruction* to any of his *Affairs,* thus refresh himself withal.

Wherefore all that I now add, is, that I have unspeakable Cause, to bless my Lord Jesus Christ, for teaching mee, by His Holy Spirit, before I was *twenty years of Age,* these Methods of *living* unto His glory.

[*February 1685.*] *Lord,* make my Tongue, a *Tree of Life!*

[*February 1696.*] *Memorandum.* This morning, in my study, praying for each of my Children by Name (as I use to do) I left the Name of my *Mehetabel* unmentioned. I wondred at this Omission, in myself and blam'd and chid myself, that I should bee so sottish, as having but *three* children to forgett *one* of them. Now, I had no sooner done my prayers, but the messenger gave mee to understand that the Child had been for above an Hour before, by its Death, gone beyond the reach or use, of our *Prayers.* (Alas, the Child was overlaid by the Nurse!)

[*October 1696*] I have this Day . . . wrestled with the Lord, until I have obtained it, that a mighty Convulsion shall bee given to the *French* Empire; and that *England, Scotland,* and *Ireland,* shall bee speedily Illuminated, with glorious Anticipations of the *Kingdome of God.* Moreover, a Revolution upon the *Turkish Empire,* which is now attempted by Troubles in *Asia,* I cryed unto the Lord for; that so wee may have another good Symptom of the Approach of the Time, when the *Kingdomes of this world shall become the Kingdomes of our Lord and of His Christ.*

[*February 1697.*] . . . when I was . . . prostrate in the Dust before the Lord, my Heart being poured out in Tears, received wonderful Assurances from Heaven, that the Spirit of my Lord Jesus Christ, shall fill mee, and use mee to *glorify* Him; and that His *Angels* have wonderful Things to do for mee! . . .

Considering that there is doubtless a great *Revolution,* and the great *Reformation* at hand, I judg'd it would bee a Thing, on many Accounts profitable, for mee, to single out a *select Number* of Christians, whose Appetites are strong to bee informed about the *Characters* and *Approaches* of the Kingdome of our Lord Jesus Christ, and entertain them at my Study, in fitt Seasons, with Discourses, and Researches, of those Matters, which the *Holy Angels* themselves *desire to look into.*

[*September 1698.*] *Four Dayes* this Week, I preach, and yett I do not sink under it. One of these Dayes, was *this Day;* wherein, I rode, it may bee fourteen Miles in the Morning, even to *Reading,* and rode Home, a shorter Way, of about a dozen Miles, in the Evening; and preached at *Reading,* unto a great Auditory, gathered from all the Towns in the Neighbourhood.

In my Journey, going out, I received a remarkable *Deliverance.* Riding over a *Bridge,* one of the *rotten Poles* upon it broke; and my Horse broke thro' and broke in, and *sunk down* to his very *Breast.* I chose rather to keep the *Saddle,* than go off into the *River;* and the *Horse,* to the Astonishment of my Company *rose* again, (tearing off a *Shooe* in his Rising,) and leaped over, with mee safe upon him. How happily do the *Creatures* all serve us, while wee are serving, their and our Lord, the Blessed *Jesus!*

[*December 1699.*] Observing my Father, in Discourse with him Yesterday, to bee under some Discouragement, about the Accomplishment of the *Particular Faith,* which had seemed so often infused from Heaven into our Minds, about his yett having an Opportunity to glorify the Lord Jesus Christ in *England;* I did this Day at Noon, in my Study, lay that Matter before the Lord. And as I was concluding my Petitions about it, without any special Operation from Heaven upon my mind, and just ready to conclude, I should have none, my mind suddenly felt a strange and a strong Operation from Heaven upon it, which caused mee to break forth into Expressions of this Importance; *The Lord will do it, The Lord will do it, my Father shall be carried into* England, *and he shall there have a short, but a great Opportunity to glorify my Lord Jesus Christ; In a most wonderful Way, it shall bee brought about; And it shall at last appear, that the Faith which there has been concerning it, was the wonderful Work of Heaven; and the Lord shall have Revenues of Glory from it!*

[*July 1700.*] I was once emptying the *Cistern of Nature,* and making *Water* at the Wall. At the same Time, there came a *Dog,* who did so too, before me. Thought I; "What mean, and vile Things are the Children of Men, in this mortal State! How much do our *natural Necessities* abase us, and place us in some regard, on the same Level with the very *Dogs!*"

My Thought proceeded. "Yett I will be a more noble Creature; and at the very Time, when my *natural Necessities* debase me into the Condition of the *Beast,* my *Spirit* shall (I say, *at that very Time!*) rise and soar, and fly up, towards the Employment of the *Angel.*"

. . . I am now left alone, in the Care of a vast Congregation, the largest in all these Parts of the World. I am afraid, lest now they grow foolish, and froward, and lest the Devices of Satan may some way or other prevail to scatter them, or lest some Distemper arise among them. And, I am feeble; and in this Town, I have many Enemies; indeed, all the Enemies of the evangelical Interests, are mine.

[*May 1702.*] My dear Consort, this Week . . . after previous Illness, unhappily miscarried of a Son, after being four or five Months with Child; and yett, it is possible, that not unhappily; for she had also a *false Conception,* whereof she was now delivered. She was brought into Languishments of extreme and threatening Sickness.

[*June 1702.*] But in the Afternoon, when I was alone in my Study crying unto the Lord, for sparing and healing Mercy to my Consort, my *Particular Faith* was again renewed, and with a Flood of Tears, I thought I received an Assurance from Heaven, that she should Recover this time . . .

I then went unto my Consort, and assured her, that she should live yett awhile . . .

On the Friday, my Consort's Illness grew still (if it could be,) full of more uneasy Symptomes. I saw no Likelihood of any other than Death after all. But Lord! how aggravated a Calamity must be her Death, if such a Sting, as the Disappointment of my *Particular Faith,* must be added unto it!

[*October 1702.*] Behold a strange Thing! On the Night after the Fast, my Consort had appearing to her, (she supposes, in her sleep) a grave Person, who brought with him, a Woman in the most meagre and wretched Circumstances imaginable. My Consort fell into the Praises of God, in that her Condition was not yett so miserably Circumstanced as that woman's now before her. The grave Person then told her, that inasmuch as there were at this Time, a Couple of Symptomes become insupportable to her, he would propose a Way, wherein she should obtain some Help for them. First, for her intolerable Pain in her Breast, said he, lett them cutt the warm Wool from a living Sheep, and apply it warm unto the grieved Pain. Next, for her Salivation, which hitherto nothing had releeved, said he, take a Tankard of Spring-Water, and therein over the Fire dissolve an agreeable Quantity of Mastic's, and of Gum Icinglass: Drink of this Liquor now and then, to strengthen the Glands, which ought to have been done a great while ago.

She told this on *Friday,* to her principal Physician; who mightily encouraged our trying the Experiments. We did it; and unto our Astonishment, my Consort revived at a most unexpected Rate; insomuch, that she came twice on Satureday out of her sick Chamber, unto me in my

Study; and there she asked me to give Thanks unto God with her, and for her, on the Account of the Recovery in so surprising a Degree begun unto her.

[*November 1702.*] In this Month, my lovely Consort again declines; and some latent Mischief within her, brings on a Feebleness, that give us great Apprehensions of a mortal Issue . . .

I spent much Time, with my lovely Consort. I pray'd with her as agreeably as I could. I endeavoured her most consummate Præparation for the heavenly World, by suitable Questions and Proposals. I comforted her, with as lively Discourses upon the Glory of Heaven, whereto she was going as I could make unto her. I disposed her, and myself, all that I could, unto a glorious Resignation . . .

When I saw to what a Point of Resignation, I was now called of the Lord, I resolved, with His Help therein to glorify Him. So, two Hours before my lovely Consort expired, I kneeled by her Bed-Side, and I took into my two Hands, a dear Hand, the dearest in the World. With her then in my Hands, I solemnly and sincerely gave her up unto the Lord; and in token of my real RESIGNATION, I gently putt her out of my Hands, and laid away a most lovely Hand, resolving that I would never touch it any more!

This was the hardest and perhaps the bravest Action, that ever I did. She afterwards told me, *that she sign'd and seal'd my Act of Resignation.* And tho' before that, she call'd for me, continually; she after this never asked for me any more.

She continued until near two a clock, in the Afternoon. And the last sensible Word, that she spoke, was to her weeping Father, *Heaven, Heaven will make amends for all.*

COTTON MATHER
Agricola (c. 1725)

"A BIDDYISH seriocomic martyr," is Kenneth Silverman's phrase for Cotton Mather's public reputation in his waning years. To many who watched Mather's books roll off the presses by the score, who heard his endless proposals for social improvement, he was becoming something of a public joke. And he knew it. "I have had more books written against me; more pamphlets to traduce me, and reproach me, and belie me, than any man that I know in the world." The public Mather still had a certain relish for the fight. But the private Mather showed less and less of the jauntiness of his youth. He absorbed public ridicule as the amateur leech who proposed that smallpox pustules on dying men be scraped and injected into the living; he was threatened with debtors' prison as he fended off creditors who demanded satisfaction from his mentally unstable wife; he was bewildered by the apostasy of Yale College, which he had helped to found as a congregational bastion and which was now becoming a training school for Anglicans. He was denied the presidency of Harvard; and, most of all, he was tormented by the deaths of his children, including, in 1724, his beloved son Creasy (named for Increase) who was lost at sea: "Ah my son! my son! . . . The death of my son . . . Thousands and thousands of prayers were employed for him; yet after all, a sovereign God would not accept of him. He was buried in the Atlantic Ocean."

The pressure of sorrow can be felt in all of Mather's late work, which abandons the stylized self-consciousness of the middle years and the oracular voice of the *Magnalia* and achieves a new simplicity and openness. He produced, among many other important books in his last years, *The Angel of Bethesda* (1724), a genuine contribution to American science, and the *Manuductio ad Ministerium* (1726), an effort at transmitting the Puritan legacy to a new generation of clergy. Among the most poignant of these late works is the *Agricola,* a series of sermons that restates the old preparationist hope that man, with the help of a stern but loving ministry, can render himself fit for the ravishing experience of grace. If the language of preparation had once been strenuous and complex, Mather now domesticated it, made of it a kind of proverbial vernacular. Through this accessible rhetoric, which remained, as always, a strategy in the service of conversion, his own sufferings can be vividly felt. The *Agricola* is finally a tract about the necessity of pain—relentless, inescapable pain—as the prelude to joy. In its moving sentences on death—"to die is a thing against nature. To die willingly is a thing above nature"—one hears Mather not as the platitudinous teacher who was being left behind by his times, but as the son and father who had been death's companion at many bedsides, and who was still searching for ways to help others cope with this life while awaiting the next.

The text of the *Agricola* is from the edition of 1727, pp. 5–7, 13, 18–20, 132–137, 139–141, 192–193.

Agricola

Arator. The Work of the Plow

Agricola incurvo terram molitus Aratro.[1]

Jeremiah 4:3. Break up your fallow ground.

A call from heaven which every man upon earth is deeply concerned in . . .

Let us enquire . . . what are those operations of repentance in which the plow is to break up this fallow ground?

You take it for granted, the word of God, accompanied with the influences of the Holy Spirit, is the plow with which this work of God is carried on. And now,

First: In a true repentance, the heart is broken, with a sense and grief of the sins, which the great God has been offended at . . . By sorrow of heart, the spirit is broken. The earth is not more broken by the plow tearing of it, than the heart of a repenting one is broken with the sorrow of repentance . . . The repenting one makes a sorrowful reflection on what he has done in sinning against the glorious God. With an heart-breaking regret and remorse and sorrow, he thinks, "I have sinned, and I have done very foolishly. But Oh! What have I done, when I have sinned! I have denied the God that is above, and set myself and my idols above

1. The farmer with his curved plow has softened the earth.

him . . . I have refused eternal pleasures, and incurred eternal torments; all for a mere shadow of a delight, which is but for a moment. Oh! what madness has possessed me!" Such sentiments as these enter with the wounding force of a ploughshare into the heart of a repenting one. He feels that anguish from them that makes him cry out, "My heart is broken, O God, my heart is broken. My wounded spirit, Oh! I cannot bear it!" . . .

Beholding of the earth which the plow goes into, think: In the earth I have my grave waiting for me, where I know not how soon I may be lodged. How much may this meditation quicken you to make haste in that repentance, which must be dispatched before you sleep in the dust, or else nothing on earth can keep you from an hell forever to be trembled at.

My friend, smell to the earth. 'Tis a very wholesome scent. It will contribute to the work of repentance wonderfully.

Thus you see the plow in it[s] operations. And upon the whole, what shall I say unto you? . . .

It has been counted a memorable thing that among the old Romans they sometimes fetched a man from the plow, and one that was owner of no more than four acres neither, and set him at the head of the commonwealth. Christian, keep at this plow, and God will one day raise thee out of the dust, and fetch thee out of the dunghill and set thee with princes, even with the princes of his people.

I have done. The plow has done its work and the fallow ground is well broken up if the word of God finds now a free passage into your hearts. And, oh! May your hearts be now so opened by the Lord, that in whatever word he comes unto you, your consenting hearts may say, Welcome art thou, O Lord, and welcome is every word of thine, unto me . . .

I did indeed say, I have done. But I know not how to part with my plow-man, until I have taken a little notice of something in his hand, by which the creatures which draw his plow for him are exagitated.[2] He carries a *goad* in his hand.

We read of a champion, Judges 3:31, *He slew six hundred men with an ox-goad.* We may guess a little at the shape of that ox-goad, and how fit a tool it was for such an execution, from what is related by modern travelers concerning the husbandry in those parts of the world. They tell us that in plowing, the husbandmen use goads of an extraordinary size. They are eight foot long, and at the upper end, six inches in circumference. They are armed at the lesser end with a sharp nail for the driving of the oxen, and at the other end with a small spade or paddle of iron, strong

2. Excited.

and massy for cleansing of the plow from the clay that encumbers it in working. In such a goad, behold a better weapon than a sword, for a Shamgar to employ upon his Philistines.[3]

All that I shall observe upon it is: There are so many goads in the lively oracles of God for our excitation and instigation to repentance, and a life of piety. We read, Ecclesiastes 12:11, *The words of the wise are as goads.* And such are the words of our God by which we are to be quickened. Alas, why do we no more find them so! How stupid a thing art thou, O man, if thou dost not feel such pungencies? But then, the dealings of God with thee in his providence, what are these also, but so many stimulations to repentance, and a life of piety? If they move thee not, O dull soul, and if thou do not conform unto them, there is that voice from heaven unto thee on them, Acts 9:5, *It is hard for thee to kick against the goads.* Oh! Do not by thy dilatory proceedings in the life of God, provoke him to multiply the uneasy strokes of his goads upon thee.

Desector. The Grass before the Mower

Psalms 37:2. They shall soon be cut down as the grass.

Of whom speaks the psalmist this? Those whom the spirit of God calls evil-doers and workers of iniquity . . . We find here foretold the ruin of Antichrist, in a tremendous conflagration, wherein the enemies of God shall be consumed as the fat of lambs; into smoke shall they consume away. And we find foretold the bright prosperity of the holy people, after the wicked one shall be destroyed by the brightness of the coming of the Lord . . . When the godly are cut down as the grass, 'tis that they may be lodged in the house of God; yea that our Savior may fill his hand with them. When the wicked are cut down as the grass, 'tis that they may be cast into the oven and thrown into the devouring fire. All that we shall here consider is the common lot of mankind; for this is but what mankind in general is to look for.

The doctrine with which we are now to be instructed—but Oh! that as much affected!—is this:

To be soon cut down as the grass, this is a condition which mankind is not a stranger to.

. . . All the children of men are liable to the stroke of death; every leaf of this grass must be cut down by the scythe of death . . .

Uncertain the time when the mower will come, the offspring of the

3. Shamgar cleared the roads with his ox-goad (Judges 3:31).

earth is not always of one age and of one bulk when the mower applies the scythe unto it. Old Isaac was not the only person who may say, Genesis 27:2, *I know not the day of my death*. All the spires of grass that are cut down are not of an equal growth, but the stroke of death is given with a promiscuous excision among them. And, *mista senum et juvenum densantur funera*.[4] The scythe not only comes upon a Methuselah; but it comes upon an Abijah too; and the child died. We read of some, Job 36:14, *They die in youth*. How often has the report been made, since the days of the sons of Job, "The young men are dead!" We read of children dying. Read of such things! Yea we see them every day. The Zareptans and the Abunamites[5] are not the only ones whose children have died. It is a passage: Canticles 2:12, *The flowers appear on the earth, the time of singing is come*. It may be rendered, the time of cutting is come. The flowers of the grass do no sooner appear, but the time of cutting presently comes upon them. The coming forth of man is quickly followed with his cutting down. It is a frequent dying; there are skulls of all sizes in Golgotha. We are warned concerning the time when the scythe is to come into its operation; Ecclesiastes 9:12, *Man knoweth not his time*. They that have made nice remarks on bills of mortality will tell you that the half of those that are born don't live seventeen years; that about forty of an hundred are found alive at sixteen years; that but ten out of an hundred, at forty-six; but six, at fifty-six; but three at sixty-six; but one at seventy-six. When God pronounced the sentence of death upon mankind, it ran so: Genesis 3:19, *Until thou return unto the ground*. It is a descant which one of the ancients made upon it; he does not say, "Until thou hast passed through so many years"; but he speaks indeterminately, *until the time come. A time which I will keep uncertain to thee, when it will come*. Truly about the execution which the scythe of death is to do upon us, we must say, of that day and hour knoweth no man. The mower comes at that rate; Luke 12:40, *At an hour when ye think not*.

Here again, how can I do any other than make a stop; and make it a season to bring what will always be a word in season? It will here be a seasonable admonition; the uncertainty of death should quicken us to labor for, and hasten to, a certainty that it will go well with us when we die? God forbid, that any leaf of grass, the smallest as well as the largest, the youngest as well as the oldest, should reckon themselves excused from that grand concern, a serious preparation for death. My friends, embrace an offered Savior in all his offices. Accept the covenant of life, with all

4. The funerals are thick with young as well as old.
5. Luke 4:25.

its proposals. Be importunate with the God of all grace for a sanctifying work of his grace upon you; unpacified until you find in yourselves the comfortable marks of a soul in good terms with heaven. This must be done before you feel the scythe. Undone, undone are you, if you die before this be done. Mind, I beseech you, what comes now to you from the mouth of the glorious God; if the scythe find you unprepared, and strike you while you are yet in your sins, your doom will be that, Psalms 92:7, *When the wicked spring as the grass, it is that they shall be destroyed forever.* Verily, the scythe will consign you over to a destruction from God, which, why, why is it no more of a terror to you! Oh! Be able to say, with him,[6] *O Lord, I thought on my ways and I turned my feet unto thy testimonies; I made haste, and I delayed not to keep thy commandments.*

When the children of men who are the children of death are taken away with a stroke, and the mortal scythe cuts us down as the grass, 'tis not without something of a violence that the stroke does what it comes for. This expression, *they shall be cut down,* denotes a violence in what is done; 'tis violently done. First, the death which we call violent, as it is opposed unto the natural; this is no rare thing among the prisoners of the earth. 'Tis no rare thing to die by casualties, or to die by adversaries, to die like them on whom the tower of Siloam fell,[7] or to die like them whose blood Pilate sacrificed. Sometimes the scythe strikes with a damage that happens accidentally, sometimes with a mischief that is done intentionally. We read of some whom the scythe handles at that rate; Job 21:13, *In a moment they go down to the grave.* Many a death is brought by external occurrences; by invasions from abroad; so died the first man that ever died; while others may with Hezekiah say, *He will cut me off with pining sickness.* But men, in the death which is most natural, there is yet a violence done to nature. To die, is a thing against nature. To die willingly, is a thing above nature . . .

Gaudentius. The Joyful Harvest

Galatians 6:9. In due season we shall reap, if we faint not.

The joy of harvest is now before us. Here is an husbandry that never will, never can, miss of a glorious harvest. The husbandry prosecuted in the fields of nature often misses of the harvest expected by the husbandman. Our apostasy from God has brought a curse upon the earth, and

6. David (Psalm 119:59–60).
7. Luke 13:4.

a failing of the harvest which we have labored for. After much labor, the issue often is that; Joel 1:11–12, *Be ye ashamed, O ye husbandmen, because the harvest of the field is perished. Joy is withered away from the sons of men.* But in the husbandry of piety, a blessed and a joyful harvest is never missed of. We are advised from heaven of it; it shall have a sure reward. The reward of piety is the harvest of it. Of this, the Holy Spirit of God has here given us this assurance; *Let us not be weary in well-doing, for in due season we shall reap, if we faint not.* It seems the work of piety may not be without its wearisome difficulties: things which our carnal minds may dispose us to be too soon weary of. But hold on, hold out, O unwearied piety. There will be an harvest, wherein thou shalt reap what will be a great reward, yea a full reward of all. The oracles of our God have expressly called it so. But it is a season that must be waited for . . .

COTTON MATHER
The Wonders of the Invisible World (1692)

"THE INTELLECTUAL HISTORY of New England," wrote Perry Miller about the witchcraft crisis at Salem, ". . . can be written as if no such thing ever happened." It could be, perhaps, but it never will be—not as long as writers and readers retain their fascination with America's first large-scale witch-hunt, an interest that has proven no less durable for the fact that the phenomenon remains resistant to explanation. Still, there is something to Miller's dismissal—the events at Salem, despite their compelling human horror, were finally a subsidiary moment within a slow cultural development. What happened at Salem was an outburst of the same bewilderment and self-doubt that had afflicted New Englanders since the beginning. It was a terribly clear articulation of something more often hinted at than stated: that the Puritan appetite for moral clarity was being more frustrated than satisfied in their New Canaan.

The bare facts are well known: in the winter of 1691–92 some erratic behavior was noticed among a few young girls—"fits" and "foolish ridiculous speeches," as Robert Calef called them. When they failed to subside into the usual rhythm of adolescence, "witchcraft" began to be murmured as an explanation. "Natural" causes could not be found—or so the doctors who had been summoned said—and by the end of February legal authorities from outside Salem were brought in to examine three women who had been detained on charges of "entertaining Satan." One of them, a slave from the West Indies named Tituba, confessed to mixing potions with young girls and reveling in the woods at night with the devil himself—whom she described as an apelike figure of distorted human feature. Tituba's confession opened the floodgates: by spring the prisons of Essex county were jammed with unconfessed "witches," but not one had been brought to trial. This was partly because of a general uncertainty on how to proceed, but also because the validity of the entire Massachusetts legal system had been open to question since the loss of the charter in 1684. The new governor, William Phips, appointed a "Court of Oyer and Terminer" (to hear and determine) upon his arrival in May, of which Samuel Sewall and John Hathorne (Nathaniel's ancestor of "persecuting spirit") were members. By the end of September nineteen persons had been hanged and one pressed to death by stones.

It is easier to say how it stopped than why it began. (There had been many isolated incidents of witchcraft in New England before Salem, but none had ever grown to such proportions.) As the bodies of executed witches accumulated ("dragged," in Calef's words, for burial "to a Hole, or Grave, between the rocks"), the juries and judges began to waver. More specifically, the ministers of Boston—led by Increase Mather, who had previously sounded an occasional note of caution—turned against the whole grisly business. In a work called *Cases of Conscience* that was first circulated in manuscript, then hastily published, Mather called for a halt to the trials, which he knew had been conducted all along on shaky evidence and authority. The strongest cases were built on outright confession, which became the chief object of official desire. These were sometimes bolstered by "medical" evidence; usually the identification of a "witch's teat," a "preternatural excrescence of flesh" thought to be used for suckling a Satanic imp. But mostly the court had to depend on spectral evidence—the victim's claim that he or she had been visited by a specter of the accused, or of someone recently dead who identified the defendant as an ally of Satan. This kind of convicting evidence had always made the Boston ministers uneasy, and now the elder Mather put his doubts in plain language: "It were better that ten suspected witches should escape, than that one innocent person should be condemned." From that moment, the authority of the court was broken. In October Phips dissolved it.

All this, Miller insisted, "had no effect on the ecclesiastical or political situation, [nor did it] figure in the institutional or ideological development" of New England. Strictly speaking, he was right—but only if we take the narrow view of "effect." For one thing, the shame stayed: it stayed for Samuel Sewall, who made his public confession of complicity five years later; indeed for the whole colony, whose General Court reversed the bills of attainder in 1711 against all executed witches whose families wished it. But more than this residue of guilt, the events at Salem left the religious ideas themselves that had sanctioned the community's vengeance—as well as the men who proclaimed them—in a state of new vulnerability. Cotton Mather's reputation, as Robert Calef made certain, would never recover. (Mather had become something of an authority on witches during the 1680s, when he tended the Goodwin household, whose daughters were suspiciously afflicted. And in an act that still divides historians between reproach and defense, he refused to sign the preface to his father's book.) Calef was not alone in using the witchcraft episode to ridicule the clergy. "The reasonable part of the world," wrote Thomas Brattle, "will laugh" at the "Salem gentlemen." Urbane men like Brattle were perhaps less morally outraged than pained by the sound of the great world's mockery—but whatever the source of their indignation, the disaster at Salem had reduced the idea of Satan's meddling presence from a necessary article of Puritan faith into a superstition. The Mathers had thought that by showing his hand so recklessly the devil might revive in the hearts of New Englanders a vivid sense of the world as a battleground between God and the Prince of Darkness. They were wrong: evil was made not more but less recognizable by the spectacle of innocence defiled.

The text of *Wonders of the Invisible World* is from the edition of 1693, Sig A6 recto–Sig A7 verso.

The Wonders of the Invisible World

. . . The New Englanders are a people of God settled in those which were once the devil's territories; and it may easily be supposed that the devil was exceedingly disturbed when he perceived such a people here accomplishing the promise of old made unto our blessed Jesus, *That he should have the utmost parts of the earth for his possession*. There was not a greater uproar among the Ephesians when the gospel was first brought among them, than there was among the powers of the air (after whom those Ephesians walked)[1] when first the silver trumpets of the gospel here made the joyful sound. The devil, thus irritated, immediately tried all sorts of methods to overturn this poor plantation, and so much of the church as was fled into this wilderness immediately found, *The serpent cast out of his mouth a flood for the carrying of it away*. I believe that never were more satanical devices used for the unsettling of any people under the sun than what have been employed for the extirpation of the vine which God has here planted, casting out the heathen and preparing a room before it, and causing it to take deep root and fill the land, so that it sent its boughs unto the Atlantic Sea eastward, and its branches unto the Connecticut River westward, and the hills were covered with the shadow thereof. But all those attempts of hell have hitherto been

1. Ephesians 2:2: "in time past ye walked according to the course of this world, according to the prince of the power of the air."

abortive; many an Ebenezer has been erected unto the praise of God by his poor people here, and, having obtained help from God, we continue to this day. Wherefore the devil is now making one attempt more upon us; an attempt more difficult, more surprising, more snarled with unintelligible circumstances than any that we have hitherto encountered; an attempt so critical that if we get well through we shall soon enjoy halcyon days with all the vultures of hell trodden under our feet. He has wanted his incarnate legions to persecute us, as the people of God have in the other hemisphere been persecuted: he has therefore drawn forth his more spiritual ones to make an attack upon us. We have been advised by some credible Christians yet alive that a malefactor, accused of witchcraft as well as murder, and executed in this place more than forty years ago, did then give notice of an horrible plot against the country by witchcraft; and a foundation of witchcraft then laid, which if it were not seasonably discovered, would probably blow up, and pull down all the churches in the country. And we have now with horror seen the discovery of such a witchcraft! An army of devils is horribly broke in upon the place which is the center, and after a sort, the first-born of our English settlements. And the houses of the good people there are filled with the doleful shrieks of their children and servants, tormented by invisible hands with tortures altogether preternatural. After the mischiefs there endeavored, and since in part conquered, the terrible plague of evil angels hath made its progress into some other places, where other persons have been in like manner diabolically handled. These our poor afflicted neighbors, quickly after they become infected and infested with these demons, arrive to a capacity of discerning those which they conceive the shapes of their troublers; and notwithstanding the great and just suspicion that the demons might impose the shapes of innocent persons in their spectral exhibitions upon the sufferers (which may perhaps prove no small part of the witch plot in the issue), yet many of the persons thus repesented being examined, several of them have been convicted of a very damnable witchcraft: yea, more than one—twenty have confessed that they have signed unto a book which the devil showed them and engaged in his hellish design of bewitching and ruining our land. We know not, at least I know not, how far the delusions of Satan may be interwoven into some circumstances of the confessions; but one would think all the rules of understanding human affairs are at an end if, after so many most voluntary harmonious confessions, made by intelligent persons of all ages in sundry towns at several times, we must not believe the main strokes wherein those confessions all agree, especially when we have a thousand preternatural things every day before our eyes, wherein the confessors do acknowledge their concernment and give demonstration of their being so concerned. If the devils now can strike the minds of men with any poisons of so fine a composition and operation that scores of innocent people shall unite in confessions of a crime which we see actually committed, it is a thing prodigious, beyond the wonders of the former ages, and it threatens no less than a sort of a dissolution upon the world . . .

SUSANNA MARTIN

Examination of Susanna Martin (1692)

BEFORE THEY CAME to trial, those charged with witchcraft were customarily interrogated by representatives of the court, who then drew up a deposition to be entered as evidence against them. The records of such interrogations preserve with great immediacy the heat of confrontation, as the court, by pitting accusers against accused, sought to extract what it wanted most: confession. In confession lay not only the defendant's best chance of acquittal (none who confessed were executed), but also the prospect for a communal sense of victory over Satan, who, it was believed, had ordered his minions to dissemble, deceive, and deny their fellowship with him. In the bristling defiance of one such defendant, Susanna Martin, we encounter not only a brave woman, but also the general dilemma in which New England found itself: innocent people were being tempted to admit crimes which they had not committed. To save their lives they were being asked to make a mockery of repentance, which had always been an act of absolute centrality in the Puritan concept of covenant obligation. "He that hides his sins shall not prosper," Robert Keayne had said in faithful articulation of the orthodox attitude toward confession, "but he that confesseth and forsaketh them shall find mercy." Susanna Martin was faced with a choice between mercy and self-respect. At both of her examinations, she chose the latter. A few weeks later she was hanged.

The text is from William E. Woodward, *Records of Salem Witchcraft* (Roxbury, Mass., 1864), I, 196–200.

The examination of Susanna Martin, 2 May 1692.

As soon as she came in many had fits.

"Do you know this woman?"

Abigail Williams saith, "It is Goody Martin; she hath hurt me often." Others by fits were hindered from speaking. Elizabeth Hubbard said she hath not been hurt by her. John Indian said he hath not seen her. Mercy Lewis pointed to her and fell into a little fit. Ann Putnam threw her glove in a fit at her. The examinant laughed.

"What, do you laugh at it?"

"Well I may at such folly."

"Is this folly? The hurt of these persons?"

"I never hurt man, woman, or child."

Mercy Lewis cried out, "She hath hurt me a great many times and pulls me down."

Then Martin laughed again.

Mary Walcott saith, "This woman hath hurt me a great many times." Susan Sheldon also accused her of afflicting her.

"What do you say to this?"

"I have no hand in witchcraft."

"What did you do? Did not you give your consent?"

"No, never in my life."

"What ails this people?"

"I do not know."

"But what do you think?"

"I do not desire to spend my judgment upon it."

"Do not you think they are bewitched?"

"No, I do not think they are."

"Tell me your thoughts about them?"

"Why, my thoughts are my own when they are in; but when they are out they are another's."

"You said 'their master'—who do you think is their master?"

"If they be dealing in the black art you may know as well as I."

"Well, what have you done towards this?"

"Nothing."

"Why, it is you or your appearance."

"I cannot help it."

"That may be your master."

"I desire to lead myself according to the word of God."

"Is this according to God's word?"

"If I were such a person I would tell you the truth."

"How comes your appearance just now to hurt these?"

"How do I know?"

"Are not you willing to tell the truth?"

"I cannot tell: he that appeared in Samuel [the] shape [of] a glorified saint can appear in anyone's shape."[1]

"Do you believe these do not say true?"

1. A reference to the visitation by the shade of Samuel to Saul (I Samuel 28:14–15).

"They may lie for aught I know."

"May not you lie?"

"I dare not tell a lie if it would save my life."

"Then you will speak the truth."

"I have spoke nothing else. I would do them any good."

"I do not think you have such affections for them whom just now you insinuated had the devil for their master."

Elizabeth Hubbard was afflicted and then the marshall who was by her said she [Martin] pinched her hand.

Several of the afflicted cried out they saw her upon the beam.

"Pray God discover you, if you be guilty."

"Amen, amen. A false tongue will never make a guilty person."

"You have been a long time coming to the court today; you can come fast enough in the night," said Mercy Lewis.

"No, sweetheart," said the examinant, and then Mercy Lewis and all or many of the rest were afflicted.

John Indian fell into a violent fit and said, "It was that woman, she bites, she bites," and then she was biting her lips.

"Have you not compassion for these afflicted?"

"No, I have none."

Some cried out there was the black man with her, and Goody Vibber, who had not accused her before, confirmed it.

Abigail Williams upon trial could not come near her, nor Goody Vibber, nor Mary Walcott. John Indian cried he would kill her if he came near her, but he was flung down in his approach to her.

"What is the reason these cannot come near you?"

"I cannot tell: it may be the devil bears me more malice than another."

"Do not you see how God evidently discovers you?"

"No. Not a bit for that."

"All the congregation think so."

"Let them think what they will."

"What is the reason these cannot come near you?"

"I do not know but they can if they will, or else if you please I will come to them."

"What is the black man whispering to you?"

"There was none whispered to me."

MARY EASTY

Petition of Mary Easty (1692)

ANOTHER of the nineteen persons convicted of the crime of witchcraft, Mary Easty, offered a petition to Governor Phips a few weeks before her hanging in the summer of 1692. Easty's moving plea is not a request for clemency for herself, but an appeal on behalf of others under indictment and those who might be accused in the future. Her brief statement is remarkable not only for its enormous dignity, but for the way in which it refuses to relinquish belief in New England's capacity to be just. Even as she proclaims her innocence and prepares for her death, Easty commits herself not to revenge but to helping the Puritan authorities see the truth. Hers is an expression of submission without servility. It is a statement of one person's faith that New England can still be saved from itself.

The text of Mary Easty's petition is from Woodward, *Records of Salem Witchcraft*, II, 44–46.

Petition of Mary Easty (20th May, 1692)

The humble petition of Mary Easty unto his Excellencies Sir William Phips, and to the Honored Judge and bench now sitting in judicature in Salem, and the Reverend Ministers, humbly sheweth:

That whereas your poor and humble petitioner, being condemned to die, do humbly beg of you to take it in your judicious and pious considerations that your poor and humble petitioner, knowing my own innocencie—blessed be the Lord for it—and seeing plainly the wiles and subtility of my accusers, by myself cannot but judge charitably of others that are going the way of myself, if the Lord steps not mightily in. I was confined a whole month upon the same account that I am condemned now for, and then cleared by the afflicted persons, as some of your Honors know. And in two days time I was cried out upon by them and have been confined and now am condemned to die. The Lord above knows my innocencie then and likewise does now, as at the great day will be known to men and angels. I petition to your Honors not for my own life, for I know I must die and my appointed time is set, but (the Lord knows it is) that if it be possible, no more innocent blood may be shed, which undoubtedly cannot be avoided in the way and course you go in. I question not but your Honors does to the utmost of your power in the discovery and selecting of witchcraft and witches, and would not be guilty of innocent blood for the world; but by my innocencie I know you are in the wrong way. The Lord in his infinite mercy direct you in this great work, if it be his blessed will that no more innocent blood be shed. I would humbly beg of you that your Honors would be pleased to examine these afflicted persons strictly and keep them apart some time, and likewise to try some of these confessing witches, I being confident there is several of them has belied themselves and others, as will appear if not in this world I am sure in the world to come, whither I am now a-going. And I question not but you'll see an alteration of these things they say myself and others, having made a league with the devil, we cannot confess. I know and the Lord knows, as will shortly appear, they belie me and so I question not but they do others. The Lord above, who is the searcher of all hearts, knows that as I shall answer it at the tribunal seat that I know not the least thing of witchcraft—therefore I cannot, I dare not, belie my own Soul. I beg your Honors not to deny this my humble petition from a poor dying innocent person, and I question not but that the Lord will give a blessing to your endeavors.

To his Excellency Sir William Phips, Governor, and to the Honored Judge and magistrates now sitting in judicature in Salem.

ROBERT CALEF (1648–1719)
More Wonders of the Invisible World (1697)

IN THE FALL of 1693, beginning his work on what would become the *Magnalia* (the life of Phips was first published in 1697), Cotton Mather learned that a seventeen-year-old Boston woman named Margaret Rule was showing symptoms much like those of the bewitched in Salem. Alarmed by the possibility that the horror was spreading, he resolved to examine her for signs that she was the victim of witchcraft. Along with Mather's father and many other leading citizens, a concerned merchant named Robert Calef was present on the occasion of the bedside examination. "Calef was appalled," as David Levin bluntly puts it, "by what he saw and heard"—a reaction that marked the beginning of a feud with Mather that eventually led to the publication (in London, since no Boston printer would risk the Mathers' wrath) of Calef's *More Wonders of the Invisible World* in 1700.

It is not hard to understand why Mather found Calef's report of what he saw that day a piece of venomous libel: "she was in a fit," Calef wrote, "and he . . . rubbed her breast, etc. . . . and put his hand upon her breast and belly, viz. on the clothes over her, and felt a living thing, as he said, which moved the father also to feel, and some others." When Mather declares that questions about the "black man" struck her dumb, Calef reports "a pause without any answer." In such divergences one sees a rift that now ran deep through New England culture: Mather was still speaking the old language of righteous combat; Calef's was the language of skeptical reason.

If he pressed his crusade against the Mathers with wit and skill, Calef also added some distortion and sensationalism. Recognizing this, historians have treated him alternately as an enlightened hero waging the good fight against medieval superstition, or as an opportunist who found the right issue upon which to torment the clerical elite whom he despised. Whatever Calef's motives may finally have been, his mocking answer to Mather's *Wonders of the Invisible World* is a demonstration of how tenuous the ministry's hold was on the respect, let alone the reverence, of the people.

The text of *More Wonders of the Invisible World* is from the edition of 1700, pp. 103–104, 151–154.

More Wonders of the Invisible World

. . . In the times of Sir Edmond Andros his government, Goody Glover, a despised, crazy, ill-conditioned old woman, an Irish Roman Catholic, was tried for afflicting Goodwin's children; by the account of which trial, taken in shorthand for the use of the jury, it may appear that the generality of her answers were nonsense, and her behavior like that of one distracted. Yet the doctors, finding her as she had been for many years, brought her in *compos mentis;* and setting aside her crazy answers to some insnaring questions, the proof against her was wholly deficient. The jury brought her [in] guilty.

Mr. Cotton Mather was the most active and forward of any minister in the country in those matters, taking home one of the children, and managing such intrigues with that child, and after printing such an account of the whole in his *Memorable Providences* as conduced much to the kindling [of] those flames that in Sir William [Phips's] time threatened the devouring [of] this country.

. . . Sir William, when the witchcrafts at Salem began (in his esteem) to look formidable, that he might act safely in this affair, he asked the advice of the ministers in and near Boston. The whole of their advice and answer is printed in *Cases of Conscience,* the last pages. But lest the world should be ignorant who it was that drew the said advice, in this book of the life of Sir William Phips[1] are these words, *The ministers made unto his excellency and the council a return, drawn up at their desire, by Mr. Mather the younger, as I have been informed.* Mr. C.M. therein intending to beguile the world, and make them think that another, and not himself, had taken that notice of his (supposed) good service done therein, which otherwise would have been ascribed to those ministers in general; though indeed the advice then given looks most like a thing of his composing, as carrying both fire to increase, and water to quench, the conflagration; particularly after the devil's testimony by the supposed afflicted had so prevailed as to take away the life of one and the liberty of an hundred, and the whole country set into a most dreadful consternation, then this advice is given, ushered in with thanks for what

1. Mather's *Life of Phips* in the *Magnalia,* first published separately in 1697.

was already done, and in conclusion putting the government upon a speedy and vigorous prosecution, according to the laws of God and the wholesome statutes of the English nation; so adding oil, rather than water, to the flame: for who so little acquainted with [the] proceedings of England, as not to know that they have taken some methods with those here used, to discover who were witches? The rest of the advice, consisting of cautions and directions, are inserted in this [book] of the life of Sir William: so that if Sir William, looking upon the thanks for what was past, and exhortation to proceed, went on to take away the lives of nineteen more, this is according to the advice said to be given him by the ministers; and if the devil, after those executions, be affronted by disbelieving his testimony and by clearing and pardoning all the rest of the accused, yet this also is, according to that advice, but to cast the scale. The same that drew this advice saith, in *Wonders of the Invisible World, Enchantments Encountered,* that to have a hand in anything that may stifle or obstruct a regular direction [detection?] of that witchcraft is what we may well with a holy fear avoid: their majesties' good subjects must not every day be torn to pieces by horrid witchcraft, and those bloody felons be wholly left unprosecuted; the witchcraft is a business that will not be shammed . . . But this is not all; though this book pretends to raise a statue in honor of Sir William, yet it appears it was the least part of the design of the author to honor him, but it was rather to honor himself and the ministers; it being so unjust to Sir William as to give a full account of the cautions given him, but designedly hiding from the reader the incouragements and exhortations to proceed that were laid before him (under the name of the ministers' advice), in effect telling the world that those executions at Salem were without and against the advice of the ministers, expressed in those cautions, purposely hiding their giving thanks for what was already done, and exhorting to proceed, thereby rendering Sir William of so sanguine a complexion that the ministers had such cause to fear his going on with the tragedy, though against their advice, that they desired the president to write his *Cases of Conscience, &c.* To plead misinformation will not salve here, however it may seem to palliate other things, but is a manifest, designed travesty, or misrepresentation, of the ministers' advice to Sir William, a hiding the truth and a wronging the dead, whom the author so much pretends to honor; for which the acknowledgments ought to be as universal as the offense. But though the ministers' advice, or rather Mr. C. Mather's, was perfectly ambidexter, giving as great or greater encouragement to proceed in those dark methods than cautions against them, yet many eminent persons being accused, there was a necessity of a stop to be put to it. If it be true, what was said at the council-board in answer to the commendations of

Sir William for his stopping the proceedings about witchcraft, viz. that it was high time for him to stop it, his own lady being accused; if that assertion were a truth, then New England may seem to be more beholden to the accusers for accusing her, and thereby necessitating a stop, than to Sir William, or to the advice that was given him by his pastor.

Mr. C.M. having been very forward to write books of witchcraft, has not been so forward either to explain or defend the doctrinal part thereof; and his belief (which he had a year's time to compose) he durst not venture, so as to be copied. Yet in this [book] of the life of Sir William he sufficiently testifies his retaining that heterodox belief, seeking by frightful stories of the sufferings of some and the refined sight of others, &c., to obtrude upon the world and confirm it in such a belief as hitherto he either cannot or will not defend, as if the blood already shed thereby were not sufficient . . .

GERSHOM BULKELEY (1636–1713)
Will and Doom (1692)

IN CONTRAST to the chartered colony of Massachusetts, Connecticut during its first quarter-century had no clear legal foundation. "The two southern colonies Conecticott and Newhaven, "wrote one disgruntled observer in 1661, "have no patents . . . but govern by combination amongst themselves, but in a strange confused way, and in this confusion are the govts in New England at present, and I conceive will be no otherwise until his Majesty be pleased to call all again into his own hands." Connecticut had been settled in the mid-1630s by migrants from several towns in the Bay (led by Hooker's Newtowne congregation) who established villages at Hartford, Weathersfield, and Windsor. In 1638, after the Antinomian crisis had passed, John Davenport led another exodus—this time to Quinnipiac, later renamed New Haven—which remained a separate colony until after the Restoration. This sprinkling of Englishmen along the Connecticut River found itself quickly at odds with a group of Puritan investors in England, who dispatched young John Winthrop, Jr., with instructions to enforce their claims to rich tracts of land in the valley. Thus began a series of disputes that stretched over the whole century—sometimes resolved into cooperative unity against Dutch and Indian enemies, but more often breaking into open strife.

Modeling their church and state polities on those of Massachusetts, the Connecticut settlers inclined perhaps to a somewhat broader franchise and to more liberal church admissions, but they were nothing like the pioneer democrats legend has made them out to be. With the Restoration, the need became inescapable for some legal definition of the colony's boundaries and privileges. After hard politicking and large expenditures, the younger Winthrop finally secured a charter from the government of Charles II in 1662. (Roger Williams, with characteristic extremity, estimated the cost of Whitehall's favor at £6000 .) Winthrop's success did not, however, mark an end to internal contention. His achievement came partly at the expense of New Haven, whose brazen protection of two fugitives who had signed Charles I's death warrant made the Connecticut supplicants seem loyal and contrite.

Winthrop's charter functioned until 1687, when Sir Edmund Andros seized control at Hartford, and, following instructions from England, annexed Connecticut for what was now called the Dominion of New England. His ascendancy lasted less than two years—during which he enforced customs duties and the Navigation Acts limiting commerce to British ships. But Andros also moved to challenge land deeds issued under the old charter, and this shift from financial stringency (which could, under the right circumstances, be evaded) to outright dismissal of the colony's substantial landowners led to his downfall. He lost his allies among propertied men when their estates came into jeopardy. In 1689, led by James Fitch, a man of unpolished manner, the General Assembly moved to overthrow the royal government. It is this action that furnished the immediate background to Gershom Bulkeley's *Will and Doom.*

Fitch was an enormously gifted politician (Bulkeley thought him a demagogue) who instituted democratic reforms while accepting large land grants for himself from the Assembly and pressing his real-estate struggle against the Winthrop family and other established clans. The new government, which one displeased magistrate said was sinking "to almost the lowest ebb of democracy, if it did not border upon anarchy," pursued its own vigorous tax policy—threatening in 1689 and again in 1692 that if any residents failed to submit inventories of taxable property the General Court would "rate them, *will and doom,*" by confiscating their livestock. It was this provision that gave Bulkeley his title, but it was the character of the whole revolutionary government that earned his rage. Bulkeley considered Fitch and his allies little more than backwoods boors who were exploiting Andros' mistakes for their own purposes—notably social advancement. In articulating his contempt, Bulkeley brought into New England writing a gift for political satire and a candid royalism that had not been heard before. *Will and Doom* remained unpublished (though not unknown) until 1895, so American conservatives cannot really claim Bulkeley as a progenitor, but he did foreshadow later instances of antipopulist candor—a rare commodity in American political culture. Few documents in our history are so blunt as his in condemning "a leveling, independent, democratic principle" as "a very churlish drug." In the context of Puritan New England, Bulkeley's singularity can be seen in his judgment that the "root of all bitterness lurked [in] . . . the unhappy rebellion in England, against the noble prince [King Charles I]"—an event for which his father, Peter Bulkeley, had shown support, if not delight.

Just as John Wise appears a harbinger of James Otis and Sam Adams in his disrespect for monarchy (see Wise, *A Vindication of the Churches of New England,* below), so Bulkeley may be seen as a forecast of Alexander Hamilton in his caustic warning against the rule of the mob. But it should be remembered that he, like Wise, was protesting a form of taxation without representation, and among his points was the charge that the election of 1689 had been a seizure of power by a coterie of ambitious men masquerading as democratic representatives—men who made certain that votes could be cast only for or against their entire slate, not for individual candidates. In short, it was not so much democracy itself that Bulkeley rejected, as sham democracy. The legal rights of accused felons, he declared, are not respected in revolutionary Connecticut; the whole rebellion is a brutal farce. The language with which *Will and Doom* lampooned Fitch and his cronies was inflamed as much by a zeal for honor as by condescension toward the unwashed. *Will and Doom* is thus much more than an early explosion of American reaction: it is a work of dissident courage.

The text of the Preface to *Will and Doom* is from the *Collections of the Connecticut Historical Society,* 3 (1895): 81–86, 90–91.

Will and Doom

The Preface

It is an old saying *Insipientis est, dicere non putarem,*[1] and be it so: yet we must acknowledge that, considering our circumstances, we could not have thought there would have been any need for us to trouble ourselves or others with the writing or reading of this narrative. And the truth is, we have been more unwilling unnecessarily to expose those with whom we have to do than they have been either to injure us or expose themselves.

There is no reproach like that of a story which doth stigmatize so deep that it can hardly wear out again, but the dishonor will live time out of mind when the men are dead, which otherwise would be avoided if all good ends might be attained without it, as for good reasons we did hope and expect.

But, as we are hitherto disappointed of our expectation, so they have taken such measures as have compelled us to take this course if we may the better break their yoke from our necks and not entail slavery to our posterity, that we may vindicate ourselves from the most vile aspersions without any cause cast upon us, and may not prove ourselves disloyal and undutiful as well as they.

1. It is the mark of a fool to say I would never have thought . . .

The measures whereby they have so compelled us, endeavoring to enthrall and delude us at home, and to forestall us abroad, that we might be remediless under their abuses and oppression of us, the following narrative will sufficiently declare. And this could not content them: but, that we might be the fitter objects of their indignation, we are traduced and reviled as enemies to God, our country, and to wholesome laws and good government an ungoverned crew, sons of Belial, rebels, &c., because we will not rebel, but persist in our allegiance; and in particular, out of a peculiar (though altogether undeserved) malice against some of us, who have more especially declared against their illegal and unwarrantable actions, these are most opprobriously defamed, as if they were enemies to government and friends to none but popish, French, and arbitrary government, yea papists, wicked incendiaries, disturbers of the peace (because they endeavored and desired that the government and peace might have been preserved), Jacobites, Edmundites,[2] such as serve the devil and the Pope, reprobates, &c. And, having thus dressed us in bear-skins, they sport themselves in baiting of us. All this while, as they have no shadow of any warrant from their majesties[3] for the exercise of this government to which they now pretend, so they never dared to set out any declaration of the grounds and reasons of their rejection of the government of the crown of England here erected by Sir Edmund Andros, nor any vindication of the lawfulness and justice of their proceedings in the resumption, or assumption, erecting and exercising of this government, but require us to pin our faith on their sleeve, and to obey merely because they command; herein acting according to the professed principles of the papists, by whose doctrine the oath of allegiance given to our own prince may be dissolved or annulled by the Pope; and on the other hand it is for merchants, and not for great men or magistrates, to keep their oaths, and which requires an implicit faith and blind obedience . . .

It is true . . . that divers pamphlets have been published elsewhere in the country by some who, intruding into things they have not seen nor known, would justify Connecticut with themselves, if they knew how to do it; . . . all [these] are good for nothing in the world but to mislead, poison and prejudicate (otherwise honest and well-meaning, but) ignorant and not well-principled people against their majesties' true and lawful government; to make loyal subjects, who cannot concur with their exorbitances, odious, as if they were enemies to the people, and so to promote an Oliverian[4] republic, to raise and foment animosities, and

2. Those loyal to James II.
3. William and Mary.
4. Cromwellian.

animate the mobile to rebellion; by all which the country hath received much detriment, but no benefit at all, saving that hereby we see what spirit too many are of.

Also we cannot deny but that James Fitch in this colony hath scattered two scurrillous libels, one about the beginning of the year 1691 (almost two years after the revolt), entituled *A Plain Short Discourse, &c.*, the other about the beginning of 1692, entituled *A Little of the Much, & c.*, endeavoring to justify that which cannot be justified.[5]

With all these, silly people are much taken, and such as are willing to be deceived may be deceived by him. But no man of conscience and reason, desirous of truth, can receive the least satisfaction; for if nonsense, notorious falsehood, obloquy and absurdity would do his business, I must confess he hath done it substantially. Otherwise we are as wise as we were before.

The mention hereof brings to mind a passage very meet to be here taken notice of. This James Fitch is a corporation captain (forsooth), and was a prime ringleader in the late motions, and therefore takes upon him in his *Plain Discourse* (for we easily grant it to be his), to give his commands and animate his followers, in the words following: "Let those," says he, "in authority" (i.e. this new usurped authority) "be touched both in conscience of duty, office and oath, and in care of the peace and welfare of the colony, now draw forth the sword of justice, to defend and secure the peace, liberties, laws, privileges of the colony according to charter; to screw up the ink-horns, still the tongues, empty the purses, and confine the persons of our objectors, unless they will take warning and be persuaded to do their own business and study the things that make for peace. It was the saying of an able state-man, If there be distemper in a state that necessarily requires amendment, let it be done with the pruning-knife of the law, &c." Thus he.

The man, we see, is for money in the first place, and for amputation in the issue. These are his prescribed methods. The compulsion and force of prisons and fines are the cogent arguments of our conviction of the lawfulness (or otherwise unlawfulness) of their authority, which (if we may use, and better we cannot use, than the words of our late most renowned sovereign lord, King Charles the first), is the arbitrator of beasts, not of men, much less of Christians. Indeed, I understand that some of his brethren, who have more wit than he, cannot but laugh in their sleeves at the weakness and capriciousness of this goat, discovered in these papers: yet they have been too ready to follow such unprofitable

5. Fitch's pamphlets, which probably circulated only in manuscript, are not known to have survived.

counsel, as would bring fish to their net and feathers to their nests. Imprisoning of our persons and emptying of our purses is a game they have eagerly followed, to the no little damage of many of their majesties' good subjects.

They zealously pursue us, but not of their will to help or relieve us. Upon sight of their majesties' coronation oath, promising to govern us according to the statutes agreed on in parliament, &c., and also of their majesties' proclamation of Feb. 14th, 1688, for the continuance of sheriffs, justices of the peace, &c., some were encouraged to apply to the justices of the peace for relief of their abuses, . . . praying them to execute their commissions according to their majesties' command, and promising obedience, aid and assistance to them, &c., but all in vain: such of them as would cannot help us, being deserted by their brethren; and the rest will not, being parties to the revolt: but instead of relieving, rail upon us, threaten us with imprisonment, and we are more hurt than helped by them.

Yea, they will not so much as hear us. This authority is much like that in Oliver's time, when a faction and fag-end of the commons set up themselves for a parliament and erected a high court of injustice; a mere *noli me tangere,*[6] that will admit of no objection or dispute, but what is wanting in authority is supplied by ferocity. What, you oppose the authority, are an enemy to or question the government? a turbulent fellow, such fellows as you must be dealt with. They have all along made it appear that they will neither give nor take reason about the matter. They stick[7] not to declare in open court, that they are not bound to give any account of their authority but to their master, and we cannot find who that is, for it seems they are not obliged to shew any commission; their authority is an absolute and fountain power; they brag, they shall never be called to an account and, therefore, are bold to do they care not what, without control or objection, for all objectors must have their tongues stilled and their ink-horns screwed up. Hereby the reader may perceive something of our state, and that if this pretended government must stand (at least alone, as it is), we may conclude *actum est de nobis,*[8] we are but as sheep for the slaughter, and must be dumb before our shearers and butchers.

And what is the reason of this? If there were any just cause for it, we might thank ourselves. Why, the cause is this: There was a time when they had, in its degree, a lawful authority of government over us, although

6. Do not touch me.
7. Hesitate.
8. It is done by us.

even then, the light of law being taken from us, we were not able to see how they exceeded it and, before we were aware, enslaved us. But, in the year 1687 and 1688, they deserted and abdicated the government, and if their own testimony be true (however it may be good against themselves), put us under and left us in the hands of an arbitrary, tyrannical, popish and French government and governor; and though this be their mistake or pretext, yet thus they represent and seem to account it; and so it might have been for all them, such was their care of us. They knew the governor and his commission long before, and yet thus they dealt with us, and this act of theirs is on their part a desertion of us, and on our part a good manumission from them: for, *servus a domino desertus liber esto.*[9]

But in truth, by this means we were (though *præter intentionem suam*),[10] restored to our proper master, and reduced under the King's legal government (for the substance of it), which was our happiness; and more happy we might have been by the continuance of it.

But, in the year 1689, repenting themselves and taking advantage of that time, they (as they now term it) resume their own government, claim a property in us, and would bring us back into thralldom unto them again . . .

There are divers unhappy ingredients in our disorders and confusions in N. England, and so in Connecticut: as first, a misconstruction of charters, and a misunderstanding of the nature, privileges and power of corporations thereby created, and hence a great mistake whereby they think that, the King having incorporated them by a charter, &c., they are invested with a *summum imperium,*[11] and are become a free state . . .

Secondly. A leveling, independent, democratical principle and spirit, with a tang of the fifth-monarchy, which is a very churlish drug.

Thirdly. The abolition of the common and statute laws of England, and so of all human laws except the forgeries of our own popular and rustical shop and the dictates of personal discretion . . .

Fourthly. From these very naturally and evidently follows a fourth, and that is, a principle and spirit of disloyalty and wicked prejudice against the king and his government . . .

This root of all bitterness lurked more hiddenly in its principles for a while, but that which made it sprout, spring up and become visible, was the unhappy rebellion in England, against the noble prince (*gentis Angliæ decus et opprobrium*)[12] King Charles the first. The virulent ferment of

9. Let the servant deserted by his master be free.
10. Despite their will.
11. Supreme power.
12. The honor and shame of the English people.

that measure excited the seeds that were sown before, and hereby an antimonarchical spirit, and prejudice against the king, his person and government, became so strongly rooted in the country as not to be easily or speedily, if ever, totally eradicated.

These untoward ingredients must needs make up a pernicious composition, and, consequently, there is no great cause to wonder at our enormities or calamities: here is the root and spring of all . . .

We may sorrowfully remember the years in England from 1642 to 1660. They that cleave to their sovereign are (*eo nomine*)[13] called the Malignant Party, and they who cut off his head the Godly Party. God deliver us from such godliness . . .

13. By his name.

JOHN WISE (1652–1725)

A Vindication of the Government of New England Churches (1717)

UNLIKE his contemporaries Gershom Bulkeley and Cotton Mather, John Wise was not born to the Puritan purple. His father arrived in New England as an indentured servant in the Great Migration, then evidently became a butcher, then a brewer, and made a sufficient living to send the fifth of his dozen children to Harvard. Part of the bill for John's tuition was probably paid in malt.

In the early 1670s the young graduate ministered to a congregation in Branford, Connecticut, from which he was called to serve as chaplain during King Philip's War. (Gershom Bulkeley served the same troops as surgeon.) After a short tenure at Hatfield, Wise removed to Chebacco in Essex County, Massachusetts, where a part of the Ipswich church had agitated for years to gather its own congregation. This was his home for the rest of his life.

It was in the struggle against Andros that Wise made his mark on the colony and in American history. In 1687, against the advice of his council, the royal governor decreed that "all male residents . . . must pay a poll tax" and a property tax assessed according to worth. The levy was not especially onerous, but Andros had committed what William Stoughton called an "irregular and grievous departure" from the established system of setting rates in consultation with elected representatives. Wise became a leading spokesman for resistance, and declared that "it was not the town's duty . . . to assist [this] method of raising money." In short, there was to be no tax collected in Ipswich. He later recanted his stand, not as the seditious act of which he now stood accused, but as a manifestation of his own naive credulity: "We too boldly endeavored to persuade ourselves we were Englishmen and under privileges." Jailed at Boston in September 1687, he was tried, convicted, and fined in short order. Two years later, sitting on the General Court that dealt with the deposed governor, he sued Joseph Dudley, formerly a member of Andros's council, for having denied him a writ of habeas corpus.

After another stint as a military chaplain—this time with the new Governor Phips's ill-fated expedition against Quebec—Wise returned to an Essex filled with the cry of "witchcraft." He signed the preface to Increase Mather's *Cases of Conscience,* the work that discredited spectral evidence as legitimate grounds for conviction. When the witchcraft madness passed, Wise settled quietly into his pastorate.

But in 1710 he was again engaged in a polemic against the authority of Boston. This time he identified his opponents as the Mathers, who had been smoldering since the founding in 1699 of the Brattle Street Church, which they considered insolently defiant of congregational practice. By 1700 they were involved in an annual ministerial "association" to check innovation in the churches. Finally, the meeting of 1705 produced a document, the *Proposals,* that attacked the bedrock of congregational independence by delegating to a standing council the power to license ministers. Five years later Wise composed his response, *The Churches Quarrel Espoused* (not published until 1713), a book that has seemed to many historians a strangely belated outburst over an issue that had already faded away. Massachusetts never did adopt a formal code of church governance comparable to Connecticut's Saybrook Platform (1708), and the Mathers had been diverted by Governor Dudley and by events at Harvard from their crusade to restore church discipline. (In fact, their commitment to conciliar supervision has been exaggerated.) Outdated and misdirected or not, the *Churches' Quarrel* was an angry rejection of what Wise considered a "crude dose" of proto-Presbyterianism, which he thought an ongoing danger. His weapon was wit, with which he rebuked the Mathers for both principle and practice, declining to accept their offer of "liberty to be governed with a hook in [the] nose," and questioning not only the legitimacy, but also the feasibility of their program: "had we in all corners of our country doves trained up to carry mails or pacquets of letters . . . there might be some hopes" that a central association could guide the churches.

It was "in service of my country, and in defense of their sacred liberties" that Wise allowed himself such irreverence. In his defense he based his arguments for democratic localism more and more on what he called "right reason, which is the soul of man," thereby indicating how far New England had come since John Cotton's announcement in the 1630s: "Democracy, I do not conceive th[at] ever God did ordain as a fit government either for church or commonwealth." Wise develops his rationalist theme further in *A Vindication of the Churches of New England.* In this work's suspicion of authority imposed on well-settled churches, and its candid attribution of individual rights to "natural law," Wise displayed a mind steeped in Puritan biblicism but responsive to the winds of Enlightenment. With this combination, he exemplifies the difficulty of sorting out the early American roots of what we now call conservatism from those of what we call liberalism. Each camp has periodically claimed Wise for its own.

The text of *A Vindication of the Government of New England Churches* is from the edition of 1772, pp. 22–26, 28–29, 31–33, 35, 39, 43–44.

A Vindication of the Government of New England Churches

I shall disclose several principles of natural knowledge, plainly discovering the law of nature or the true sentiments of natural reason with respect to man's being and government; and in this essay I shall peculiarly confine the discourse to two heads, viz.

1. Of the natural (in distinction from the civil), and then,

2. Of the civil being of man; and I shall principally take Baron Pufendorf[1] for my chief guide and spokesman.

I shall consider man in a state of natural being as a freeborn subject under the crown of heaven and owing homage to none but God himself. It is certain civil government in general is a very admirable result of providence and an incomparable benefit to mankind, yet must needs be acknowledged to be the effect of human free-compacts and not of divine institution . . . I shall more distinctly explain the state of human nature in its original capacity, as man is placed on earth by his maker, and clothed with many investitures and immunities which properly belong to man separately considered. As,

The prime immunity in man's state is that he is most properly the subject of the law of nature. He is the favorite animal on earth, in that this part of God's image, viz. reason, is congenate with his nature, wherein by a law immutable, instamped upon his frame, God has provided a rule for men in all their actions, obliging each one to the performance of that which is right, not only as to justice but likewise as to all other moral virtues, the which is nothing but the dictate of right reason founded in the soul of man . . . That which is to be drawn from man's reason, flowing from the true current of that faculty, when unperverted, may be said to be the law of nature, on which account the Holy Scriptures declare it

1. Samuel von Pufendorf's *De Jure Naturae et Gentium* (*On the Law of Nature and Nations;* 1672) was translated into English in 1703, and quickly became one of the leading statements of the theory of contractual government. With the Glorious Revolution of 1688, English legalists placed a new stress on the covenantal obligations of the king.

written on men's hearts. For being endowed with a soul, you may know from yourself how and what you ought to act. Romans 2:14, *These having not a law, are a law to themselves*. So that the meaning is, when we acknowledge the law of nature to be the dictate of right reason, we must mean that the understanding of man is endowed with such a power as to be able, from the contemplation of human condition, to discover a necessity of living agreeably with this law; and likewise to find out some principle by which the precepts of it may be clearly and solidly demonstrated. The way to discover the law of nature in our own state is by a narrow watch and accurate contemplation of our natural condition and propensions . . . But more particularly in pursuing our condition for the discovery of the law of nature, this is very obvious to view, viz.

A principle of self-love and self-preservation is very predominant in every man's being;

A sociable disposition;

An affection or love to mankind in general.

And to give such sentiments the force of a law, we must suppose a God who takes care of all mankind and has thus obliged each one as a subject of higher principles of being than mere instincts. For that all law properly considered supposes a capable subject and a superior power, and the law of God, which is binding, is published by the dictates of right reason as other ways. Therefore, says Plutarch, "To follow God and obey reason is the same thing" . . . Man is a creature extremely desirous of his own preservation; of himself he is plainly exposed to many wants, unable to secure his own safety and maintenance without assistance of his fellows; and he is also able of returning kindness by the furtherance of mutual good. But yet man is often found to be malicious, insolent, and easily provoked, and as powerful in effecting mischief as he is ready in designing it. Now that such a creature may be preserved, it is necessary that he be sociable; that is, that he be capable and disposed to unite himself to those of his own species and to regulate himself towards them that they may have no fair reason to do him harm, but rather incline to promote his interests and secure his rights and concerns. This then is a fundamental law of nature, that every man as far as in him lies do maintain a sociableness with others, agreeable with the main end and disposition of human nature in general. For this is very apparent, that reason and society render man the most potent of all creatures. And finally, from the principles of sociableness it follows as a fundamental law of nature that man is not so wedded to his own interest but that he can make the common good the mark of his aim. And hence he becomes capacitated to enter into a civil state by the law of nature; for without this property in nature, viz. sociableness, which is for cementing of parts, every government would soon molder and dissolve.

The second great immunity of man is an original liberty instamped upon his rational nature. He that intrudes upon this liberty violates the law of nature . . .

The third capital immunity belonging to man's nature is an equality amongst men which is not to be denied by the law of nature till man has resigned himself with all his rights for the sake of a civil state; and then his personal liberty and equality is to be cherished and preserved to the highest degree as will consist with all just distinctions amongst men of honor and shall be agreeable with the public good . . .

To consider man in a civil state of being, wherein we shall observe the great difference between a natural and political state; for in the latter state many great disproportions appear, or at least many obvious distinctions are soon made amongst men; which doctrine is to be laid open under a few heads.

Every man considered in a natural state must be allowed to be free and at his own dispose; yet to suit man's inclinations to society, and in a peculiar manner to gratify the necessity he is in of public rule and order, he is impelled to enter into a civil community and divests himself of his natural freedom and puts himself under government, which amongst other things comprehends the power of life and death over him, together with authority to enjoin him some things to which he has an utter aversion, and to prohibit him other things for which he may have as strong an inclination; so that he may be often, under this authority, obliged to sacrifice his private for the public good. So that though man is inclined to society, yet he is driven to a combination by great necessity. For that the true and leading cause of forming governments and yielding up natural liberty, and throwing man's equality into a common pile to be new cast by the rules of fellowship was really and truly to guard themselves against the injuries men were liable to interchangeably; for none so good to man as man, and yet none a greater enemy . . .

Let us conceive in our mind a multitude of men, all naturally free and equal, going about voluntarily to erect themselves into a new commonwealth. Now their condition being such to bring themselves into a politic body, they must needs enter into divers covenants.

They must interchangeably each man covenant to join in one lasting society, that they may be capable to concert the measures of their safety by a public vote.

A vote or decree must then nextly pass to set up some particular species of government over them. And if they are joined in their first compact upon absolute terms to stand to the decision of the first vote concerning the species of government, then all are bound by the majority to acquiesce in that particular form thereby settled, though their own private opinion incline them to some other model.

After a decree has specified the particular form of government, then there will be need of a new covenant, whereby those on whom sovereignty is conferred engage to take care of the common peace and welfare; and the subjects on the other hand, to yield them faithful obedience. In which covenant is included that submission and union of wills by which a state may be conceived to be but one person. So that the most proper definition of a civil state is this, viz., A civil state is a compound moral person whose will (united by those covenants before passed) is the will of all; to the end it may use and apply the strength and riches of private persons towards maintaining the common peace, security, and well-being of all, which may be conceived as though the whole state was now become but one man . . .

The forms of a regular state are three only, which forms arise from the proper and particular subject in which the supreme power resides. As,

A democracy, which is when the sovereign power is lodged in a council consisting of all the members, and where every member has the privilege of a vote. This form of government appears in the greatest part of the world to have been the most ancient. For that reason seems to show it to be most probable that when men (being originally in a condition of natural freedom and equality) had thoughts of joining in a civil body, would without question be inclined to administer their common affairs by their common judgment, and so must necessarily to gratify that inclination establish a democracy . . .

The second species of regular government is an aristocracy; and this is said then to be constituted when the people or assembly united by a first covenant and having thereby cast themselves into the first rudiment of a state, do then by common decree devolve the sovereign power in a council consisting of some select members; and these having accepted of the designation are then properly invested with sovereign command; and then an aristocracy is formed.

The third species of a regular government is a monarchy, which is settled when the sovereign power is conferred on some one worthy person. It differs from the former because a monarch who is but one person in natural as well as in moral account, and so is furnished with an immediate power of exercising sovereign command in all instances of government; but the forenamed must needs have particular time and place assigned; but the power and authority is equal in each.

Mixed governments, which are various and of divers kinds (not now to be enumerated) yet possibly the fairest in the world is that which has a regular monarchy, settled upon a noble democracy as its basis. And each part of the government is so adjusted by pacts and laws that render the whole constitution an Elysium. It is said of the British empire that it is such a monarchy as that by the necessary subordinate concurrence of the Lords and Commons, in the making and repealing all statutes or acts of Parliament, it hath the main advantages of an aristocracy and of a democracy, and yet free from the disadvantages and evils of either. It is such a monarchy as by most admirable temperament affords very much to the industry, liberty, and happiness of the subject, and reserves enough for the majesty and prerogative of any king who will own his people as subjects, not as slaves. It is a kingdom that of all the kingdoms of the world is most like to the kingdom of Jesus Christ, whose yoke is easy and burden light . . .

I shall now proceed to enquire whether any of the aforesaid species of regular, unmixed governments can, with any good show of reason, be predicable of the church of Christ on earth . . .

A democracy. This is a form of government which the light of nature does highly value, and often directs to, as most agreeable to the just and natural prerogatives of human beings. This was of great account in the early times of the world; and not only so, but upon the experience of several thousand years, after the world had been tumbled and tossed from one species of government to another at a great expense of blood and treasure, many of the wise nations of the world have sheltered themselves under it again, or at least have blendished and balanced their governments with it . . .

But to wind up the whole discourse in a few words . . .

Three particulars, or so many golden maxims, securing the honor of congregational churches:

Particular 1. That the people or fraternity under the gospel are the first subject of power, or else religion sinks the dignity of human nature into a baser capacity with relation to ecclesiastical, than it is in, in a natural state of being with relation to civil government.

Particular 2. That a democracy in church or state is a very honorable and regular government according to the dictates of right reason. And therefore,

Particular 3. That these churches of New England, in their ancient constitution of church order, it being a democracy, are manifestly justified and defended by the law and light of nature . . .

JEREMIAH DUMMER (1679–1739)
A Defense of the New England Charters (1715)

JEREMIAH DUMMER spent most of his life in England, where he served, from the reign of Queen Anne to the Hanoverian succession, as a political representative for his native New England. In 1710, before he had turned thirty, he became the official agent for Massachusetts, an appointment conferred upon him with less than unanimous confidence: "Barter away none . . . of our religious privileges," Samuel Sewall warned him, "though you might have millions in lieu of them." This kind of nervous cajoling hounded Dummer all his life. In 1704 Increase Mather had commended Dummer's *Discourse on the Holiness of the Sabbath* so that "he might vindicate himself from the calumny of being an anti-Sabbatarian." A decade later Dummer was rankling at similar "slander"—this time that he "had filled the [Yale] Library" with Anglican books in order to undermine the infant congregational college. This was one of many situations in which he found himself vilified by groups on both sides of a controversy. Among his projects from afar had been to persuade Thomas Hollis, a rich benefactor of Harvard, to divert some of his wealth to the new school at New Haven. "Dummer's management for Yale College," Hollis reacted, "led me to suspect a snake in the grass"; he declined the request. Those, meanwhile, who did want an orthodox alternative to Harvard were saying that the notorious "defection from the religion of their country" by Samuel Johnson and Timothy Cutler (Yale tutors who embraced the Church of England) "was owing to the library [that Dummer] had sent over." Somehow, Dummer's advocacy was always construed as a ruse for his own dastardly purposes.

So while he worked with remarkable effectiveness to thwart parliamentary motions to recall New England's charters, Dummer was never quite trusted at home. To his less adventurous countrymen he seemed unwholesome, a prodigal son seduced by the enchantments of England. "In his latter days," it was said, "he grew a libertine and kept a seraglio of misses around him." One shocked visitor from the American provinces found him surrounded by ladies "sipping raspberry punch" after dinner.

In fact Dummer did aspire without embarrassment to the aristocratic mode of cultivated leisure, if not to dissipation. In a poem published near the end of his life in the *Gentleman's Magazine,* he pays homage, in rather insistent rhyme, to Alexander Pope:

> O could I chant like him, the country swains
> Should leave their bleating flocks upon the plains,
> And ravish'd listen to my rural strains.

It is a nice irony that while Dummer celebrated the manorial country life near London and far from his rural homeland, and while he expressed fatigue with the grimy world of politics and finance, he produced an argument on behalf of New England that is dominated by the value of its exports and expenditures. The *Defense of the New England Charters* is a candidly utilitarian statement: "The sum of my argument," it concludes, "is, that the benefit which Great Britain receives from the plantation, arises from their commerce." New England "is a good nursery of seamen for the navy . . . [it] assists the islands that [make sugar] . . . [it] buys every sort of British manufacture." In short, the *Defense* amounts to a concession that New England was settled "at a vast expense" and an assertion that it was paying its debt with interest. This deferential argument carried the day. The colonists kept their charters.

To the historian interested in such an elusive subject as the New England mind, a different calculation of cost may occur upon reading Dummer's *Defense.* Dummer himself was a marginal American, but the premises of his advocacy, and the support he enjoyed from such figures as Cotton Mather, who endorsed his "fidelity and assiduity, in our service," are clues to a fundamental shift in New England's understanding of itself. Already by 1700 the Brattle Street organizers were scoffing at those who believed that "the design of our first planters . . . consisted in some little rites, modes, or circumstances of church discipline." In looking back to those founders, Dummer is equally quick to say what they were not—"neither criminals nor necessitous"—but he leaves us wondering what they were. This question is not centrally at issue in Dummer's *Defense*—a work whose purpose is to protect New Englanders of the present rather than to explain those of the past. But one may wonder just what was left to New England when Dummer saved it from the Tories. No mature culture could rest upon an image of itself as a service station for Mother Britain. By the time John Adams came to cite the *Defense* as a waking moment in the prehistory of the Republic, such a form of American self-defense had been examined and found wanting.

The text of the *Defense* is from the edition of 1721, pp. 7–13, 15–16, 73, 76–78.

A Defense of the New England Charters

. . . To increase the nation's commerce and enlarge her dominions must be allowed a work of no little merit, if we consider the hardships to which the adventurers were exposed; or the expense in making their settlements . . . After many dangers in their voyages over the Atlantic, which was not such an easy navigation a hundred years ago as it is now, they arrived at an inhospitable shore and a waste wilderness, where there were few of the necessaries, and not one of the accommodations of life; where the climate was so extreme, the summer heats so scorching, and the winters so long and so cold, that the country seemed hardly habitable. To sum up their misfortunes . . . by fatigue and famine, by the extremity of the seasons, and by a war with the savages, the first planters soon found their graves, leaving the young settlements to be perfected by their survivors.

To omit all this, I shall only be particular in the expense, which was above 200,000 £ pounds sterling in settling the single province of the Massachusetts Bay. The account stands thus: the freight of the passengers cost 95,000 £. The transportation of their first stock of cattle came to 12,000 £. The provisions laid in for subsistence, till by tillage more could be raised, cost 45,000 £. The materials for building their first little cottages came to 18,000 £. Their arms and ammunition cost 192,000 £, not taking into account the very great sums which were expended in things of private use, that people could not be without, who were going to possess an uninhabited land. I must add that 192 ships were employed in making this great plantation, and twelve years were spent before it was brought to any tolerable degree of perfection.

As great, however, as this expense was, I believe it will appear that the settlement of New England was not more chargeable to the adventurers, than it has been in its consequence profitable to Great Britain. There is no sort of British manufacture, but what the subjects there demand in a greater or less proportion, as they have ability to pay for it; everything for the use, convenience, ornament, and (I say it with regret) the luxury and pride of life. Some of the oldest and most experienced traders to those parts have by computation made these exports arise to the value of 300,000 £ per annum. The imports from thence are equally beneficial to the kingdom. They brought home bullion as long as they had any left; and now they are so exhausted they can no longer send it directly, they continue to remit it by way of Spain, Portugal, and the Straits: it is there they sell their fish, and the produce of it comes hither in gold and silver, or bills of exchange, which is the same thing.

Other and better returns than money itself they make in masts, the fairest and largest in the whole world, besides pitch, turpentine, rosin, plank, knees for ships, and other species of timber for various uses . . . What we take of these commodities from our own plantations, is brought home in our own ships, and paid for with our manufactures . . .

Other articles might be mentioned, as whale oil and fins, which are yearly imported from New England in no contemptible quantities . . .

'Tis true, New England makes no sugar, but it assists the islands that do; without which assistance they could not make it, at least not cheap enough and in sufficient quantities to answer the markets in Europe . . .

It may be added that New England is a good nursery of seamen for the navy. I believe I may affirm that there was hardly a ship during the last war, in the royal navy, without some of *their* sailors on board, which so distressed the New England merchants, that they were obliged to man their ships with Indians and Negroes.

What I have said amounts to this: that New England received her charters on this express condition, of settling colonies for the benefit of the crown: that she has at a vast expense, and through incredible difficulties accomplished the work even beyond what was ever hoped or expected.

And then the conclusion that I would draw from these premises is this, that to strip the country of their charters after the service has been so successfully performed, is abhorrent from all reason, equity, and justice . . .

It seems therefore a severity without a precedent, that a people who have the misfortune of being a thousand leagues distant from their sovereign, a misfortune great enough in itself, should unsummoned, unheard, in one day be deprived of all their privileges which they and their fathers have enjoyed for near an hundred years . . .

It's indeed very reasonable that all public affairs be subject to the determination of the public wisdom, and there is no occasion to notify anybody, because everybody is supposed to be present in the representative body of the whole; but here the provinces to be censured and deprived have no representative in Parliament, and consequently must be considered as absent persons, suffering unheard . . .

BENJAMIN COLMAN (1673–1747)

Practical Discourses on The Parable of the Ten Virgins (c. 1705)

LED BY Thomas Brattle, the urbane Treasurer of Harvard College (who during the witchcraft years had pointedly excluded New England from "the reasonable part of the world"), a group of Boston's well-to-do merchants undertook in 1699 to build a meeting house where they could worship in style. "Every baptized adult person," they declared, "who contributes to the maintenance," was to have a voice in choosing the pastor of this new church, and public professions of faith were no longer to be required, not even in written form as the South Church had been allowing for some time.

These intentions amounted to much more than a frittering away of time-honored convention. To some historians, the Mathers have seemed extravagantly defensive in accusing these "innovators" of plotting "utterly to blow up all." In the final analysis, however, they were right: the *Manifesto* (1699) of the new church, and more explicitly a pamphlet entitled *The Gospel Order Revived* (1700), both written mainly by Benjamin Colman, amounted to flat declarations that the basic Puritan concept of the gathered church was obsolete. "Our Lord Jesus Christ has nowhere appointed," the authors of the pamphlet declared, "that there should be a covenant entered into by some persons of a Christian society, exclusive of the rest, whereby they being in covenant one with another, should thereby call themselves a Church of Christ." The kind of church that remained after this demolition was to be a community of worshippers "knowing and sound in the fundamental doctrines of the *Christian Religion,* without scandal in their lives"—no more, no less. If a driving Puritan impulse had once been to bring the visible and invisible church as close to congruence as human means would allow, the Brattle Street group was now pronouncing that ministers "are not heart searchers." To the Mathers this was a surrender to a world where the appetite for self-promotion had grown but the willingness to test inner assurance had vanished. This, they thought, was plain and simple treason to the meaning of New England. For those who had once been called "formal hypocrites" and had been excluded from full church membership, there was nothing now to keep them out except their own indifference.

Benjamin Colman, the man chosen as first minister of the Brattle Street Church, was a child during the ravages of the 1670s and barely twelve years old when Massachusetts lost her charter in 1684. Such patriarchs as Increase Mather, encouraging and excoriating the people of New England in the name of the fathers, were for Colman, if not quite storybook legends, not quite real presences either. With Davenport gone, John Eliot grown old, and the Mathers slipping, Colman came into adulthood on the verge of a new age.

As a frail young graduate of "thin and slender appearance . . . soft and delicate voice . . . [with] red spots in his cheeks [that] suggested consumption," Colman sailed to England to add some finish to his Harvard education. There he preached under appointment of the Presbyterian Board—an act inconceivable for a New England minister of an earlier day. For a time it appeared that he might stay in England, but in 1699 he accepted the call from the founders of the Brattle Street Church. He returned home, married, and lived long enough to be, as Clifford Shipton puts it, "in his time both the youngest and the oldest minister in Boston."

Colman quickly became a master of the pulpit. He offered, in the opinion of one eighteenth-century admirer, "the choicest matter presented in elegant language . . . [in a] style [that] was . . . grand and polite." Officiating at a church known in some circles as the "Presbyterian brat," he aimed in his preaching, as in the following phrases from the *Discourses on the Parable of the Ten Virgins,* not to inflict spiritual pain or joy but to provide an enticing model of Christian "conversation." His was by no means a superficial mind concerned with externals, but he did turn his rhetorical gifts toward imparting a feeling, a taste, for what might be called the right style for salvation: "We should resemble virgins in *purity* . . . think and speak *scripturally;* never . . . take that for knowledge which does not influence to agreeable practice . . . Good men . . . know the worth, and what price to put on the grace of God . . . the renewed soul beholds himself with complacency, loves his own form and comeliness, rejoices in his safety." With such formulations, Colman made alluring the advantages of grace and displayed a model of the saint's deportment. In less abstract passages, he layered his words upon scriptural illustrations—not so much to elucidate doctrine as to create an atmosphere, to play pleasing variations upon his theme. His image-making delights the eye; he became, above all, proficient at exploiting the intimate connection between vision and mood.

Colman portrayed the saint not as a transfigured man but as one who has been promoted to an echelon above anxiety. To his congregation he both recommended and exemplified the virtues of balance and calm. While the Mathers railed that a "*Satanic energy* [was] on the people in this town," and the whole colony was considered in some English quarters to be a collection of misfits, Colman's well-to-do supporters, as Teresa Toulouse points out, "needed an image of themselves that . . . provided them with a sense of social stability." He supplied that need with a sophistication and authority that left the language and even the purpose of the New England pulpit permanently changed.

The text of the *Ten Virgins* is based on the edition of 1707, pp. 2–3, 28–30, 40–41, 62–63, 65, 86–88, 96–97, 372–377.

Practical Discourses on the Parable of the Ten Virgins

The scope and design of the parable is plainly given us in the close of it: to put us on a constant, careful, exact watch, lest the summons of death surprise us unprepared . . .

The parables of our Savior in general, they are similitudes taken from known customs and actions of men, and made use of to inform us in spiritual doctrines. According as they are managed, they are either a familiar and easy, or an obscure and covert way of communicating one's mind. It was a usual mode of teaching with the Jewish doctors, and we have several of their parables to their disciples in our hands to this day. It is obvious that spiritual truths may be very plainly delivered in this allusive way, and when they are so, there is this advantage—that they strangely draw men's attention and fix on the memory while they take the fancy. For we find people will listen to a story or example in a sermon, who sit very careless while the doctrines and laws of Christ are more simply preached . . .

Like espoused virgins we should be expecting, desiring, waiting and preparing for the coming of our Lord; and that whether in the visits he makes to the souls of saints in this life, or his calling them to himself by death. We should look for him, and give him welcome when we meet him . . .

How much more should we with raptures think of and wish for heaven, the place and time of full communion and vision? In this we groan earnestly, in the hope and expectance of the appointed hour for our going to Christ. You know the impatiences of an expecting love, the preparations against the day of the consummations of our desires, and how joyfully it is welcomed when arrived; nor is there any indecency herein. Can the bride forget to provide her ornaments and attire against the time?

No more the believer his, the graces of the spirit of God, and the righteousness which is through the faith of Christ. Death is to the believer the servant and messenger of Christ, attended by a guard of bright and holy angels, to wait on and conduct him to his rest. Why should we not run to meet the smiling vision, as those that are found alive at Christ's second coming will fly up to meet him in the air.

We should resemble virgins in purity. This is eminently that which the comparison in the text is brought for. And so the Apostle expressly uses it in his Epistle to the Corinthians; *I have espoused you to one husband that I may present you as a chaste virgin to Christ.* The metaphor seems far too glorious for us in this sinful flesh—a chaste virgin—for we come polluted into the world; from the moment of our conception we are unclean. We have also in our life actually defiled ourselves with adulterous loves. In how poor a sense then shall we answer the names of innocence, purity, uncorrupt, inviolate chastity? Or, shall we defile ourselves no more from this day forward? What man can promise this either? . . .

The filthiness both of flesh and spirit must be supposed, and the cleansing of both, and this in order to the perfecting holiness . . . There must be a cleansing therefore from sin, wherefore the scripture speaks of our being washed, purged, &c. By imputation the blood of Christ cleanseth from all sin, in which sense cleansing sounds the same with pardon . . . The impure thoughts which the corrupt mind once liked are now banished, the wanton imaginations it once surfeited on find no more place or license. They may break in, but their intrusion does offend. There is an antipathy to them—"I hate vain thoughts." They pollute as well as hinder the soul in holy exercises; like swarms of flies gathering about the sacrifice, that distract the offerer and leave their ordure on the altar . . .

Use: To conclude, you see how foul you are in the eyes of heaven without the spirit of holiness. You may wash and dress, paint and patch, and outwardly admire yourselves as you will; but there is a scurf[1] and scabbiness within. You are to God's pure eyes as those beastly salvages would be to yours, who dress themselves with the entrails of beasts with all the filth in them. So you twine your lusts about your breasts, and hang 'em as bracelets on your neck and arms . . .

All the further use I shall make of the doctrine is in this one inference—that if a profession is necessary, much more is it so to live according to our profession. Your profession is of holiness: let your care be to live holily. Hypocrisy is in many respects as bad as avowed profaneness . . .

The defect of many in their profession should be reproved. Some call

1. A scaly skin condition.

themselves Christians, and yet seek not baptism for themselves or their families.[2] Is this as the last words of the ascending Savior do require and enjoin? Yet how many do forget 'em, and live easy without owning Christ in this appointed way! Who though they see here is water, and are told that so all nations are to be discipled, nay, though they will be ready to say they believe in the Lord Jesus Christ with all their hearts, yet have never so much as asked, *What doth hinder that I should be baptized?* A shameful defect on us, so peculiarly our own in this land, and one woeful effect of the narrow principles our fathers generally began upon in the founding of these churches, that I believe no professing people under heaven has the like to show and blush at.

As for the public and solemn recognition of the baptismal vow by those that have been baptized in their infancy, it is a thing unknown almost among us, unless when people come up to the Lord's table, which very few do considering our numbers, or when they seek baptism for their children. Whereas the profession of all our youth is maimed for lack of this, they having never taken their baptismal engagements on themselves since they are grown up, and are externally Christians no further than as their parents made them, by no sufficient solemn act of their own have signified their free consent to the covenant they are under. The pastors of this country are very sensible of this lameness and disorder upon us . . .

The general neglect of the Lord's Supper is another scandalous stain upon the profession of this people. It looks as if men had forgot or renounced their baptism, or, as if the cross of Christ were an offense to them, and they were ashamed of it. What a strange thing is it, that all our hopes are built on the death of Christ, and there is this one standing memorial of his death in the church, and yet men and women of thirty or fifty years of age have never once shown forth their Savior's death according to his commandment! . . .

How happy are they that live forever in his presence, and minister unto him, beyond those of the wise and magnificent Solomon, whom queens themselves could envy? Would not the noble spirit court only this, knew he of any such transcendent and unfading honor attainable? Would he not tread on crowns and scepters, and spurn at palaces and thrones, if they would clog his way to a better and more lasting state of renown? The very prince on earth being but a vassal and the worm before the most high God, and if he be compared to an angel of his, it is a flight

2. Michael Colacurcio puts the matter succinctly: "The burning issue of the decade after 1679 was . . . the failure of the New England Congregational churches to replenish themselves with an ample supply of 'saints.' "

in his honor, too high for his mortal state. Again, do you think the voluptuous man knows anything of the joys of heaven, that never cloy or sour? Knew he the least part of the sweetness of the sense of God's love, and the unspeakable joys he can fill and satiate the soul with; knew he the ravished elder's transports while they sing the praises and victories of the Lamb, their hearts rising with their notes, and keeping way with their voice; knew he the deliciousness of those eternal greens and living fountains of waters, where the Lamb, which is in the midst of the throne, shall lead and feed his redeemed? Did the sinner know anything of this place of pure and full endless pleasure, would he, could he, hanker any longer after the dreggy cheap pleasures of sin? No, no! He would despise and hate and loathe them; his stomach would turn at 'em; his enobled soul would not relish 'em; his past surfeits would soon end in antipathy . . . In a word, irreligion shows a man to be a stranger to himself, ignorant of his own frame and make, that he has a soul in the delight and perfection whereof his happiness consists. One would think the man esteemed himself only of the upper order of brutes, to graze with and perish like 'em. Our alliance to the spiritual world, the unseen vital substance, the glory of our nature, is forgotten. Nor can there be a more gross piece of ignorance than this, even in the first thing that we have to learn: the frame of our nature, and our relation to a better world. Herein the sinner is ignorant of the grasp and reach of his own nature, which no finite good can ever satisfy but it will be cheated after all, hungry, and calling for more. We may as well throw a shrimp to a whale, or hold a thimble-full of water to Behemoth to drink, when as *he trusteth that he can draw up Jordan into his mouth,* Job 40:23–24, *Behold he drinketh up a river, he taketh it with his eyes.* To conclude, sinners seem not to know, or at all imagine, that truth is the proper food and nourishment of a rational mind, and that husks are only for swine, that his soul can't be nourished by the gross diet of sense, but is oppressed and starved in the luxurious surfeits of the body. Thus sinners publish their own ignorance of themselves, and the world they live in, of their own mortality and immortality too. For they lay in as it were for the body's everlasting subsistence here below, but make no provision for the immortal spirit when it shall take its flight . . .

The folly of irreligion is, that it has no foresight. 'Tis blind, and intent only on present gains and pleasures, having no sense of the soul's duration, nor the body's frailty, not indeed of anything but what it sees and feels. This is such stupidity as we should be utterly ashamed of, for we are not beasts that know not they must die, and that perish when they do die. The wisdom of mankind is to consider their latter end. The good man thinks much of this, weighs it well, and prepares for the black day. He acts upon this sense, that he is to live forever in another world, and shall need to be happy then as much as now. Therefore all the days of his appointed time he waits till his change comes.

This has always been accounted the highest wisdom of man, to govern his life here by the thoughts of dying and of eternity. Seneca has many wise and excellent instructions on this head, which might raise both wonder and shame in most Christians. It is storied of the Indian wise men, called "Brachmans," that they had "their sepulchers at their doors, that both upon their going out and coming in they might remember their approaching change, and govern their lives by the monitory sight of their graves." Some have kept their coffins by them to keep their dissolution in mind. Some have chosen mottoes of such a nature for themselves, and those that are usually written on dials bear this sense. In short, it is the universal sense of mankind that one of the most effectual courses for our good conduct in this world is to be frequent in the serious remembrance of another . . .

Our present peace, and proficiency, and future safety, does much depend on it. It keeps the mind serious and under great awe, it prevents many a sin and as many disquiets of conscience, it promotes good frames in the soul, gives great force to the motives of the gospel, and makes men have a single respect to conscience and duty. It sets the world in a true light, an empty, vain deceitful thing as it is; and it shows sin in its true colors, as the mischief and enemy of our souls. It shows a man himself, and the measure of his days, how frail he is; and it leads him to consider the state of his soul, and the misery that awaits him unless he repent; and it is a spur and goad in his side that he timely do so. And these are such weighty useful thoughts, that no man can be content to be without, and not show himself a fool . . .

Matthew 25:11. Afterward came also the other virgins, saying, Lord, Lord, open to us.

The last refuge of perishing impenitent sinners is to cry for mercy, and try what supplication will do . . . They cry for entrance, not ignorant, we may think, that nothing entereth that defileth. Are they then indeed willing to be made holy? Yes, to escape damnation they think they could now bear it, nay passionately crave and prefer it . . .

But I lay aside these various glosses, which a fruitful fancy might suggest to itself; and shall only attend to the nature and scope of this supplication of the foolish—which is this: a miserable soul's sense of its state, and the anguish that follows thereupon. For now they see their lost condition and bewail it, and their prayer speaks nothing but despair and sorrow. The ardor of their cry is from their anguish . . .

I shall only therefore spend a few thoughts on the unspeakable anguishes of wretched souls when they find themselves determined to certain and remediless misery. The scripture sufficiently signifies to us what a quick sense the damned will have of misery, and in what accents they will express it. Eternity will not be passed away stupidly, as their life here is under the curse of God. No more can they be vain and merry and make a mock of sin; the flames or darkness afford no scenes for these. 'Tis the state of torment, and the natural fruit of that is inward anguish, and the effect of that weeping and wailing and gnashing of teeth. The anguishes of the wicked will answer to the cause: the wrath of God and the loss of him and heaven, the lashes of conscience, the rage and tumult of their passions, the malice of devils, the piercing of devouring flames, and the amazing prospect of the eternal duration of all these. Incessant restlessness and convulsions must needs come of these hideous causes; for what should follow upon indignation and wrath but tribulation and anguish? And what of that but flowing tears, and gnashing teeth, and dolorous plaints, the eyes rolling, the hands wringing, the hair torn, and all the tokens of extreme grief.

The sad occasion in the text justifies all this, to see the door of heaven shut and barred upon 'em . . .

The contempt herein done the sinner will confound and pierce him, and no contempt can be greater than to have the door shut against him. As if the master of the house should say, presumptuous wretch, you think of admission hither! Heaven made for you! Imagine you! You a companion of angels, and heir of God, and to reign with Christ? Shall heaven be so prostituted! O child of hell, come no nearer! Away to your prepared place, you may know it by your likeness to it; you resemble your father the devil, and one would think should know him, and not take the Holy One for your Lord, nor hope that he'll own you. Say, speechless man, why should you come in hither, not having a wedding garment? The shame of thy nakedness appears; begone and cover it in the shades below! Is this a pickle[3] to come in unto the marriage? To be an offensive stench to the elect guests! So the door is shut in slight and scorn, and they go to shame and everlasting contempt, and shame as well as fear hath torment . . .

Excluded from God and Christ, it is to be left to devils to be their prey. So when a disarmed person flies, from a strong and wrathful foe pursuing at his heels, to some city or castle where he may be safe, sees to his amazement the bridge drawn up, or the gates clapped to against him and himself abandoned to the enemy's lust; such is the case of those whom heaven excludes—left to the will of devils, without among the

3. A rowdy, unsavory man.

dogs, cursed spirits so mean and sordid and quarrelsome. Seized by the greedy fiends, and born away in the teeth of the devouring lion, they cast back a longing eye, and bite their tongues as they lose all sight and hope of the blissful place. Lost and undone forever, say they of themselves, and save the devourer the cruel labor of tearing off their flesh. "Forever? fatal word! Forever? Who can bear the doom of everlasting woe?"

So methought I once saw a little image of the last distress and outcries of condemned sinners at a melancholy assize, where the sentence had no sooner passed the judge's lips but they joined in one shriek, "Mercy, my Lord! Mercy—Mercy?" in gestures, and looks, and tone enough to pierce every heart, and draw tears from every eye . . .

SIX

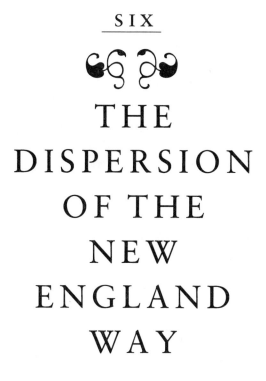

THE DISPERSION OF THE NEW ENGLAND WAY

THE SPLINTERING of New England's uniformity—institutionally and intellectually—was most evident in the Bay Colony: in the drawing of party lines among the clergy of eastern Massachusetts, in the ongoing crisis of Harvard College, in the rift between the Mathers and "Pope" Stoddard of Northampton, even within the mind of Cotton Mather himself as he strained to hold together the new implications of "reason" with a felt resurgence of "piety." Thomas Prince, commemorating the centennial of Winthrop's landing in 1730, was at a loss to chronicle an enduring unity within Massachusetts itself, much less to point with any assurance to a persistent New England Way. For within the first quarter of the new century, not only was each of the once "United Colonies" suffering from internal divisions, but Connecticut was going its own separate way.

Out of Connecticut's internal conflicts and the resulting migrations emerged a "greater New England," encompassing Long Island, Westchester County, and above all large portions of New Jersey. New England's diaspora had effectively begun after the synod of 1662 and the granting of a charter to the Hartford government that embraced a once-separate New Haven within a broader "Connecticut" jurisdiction. When in 1664 the General Assembly of Connecticut recommended that all the churches of the colony adopt the Half-Way Covenant, John Davenport described "Christ's interest in New Haven Colony as miserably lost." Davenport's friend Abraham Pierson was so outraged—until then the clergy of New Haven had never bowed to the secular arm—that he and his entire congregation moved to New Jersey. Thereby was established, at New-Ark, a New England Puritan base that was to expand and to play, in the eighteenth century, a critical role in the formation and definition of Middle Colony Presbyterianism.

The displaced New Englanders were increasingly served by graduates of a New College, ultimately named Yale, which was founded at Branford in 1701 by ministers of the old New Haven colony and which, after a brief stay in Saybrook, settled in New Haven. The new college ironically served also in a variety of ways as the locus for a rediscovery of the values of Old England: most dramatically, the value of Episcopacy itself, which seemed to many to offer respite from the seeming anarchy of Connecticut's churches, with their incessant squabbling over forms of church government. But Old England was rediscovered in other ways as well, most notably, in Connecticut, by those who believed with Gershom Bulkeley that the English constitution provided the only hedge against the clownish mobocracy of the province. Disdain for an antiquated New England Way led some to travel to Old England, others to imbibe its new intellectual dispensations, and many to remove to the more stable Royal Colony of New York. Out of Boston too there was movement to other colonies and to England, accompanied by a disposition to embrace a wider cosmopolitan and continental vision.

Finally, with the coming out of England in 1740 of the "grand itinerant," George Whitefield, New England experienced the Great Awakening, a religious revival that for many erased the old provincial self-definition and gave the descendants of the Puritans a sense of common experience and destiny shared with the faithful from New Jersey to Georgia. The pre-eminent architect and spokesman of the Awakening, Jonathan Edwards, spent most of his adult life in Northampton, Massachusetts. But after his education at Yale Edwards had briefly held a pulpit in New York City, and he ended his days as president of the College of New Jersey—where, it was assumed, the stock of the Puritans still lived. His vision, as it emerged in the Great Revival and developed in its aftermath, made manifest the final repudiation of New England tribalism, hymning as it did the possibility of the redemption, not of "God's people in *America*" merely, but, as in the days of the first reformers, of the whole of humanity.

JOSEPH MORGAN (1671–c. 1745)
The History of the Kingdom of Basaruah (1715)

THE NEW ENGLANDERS who settled in New Jersey carried with them ideas and principles that allowed, at first, an easy settling into the Presbyterianism of the Middle Colonies. Eventually, however, by virtue of their New England inheritance they were drawn up in battle array, clashing with the Scots-trained ministry that strove to dominate the Philadelphia synod. The acknowledged leader of the New Englanders at the time of the rift was Jonathan Dickinson, who had been born and raised in the Connecticut Valley of Massachusetts in the years of Stoddard's dominion. Dickinson graduated from Yale in 1706, then pursued further study until he settled in Elizabethtown, New Jersey, where he was formally installed as minister in 1709. The sermon at his installation was preached by Joseph Morgan, whose own career was ample evidence that even in the earliest years of the new century New England was no longer a simply defined geographical area. Morgan, born and raised in Connecticut, assumed his first ministry at Greenwich, but by 1700 he was settled in Westchester County, New York, where he served a number of churches of transplanted New Englanders. The royal governor of New York, impatient with all nonconformity, tried to force Morgan and his congregations into the Church of England. Morgan failed in his resistance and returned to Greenwich in 1704. In 1708 he moved to Freehold, New Jersey, where he served as minister for twenty years, producing at least ten published works and maintaining a correspondence with Cotton Mather. Morgan, who had not attended college, was granted an honorary A.M. by Yale in 1719, in attestation of his intellectual stature among the leaders of a "greater New England."

Admitted to the Presbytery of Philadelphia in 1710, Morgan allied himself with those (led by Dickinson) who resisted the demand that all ministers "subscribe" to the Westminster Confession. He also thundered forth sermons attacking usury and other forms of covetousness, insisting that earthly happiness was to be found in neither worldly goods nor sensual pleasures. His principles and themes were thus, in sum, very much those of Dickinson, Theodorus Freylinghuysen, and William Tennent and his sons: the instruments and inspiration of what was to be the Great Awakening in the Middle Colonies. Morgan was not so much an avatar of the Awakening, however, as its prophet, for a full quarter-century before the Great Revival of 1740 he had diagnosed the psychosocial malaise out of which the Awakening arose. *The History of the Kingdom of Basaruah,* published in 1715, can rightly be read as a recapitulation of seventeenth-century covenant theology, indeed as a summation of three generations of New England thought. In form an allegory, deeply indebted to John Bunyan's *The Holy War,* it is also a commentary on nearly a century of Puritan experience in the New World. Bearing on its title page the notation that it was written "for the abundant instruction that may be learned therefrom, in these remote parts," Morgan (perhaps unintentionally) offered a diagnosis of the impact of the wilderness on the stock of the Puritans, wherever they had wandered.

The text is from the edition by Richard Schlatter (Cambridge, Mass.: Harvard University Press, 1946), pp. 56–57.

The History of the Kingdom of Basaruah

Chapter V. A Description of the Wilderness of Basaruah[1] and the Peoples' Behaviour there in their Banishment

In the next Place the King *drove* them out of the Pleasant Country, into the Wilderness of *Basaruah,* and never suffered them to return more, lest they should attempt to travel the High-Road to the Country of *Shamajim,*[2] and be drowned in the River; for this high Road led out of no part of *Basaruah,* except the pleasant Country, and was now cut off by the River.

2 So into the Wilderness they came, which is a hideous barren Country, full of Terrible *wild Beasts* of all sorts (which have yet this quiet property, that so long as men let them alone, they do them little harm, but they will come and fawn upon Men, and if they go to play with them, they bite terribly, and with great Venom).

3 The Land bears a few things (by hard Labour) which are good for *present use,* but it bears nothing that will keep for *Time to come;* And those things that are of use, if they be taken either *immoderately,* or

1. Flesh-spirit.
2. Heaven.

unseasonably, or *out of the right manner,* will surfeit the blood, and breed many Diseases.

4 But the common Produce of the Land is a *multitude of Fruits,* that look very beautiful afar off, but when men come to eat them, they loose their *Taste* before they are well swallowed, and commonly leave a bitter Tang in the stomach, but are alwayes as unwholsom as they appear lovely to look upon, and breed many Epidemical Diseases; yet such as know not the Taste of better, admire them.

5 The People were no sooner come into this Country, but they fell to digging up the imaginary Riches of it, as if they thought to abide there forever; and as for the *Pleasant Country,* most of them soon forgot that ever they had been there, and the loss of the *Celestial Country* was little regarded, and many would not believe that the King would deprive them of it for so small an offence, as they thought their Rebellion was; But the Reason of this Imagination was, because their Law-Books were little Legible since they had sullied them by their Rebellion, and they took little Pains, to read what was legible therein.

6 However, their main study was to make themselves happy where they were; and the less Satisfaction they found in the imaginary pleasures of the Wilderness, the more they strove after them, thinking the *Defect* was only in that they had not enough of them, and so they pleased themselves with the Expectation of greater things, which they seldom ever obtained, and if they did obtain them, they never answered their Expectations, but were *altogether Vanity and vexation of Spirit.*

7 Thus they *disquieted themselves in vain,* and the more Troubles and Disappointments they had, the more eager they were to get the Wilderness Pleasures, instead of seeking a *better Country,* which was the end for which the King sent them hither, *viz.* to move them to go over the River for a better Habitation.

SOLOMON STODDARD

An Examination of the Power of the Fraternity (c. 1715)

THREE YEARS AFTER the publication of Morgan's allegory, Solomon Stoddard published one of the last, and perhaps the most revealing, of his many utterances justifying the ecclesiastical innovations he had begun in the 1670s. Those innovations, representing yet another response to the spiritual life of New Englanders in "remote parts," he had first publicly espoused in 1700, with the publication of *The Doctrine of Instituted Churches*. Stoddard's ecclesiology struck the Mathers as identical with that of the Brattle Street Church in that he, in what seemed a Presbyterian gesture, opened the Lord's Supper to nearly all. But Stoddard was hardly a latitudinarian in his views of the church: his motives (something like those of Hooker before him) seem to have been to expand church membership so as to bring the entire community under his control. Like Hooker too, Stoddard made his alliances with the oligarchs of his congregation, but he proved more than a match for the "crafty," not only in Northampton, but throughout Western Massachusetts and large parts of Connecticut, mainly by translating the traditional ministerial "Consociation" into a clerical body as powerful as any Presbyterian synod. The Saybrook Platform, adopted by a Connecticut synod in 1708, clearly owed as much to Stoddard's influence and example as it did to the Matherian proposals for "ordering the interest of the churches" of eastern Massachusetts—proposals so vehemently and eloquently repudiated by John Wise.

Indeed, Stoddard's notions of church government went far beyond those of the Mathers in repudiating the very "democracy" that Wise saw threatened. Although Stoddard's Northampton congregation was periodically refreshed by "harvests" as he continued to preach the evangelical doctrines of *The Safety of Appearing at the Day of Judgment,* he interpreted these outpourings of the spirit as bringing only "convictions." Having seemingly opened the sluices of divine grace, he treated everyone equally—as equally short, that is, of sainthood. He had repudiated Hooker's psychology, but he in effect extended the process of "preparation" until it encompassed one's entire life. He differed from Hooker, however, in offering his people neither "duties" nor "works" through which they might act to forward their work of redemption. Over the years, moreover, Stoddard had moved from an emphasis on the need and value of "assurance" to one more than reminiscent of Hooker's rhetorical stance in Hartford: God, Stoddard proclaimed in an ordination sermon of 1718 (*The Presence of Christ*), "doesn't bless cordials to take away stubborn humors . . . men need to be frightened and not pleased." In *An Examination of the Power of the Fraternity* Stoddard revealed a contempt for the mind of the multitude that surpassed in scornfulness even some of the venom of Gershom Bulkeley. He had left behind not the jeremiad merely, but the Cambridge Platform and nearly a century of New England faith and practice. But most important, he had left behind the hope of an elect people, distinguishable from others, who collectively might work out not merely their own salvation but the redemption of all mankind.

An Examination of the Power of the Fraternity was appended to *The Presence of Christ with the Ministers of the Gospel,* also by Solomon Stoddard, and published in Boston in 1718. The text is from that edition, pp. 1–3, 10–11.

An Examination of the Power of the Fraternity

The mistakes of one generation many times become the calamity of succeeding generations. The present generation are not only unhappy by reason of the darkness of their own minds, but the errors of those who have gone before them have been a foundation of a great deal of misery. Posterity is very prone to espouse the principles of ancestors, and from an inordinate veneration of them to apprehend a sacredness in their opinions, and don't give themselves the trouble to make an impartial examination of them, as if it were a transgression to call them into question, and bordered upon irreligion to be wavering about them . . .

The first planters drew up a Platform of Church Discipline before they had much time to weigh those things, and when they were under prejudices from the experience of their sufferings in England; and some of their posterity are mightily devoted to it, as if the Platform were the pattern in the mount, and all deviations from it are looked upon as a degree of apostasy; others have taken the liberty to examine it and can discover no foundation in the word of God for many positions therein. These differences do much interrupt our quiet and hinder the flourishing of religion. Some persons place a great part of their religion in their being of this or that party; and others who have better principles spend more of their zeal in those controversies than is meet, and thereby it comes to pass that weightier matters are too much neglected, men's corruptions are drawn forth, offense is given, and sometimes offense is taken, to the great disadvantage of the interest of religion. There is a necessity of the vindicating the truth, yet we cannot do it without making some disturbance.

In the platform it is affirmed, *That the brethren have power of judgment in matters of censure and power in admitting of members.*

This principle is very popular; it is taking with them to see themselves advanced to a share in the government: they have a greater fondness for power than ability to use it, and nothing but light as clear as the light of the sun at noon-day will prevail with some men to part with one inch of that power, which they are told doth belong to them.

But I shall endeavor to clear it up, *That the government of the church is given unto the elders, that the fraternity have no power in binding and loosing . . .*

It was the ministers' work of old to judge in spiritual causes, so it is now: men yield the case, only they say, *That the multitude have a negative voice, and if they think meet may stop their proceedings.* As if the people were to have more privilege and power under the gospel, and the minister have less . . .

The community are not fit to judge and rule in the church. They must be men of understanding that are to judge in civil causes, Exodus 18:21, *Thou shalt provide out of all the people able men.* Deuteronomy 1:13, *Take you wise men and understanding, and known among your tribes, and I will make them rulers over you.* There is a great deal of intricacy many times in causes and many things are offered to blind the eyes: there may be fair pretenses for foul actions. Sometimes it is difficult to find out matter of fact; sometimes to find out matter of law. So that there is great need of understanding . . . But the community are not men of understanding. Wise men are but here and there to be found. Many of them have not had the advantage of reading and study. Some of them are men of very weak abilities, some of them are rash, some of them are young, hardly sixteen years of age, some of them are servants; a crafty man may lead a score of them by the nose; they are uncapable to see into an abstruse thing. Let the government be put into their hands, and things will be carried headlong by a tumultuous cry. If the multitude were to be judges in civil causes, things would quickly be turned upside down.

SAMUEL JOHNSON (1696–1772)
"My Present Thoughts of Episcopacy" (1719, 1722)

AMONG THE MANY ironies of New England's thought and expression in the early eighteenth century was that Yale College, designed by some of the ministers of what had been New Haven Colony, endorsed and supported by Mather, produced among its first fruits what seemed at the time to be an epidemic of reversions to Episcopacy. Within a half-century of its founding Yale was to be pressed to remold its curriculum, as had Harvard, to befit a plantation of trade rather than of religion, but this demand (which helped to produce Dartmouth College, as it had, even earlier, Princeton) was seemingly irrelevant to the massive trauma suffered by Yale in 1722. In March 1719 the college asked Timothy Cutler (Harvard, 1701) to serve as rector. All seemed in joyous order until, the day after the 1722 commencement, Cutler presented a paper, signed by himself, one of his Yale tutors, and several local ministers, stating: "Some of us doubt of the validity, and the rest are more fully persuaded of the invalidity, of Presbyterian ordination, in opposition of Episcopal." Mather and others had often suspected that President Leverett (and his ally William Brattle) had long been quietly tempting Harvard students with the delights of Episcopacy, but Cutler's statement nevertheless came as a bombshell. A public debate was arranged between the trustees of the college and the advocates of the divine right of Episcopacy; Cutler was joined by Samuel Johnson (Yale, 1719) in arguing the affirmative. In October Cutler was dismissed from the rectorship, and in November he, Johnson, and Daniel Browne (Cutler's cosigning tutor) sailed for England to receive Episcopal ordination.

That Johnson had not easily arrived at his decision is attested by the "case of conscience" he had addressed to himself as early as 1719. The document is extraordinary, if only because it stands as one of the few pieces of "casuistry" to come out of New England's first century. In Old England, in the 1620s, books of casuistry had abounded, in part because many vexed nonconformists had no sympathetic clergy to turn to personally, in part because social and economic change seemed so rapid as to make each day one of ethical torment to those who would contend for the faith. Perhaps because New England's churches were well-stocked with soul-physicians, perhaps because (despite all public declamation) social change had in fact occurred slowly and quietly enough to be adapted to (this was, after all, the complaint of the jeremiads, who saw declension sneak up on New England like an armed man), the only major compendia of cases of conscience to emerge in New England's first century were a volume produced by Increase Mather during the backlash from the witchcraft crisis and another, as late as 1722, by Solomon Stoddard. To be sure, more than one Puritan diarist, like Samuel Sewall, had racked his conscience over whether he was properly "prepared" to receive the sacrament. Stoddardeanism rendered such torment irrelevant, just as the "Preparatory Meditations" of Edward Taylor—Stoddard's most vehement critic in western Massachusetts—can be read, in part, as private cases of conscience. But Johnson's "Present Thoughts" is comparable to very little else in the New England canon; indeed, being intensely personal as well as unpublished, it also differed markedly from his own public utterances after he had embraced Episcopacy.

The *Letters to Dissenters* Johnson published in the 1730s began by questioning the ecclesiastical constitution of Connecticut, even by asking whether it was not a very mixed bag being clung to by defenders of the "old way": "some of your teachers hold the sacrament a converting ordinance, which the writers of our church deny." But he quickly moved from pointing to "the many disorders, contentions, and confusions" arising from the variety of amendments to the Cambridge Platform then prevailing ("I believe I think as charitably of your fathers as any of you do; . . . they meant well") to railing against the "ill breeding" of those who argued against Episcopacy. For one who had once doubted that he had the "politeness" requisite to Anglican orders, Johnson's visit to London seems to have worked a remarkable social sea-change, as well as psychological wonders: now he could parry any of his respondents' thrusts with the observation that his opponent showed "himself so little of the gentleman." It may be more than relevant that Johnson had in 1729 made the acquaintance of Bishop Berkeley, then residing in Newport, Rhode Island. Johnson persuaded Berkeley to donate books to Yale, and himself that he was somehow Berkeley's vicar in the New World. Soon he was espousing Berkleian philosophy, which he embodied in his most noteworthy book, *Elementa Philosophica,* published by Franklin in Philadelphia in 1752. Two years later Johnson was installed as president of what was to be until the Revolution, the bastion of Anglican thought in the northern colonies—King's College of New York—where he served until in 1766 a long succession of illnesses brought his resignation.

During his time as president of the Anglican college in New York and the six years of his life that remained after his return to New England, Johnson's efforts as a scholar and pamphleteer established him as the embodiment of a type that was to flourish throughout New England's eighteenth century: the self-defined Englishman residing in the New World. To be sure, many of the founders of the Bay Colony and of New Haven had briefly thought of themselves as such, but hardly in the manner of Johnson, who in his writings, published and unpublished, over and again stressed the need to bring the "Genius of English America" more into tune with the values and institutions of what to him was now the "home country." He was among the many New England Anglicans who argued strenuously, in the 1760s, for the appointment of a bishop of the Church of England for the colonies, and his arguments on the need for order in colonial affairs grew increasingly reminiscent of Richard Hooker's *Laws of Ecclesiastical Polity.*

Unquestionably a fair estimate of Johnson's career would stress his later writings, particularly the nonpolemical ones, for he is rightly celebrated as one of the pillars of early American philosophic thought. But the "Thoughts" of 1719, which showed an American conscience coming full circle from where it had once been placed by William Ames in his *Cases of Conscience,* may well be Johnson's most eloquent utterance. Filled with self-doubts, lacking any of the pretentiousness later inspired by his journey to London and the English honors accorded him (in 1743 he was made a Doctor of Divinity by Oxford), it stands as the heartfelt response of one genuinely troubled by the seeming chaos into which the ancestral worship of New England had fallen.

The text of "My Present Thoughts" is from *The Life and Writings of Samuel Johnson,* ed. Herbert and Carol Schneider (New York: Columbia University Press, 1929), III, 3–8.

My Present Thoughts of Episcopacy with what I conceive may justify me in accepting Presbyterial Ordination. Written at West Haven, Dec. 20, Anno Dom. 1719.

Concerning Episcopacy and particularly with relation to me under my present circumstances I shall in the following paragraphs:

I. Set down my present apprehensions formed from the best light I can obtain, and

II. I shall consider what may be matter of justification to me under my present circumstances in receiving Presbyterial ordination . . .

So remote are the days of the primitive church, so obscure the accounts of it, and in some respects so different (men being then in many particulars of different apprehensions and tempers, as well as now) and therefore so liable to be interpreted to a different sense, according to the different hypotheses advanced, and so great the ignorance which had invaded and overspread the church in the greatest darkness of popery, and finally so little the ability or opportunity of most of the first reformers, just then emerging out of it, to examine thoroughly into the state of the primitive church, that it is more to be lamented than wondered at, that when they first set upon reformation they fell into so many different sects and parties, every one still esteeming themselves the most pure and primitive. And therefore I imagine that the separation of one particular church or sect of Christians, from another is a much more excusable evil now than it was in the first ages of Christianity, justly esteemed by the ancient fathers of the primitive church.

But to proceed, the church I conceive to be a well formed and well regulated society under regulations peculiar to itself, and therefore as well as all other well regulated societies, must consist of a *pars regens* and a *pars regenda*.[1] It must be under the direction of officers to whom the management of the public affairs of it doth belong, and what those offices are and who the officers, and how many degrees and orders of them are, are to be considered.

Now as to the two inferior orders of elders and deacons. There is no question with respect to them at present. But whereas there has been and still is in some parts of the church an order of men called bishops, whose office as such has been held to be the inspection and government of the church both clergy and laity, and the imposition of hands in the ordination of the clergy and confirmation of the laity within their respective districts, I am now concerned to be determined whether this order be of divine right and who these offices are by divine appointment appropriated to, so as to render it unlawful even upon the most urgent emergencies to recede from it?

And to this I answer that all prejudices laid aside, and so far as I can inform myself, I must confess that I am firmly persuaded and am constrained from as good evidences as the nature of the thing is now capable of, supposing it were really so, firmly to believe that Episcopacy was truly the primitive and apostolical form of church government, and that the apostolic office was designed to be a settled standing office in the church to the end of the world . . .

And not only so, but in the next place I must own that I am fully convinced that such a condition is indeed most excellent in itself, as being in the best manner imaginable suited for the answering the ends for which

1. A ruling part and a part to be ruled.

any supposed constitution whatsoever can be calculated, exactly adapted to the nature of such a society as the church is, and of the most direct and best tendency to promote, preserve and maintain the peace and unity of the same and purity in profession and practice of the true religion therein.

And such is my opinion of it, and affection to it on the account hereof, that I would with a full approbation and complacency of mind and with the greatest delight and satisfaction submit to the orders of it, and should rejoice with all my heart if Providence should place me under such circumstances as should make it my duty so to do. And if I am misled in any of these my apprehensions concerning either the church or the constitution and government of it, I should be glad upon many accounts to be led into a better sense of things.

Having thus stated the case, I leave it to impartial advice, whether this be good divinity or not, that any circumstances will justify me in what I propose to do? And if so, I submit it also to be considered whether my circumstances are such? Which are these:

1. The passionate entreaties of a tender mother.

2. That my breaking forth upon an attempt of that nature would be of vastly more dis-service to the best interest of the church itself than my going over to it could be of service to it.

3. That it can't be without most fatal jealousies to the college, and the effects of it must be mischievous.

4. That I must thereby be exposed to great dangers and difficulties, to which I am a great stranger.

5. My want of that politeness and those qualifications which would be requisite in making such an appearance.

6. That in order to taking Episcopal order there are many things to be complied with which I do not sufficiently understand.

7. That the times, 'tis to be feared, are very difficult at home, and its likely not so good encouragement to such designs as might be wished for.

8. That although I seem tolerably well satisfied in these my thoughts, of the right of Episcopacy, yet considering the meanness of my advantages and the scantiness of my time hitherto, I have reason to be very jealous whether I have not too much precipitated into these opinions.

And then finally perhaps I may in the meantime be doing some service to promote the main interest of religion, though it be not in a method so desirable.

FINIS

Upon these principles I continued easy about two years and then upon a more careful examination of the matter, I found I could not with a good conscience continue to administer in the name of Christ when I was under a persuasion that I had never had a regular mission from him, and thereupon I thought it my bounded duty to come over to the Episcopal side that I might live and die in the unity of the church. Accordingly I with Dr. Cutler, Mr. Hart, Mr. Whittelsey, Mr. Eliot, Mr. Wetmore, and Mr. Browne, made our public declaration for the Church, September 13, 1722, at Yale College, New Haven.

BENJAMIN FRANKLIN (1706–1790)
Dogood Paper No. 4: On the Higher Learning (1722)

THE FRAGMENTATION among New England's traditional intellectual elite was hardly the entire tale of the twilight of Puritanism in America. New voices—in part heirs to the Puritan heritage, in larger part alienated from it—emerged to swell the chorus of criticism of ancient institutions. Among them was Benjamin Franklin, so well known to students of American literature as to require no formal introduction, and one of two eighteenth-century writers clearly to deserve an anthology of his own. Though Franklin, through his almanacs, satires, and classic *Autobiography,* is ordinarily identified with Philadelphia and London, he began his literary career as a Bostonian—as an anonymous contributor to his brother's *New-England Courant* when he was barely sixteen years of age. His pseudonym, "Silence Dogood," was a clearly intentional mockery of Cotton Mather's *Bonifacius: An Essay upon the Good* (1710), which later came to be known by its running title, "Essays to do Good."

Yet Benjamin Franklin, who later often acknowledged an indebtedness to *Bonifacius* in the formation of his own ethical views, was, even as a brash youngster, attacking many of the same institutions that had aroused the ire of the Mathers. Increase Mather had been ousted from the presidency of Harvard, and Cotton, confiding to his *Diary* that he dreamed of being called to that eminence, was reduced to private carping—"There are many unwise things done" at Harvard, he advised himself, "about which I must watch for opportunities, to bear public testimonies"—and to peripheral gestures. His *Manuductio ad Ministerium* (1726) was a proposed curriculum, not for Harvard so much as for those Harvard graduates who were not, he was convinced, receiving a proper training for the ministry. Indeed, long before 1726 Cotton Mather, persuaded that Harvard had been converted by President Leverett into a nursery of merchants—or of merchants' sons—had helped to found a new college in Connecticut. He had offered its founders a "Scheme for a College" on the ancient model and in 1718 had secured the gift from Elihu Yale that led, at Mather's suggestion, to its eventual naming.

In this context, Franklin's satire of Harvard College—in which he displays most clearly his debt to John Bunyan—differed little in substance from some of Cotton Mather's own laments. To be sure, Franklin does not stand in judgment from the perspective of the "good old way." In fact his own grandfather Peter Folger had been among the first to satirize New England's tribalism. "New England they are like the Jews," Folger had written in *A Looking-Glass for the Times* (1676), a Baptist plea for toleration, "as like as like can be." Benjamin Franklin wrote not as a Baptist but as one of the *novi homines* who, over the next decades, would rise to eminence in New England overshadowing the privileged offspring of the old order, or, like himself, would carry more than a bit of New England with them as they sought fame and fortune elsewhere.

The text is from Leonard W. Labaree's standard edition of *The Papers of Benjamin Franklin* (New Haven: Yale University Press, 1959–), I, 14–18. Copyright © 1959 by Yale University Press.

Silence Dogood, No. 4
On the Higher Learning

An sum etiam nunc vel Graecè loqui vel Latinè docendus?[1]
Cicero.

To the Author of the *New-England Courant.*

May 14, 1722

SIR,

Discoursing the other Day at Dinner with my Reverend Boarder, formerly mention'd, (whom for Distinction sake we will call by the Name of Clericus,) concerning the Education of Children, I ask'd his Advice about my young Son William, whether or no I had best bestow upon him Academical Learning, or (as our Phrase is) *bring him up at our College:* He perswaded me to do it by all Means, using many weighty Arguments with me, and answering all the Objections that I could form against it; telling me withal, that he did not doubt but that the Lad would take his Learning very well, and not idle away his Time as too many there now-a-days do. These Words of Clericus gave me a Curiosity to inquire a little more strictly into the present Circumstances of that famous Seminary of Learning; but the Information which he gave me, was neither pleasant, nor such as I expected.

As soon as Dinner was over, I took a solitary Walk into my Orchard,

1. And must I now be taught to speak Greek or Latin?

still ruminating on Clericus's Discourse with much Consideration, until I came to my usual Place of Retirement under the *Great Apple-Tree;* where having seated my self, and carelessly laid my Head on a verdant Bank, I fell by Degrees into a soft and undisturbed Slumber. My waking Thoughts remained with me in my Sleep. and before I awak'd again, I dreamt the following DREAM.

I fancy'd I was travelling over pleasant and delightful Fields and Meadows, and thro' many small Country Towns and Villages; and as I pass'd along, all Places resounded with the Fame of the Temple of LEARNING: Every Peasant, who had wherewithal, was preparing to send one of his Children at least to this famous Place; and in this Case most of them consulted their own Purses instead of their Childrens Capacities: So that I observed, a great many, yea, the most part of those who were travelling thither, were little better than Dunces and Blockheads. Alas! alas!

At length I entred upon a spacious Plain, in the Midst of which was erected a large and stately Edifice: It was to this that a great Company of Youths from all Parts of the Country were going; so stepping in among the Crowd, I passed on with them, and presently arrived at the Gate.

The Passage was kept by two sturdy Porters named *Riches* and *Poverty,* and the latter obstinately refused to give Entrance to any who had not first gain'd the Favour of the former; so that I observed, many who came even to the very Gate, were obliged to travel back again as ignorant as they came, for want of this necessary Qualification. However, as a Spectator I gain'd Admittance, and with the rest entred directly into the Temple.

In the Middle of the great Hall stood a stately and magnificent Throne, which was ascended to by two high and difficult Steps. On the Top of it sat LEARNING in awful State; she was apparelled wholly in Black, and surrounded almost on every Side with innumerable Volumes in all Languages. She seem'd very busily employ'd in writing something on half a Sheet of Paper, and upon Enquiry, I understood she was preparing a Paper, call'd, *The New-England Courant.* On her Right Hand sat *English,* with a pleasant smiling Countenance, and handsomely attir'd; and on her left were seated several *Antique Figures* with their Faces vail'd. I was considerably puzzl'd to guess who they were, until one informed me, (who stood beside me,) that those Figures on her left Hand were *Latin, Greek, Hebrew,* &c. and that they were very much reserv'd, and seldom or never unvail'd their Faces here, and then to few or none, tho' most of those who have in this Place acquir'd so much Learning as to distinguish them from *English,* pretended to an intimate Acquaintance with them. I then enquir'd of him, what could be the Reason why they continued vail'd, in this Place especially: He pointed to the Foot of the

Throne, where I saw *Idleness,* attended with *Ignorance,* and these (he informed me) were they, who first vail'd them, and still kept them so.

Now I observed, that the whole Tribe who entred into the Temple with me, began to climb the Throne; but the Work proving troublesome and difficult to most of them, they withdrew their Hands from the Plow, and contented themselves to sit at the Foot, with Madam *Idleness* and her Maid *Ignorance,* until those who were assisted by Diligence and a docible Temper, had well nigh got up the first Step: But the Time drawing nigh in which they could no way avoid ascending, they were fain to crave the Assistance of those who had got up before them, and who, for the Reward perhaps of a *Pint of Milk,* or a *Piece of Plumb-Cake,* lent the Lubbers a helping Hand, and sat them in the Eye of the World, upon a Level with themselves.

The other Step being in the same Manner ascended, and the usual Ceremonies at an End, every Beetle-Scull seem'd well satisfy'd with his own Portion of Learning, tho' perhaps he was *e'en just* as ignorant as ever. And now the Time of their Departure being come, they march'd out of Doors to make Room for another Company, who waited for Entrance: And I, having seen all that was to be seen, quitted the Hall likewise, and went to make my Observations on those who were just gone out before me.

Some I perceiv'd took to Merchandizing, others to Travelling, some to one Thing, some to another, and some to Nothing; and many of them from henceforth, for want of Patrimony, liv'd as poor as Church Mice, being unable to dig, and asham'd to beg, and to live by their Wits it was impossible. But the most Part of the Crowd went along a large beaten Path, which led to a Temple at the further End of the Plain, call'd, *The Temple of Theology.* The Business of those who were employ'd in this Temple being laborious and painful, I wonder'd exceedingly to see so many go towards it; but while I was pondering this Matter in my Mind, I spy'd *Pecunia* behind a Curtain, beckoning to them with her Hand, which Sight immediately satisfy'd me for whose Sake it was, that a great Part of them (I will not say all) travel'd that Road. In this Temple I saw nothing worth mentioning, except the ambitious and fraudulent Contrivances of Plagius, who (notwithstanding he had been severely reprehended for such Practices before) was diligently transcribing some eloquent Paragraphs out of Tillotson's[2] *Works,* &c., to embellish his own.

Now I bethought my self in my Sleep, that it was Time to be at Home, and as I fancy'd I was travelling back thither, I reflected in my Mind on

2. Archbishop John Tillotson, chaplain to Charles II and later a favorite of William and Mary, took the English church in the direction of deistic rationalism.

the extream Folly of those Parents, who, blind to their Childrens Dulness, and insensible of the Solidity of their Skulls, because they think their Purses can afford it, will needs send them to the Temple of Learning, where, for want of a suitable Genius, they learn little more than how to carry themselves handsomely, and enter a Room genteely, (which might as well be acquir'd at a Dancing School,) and from whence they return, after Abundance of Trouble and Charge, as great Blockheads as ever, only more proud and self-conceited.

While I was in the midst of these unpleasant Reflections, Clericus (who with a Book in his Hand was walking under the Trees) accidentally awak'd me; to him I related my Dream with all its Particulars, and he, without much Study, presently interpreted it, assuring me, *That it was a lively Representation of* HARVARD COLLEGE, *Etcetera*. I remain, Sir, Your Humble Servant,

SILENCE DOGOOD

JOHN BULKELEY (1679–1731)
Preface to Roger Wolcott, *Poetical Meditations* (1725)

JOHN BULKELEY was Gershom's son and, like his father, a Connecticut clergyman after his graduation from Harvard. Like his father also, he was distressed by the democratic and anarchic spirit of Connecticut (what Samuel Johnson was to call its "wretched, mobbish" mode of government) and preferred a form of government more closely modeled on that of the mother country. He did not follow Gershom in implicitly calling for reinstitution of the Church of England, but in his long preface to Roger Wolcott's *Poetical Meditations* he did insist that the British constitution provided "a model of government so perfect and well adapted to the ends of government" that wherever the Connecticut charter deviated from its principles that charter deserved to be voided. Such truths, Bulkeley explained, would be appreciated only by men capable of understanding the theories of John Locke—"that man of deep thoughts"—and would remain inaccessible to "the multitude (who generally speaking have too much rubbish in their brain to think of anything with distinctness)." Locke's *Essay on Human Understanding* thus proved as useful to the younger Bulkeley as his *Treatises on Government,* perhaps even more useful; for Bulkeley's effort at political theorizing was sustained more by views of human psychology than by views of proper forms of government. Whereas his father had once found the clowns of Connecticut guilty of "simplicity of the head," John Bulkeley, no less persuaded that the populace was "trained up, but too much, in *principles* of *rebellion,*" could more precisely indict them for "enthusiastic" conceits, and could argue, as had Solomon Stoddard with respect to the church, that control must be given to those with clear and distinct ideas.

Unlike Stoddard, however, Bulkeley seems not to have been tormented by the moral questions concerning the New Englanders' treatment of the Indians. In *An Answer to Some Cases of Conscience Respecting the Country,* Stoddard, always eminently practical in his selection of issues, had focused on the question, "Did we wrong the Indians in buying their land at a small price?" His resolution touched briefly on the traditional argument that the first white settlers of New England had found it a "waste place," but final assurance came with his conclusion that a deal, after all, is a deal: "we came to their market, and gave them their price." In fact, Stoddard insisted, we paid them more than necessary, for the land was worth nothing when occupied by the Indians: it was "our dwelling in it, and our improvements, that have made it to be of worth." Stoddard himself persisted in the New England ambivalence toward the Indians, publishing in 1723 a discourse asking *Whether God is not angry with the Country for doing so little towards the conversion of the Indians.* But Bulkeley argued in a tract of 1724 that the "aboriginal natives" had precious little right to the American land; and his introduction to Wolcott's poetry lays bare the premise on which he based his argument that the lazy and shiftless Indians had forfeited all rights to the land: they had failed to mix their labor with the soil, which, as John Locke had demonstrated, was essential to the creation of "a property" that men could rightly call their own.

Wolcott's *Poetical Meditations* were dedicated to Timothy Edwards, Stoddard's son-in-law and the father of Jonathan Edwards, who within the decade was to begin giving John Locke quite different meaning and import. But in 1725 Locke, and the Augustan mode his works helped to inspire in New England, sustained not only the curious intermixture of politics and aesthetics that occupied Bulkeley's Preface but the poetry of Wolcott as well. Balance, order, even tranquillity, were the pervasive themes. In his effort to celebrate the epic of Connecticut, Wolcott attributed to the Connecticut Valley a pastoral quiescence that contrasts sharply with the "waste and howling" wilderness once described as the challenge justifying New England's claims and achievements. Wolcott was probably as familiar with Alexander Pope's *Windsor Forest* as was Bulkeley with Pope's *Essay on Criticism.* Wolcott's Connecticut River marks the first appearance in American literature of the English meander that was to delight generations of American poetasters who hoped to impose tranquillity on the American scene. In the following passage, John Winthrop, Jr., recounts some of the splendors of the Connecticut Valley to a recently restored King Charles II:

> Great Sir, Since Reconciled Heaven Restores
> You to the Throne of Your High Ancestors,
> See how each Subject Emulating tries,
> To Express our National Felicities;
> The Joy of Your Accession to the Throne,
> Is like the Lustre of the Morning Sun;

Which from the East Salutes the Western Shores,
Still trampling under foot Nights horrid Powers:
So the loud Accents of this boundless Joy,
Ecchoing in our Ears from *Britanny,*
Gave Light and Gladness where-so'ere it came,
And fill'd our joyful Hearts with equal Flame.
The sad Remembrance of those days of Wo,
Which in Your Absence we did undergo,
Transports our present Joys to that Excess,
As passeth all Expressions to express.

. . . . .

This gallent *Stream* keeps running from the Head
Four Hundred Miles ere it with *Neptune* bed,
Passing along hundreds of *Rivolets,*
From either bank its Christial waves besets,
Freely to pay their Tributes to this Stream,
As being Chief and Sovereign unto them,
It bears no torrent nor Impetuous course
As if 'twere driven to the Sea by force.
But calmly on a gentle wave doth move;
As if 'twere drawn to *Thetis* house by love.

The Waters Fresh and Sweet, and he that swims
In it, Recruits and Cures his Surfeit Limbs.
The *Fisherman* the *Fry* with Pleasure gets,
With Seins, Pots, Angles, and his Tramel-nets.
In it Swim *Salmon, Sturgeon, Carp* and *Eels,*
Above fly *Cranes, Geese, Duck, Herons* and *Teals;*
And *Swans* which take such Pleasure as they fly,
They Sing their Hymns oft long before they Dy.

Wolcott, as this excerpt suggests, was only incidentally a poet. A native of Windsor, Connecticut, he was a man of public affairs, major general at the capture of Fortress Louisburg, assemblyman, chief justice, and eventually governor of Connecticut. His attempt at an epic of Connecticut was a *political* document, justifying the Restoration, the expropriation of New Haven, and the unquestioned Englishness of the descendants not merely of Hooker's despairing migrants but of those who had, with Davenport, eagerly and with fresher hopes transplanted themselves from England's green and pleasant land.

The text of Bulkeley's Preface is from the edition published in New London, Connecticut, in 1725, pp. ix-xii, xiv-xv.

Poetical Meditations The Preface

. . . Some there are that have remarked that the accomplished poet and the great man are things seldom meeting together in one person, or that it's rare those powers of mind that make the one are found united with those that constitute the other. And perhaps it may be a truth which for the main holds true. For whereas what is properly called wit (which is no other than a ready assemblage of ideas or a putting those together with quickness and variety wherein there can be found any congruity or resemblance; or to speak more plain, an aptness at metaphor and allusion) is what, as I take it, makes the accomplished poet; exactness of judgment, or clearness of reason (which we commonly and truly say makes the great man), on the other hand, lies in an ability of mind nicely to distinguish its ideas the one from the other, where there is but the least difference, thereby avoiding being missed by similitude, and by affinity to take one thing from another. And the process of the mind in these two things being so contrary the one to the other, 'tis not strange if they are powers not ever united in the same subject. Yet this notwithstanding, all must say, this is not a remark that universally and without exception will hold true; but that how contrary and inconsistent soever the process of the mind in the exercise of these two powers may seem to be, yet there are instances wherein they are united in a wonderful measure. And many men in whom we find a great deal of pleasantry or wit are notwithstanding very judicious and rational . . .

For my own part, whatever opinion some may have of me as to my principles in politics, and though perhaps our present frame or model of government is not the best that might be, but capable of a change in some points to the better, yet I can freely confess that I look upon it as an indulgence and favor of heaven, a just ground of gratitude; and that as it's a constitution capable of rendering us a people more happy than we are, so that the infelicities we labor under in the present day, which truly are not few or small, are rather owning to the want of a due use, or rather an abuse of it, than the constitution itself.

I am no admirer of those despotic forms of government which, as they obtain in some places, so are not without their advocates in others, where the blessings they enjoy under the good and gentle administrations of better forms might convince them of their folly and teach them better. I firmly believe that the law of nature knows no difference or subordination among men, besides those of children to their parents and wives to their husbands, and that these relations only excepted, all men are otherwise equal . . .

I presume there are not many in this popular, leveling day who will not readily subscribe to this doctrine, and more than that, who will not say that in lawful governments that are founded in compact, the more general error is that so much power is given up by the community, and vested in their rulers. I am very sure among us at least there are not many who (pardon me if what I say may be amiss), generally speaking, are a people trained up but too much in principles of rebellion and opposition to government; and who as to the constitution obtaining among us, as popular as it is, yet think it defective by error on the other extreme? Yet all this notwithstanding, certain it is, despotic forms are not the only that are prejudicial to the ends of government, but those erring on the other extreme are perhaps as inconsistent with them, and of this, besides their but too often exemplifying the condition of Ephesus at a certain time when Paul was there, Acts 19.[1] We need not go far from home for evidence. Our English constitution at home seems to be an happy mean between these two extremes, wisely contrived to secure from the ill consequents of either of them. A constitution it is wherein as one says, though the executive power be lodged solely in the king, yet the legislative power is divided between him and his people, by which as the king has bounds set to his prerogative, so the people have their privileges which assert their liberty. Such a constitution it is as allows enough to a king of no tyrannical a temper, and what is sufficient to secure the ends of government, and enough to the people to preserve them from slavery. There is monarchy without slavery, a great king, and yet a free people; such a monarchy as has the main advantages of an aristocracy in the Lords, and of a democracy in the Commons, without the inconveniences of either. In a word, a model of government so perfect and well adapted to the ends of government does it seem to be, that as the things wherein other constitutions (and in particular *ours* in this colony) harmonizes with it seem to be its great perfects, and those wherein it differs its great imperfections . . .

1. Paul finds "the whole city . . . filled with confusion . . . some therefore cried one thing, and some another . . . for the assembly was confused; and the more part knew not wherefore they were come together" (Acts 19:29, 32).

AFTERWORD

WOLCOTT'S soothing reconstruction of New England history may be read both as ending the Puritan era in New England literature and as beginning its Augustan voice—a chorus that rose in volume down to and through the American Revolution. Indeed, both Wolcott's poetry and Bulkeley's prose gave a radically new definition to the errand of New Englanders into the wilderness. Like Gershom Bulkeley they repudiated New England tradition, but they were by no means unabashedly loyal to the Crown of England. The elder Bulkeley had appealed to William and Mary to bring in something of the Old World, as it were, to redress the imbalances of the new; even as Paul Dudley (grandson of one of the builders of the Bay colony) had complained that America would "never be worth living in, for lawyers and gentlemen" until the Massachusetts charter was replaced by the judicial system and the common law of England. The question, at bottom, was not one of political philosophy, but the most practical of matters: the sober and solid citizens of Connecticut, Gershom Bulkeley had complained, would seek their "fortunes" elsewhere if their majesties did not heed their cry for help. It was coming to be understood that New England was in fact a plantation of trade, not of religion; as Dummer had informed the Lords Commissioners, his people had come to New England, not to illumine the world with the brightness of Christ's appearing, but "to increase the nation's commerce and enlarge her dominions."

The literature of Augustan New England can be read as revolving about a single theme: the need to embody, in the life and institutions of the New World, the values of a more "civilized" mother country. The imperatives of Wolcott's reconstruction of the seventeenth-century New England landscape found their ultimate prerevolutionary expression in Thomas Hutchinson's *History of Massachusetts Bay* (1764–1767), where the witchcraft frenzy was explained as arising from "a turn of mind" inevitable among a people dwelling in "a wilderness without limits" and isolated from all European "delights of life." Such a view was already implicit in William Douglass' *A Summary Historical and Political . . . of the British Settlements in North America* (1749–1751). Douglass' bias was "scientific," and although he is remembered chiefly for his opposition to smallpox inoculation, his history is marked by an animus against all the "enthusiasms" of his enemy Cotton Mather and against both Mather's ancestors and his spiritual heirs.

A more measured expression of the emerging scientific spirit was offered in 1743 by Benjamin Franklin in *A Proposal for Promoting Useful Knowledge among the British Plantations in America.* This document transcended a definition of the New World in terms of John Locke's conception of property and embodied Francis Bacon's nobler vision of encouraging "philosophical experiments that let light into the nature of things, tend to increase the power of man over matter, and multiply the conveniences and pleasures of life." Franklin, long gone from Boston (where he had both admired and satirized Cotton Mather), was by 1743 settled permanently—until dispatched as America's first ambassador to the Old World—in Philadelphia. His *Proposal* thoughtfully signaled the beginning of an era in which the Americans' errand was to be newly defined by the very wilderness that lay before them:

> The English are possessed of a long tract of continent, from Nova Scotia to Georgia, extending North and South thro' different climates, having different soils, producing different plants, mines and minerals, and capable of different improvements, manufactures, &c.
>
> The first drudgery of settling new colonies . . . is now pretty well over; and there are many in every province in circumstances that set them at ease, and afford leisure to cultivate the finer arts, and improve the common stock of knowledge.

Franklin, to be sure, was no longer writing as a New Englander; indeed, he seemed to view America from a position halfway between, as it were, Philadelphia and London. But his description of the New World as a vast stock of raw materials, a bundle of resources that ought to engage the minds of the scientifically inclined and the energies of all (lest they lapse into the new American original sin of "laziness") was previsioned in New England as well. Jared Eliot (grandson of the apostle to the Indians) was not Franklin's Connecticut correspondent merely, but truly one of his coadjutors. Eliot had signed Timothy Cutler's queries as to the validity of Presbyterian ordination but had eventually resolved his doubts in favor of New England tradition. Besides a clergyman, he was a physician, botanist, mineralogist, and, above all, like Franklin, an ardent advocate of "scientific agriculture." His *Essays upon Field Husbandry in New England,* written in 1747 though not published until 1760, were Franklinian in style as well as doctrine. "Manure," Eliot insisted, "is the one thing needful."

Also in 1747 was published the *chef d'oeuvre* of American Augustan poetry: William Livingston's *Philosophic Solitude, or the Choice of a Rural Life.* This poem, which enjoyed thirteen separate editions by 1790 and was a favorite of anthologizers in the early Republic, was quickly embraced and dispatched abroad as evidence that Englishmen held a "wrong opinion" of American "ignorance and barbarism." But it was by no means the sole venture into *belles lettres* in the 1740s, which witnessed several efforts to produce journals of literary as well as scientific and political interest. In 1741 Franklin himself had produced *The General Magazine,* a compendium of reprints from English publications along with some original essays and even occasional poetry. He had included several poems by Mather Byles, Cotton Mather's nephew, who served as the center for what passed as cultural life in Boston. Byles's *The American Magazine and Historical Chronicle* was published in Boston from 1743 to 1745, and in 1744 Byles put together a collection of his own efforts, *Poems on Several Occasions.* Yet one of the more intense literary coteries of mid-century America emerged not in either of the larger cities but in Connecticut, where the literati were widely dispersed, and where neither the capital nor the college city could pose as a burgeoning metropolis.

William Livingston came out of the Yale class of 1741, the source of what remained a close-knit band of literarily inclined brothers. Livingston, the youngest of six sons of an aristocratic New York family, set up briefly after graduation as a law clerk in New York City. But he was soon denouncing the system—of the law as well as of apprenticeship—for making a "young fellow trifle away the bloom of his age." Like Franklin resentful of all that stood in the way of youth's ambition, Livingston may have been as well something of an eighteenth-century Bartleby: he succeeded, during his legal clerkship, in composing two short poems and a treatise on the drama. The latter so impressed his classmate Noah Welles that he proposed submitting it to Byles' magazine, but Livingston demurred, judging the piece "too incorrect and superficial to obtrude on the public." He showed considerably less diffidence with his much longer piece of verse, *Philosophic Solitude.* This poem is often read as a feeble imitation of John Pomfret's *The Choice,* which indeed was to be the model for Benjamin Church's *The Choice, a Poem after the Manner of M. Pomfret* (1757). But Livingston's numerous Yale admirers knew better: "a second *Windsor* starts in every line," announced Welles in one of several adulatory pieces of verse prefaced to *Philosophic Solitude*. For though Livingston, like Pomfret, dwelled on the choice of a properly virginal wife to share his rural life, the central issue for him, as for many another colonial poetaster, was that raised in Pope's *Windsor Forest*. What Pope offered Livingston and others in mid-eighteenth-century America was an opportunity to reject a way of life—not just Ranelagh and Vauxhall but the hurly-burly of London—that was never in fact a likely option in an as-yet-underdeveloped country.

In fact Livingston, after sharing his verses with his Connecticut coterie, plunged back into New York City, where he began a new career, first as a pamphleteer arguing for the establishment of a "dissenting" college to rival that presided over by Samuel Johnson (King's College, later Columbia). Along with Welles and other Connecticut friends he soon took up the cudgels against the rumored plot to establish an American bishop. He also published vitriolic assaults on Governor Clinton, leader of his family's ancient enemies, and in 1752 he began to publish *The Independent Reflector,* a magazine that for three years engaged the energies of many a Yale graduate in New York. Though excerpts from Pope were quoted (often serving as epigraphs), the main thrust of the magazine was partisan and polemical, assailing every aspect of the Anglican culture in New York, which to Livingston, as Milton M. Klein has observed, represented an "intellectual wasteland." Seemingly oblivious to, say, Johnson's *Elementa Philosophica,* and unsuccessful in his efforts to erect a competing college in New York, Livingston increasingly identified with the young College of New Jersey at Princeton. When the Clintonians were victorious politically, Livingston finally moved to New Jersey, from which he was sent as delegate to the Continental Congresses. He served as governor of New Jersey for the first fourteen years of independence.

Mere mention of the College of New Jersey is a reminder that the thought of New England cannot be traced, in the post-Puritan era, on one straight line from Bulkeley and Wolcott to Thomas Hutchinson, or even to Franklin's *The Way to Wealth* (1758), his profoundly "Puritan" self-satire on his own maxims for self-improvement. To be sure, science, literature, politics had come to seem, to many in and of New England, the truly new dispensation, one that freed the New England mind at last from its religious obsession, and one that recognized as well that the written word—prose satire as well as verse, Addisonian essay, political pamphlet—had replaced the sermon as the proper literary diet for the New World. "The press," proclaimed one of Livingston's critics, was to him and his allies "what the pulpit was in times of Popery"—as if the preaching and the hearing of the word had been central in only the remotest of European antiquities.

In fact, the half-century after 1725 may have been the most prodigious era of sermonizing in American history. In 1742, a year before Franklin's *Proposal,* appeared Jonathan Edwards' *Some Thoughts concerning the Present Revival of Religion in New England,* a sustained defense of the "great and general awakening" that had for two years or more engrossed the attention of vast multitudes throughout the colonies. Four years later Edwards published *A Treatise Concerning Religious Affections,* first preached in sermon form and thereafter expanded into a radically new analysis of religious psychology—possibly the greatest of all American efforts in this vein—in which he both repudiated the "faculty psychology" of his Puritan forebears and provided a revitalized Calvinism with an understanding of the mind's operations derived from his own sensitive and imaginative reading of Locke. However one defines it—Perry Miller insisted that the Awakening, and the controversy between Edwards and his mighty "rationalist" opponent Charles Chauncy, shifted the focus away from the nature of God to the nature of man—what is clear is that another epoch had opened for the mind of New England and all America: one quite different from what Franklin envisioned as the age of "drudgery" ended. Edwards and those who accepted his intellectual leadership did not aspire to the "civilized" ways of Old England; indeed, what they feared most was that American culture and ideals were in danger of being "assimilated" to those of the once-Mother Country. They hoped—indeed expected—that a wholly different society, the kingdom of God itself, would emerge out of the as-yet-unformed wilderness, and that not only a decadent Europe but all humanity would become part of God's spiritually thriving kingdom on earth.

Perhaps above all the Awakening brought an end to the regional and tribal consciousness that had been so manifest throughout New England's first century. That aspect of the revival, and indeed the whole of the Awakening, have received their own anthologies, and Edwards himself deserves a continued singular attention. Born in 1703 in East Windsor, Connecticut, Edwards entered Yale (then the College of New Haven) in 1716 and was graduated four years later. For two more years he studied theology in New Haven, then served for a year as minister to a Presbyterian church in New York City. Edwards returned to Yale until 1726, when he left to become a colleague of his grandfather Stoddard in Northampton. In 1731 the first of his published sermons appeared, delivered as a doctrinal challenge to the Boston clergy at their "Thursday lecture." Over the next quarter-century Edwards produced a corpus of prose unmatched in the American canon for its intellectual vigor and its verbal architecture.

Edwards is commonly identified not simply as a Calvinist (with special attention to his late-life treatises on the *Freedom of the Will* and *Original Sin*) but, despite a half-century of republication and scholarship, as a preacher of "hell-fire" sermons. Attention to his language, however, or even to his doctrine, clearly shows that Edwards, like Cotton, conceived sin to be privative, not positive, and hell not a place of burning sulphur but a state of mind: an eternal torment in the absence of God. Spiders, arrows, flames, were for Edwards metaphors; it may well be that in the final analysis his highest achievement, as a theologian and as a preacher, lay in his ability to infuse old doctrines with new meaning through a novel, even radical, reformulation of language. In 1734, for instance, he delivered a series of sermons, published in 1738 as *Justification by Faith Alone,* in which, aware not merely of reversions to Episcopacy but of Arminian tendencies within New England's traditional churches (even his own), he reasserted what he styled "the principal hinge of Protestantism." The "evangelical scheme" he espoused, however, represented not so much a rejection of the theology of the covenant as an infusing of it with radically new meanings derived from his reading of Isaac Newton:

> I do not now pretend to define justifying faith, or to determine precisely how much is contained in it, but only to determine thus much concerning it, viz., that it is that by which the soul that before was separate and alienated from Christ, unites itself to him, or ceases to be any longer in that state of alienation, and comes into that forementioned union or relation to him, or, to use the scripture phrase, that it is that by which the soul comes to Christ, and receives him: and this is evident by the scripture's using these very expressions to signify faith . . . If it be said that these are obscure figures of speech, that, however they might be well understood of old among those that then commonly used such metaphors, yet they are difficultly understood now; I allow that the expressions, *receiving* Christ, and *coming* to Christ, are metaphorical expressions: and if I should allow them to be obscure metaphors, yet so much at least is certainly plain in them, viz., that faith is that by which those that before were separated, and at a distance from Christ (that is to say, were not so related and united to him as his people are), do cease to be any longer at such a distance, and do come into that relation and nearness . . .

"Metaphor" may well be the clue not only to Edwards' literary achievement but to the entire intellectual universe he unfolded for his and later generations. From the earliest sermons through the posthumously published dissertations *True Virtue* and *The End for which God Created the World,* he regularly dilated on the most metaphoric of scriptural sources, ordaining for them meanings of his own. Not just any meanings, however, or arbitrary ones: if any single thread unites all his utterances it is the one encapsulated in a single entry in his private notebooks—"gravity," he declared after exploring the inherent qualities of Newton's universe, "is a type of love." Love as a unifying force among intelligent beings was the central theme of the *Religious Affections,* as well as the memoir of David Brainerd, Edwards' son-in-law, whom he hymned as an exemplum of the "experimental religion" set out in the *Affections.* It informed also his millenarian writings, most particularly his *Humble Attempt* to bring into "visible union" not merely Northampton's church but "all God's people in America." At the end (in *The Nature of True Virtue*) he defined the ultimate divine excellency as "a society of intelligent beings, sweetly united in benevolent agreement of heart," and the beatific vision of *The End for which God Created the World* was one in which atomized humanity was being drawn into a more perfect union by the gravitational powers of divine and human love:

> Thus we see that the great and last end of God's works which is so variously expressed in Scripture, is indeed but *one;* and this *one* end is most properly and comprehensively called, THE GLORY OF GOD; by which name it is most commonly called in Scripture: and is fitly compared to an effulgence or emanation of light from a luminary, by which this glory of God is abundantly represented in Scripture. Light is the external expression, exhibition and manifestation of the excellency of the luminary, of the sun for instance: it is the abundant, extensive emanation and communication of the fulness of the sun to innumerable beings that partake of it. It is by this that the sun itself is seen, and his glory beheld, and all other things are discovered; it is by a participation of this communication from the sun, that surrounding objects receive all their lustre, beauty and brightness. It is by this that all nature is quickened and receives life, comfort and joy . . .
>
> The emanation or communication of the divine fulness, consisting in the knowledge of God, love to God, and joy in God, has relation indeed both to God, and the creature; but it has relation to God as its fountain, as it is an emanation from God;

and as the communication itself, or thing communicated, is something divine, something of God, something of his internal fulness, as the water in the stream is something of the fountain, and as the beams of the sun, are something of the sun. And again, they have relation to God, as they have respect to him as their object; for the knowledge communicated is the knowledge of God; and so God is the object of the knowledge, and the love communicated is the love of God; so God is the object of that love, and the happiness communicated is joy in God; and so he is the object of the joy communicated. In the creature's knowing, esteeming, loving, rejoicing in, and praising God, the glory of God is both exhibited and acknowledged; his fulness is received and returned. Here is both an *emanation* and *remanation*. The refulgence shines upon and into the creature, and is reflected back to the luminary. The beams of glory come from God, and are something of God, and are refunded back again to their original. So that the whole is *of* God, and *in* God, and *to* God, and God is the beginning, middle and end in this affair . . .

Let the most perfect union with God be represented by something at an infinite height above us; and the eternally increasing union of the saints with God, by something that is ascending constantly towards that infinite height, moving upwards with a given velocity, and that is to continue thus to move to all eternity. God, who views the whole of this eternally increasing height, views it as an infinite height. And if he has respect to it, and makes it his end, as in the whole of it, he has respect to it as an infinite height, though the time will never come when it can be said it has already arrived at this infinite height . . .

It is no solid objection against God's aiming at an infinitely perfect union of the creature with himself, that the particular time will never come when it can be said, the union is now infinitely perfect. God aims at satisfying justice in the eternal damnation of sinners; which will be satisfied by their damnation, considered no otherwise than with regard to its eternal duration. But yet there never will come that particular moment, when it can be said, that now justice is satisfied. But if this does not satisfy our modern freethinkers, who do not like the talk about satisfying justice with an infinite punishment; I suppose it will not be denied by any, that God, in glorifying the saints in heaven with eternal felicity, aims to satisfy his infinite grace or benevolence, by the bestowment of a good infinitely valuable, because eternal; and yet there never will come the moment, when it can be said, that now this infinitely valuable good has been actually bestowed.

Two months after his installation as president of Princeton in January 1758, Edwards died of smallpox, following an inoculation he had insisted on for his students. In life, as in thought, he was both of New England and not of it, ranging in person, and even more in imagination, well beyond its confines. Yet he was, as an intellect and as an artist, perhaps the ultimate New Englander, representing not its flowering but—little more than a century after the first settlements—its fruitful perfection.

BIBLIOGRAPHICAL NOTES

THIS SECTION opens with a selective survey of works (including all those quoted or referred to in the Introduction) that treat various aspects of English and American Puritanism. Next comes an alphabetical list of authors whose writings appear in this anthology, giving major works about each author. Witchcraft has its own bibliography at the end. (For works cited more than once, all references after the first are given by short title and date of publication only.)

INTRODUCTION

For the emergence of Puritanism as a distinguishable branch of English Protestantism, see John T. McNeill, *The History and Character of Calvinism* (New York: Oxford University Press, 1967); A. G. Dickens, *The English Reformation* (New York: Schocken, 1964); Patrick Collinson, *The Elizabethan Puritan Movement* (Berkeley: University of California Press, 1967); Horton Davies, *Worship and Theology in England* (Princeton: Princeton University Press), vol. 1, *From Cranmer to Hooker, 1534–1603* (1970), and vol. 2, *From Andrewes to Baxter, 1603–1690* (1975); Keith Thomas, *Religion and the Decline of Magic* (London: Weidenfeld and Nicolson, 1971); and the older but still impressive William Haller, *The Rise of Puritanism* (New York: Columbia University Press, 1938). Peter Milward has written two helpful guides, *Religious Controversies of the Elizabethan Age* (London: Scolar Press, 1977); and *Religious Controversies of the Jacobean Age* (Scolar, 1978). Useful collections of documents include J. R. Tanner, ed., *Constitutional Documents of the Reign of James I, 1603–1625* (Cambridge: Cambridge University Press, 1961); Everett Emerson, ed., *English Puritanism from John Hooper to John Milton* (Durham: Duke University Press, 1968); and H. C. Porter, *Puritanism in Tudor England* (Columbia: University of South Carolina Press, 1971). Valuable for a sense of the religious disputes is Paul Elmer More and Frank Leslie Cross, eds., *Anglicanism: The Thought and*

Practice of the Church of England Illustrated from the Religious Literature of the Seventeenth Century (London: S.P.C.K., 1935). A single-volume compilation of the essential tracts documenting the history of congregationalism in England, Holland, and New England, with invaluable commentary, is Williston Walker, ed., *The Creeds and Platforms of Congregationalism* (1893) (rpt. Philadelphia: Pilgrim Press, 1960).

The temperament of Stuart Puritanism is sensitively evoked in two books by Geoffrey Nuttall, *The Holy Spirit in Puritan Faith and Experience* (Oxford: Basil Blackwell, 1946), and *Visible Saints: The Congregational Way, 1640–1660* (Oxford: Blackwell, 1957); and in John S. Coolidge, *The Pauline Renaissance: Puritanism and the Bible* (Oxford: Oxford University Press, 1970).

For the political context in which Puritanism developed, see the groundbreaking works of Christopher Hill, a scholar who combines an essentially Marxist view with a capaciousness of mind that marks his work as an enduring achievement of the historical imagination—especially *Puritanism and Revolution* (New York: Schocken, 1964); and *Society and Puritanism in Pre-Revolutionary England* (New York: Schocken, 1967). A stimulating collection of essays that treats the larger European setting is Trevor Aston, ed., *Crisis in Europe, 1560–1660* (New York: Doubleday, 1967). Also valuable are Michael Walzer, *The Revolution of the Saints* (New York: Atheneum, 1973); and Perez Zagorin, *The Court and the Country: The Beginnings of the English Revolution* (New York: Atheneum, 1971). The ongoing effort to establish connections between Puritanism, class, and social change began with Max Weber, *The Protestant Ethic and the Spirit of Capitalism* (1904–1905) (trans. Talcott Parsons, New York: Charles Scribner's Sons, 1930). Weber was introduced to an English audience, and amplified, by his distinguished disciple R. H. Tawney, especially in *Religion and the Rise of Capitalism* (New York: Harcourt, Brace, 1926). See Paul Seaver, "The Puritan Work Ethic Revisited," *Journal of British Studies*, 19–20 (1979–81):35–53. Helpful introductions to the difficult subject of the English Revolution are Conrad Russell, ed., *The Origins of the English Civil War* (London: Macmillan, 1973); and two by Lawrence Stone, *Social Change and Revolution in England, 1540–1640* (New York: Barnes and Noble, 1965), and *The Causes of the English Revolution, 1529–1642* (New York: Harper, 1972). A small but well-chosen anthology is Stuart E. Prall, ed., *The Puritan Revolution* (New York: Doubleday, 1968). William Haller, ed., *Tracts on Liberty in the Puritan Revolution: 1638–1647* (New York: Columbia University Press, 1933), 3 vols., is a rich collection of original sources in facsimile. Still indispensable are the contemporary royalist narrative by Edward Hyde, Lord Clarendon, *The History of the Rebellion* (written 1646–48 and 1671–74) (ed. W. Dunn Macray, Oxford University Press, 1888); and Samuel R. Gardiner's seventeen volumes on *The History of England* from 1603 to 1656 (London, 1863–1901), the supreme example of Whig historiography.

The basic authority on the settlement of New England remains Charles M. Andrews, *The Colonial Period of American History* (New Haven: Yale University Press, 1934), 4 vols. Still fascinating is Thomas Hutchinson, *The History of the*

Colony and Province of Massachusetts Bay (1764–1767) (ed. Lawrence Mayo, Cambridge, Mass.: Harvard University Press, 1936), 3 vols. Although hostile in many respects to the Puritan "theocracy," James Truslow Adams, *The Founding of New England* (Boston: Little, Brown, 1921); and Charles Francis Adams, *Three Episodes in Massachusetts History* (Boston: Houghton Mifflin, 1896), retain much of their original power. Among more recent works, the transition from England to America is studied by Patricia Caldwell in *The Puritan Conversion Narrative: The Beginnings of American Expression* (New York: Cambridge University Press, 1983), which uses the surviving professions of faith (mainly those of Thomas Shepard's Cambridge congregation) to describe the emergence of a distinctively American religious expression. Charles E. Hambrick-Stowe addresses similar questions in *The Practice of Piety: Puritan Devotional Discipline in Seventeenth-Century New England* (Chapel Hill: University of North Carolina Press, 1982). Edmund Morgan's *Visible Saints: The History of a Puritan Idea* (Ithaca: Cornell University Press, 1963) traces the emergence of the congregational idea in Holland and England and describes its American transformations. An interesting psychoanalytic study of the emigrants and their descendants is David Leverenz, *The Language of Puritan Feeling* (New Brunswick: Rutgers University Press, 1980). More focused on political and social adjustment to the New World are Robert Emmet Wall, Jr., *Massachusetts Bay: The Crucial Decade, 1640–1650* (New Haven: Yale University Press, 1972); T. H. Breen, *Puritans and Adventurers: Change and Persistence in Early America* (New York: Oxford University Press, 1980); and David Grayson Allen, *In English Ways: The Movement of Societies and the Transferral of English Local Law and Custom to Massachusetts Bay in the Seventeenth Century* (Chapel Hill: University of North Carolina Press, 1981). The basic source for the political history of the Massachusetts Bay Colony is Nathaniel B. Shurtleff, ed., *Records of the Governor and Company of the Massachusetts Bay*, 5 vols. (Boston, 1853–54). Ann Kibbey, *Rhetoric, Prejudice, and Violence: The Interpretation of Material Shapes in Puritanism* (New York: Cambridge University Press, 1985), applies some techniques of current literary theory to the writings of the first generation. Andrew Delbanco, "The Puritan Errand Re-Viewed," *Journal of American Studies*, 18 (Dec. 1984), is an exploration of the emigrants' motives and experience.

There is a growing literature on the nature and development of the New England town, of which leading examples are Sumner C. Powell, *Puritan Village* (Middletown, Conn.: Wesleyan University Press, 1963); and Kenneth A. Lockridge, *A New England Town: The First Hundred Years* (New York: Norton, 1970). A study of the New England ministry from its beginnings is David D. Hall, *The Faithful Shepherd: A History of the New England Ministry in the Seventeenth Century* (Chapel Hill: University of North Carolina Press, 1972). William Cronon, *Changes in the Land: Indians, Colonists, and the Ecology of New England* (New York: Hill and Wang, 1983) is a fresh consideration of the ways in which English settlers tried to bring the land itself into conformity with their European ideas. A fascinating record of early New England life and culture is the three-volume exhibition catalog *New England Begins* (Boston: Museum of Fine Arts, 1983). David D. Hall, in "Toward a History of Popular Religion in Early New England," *William and Mary Quarterly*, 3d. ser., 41 (1984):49–55, has sketched some new approaches to the old problem of assessing the place of religious ideas in the everyday life of ordinary men and women. A good collection of documents is Edmund Morgan, ed., *The Founding of Massachusetts* (Indianapolis: Bobbs-Merrill, 1964). The migration has been considered in a number of suggestive essays, including Breen's "Moving to the New World: The Character of Early Massachusetts Immigration," (ch. 3 of *Puritans and Adventurers*) and John T. Horton, "Two Bishops and the Holy Brood: A Fresh Look at a Familiar Fact," *New England Quarterly*, 40 (1967):339–346, an article that is also a convenient review of earlier work on the subject. On the question of the emigrants' expectations, see Alan Heimert, "Puritanism, The Wilderness, and the Frontier," *New England Quarterly*, 26 (1953):361–382.

The return home of significant numbers of New Englanders after the outbreak of civil war has received little scholarly attention. See William L. Sachse, "The Migration of New Englanders to England, 1640–1660," *American Historical Review*, 53 (1948), 251–278; and Harry Stout, "University Men in New England, 1620–1660: A Demographic Analysis," *Journal of Interdisciplinary History*, 4 (1974), 375–400.

The background of millenarianism can be approached through Norman Cohn, *The Pursuit of the Millennium* (New York: Oxford University Press, 1970). For Reformation continuities and American consequences, see Ursula Brumm, *American Thought and Religious Typology* (1963) (trans. John Hoaglund, New Brunswick: Rutgers University Press, 1970); Mason Lowance, *The Language of Canaan* (Cambridge, Mass.: Harvard University Press, 1980); and several influential works by Sacvan Bercovitch: "Horologicals to Chronometricals: The Rhetoric of the Jeremiad," *Literary Monographs*, 3, ed. Eric Rothstein (Madison: University of Wisconsin Press, 1970), which is an earlier version of his *The American Jeremiad* (Madison: University of Wisconsin Press, 1978). See also Bercovitch, *The Puritan Origins of the American Self* (New Haven: Yale University Press, 1975). An important essay that has been insufficiently recognized is James P. Walsh, "Holy Time and Sacred Space in Puritan New England," *American Quarterly*, 32 (1980):79–95. On Puritan attitudes toward the Jews, see Bercovitch, "Puritan New England Rhetoric and the Jewish Problem," *Early American Literature*, 5 (1970):63–71; Peter Toon, *Puritans, the Millennium, and the Future of Israel* (Cambridge: James Clarke, 1970), ch. 7; and Richard H. Popkin, "Jewish Messianism and Christian Millenarianism," in Perez Zagorin, ed., *Culture and Politics from Puritanism to the Enlightenment* (Berkeley: University of California Press, 1980), pp. 67–90.

The great interpretive work in relation to which much subsequent scholarship stands as modification, amplification, and response is that of Perry Miller, whose chronicle of the intellectual history of colonial New England is a towering achievement of American historiography: *Orthodoxy in Massachusetts* (1933) (rpt. New York: Harper, 1970); *The New England Mind: The Seventeenth Century* (1939) (rpt. Cambridge, Mass.: Harvard University Press, 1982); *The New England*

Mind: From Colony to Province (1953) (rpt. Cambridge, Mass.: Harvard University Press, 1982); *Errand into the Wilderness* (Cambridge, Mass.: Harvard University Press, 1956); and some of the essays in *Nature's Nation* (Cambridge, Mass.: Harvard University Press, 1967).

Among the early challenges to Miller's stress on Puritan rationalism are Alan Simpson, *Puritanism in Old and New England* (Chicago: University of Chicago Press, 1955); James F. Maclear, "The Heart of New England Rent: The Mystical Element in Early Puritan History," *Mississippi Valley Historical Review,* 42 (1956):621–652; Norman Grabo, "The Veiled Vision: The Role of Aesthetics in Early American Intellectual History," in Sacvan Bercovitch, ed., *The American Puritan Imagination: Essays in Revaluation* (Cambridge: Cambridge University Press, 1974), pp. 19–33; and Richard Schlatter, "The Puritan Strain," in John Higham, ed., *The Reconstruction of American History* (New York: Harper, 1962), pp. 25–45. Notable among more recent general treatments are Darrett B. Rutman, *American Puritanism* (Philadelphia: Lippincott, 1970); and Larzer Ziff, *Puritanism in America* (New York: Viking, 1973). Francis J. Bremer, *The Puritan Experiment* (New York: St. Martin's, 1976) is a highly readable introduction. A short, penetrating essay is William G. McLoughlin, "The Puritan Awakening and the Cultural Core," in his *Revivals, Awakenings, and Reform* (Chicago: University of Chicago Press, 1972), ch. 2.

Miller's sweeping narrative of Puritanism in decline as the seventeenth century wore on has come under strenuous challenge in recent years. The richest critique is Bercovitch, *The American Jeremiad* (1978), which argues for the jeremiad as the rhetorical agent of Puritan self-affirmation, rather than as a genre of lamentation in a disintegrating culture. Robert Middlekauff's *The Mathers: Three Generations of Puritan Intellectuals* (New York: Oxford University Press, 1971) is also broadly suggestive in proposing that the piety of later Puritanism changed rather than slackened. Other works include Robert G. Pope, *The Half-Way Covenant: Church Membership in Puritan New England* (Princeton: Princeton University Press, 1969), and Emory Elliott, *Power and the Pulpit in Puritan New England* (Princeton: Princeton University Press, 1975). A thoughtful reconsideration of the later seventeenth century is David M. Scobey, "Revising the Errand: New England's Ways and the Puritan sense of the Past," *William and Mary Quarterly,* 3d. ser., 41 (1984):3–31. Everett Emerson, "Calvin and Covenant Theology," *Church History,* 25 (1956):136–144, helped to initiate the questioning of Miller's overarching theme that the "Federal Theology" represented a dilution of "pure" Calvinism. An important article that supports Miller's theory of the drift toward legalism is Michael McGiffert, "The Problem of the Covenant in Puritan Thought: Peter Bulkeley's *Gospel-Covenant,*" *The New England Historical and Genealogical Register,* 130 (1976):107–129. A thorough treatment of preparationism, mainly supportive of Miller's views, is Norman Pettit, *The Heart Prepared: Grace and Conversion in Puritan Spiritual Life* (New Haven: Yale University Press, 1966). Philip F. Gura, *A Glimpse of Sion's Glory: Puritan Radicalism in New England, 1620–1660* (Middletown, Conn.: Wesleyan University Press, 1983), calls attention to a wide range of Puritan dissidents in the early years of the colony, thus revising our sense of the Puritan "consensus" as Miller described it. A significant revision of Miller's account of Puritan intellectual life is Norman Fiering, *Moral Philosophy at Seventeenth-Century Harvard* (Chapel Hill: University of North Carolina Press, 1981).

On later phases of Puritanism and its legacies, see Miller, *The New England Mind: From Colony to Province* (1953); Richard L. Bushman, *From Puritan to Yankee: Character and Social Order in Connecticut, 1690–1765* (Cambridge, Mass.: Harvard University Press, 1967); Carl Bridenbaugh, *Mitre and Sceptre: Transatlantic Faiths: Ideas, Personalities, and Politics, 1689–1775* (New York: Oxford University Press, 1962); James Jones, *The Shattered Synthesis: New England Puritanism before the Great Awakening* (New Haven: Yale University Press, 1973); J. William T. Youngs, Jr., *God's Messengers: Religious Leadership in Colonial New England* (Baltimore: Johns Hopkins University Press, 1976); Alan Heimert, *Religion and the American Mind: From the Great Awakening to the Revolution* (Cambridge, Mass.: Harvard University Press, 1966); Jay Fliegelman, *Prodigals and Pilgrims: The American Revolution against Patriarchal Authority, 1750–1800* (New York: Cambridge University Press, 1982); Herbert L. Osgood, *The American Colonies in the Eighteenth Century* (New York: Columbia University Press, 1924). An anthology of later election sermons is A. W. Plumstead, ed., *The Wall and the Garden* (Minneapolis: University of Minnesota Press, 1968).

For more information on individual authors, see James A. Levernier and Douglas R. Wilmes, eds., *American Writers before 1800* (Westport, Conn.: Greenwood Press, 1983). Other valuable bibliographies are *Books about Early America* (Williamsburg: Institute of Early American History, 1970), and its supplement, *Books about Early America, 1970–1975*; Nelson R. Burr, *A Critical Bibliography of Religion in America* (Princeton: Princeton University Press, 1961); Alden T. Vaughn, ed., *The American Colonies in the Seventeenth Century* (New York: Appleton-Century-Crofts, 1971); Jack P. Greene, ed., *The American Colonies in the Eighteenth Century, 1689–1763* (Appleton-Century-Crofts, 1969); and those included in Sacvan Bercovitch, ed., *The American Puritan Imagination: Essays in Revaluation* (Cambridge: Cambridge University Press, 1974); H. Shelton Smith, Robert T. Handy, and Lefferts A. Loetscher, *American Christianity: An Historical Interpretation with Representative Documents* (New York: Charles Scribner's Sons, 1960), vol, 1; Frank Freidel, ed., *The Harvard Guide to American History* (Cambridge, Mass.: Harvard University Press, 1974); Bercovitch, ed., *Typology and Early American Literature* (Amherst: University of Massachusetts Press, 1972); Everett H. Emerson, ed., *English Puritanism from John Hooper to John Milton* (Durham, N.C.: Duke University Press, 1968); Perry Miller and Thomas H. Johnson, eds., *The Puritans* (Cleveland: American Book, 1938; rev. ed., 1963). Moses Coit Tyler, *A History of American Literature: 1607–1765* (1878; rpt. New York:Collier, 1962) remains the best comprehensive survey of the period. The most incisive short survey is Kenneth B. Murdock, "The Colonial and Revolutionary Period," in Arthur Hobson Quinn, ed., *The Literature of the American People* (New York: Appleton-Century-Crofts, 1951).

The works by Levernier, Bercovitch (*Typology*), Emerson, and Miller include lists of primary sources. More extensive bibliographies of primary materials may be found in vol. 2 of Henry Martyn Dexter, *Congregationalism of the Last Three Hundred Years as seen in its Literature* (1880) (rpt. New York: Burt Franklin, 1970). For full listings of published writings by authors represented in this book, the reader should consult the short-title catalogues by A. W. Pollard and G. R. Redgrave (1475–1640) (London: Bibliographical Society, 1946; I-Z rev. by Katherine Pantzer et al., 1976); Donald Wing (1641–1700) (New York: Columbia University Press, 1945); Charles Evans, *American Bibliography* (1639–1820) (New York: Peter Smith, 1941–42; rev. by Clifford K. Shipton and James E. Mooney, Worcester: American Antiquarian Society and Barre Publishers, 1969); supplement by Roger P. Bristol (Charlottesville: University of Virginia Press, 1970).

For scholarship and criticism, also consult the standard annual bibliographies: *Writings on American History* (published by the American Historical Association); the *MLA Bibliography* (Modern Language Association); and the *Index to Religious Periodical Literature* (American Theological Library Association)—known since 1977 as *Religion Index One* (articles) and *Religion Index Two* (books).

The daunting quantity of recent scholarship (of which we list only a small fraction) should not be allowed to obscure the continuing value of the great nineteenth-century historians—especially George Bancroft and John Gorham Palfrey. When all the disclosures of modern writers are brought to bear on colonial New England, a case may still be made for the works of Nathaniel Hawthorne as the most profound treatment we have of our Puritan origins: see Michael Colacurcio, *The Province of Piety: Moral History in Hawthorne's Early Tales* (Cambridge, Mass.: Harvard University Press, 1984).

WILLIAM AMES

A full-length study is Keith L. Sprunger, *The Learned Doctor William Ames: Dutch Backgrounds of English and American Puritanism* (Urbana: University of Illinois Press, 1972). Perry Miller treats Ames's importance for the first-generation American Puritans in *The New England Mind: The Seventeenth Century* (1939), esp. bk. II. Ames's *Medulla Theologica* (1623), perhaps the most important *summa* of Puritan doctrine until Samuel Willard's *A Compleat Body of Divinitie* (1726), has been newly translated in an excellent modern edition by John D. Eusden, as *The Marrow of Theology* (1968) (rpt. Durham: Labyrinth Press, 1983).

WILLIAM BRADFORD

In addition to the works on Plymouth cited under Robert Cushman, see David Levin, "William Bradford: The Value of Puritan Historiography," in Everett Emerson, ed., *Major Writers of Early American Literature* (1972); Alan B. Howard, "Art and History in Bradford's *Of Plymouth Plantation*," *William and Mary Quarterly,* 28 (1971):237–266; and Norman Grabo, "William Bradford: *Of Plymouth Plantation,*" in Hennig Cohen, ed., *Landmarks of American Writing* (New York: Basic Books, 1969).

ANNE BRADSTREET

An edition of Bradstreet's writing in modern spelling is Jeannine Hensley, ed., *The Works of Anne Bradstreet* (Cambridge, Mass.: Harvard University Press, 1967). Josephine K. Piercy has edited a facsimile edition of *The Tenth Muse* (Gainesville: Scholars' Facsimiles and Reprints, 1965). More recently, Joseph R. McElrath, Jr., and Allan P. Robb have published *The Complete Works of Anne Bradstreet* (Boston: Twayne, 1981), with full textual apparatus comparing the various seventeenth-century editions.

Criticism includes Ann Stanford, "Anne Bradstreet," in Everett Emerson, ed., *Major Writers of Early American Literature* (1972); Wendy Martin, "Anne Bradstreet's Poetry: A Study of Subversive Piety," in Sandra M. Gilbert and Susan Gubar, eds., *Shakespeare's Sisters: Feminist Essays on Women Poets* (Bloomington: Indiana University Press, 1979); Robert Daly, *God's Altar: The World and the Flesh in Puritan Poetry* (Berkeley: University of California Press, 1978), ch. 3; Samuel Eliot Morison, *Builders of the Bay Colony* (1930, ch. 11. For the effects on women of the Antinomian controversy, see Darrett B. Rutman, *Winthrop's Boston* (Chapel Hill: University of North Carolina Press, 1965), ch. 5. A sensitive discussion of Bradstreet's adjustment to New England is Albert J. von Frank, *The Sacred Game: Provincialism and Frontier Consciousness in American Literature, 1630–1860* (New York: Cambridge University Press, 1984), ch. 1. See also the interesting Foreword by Adrienne Rich to the Hensley edition. The standard biography is Elizabeth Wade White, *Anne Bradstreet* (New York: Oxford University Press, 1971). Berryman's "Homage to Mistress Bradstreet" was first published in *Partisan Review* in 1953.

GERSHOM BULKELEY

The early history of Connecticut may be followed in Charles M. Andrews, *The Colonial Period of American History* (1934), vol. 2; and in Richard S. Dunn, *Puritans and Yankees: The Winthrop Dynasty of New England, 1630–1717* (Princeton: Princeton University Press, 1962). Richard L. Bushman, *From Puritan to Yankee: Character and Social Order in Connecticut, 1690–1765* (Cambridge, Mass.: Harvard University Press, 1969), is first-rate social history.

PETER BULKELEY

A portion of *The Gospel-Covenant* has been edited by Phyllis M. Jones and Nicholas R. Jones in their *Salvation in New England* (Austin: University of Texas Press, 1971). See Michael McGiffert, "The Problem of the Covenant in

Puritan Thought: Peter Bulkeley's *Gospel-Covenant*," *New England Historical and Genealogical Register*, 130 (1976):107–129; and Sacvan Bercovitch, *The American Jeremiad* (1978), ch. 2.

BENJAMIN COLMAN

The most penetrating discussion of Colman is Teresa Toulouse, " 'Syllabical Idolatry': Benjamin Colman and the Rhetoric of Balance," *Early American Literature*, 18 (1984):257–274; also valuable are Christopher Reaske's commentary in his edition of Ebenezer Turrell, *The Life and Character of the Reverend Benjamin Colman, D.D.* (1743; rpt. Delmar, N.Y.: Scholars' Facsimiles and Reprints, 1972); and Theodore Hornberger, "Colman and the Enlightenment," *The New England Quarterly*, 12 (1939):227–240. Also see S. K. Lothrop, *History of the Brattle Street Church* (Boston, 1851).

JOHN COTTON

Cotton has begun to attract the serious attention he deserves. Full-scale studies include Larzer Ziff, *The Career of John Cotton: Puritanism and the American Experience* (Princeton: Princeton University Press, 1962), and Everett Emerson, *John Cotton* (New York: Twayne, 1965). Useful articles especially sensitive to Cotton's distinctive genius are Norman Grabo, "John Cotton's Aesthetic: A Sketch," *Early American Literature*, 3 (1968):4–10; Jesper Rosenmeier, "Clearing the Medium: A Reevaluation of the Puritan Plain Style in Light of John Cotton's *A Practicall Commentary upon the First Epistle Generall of John*," *William and Mary Quarterly*, 37 (1980):577–591; and Rosenmeier's "New England's Perfection: The Image of Adam and the Image of Christ in the Antinomian Crisis, 1634–1638," *William and Mary Quarterly*,27 (1970):435–459. Cotton's major statements on church polity have been edited by Larzer Ziff as *John Cotton on the Churches of New England* (Cambridge, Mass.: Harvard University Press, 1968).

ROBERT CUSHMAN

The best collection of Plymouth materials remains Alexander Young, ed., *Chronicles of the Pilgrim Fathers* (Boston, 1841), which reprints Cushman's 1621 sermon on self-love. George D. Langdon, Jr., *Pilgrim Colony: A History of New Plymouth, 1620–1691* (New Haven: Yale University Press, 1966), is the standard history. The colony records were edited by Nathaniel B. Shurtleff and David Pulsifer as *Records of the Colony of New Plymouth in New England* (Boston, 1855–1861). See also John Demos, *A Little Commonwealth: Family Life in Plymouth Colony* (New York: Oxford University Press, 1970).

JOHN DAVENPORT

Davenport's letters have been edited by Isabel M. Calder (New Haven: Yale University Press, 1937); her *New Haven Colony* (New Haven: Yale University Press, 1934) is also valuable. The election sermon of 1669 may be found in the *Publications of the Colonial Society of Massachusetts* 10 (1907). The controversy that followed Davenport's acceptance of the call to succeed John Wilson at the First Church is discussed in Richard C. Simmons, "The Founding of the Third Church in Boston," *William and Mary Quarterly* 26 (1969):241–252.

JEREMIAH DUMMER

Among the few substantial studies of Dummer is Sheldon S. Cohen, "The Diary of Jeremiah Dummer," *William and Mary Quarterly*, 24 (1967):397–422, which includes portions of the otherwise unpublished diary along with a commentary on Dummer's mind and career.

BENJAMIN FRANKLIN

The literature on Franklin is voluminous. Among the many general studies are Carl Van Doren, *Benjamin Franklin* (New York: Viking, 1938); Bruce Granger, *Benjamin Franklin: An American Man of Letters* (Ithaca, N.Y.: Cornell University Press, 1964); and Alfred O. Aldridge, *Benjamin Franklin, Philosopher and Man* (Philadelphia: Lippincott, 1965). The most recent biography is Ronald W. Clark, *Benjamin Franklin* (New York: Random House, 1983). The famous critique of Franklin by D. H. Lawrence in *Studies in Classic American Literature* (1923; New York: Viking, 1964) remains challenging. For the influence of Franklin's Puritan heritage, see David Levin, "The Autobiography of Benjamin Franklin: The Puritan Experimenter in Life and Art," *Yale Review*, 53 (1964): 258–275. A number of provocative essays are to be found in J. A. Leo Lemay, ed., *The Oldest Revolutionary: Essays on Benjamin Franklin* (Philadelphia: University of Pennsylvania Press, 1976). See also William Spengemann, *The Forms of Autobiography: Episodes in The History of a Literary Genre* (New Haven: Yale University Press, 1980), ch. 2. Apart from the *Autobiography* (1791), which is best read in the Yale edition, the fullest selection of Franklin's works, including some from the early period in New England, remains Chester E. Jorgenson and Frank Luther Mott, eds., *Benjamin Franklin: Representative Selections* (1936; rev. ed. New York: Hill and Wang, 1962).

THOMAS HOOKER

G. H. Williams, et al., ed., *Thomas Hooker: Writings in England and Holland* (Cambridge, Mass.: Harvard University Press, 1975) is richly annotated and invaluable. Everett Emerson has conveniently assembled and introduced facsimiles of two English sermons and one American in *Redemption: Three Sermons* (Gainesville: Scholars' Facsimiles & Reprints, 1956). Sargent Bush, *The Writings of Thomas Hooker: Spiritual Adventure in Two Worlds* (Madison: University of Wisconsin Press, 1979), is an ambitious and provocative study of the whole range of Hooker's achievement. Hooker's "democratic" inclinations have been a subject of debate ever since V. L. Parrington's *Main Currents in American Thought: The Colonial Mind* (Harcourt, Brace, 1927); Perry Miller's famous response is reprinted as "Thomas Hooker and the Democracy of Connecticut" in *Errand into the Wilderness* (1956). For discussion of Hooker's place in the meditative tradition, see Norman Grabo, "The Art of Puritan Devotion," *Seventeenth-Century News*, Spring (1968):7–9.

ANNE HUTCHINSON

The major documents of the Antinomian crisis are collected in David D. Hall, ed., *The Antinomian Controversy, 1636–1638* (Middletown, Conn.: Wesleyan University Press, 1968). A convenient gathering of commentary is Francis J. Bremer, *Anne Hutchinson: Troubler of the Puritan Zion* (Huntington, N.Y.: Robert E. Krieger, 1981). Valuable studies, some included in Bremer, are Kai T. Erikson, *Wayward Puritans: A Study in the Sociology of Deviance* (New York: Wiley, 1966); Jesper Rosenmeier, "New England's Perfection: The Image of Adam and the Image of Christ in the Antinomian Crisis, 1634 to 1638," *William and Mary Quarterly*, 27 (1970):435–459; Lyle Koehler, "The Case of the American Jezebels: Anne Hutchinson and Female Agitation during the Years of Antinomian Turmoil, 1636–1640," *William and Mary Quarterly*, 31 (1974):55–78; Patricia Caldwell, "The Antinomian Language Controversy," *Harvard Theological Review*, 69 (1976):345–367; J. F. Maclear, "Anne Hutchinson and the Mortalist Heresy," *New England Quarterly*, 54 (1981):74–103. Emery Battis, *Saints and Sectaries: Anne Hutchinson and the Antinomian Controversy in the Massachusetts Bay Colony* (Chapel Hill: University of North Carolina Press, 1962), presents demographic evidence that associates Hutchinson's followers with a merchant faction. See also Charles Francis Adams, *Three Episodes of Massachusetts History* (1896); and Larzer Ziff, *The Career of John Cotton* (1962). Two suggestive works that open the subject of the experience of women in the seventeenth century are Keith Thomas, "Women and the Civil War Sects," in Trevor Aston, ed. *Crisis in Europe* (1965); and Roger Thompson, *Women in Stuart England and America: A Comparative Study* (London: Routledge and Kegan Paul, 1974). Interesting arguments for Anne Hutchinson's presence in later American literature are Michael J. Colacurcio, "Footsteps of Ann Hutchinson: The Context of *The Scarlet Letter*," *English Literary History*, 39 (1972):459–494; Joel Porte, *Representative Man: Ralph Waldo Emerson in His Time* (New York: Oxford University Press, 1979), pp. 98–104; Amy Schrager Lang, "Antinomianism and the 'Americanization' of Doctrine," *New England Quarterly*, 54 (1981):225–242.

EDWARD JOHNSON

Several scholars have argued for the centrality of millenarian expectation to Johnson's *History:* Sacvan Bercovitch, "The Historiography of Johnson's *Wonder-Working Providence,*" *Essex Institute Historical Collections,* 104 (1968): 138–161; Ursula Brumm, "Edward Johnson's *Wonder-Working Providence* and the Puritan Conception of History," *Jarbuch für Amerikastudien,* 14 (1969):140–151; and Cecelia Tichi, *New World, New Earth: Environmental Reform in American Literature from the Puritans through Whitman* (New Haven: Yale University Press, 1979), ch. 2. See also Edward J. Gallagher, "An Overview of Johnson's *Wonder-Working Providence,*" *Early American Literature,* 5 (1971):30–49. *Wonder-Working Providence* is best read in J. Franklin Jameson's edition (1910; rpt. New York: Barnes and Noble, 1967).

SAMUEL JOHNSON

A comprehensive study of Johnson is Joseph J. Ellis, *The New England Mind in Transition: Samuel Johnson of Connecticut, 1696–1772* (New Haven: Yale University Press, 1973). The four-volume Columbia University Press edition of Johnson's work (1929), ed. Herbert and Carol Schneider, contains invaluable commentary. On the rise of an Anglican party, see Thomas C. Reeves, "John Checkley and the Emergence of the Episcopal Church in New England," *Historical Magazine of the Protestant Episcopal Church,* 34 (1965):349–360. The most suggestive study of Anglicanism in colonial New England remains unpublished: Alan M. Kantrow, "Jacob's Ladder: Anglican Traditionalism in New England" (Ph.D. diss., Harvard, 1979).

ROBERT KEAYNE

A helpful collection is Stuart Bruchey, ed., *The Colonial Merchant: Sources and Readings* (New York: Harcourt, Brace, 1966). The major study is Bernard Bailyn, *The New England Merchants in the Seventeenth Century* (Cambridge, Mass.: Harvard University Press, 1955).

COTTON MATHER

Four contemporary scholars have led the restoration of Cotton Mather to a place of dignity and eminence in American letters: Robert Middlekauff, in *The Mathers: Three Generations of Puritan Intellectuals* (New York: Oxford University Press, 1970); Sacvan Bercovitch, "Cotton Mather," in Everett Emerson ed., *Major Writers of Early American Literature* (1972); David Levin, *Cotton Mather: The Young Life of the Lord's Remembrancer* (Cambridge, Mass.: Harvard University Press, 1978); and Kenneth Silverman, *The Life and Times of Cotton Mather* (New York: Harper and Row, 1984). Silverman has also edited *The Selected Letters of Cotton Mather* (Baton Rouge: Louisiana State University

Press, 1971). Kenneth B. Murdock, *Cotton Mather: Selections* (1926; rpt. New York: Hafner, 1960), remains the only serviceable anthology. David Levin has edited *Bonifacius: An Essay upon the Good* (Cambridge, Mass.: Harvard University Press, 1966). The 1852 Hartford edition of *The Magnalia* (2 vols.) has been reprinted by The Banner of Truth Trust, Carlisle, Pennsylvania, 1979. A facsimile edition by Josephine Piercy of *The Christian Philosopher* (1721) is available from Scholars' Facsimiles and Reprints, Gainesville, Florida, 1968. Kenneth B. Murdock and Elizabeth W. Miller completed only Books I and II of the *Magnalia* (Cambridge, Mass.: Harvard University Press, 1977) before their deaths. It is a splendid edition.

Among older studies, Barrett Wendell's *Cotton Mather: The Puritan Priest* (1891; rpt. New York: Harcourt, Brace, 1963), with an introduction by Alan Heimert, has continuing value. Also interesting is Katherine Anne Porter's "Affectation of Praehiminincies," *Accent,* 2 (1942):131–138. Among the many more recent studies, see Mitchell Breitwieser, *Cotton Mather and Benjamin Franklin: The Price of Representative Personality* (New York: Cambridge University Press, 1984); Richard F. Lovelace, *The American Pietism of Cotton Mather: The Origins of American Evangelism* (Grand Rapids, Mich.: William B. Eerdman's, 1979).

INCREASE MATHER

One of the books that helped launch the modern reconsideration of Puritanism is Kenneth B. Murdock, *Increase Mather: The Foremost American Puritan* (Cambridge, Mass.: Harvard University Press, 1926). A recent study is Mason Lowance, *Increase Mather* (New York: Twayne, 1974).

THOMAS MORTON

See Samuel Eliot Morison, *Builders of the Bay Colony* (1930; rev. ed. Boston: Houghton Mifflin, 1962), ch. 1; and John Seelye, *Prophetic Waters: the River in Early American Life and Literature* (New York: Oxford University Press, 1977), ch. 6.

JOHN NORTON

Abel Being Dead Yet Speaketh has been reprinted (Delmar, N.Y.: Scholars' Facsimiles and Reprints, 1978) with an introduction by Edward J. Gallagher. See also James Jones, *The Shattered Synthesis*, ch. 1. Two helpful discussions of the complex issues of toleration and the relation of Massachusetts to Restoration England are Paul R. Lucas, "Colony or Commonwealth: Massachusetts Bay, 1661–1666," *William and Mary Quarterly*, 24 (1967):88–107; and E. Brooks Holifield, "On Toleration in Massachusetts," *Church History*, 38 (1969):188–200.

MARY ROWLANDSON

Rowlandson's captivity narrative has been fully reprinted many times, most recently in two collections that help to place it within the genre of which it is the leading example: Richard Slotkin and James K. Folsom, eds., *So Dreadfull a Judgment: Puritan Responses to King Philip's War, 1676–1677* (Middletown: Wesleyan University Press, 1978); and Alden T. Vaughan and Edward W. Clark, eds., *Puritans Among the Indians: Accounts of Captivity and Redemption, 1676–1724* (Cambridge, Mass.: Harvard University Press, 1981). See also Roy Harvey Pearce, "The Significances of the Captivity Narrative," *American Literature*, 19 (1949):1–20; and Slotkin, *Regeneration Through Violence: The Mythology of the American Frontier, 1600–1860* (Middletown: Wesleyan University Press, 1973).

SAMUEL SEWALL

There are biographies by Ola E. Winslow, *Samuel Sewall of Boston* (New York: Macmillan, 1964), and T. B. Strandness, *Samuel Sewall: A Puritan Portrait* (East Lansing: Michigan State University Press, 1967). A vivid reconstruction of the texture of Sewall's daily experience is David D. Hall, "The Mental World of Samuel Sewall," *Proceedings of the Massachusetts Historical Society,* 92 (1980):21–44. Robert Middlekauff, in an important article, argues that "ideas instructed [Sewall] in what to feel": "Piety and Intellect in Puritanism," *William and Mary Quarterly,* 22 (1965):457–470. On Sewall's interest in the apocalypse, see Mukhtar Ali Isani, "The Growth of Sewall's *Phaenomena quaedam Apocalyptica,*" *Early American Literature,* 7 (1972): 64–75. For the context of his antislavery opinions, see Lorenzo J. Greene, *The Negro in Colonial New England* (1942; rpt. New York: Athenaeum, 1968).

THOMAS SHEPARD

The fullest biography of Shepard remains that by John Albro, in volume I of Albro's edition of *The Works of Thomas Shepard* (1853) (rpt. New York: AMS Press, 1967). Michael McGiffert has edited the *Journal* and *Autobiography,* with valuable notes and commentary, as *God's Plot: The Paradoxes of Puritan Piety* (Amherst: University of Massachusetts Press, 1972). A recent contribution to our understanding of Shepard is the edition by George Selement and Bruce C. Woolley of the *Confessions* of his Cambridge congregation that he took down in the early 1640s, *Publications of the Colonial Society of Massachusetts,* vol. 58 (1981). These documents are the subject of Patricia Caldwell's *The Puritan Conversion Narrative* (1983). See also Jesper Rosenmeier, "New England's Perfection," and Andrew Delbanco, "Thomas Shepard's America: The Biography of an Idea," in Daniel Aaron, ed., *Studies in Biography* (Harvard English Studies, no. 8) (Cambridge, Mass.: Harvard University Press, 1978), 159–182. For discussion of the date of composition of *The Sound Believer*, see Susan Drinker

Moran, "Thomas Shepard and the Professor: Two Documents from the Early History of Harvard," *Early American Literature*, 27, 1 (1982): 24–42; and Phyllis and Nicholas Jones, *Salvation in New England*, p. 18.

THOMAS SHEPARD, JR.

Apart from the general studies treating the later seventeenth century, A. W. Plumstead, *The Wall and The Garden: Selected Massachusetts Election Sermons* (1968) is helpful in establishing the context of the jeremiad.

SOLOMON STODDARD

Modern study of Stoddard begins with Miller's "Solomon Stoddard, 1643–1729," *Harvard Theological Review*, 34 (1941):277–320, which is somewhat expanded in Book II of *From Colony to Province* (1953). Robert Pope, in *The Half-Way Covenant* (1969), and E. Brooks Holifield, *The Covenant Sealed: The Development of Puritan Sacramental Theology in Old and New England, 1570–1720* (New Haven: Yale University Press, 1974), challenge Stoddard's priority as an innovator in sacramental theory. See also Thomas Schafer, "Solomon Stoddard and the Theology of the Revival," in Stuart Henry, ed., *A Miscellany of American Christianity* (Durham: Duke University Press, 1963), pp. 328–361; James P. Walsh, "Solomon Stoddard's Open Communion: A Reexamination," *New England Quarterly*, 43 (1970): 97–114; and Paul R. Lucas, *Valley of Discord: Church and Society Along the Connecticut River, 1636–1725* (Hanover, N.H.: University Press of New England, 1976). A recent biography is Ralph J. Coffman, *Solomon Stoddard* (Boston: Twayne, 1978).

EDWARD TAYLOR

The standard edition is Donald Stanford ed., *The Poems of Edward Taylor* (New Haven: Yale University Press, 1960). Thomas M. and Virginia L. Davis have edited Taylor's *"Church Records" and Related Sermons* (Boston: Twayne, 1981), *Edward Taylor vs. Solomon Stoddard: The Nature of the Lord's Supper* (Twayne, 1981), and *Edward Taylor's Minor Poetry* (Twayne, 1981). Norman Grabo's editions of the *Treatise Concerning the Lord's Supper* (East Lansing: Michigan State University Press, 1965), and a series of sermons that correspond to Meditations 42–56 of the second series, entitled *Christographia* (New Haven: Yale University Press, 1962), are of central importance. Charles W. Mignon is preparing an edition of the sermons in the "Nebraska manuscript," described by him in *Early American Literature*, 12 (1977–78):296–301. Louis Martz contributed an important foreword to Stanford's text, in which he sets out the case for Taylor as a "meditative poet" in the Ignatian tradition as defined in his *The Poetry of Meditation* (New Haven: Yale University Press, 1954). Since Martz, our understanding of Protestant meditation has been significantly revised by Barbara Lewalski in *Donne's Anniversaries and the Poetry of Praise: The Creation of a Symbolic Mode* (Princeton: Princeton University Press, 1973), and in her *Protestant Poetics and the Seventeenth-Century Religious Lyric* (Princeton: Princeton University Press, 1979), the final chapter of which is devoted to Taylor. See also Kathleen Blake, "Edward Taylor's Protestant Poetic: Nontransubstantiating Metaphor," *American Literature,* 43 (1971):1–24.

Taylor has attracted more attention in recent years than any other Puritan writer, in part because of his recent appearance in print but also, no doubt, because of a critical appetite for poetry that had been largely unsatisfied by other early American efforts. Detailed listings of criticism before the last decade may be found in Bercovitch, *The American Puritan Imagination* (1974). Especially valuable are Alan B. Howard, "The World as Emblem: Language and Vision in the Poetry of Edward Taylor," *American Literature,* 44 (1972):359–384; Ursula Brumm, "Edward Taylor and the Poetic Use of Religious Typology," in Bercovitch, *Typology and Early American Literature* (1972); Albert Gelpi, *The Tenth Muse: The Psyche of the American Poet* (Cambridge, Mass.: Harvard University Press, 1975), ch. 2; Karl Keller, *The Example of Edward Taylor* (Amherst: University of Massachusetts Press, 1975); William Scheick, *The Will and the Word* (Athens: University of Georgia Press, 1976); and Michael J. Colacurcio, "God's Determinations Touching Half-Way Membership: Occasion and Audience in Edward Taylor," *American Literature,* 39 (1967):298–314, which opened up the subject of the relation between Taylor's ecclesiastical convictions and the compassion of his art. Norman Grabo, *Edward Taylor* (Boston: Twayne, 1961) is a good general introduction.

THOMAS TILLAM

There is a sketch of Tillam's life by Ernest Payne, *Baptist Quarterly,* 17 (1957):61–66. See also B. S. Capp, *The Fifth-Monarchy Men* (London: Faber and Faber, 1972), 140–141, 200–201.

HENRY VANE

A recent biography of Vane is J. H. Adamson and H. F. Folland, *Sir Harry Vane* (Boston: Gambit, 1973). Still valuable is James K. Hosmer, *The Life of Young Sir Henry Vane, Governor of Massachusetts Bay and leader of the long Parliament* (Boston, 1889).

NATHANIEL WARD

See Robert D. Arner, "*The Simple Cobbler of Aggawam:* Nathaniel Ward and the Rhetoric of Satire," *Early American Literature,* 5 (1971):3–16; and Morison, *Builders of the Bay Colony* (1930), ch. 7. Paul M. Zall's edition of *The Simple Cobbler* (Lincoln: University of Nebraska Press, 1969) contains useful annotations, to which Mr. Delbanco is indebted.

MICHAEL WIGGLESWORTH

The fullest biography is Richard Crowder, *No Featherbed to Heaven: A Biography of Michael Wigglesworth, 1631–1705* (East Lansing: Michigan State University Press, 1962). Wigglesworth's diary, including four professions of faith made in his church, has been edited by Edmund Morgan in *Publications of the Colonial Society of Massachusetts,* 35 (1951):311–444 (rpt. New York: Harper, 1965). Although no adequate edition of Wigglesworth's works has been published, Ronald A. Bosco has one in preparation.

ROGER WILLIAMS

The six-volume Narragansett edition of Williams' *Writings* (1867) has been reprinted (New York: Russell and Russell, 1963) with a seventh volume of material introduced by Perry Miller. Miller's *Roger Williams: His Contribution to the American Tradition* (New York: Atheneum, 1953), although its claims for the uniqueness of Williams' typological imagination have now been challenged, remains the best combination of selections and commentary. For further discussion see Edmund Morgan, *Roger Williams: The Church and the State* (New York: Harcourt, Brace, 1967); Sacvan Bercovitch, "Typology in Puritan New England: The Williams-Cotton Controversy Reassessed," *American Quarterly* 19 (1967):166–191; Jesper Rosenmeier, "The Teacher and the Witness: John Cotton and Roger Williams," *William and Mary Quarterly* 25 (1968):408–431; Richard Reinitz, "The Separatist Background of Roger Williams' Argument for Religious Toleration," in Bercovitch, *Typology and Early American Literature* (1972); and W. Clark Gilpin, *The Millenarian Piety of Roger Williams* (Chicago: University of Chicago Press, 1979.)

JOHN WINTHROP

A casebook devoted to Winthrop's decision to emigrate to America is Darrett B. Rutman, *John Winthrop's Decision for America: 1629* (Philadelphia: Lippincott, 1975); the leading modern study is Edmund S. Morgan, *The Puritan Dilemma: The Story of John Winthrop* (Boston: Little, Brown, 1958). The basic source for study of Winthrop, and for the early years of Massachusetts Bay, is the Massachusetts Historical Society's five-volume *The Winthrop Papers* (1929–1947), which gathers the documents previously published in its *Proceedings.* An illuminating essay is Richard S. Dunn, "John Winthrop Writes His Journal," *William and Mary Quarterly,* 41 (1984):185–212. Dunn, with Laetitia Yeandle, is preparing a new edition of the Journal, to be published by the Massachusetts Historical Society.

JOHN WISE

Apart from the works on political thought cited earlier, see Clinton Rossiter, "John Wise: Colonial Democrat," *New England Quarterly* 22 (1949):3–

32. Useful for establishing context is Edmund Morgan, ed., *Puritan Political Ideas: 1558–1794* (New York: Bobbs-Merrill, 1965). See also T.H. Breen, *The Character of the Good Ruler: A Study of Puritan Political Ideas in New England, 1630–1730* (New Haven: Yale University Press, 1970), and Stephen Foster, *Their Solitary Way: The Puritan Social Ethic in the First Century of Settlement in New England* (New Haven: Yale University Press, 1971).

WITCHCRAFT

The literature on witchcraft has always been large and lively; for the European background, see E. William Monter, ed., *European Witchcraft* (New York: Wiley, 1969); and Alan Macfarlane, *Witchcraft in Tudor and Stuart England: A Regional and Comparative Study* (New York: Harper, 1976). On New England, the treatment in George Bancroft's great *History of the United States* (Boston, 1837), vol. III, remains of penetrating insight. Miller's discussion is in *The New England Mind: From Colony to Province* (1953), ch. 13. David Levin, *Cotton Mather: The Young Life of the Lord's Remembrancer* (1978), contains a measured defense of Mather; Sacvan Bercovitch, "Cotton Mather," in Emerson, ed., *Major Writers of Early American Literature* (1972), argues that Mather construed the events at Salem as harbingers of the millennium. A persuasive and innovative study is Paul Boyer and Stephen Nissenbaum, *Salem Possessed: The Social Origins of Witchcraft* (Cambridge, Mass.: Harvard University Press, 1974), which argues that the crisis grew out of social conflict between the rising entrepreneurs of Salem Town and the struggling subsistence farmers of Salem Village: usually the "witches" were among the former, the accusers among the latter. Chadwick Hansen, *Witchcraft at Salem* (New York: Braziller, 1969), presents the pioneering thesis that witchcraft was so much a part of Puritan culture that some who were accused actually did attempt to practice it. Useful sourcebooks are George L. Burr, ed., *Narratives of the Witchcraft Cases* (New York: Scribner's, 1914); David Levin, ed., *What Happened in Salem?* (New York: Harcourt, Brace, 1960); and Paul Boyer and Stephen Nissenbaum, eds., *Salem Village Witchcraft: A Documentary Record of Local Conflict in Colonial New England* (Belmont, Calif.: Wadsworth, 1972). See also Ann Kibbey, "Mutations of the Supernatural: Witchcraft, Remarkable Providences, and the Power of Puritan Men," *American Quarterly* 34, 2 (1982):125–148. The most remarkable scholarly work yet achieved is John Demos, *Entertaining Satan: Witchcraft and the Culture of Early New England* (New York: Oxford University Press, 1982). Demos deals very little with Salem directly in his moving book; rather, he treats witchcraft generally as an idea imposed to explain away the sometimes threatening behavior of those—often spinsters and other "unsocialized" women—who had to cope with the exigencies of misfortune. Finally, the value of Arthur Miller's great play, *The Crucible* (1953), should not be underestimated as a portrayal of the forces that drove people to accusation, fantasy, revenge, and heroic resistance.

INDEX

Note: Works included in the anthology are indicated by page numbers in bold type.